AF898760

Making Money in Ancient Athens

Making Money in Ancient Athens

Michael Leese

University of Michigan Press
Ann Arbor

Copyright © 2021 by Michael Leese
All rights reserved

For questions or permissions,
please contact um.press.perms@umich.edu

Published in the United States of America by the
University of Michigan Press
Manufactured in the United States of America
Printed on acid-free paper
First published October 2021

A CIP catalog record for this book is available from the British Library.

Library of Congress Cataloging-in-Publication data has been applied for.

Library of Congress Control Number: 2021944315
LC record available at https://lccn.loc.gov/2021944315

ISBN 978-0-472-13276-8 (hardcover : alk. paper)
ISBN 978-0-472-12944-7 (e-book)

Cover illustration: Silver coin hoard F 13:4. American School of Classical Studies at Athens: Agora Excavations.

For Amy

Contents

Digital materials related to this title can be found on the Fulcrum platform via the following citable URL: https://doi.org/10.3998/mpub.11553427

Preface

The title of this book was originally intended to be *Making Money in Ancient Greece*, because Athenocentrism and Athenian exceptionalism have been long cited as methodological problems when it comes to the study of the ancient economy. The book therefore has a more narrow title than I would have preferred, because some may initially be put off by the geographical limitations implied in the title and will believe this book's argumentative force sidesteps some of the central debates among economic historians about the applicability of Athenian evidence to the ancient economy more broadly. Athens was not a hermetically sealed system, however, as its economic system was intricately intertwined with those of the other *poleis* and regions of the wider Mediterranean basin. Therefore, much of my intent is to demonstrate how the patterns observable (admittedly in much greater detail) in Athens are also reflected in the evidence preserved from other *poleis*. Accordingly, I often use the broader terms "Greece" and "Greek" in contexts where it is not certain that evidence is restricted to Athens alone.

Some will find my transliteration of Greek proper names into the Roman alphabet inconsistent or capricious, as I tend to follow Latinized convention for more famous figures, while I resort to the use of the letter "k" for less familiar individuals to facilitate the consultation of Davies' *Athenian Propertied Families* in particular.

Acknowledgments

For a project so long in the making, it is hard to sum up in a brief statement how many people have been so helpful in bringing it to fruition. This book began as a dissertation in the Interdepartmental Program in Greek and Roman History at the University of Michigan, which was the best possible place to do an interdisciplinary project like this. My co-chairs Sara Forsdyke and Bruce Frier guided the project from its original inception through every stage of development, down through the critical stages of revising the new material I wrote for the monograph. The rest of my committee, Ian Moyer, David Potter, Ruth Scodel, and Ray Van Dam all contributed significantly to the shape the project took, and gave invaluable advice for how to revise it into a book.

The Responsible Governance and Sustainable Citizenship Project and the Department of History at the University of New Hampshire both supported this project with semesters of research leave. David Bachrach, Jeff Bolster, and Stephen Trzaskoma all provided me with extensive substantive criticism on written drafts of different chapters, as did Vince Rosivach, who helped me with the difficult task of presenting and framing my overall approach to the various issues I was grappling with. Graham Oliver, Edward Harris, and Donald W. Jones also gave useful feedback on earlier drafts of written material. My ideas were further honed through a number of conversations about the material over the years with Alain Bresson, Jean Andreau, Henry Colburn, Franco De Angelis, Dennis Kehoe, and Edgardo Pérez Morales, as well as with my colleagues in the Department of History at UNH, especially Jan Golinski, Jess Lepler, Fred Meiton, Liz Mellyn, and also my fellow classicists Harriet Fertik, Joanna Kenty, and Scott Smith. I received helpful feedback on my arguments from audiences in the classics departments at Brown University, and the Universities of Illinois, Michigan, and Pennsylvania. The anonymous reviewers at University of Michigan Press, with their incisive critiques, were instrumental in determining the final state of the book and the organization of the chapters. I would like to thank Kevin Rennells for deftly handling the production of the manuscript,

Andrew Jones for his meticulous index work, and Ellen Douglas for her superb copyediting.

Most of all, however, I want to thank Amy Warhaft for her unwavering support during my times of doubt and the encouragement to keep going in the face of the numerous unforeseen difficulties and setbacks throughout this entire long process. With her tireless commitment to this project, she read drafts, copyedited, and gave constructive comments. Her years as a steadfast companion have made this book what it is. She is largely responsible for the quality of the final product, which is dedicated to her.

Introduction

At the end of Plato's *Apology*, while facing the death penalty, Socrates has the opportunity to propose an alternative punishment to the Athenians. But instead of humbly suggesting a lighter penalty, he deflects the charges against him and snarkily declares that he actually deserved to be supported at state expense as a reward for the good services he rendered his fellow citizens throughout his life:

> τί ἄξιός εἰμι παθεῖν ἢ ἀποτεῖσαι, ὅτι μαθὼν ἐν τῷ βίῳ οὐχ ἡσυχίαν ἦγον, ἀλλ' ἀμελήσας ὧνπερ οἱ πολλοί, χρηματισμοῦ τε καὶ οἰκονομίας καὶ στρατηγιῶν καὶ δημηγοριῶν καὶ τῶν ἄλλων ἀρχῶν καὶ συνωμοσιῶν καὶ στάσεων τῶν ἐν τῇ πόλει γιγνομένων . . . ἐπιχειρῶν ἕκαστον ὑμῶν πείθειν μὴ πρότερον μήτε τῶν ἑαυτοῦ μηδενὸς ἐπιμελεῖσθαι πρὶν ἑαυτοῦ ἐπιμεληθείη ὅπως ὡς βέλτιστος καὶ φρονιμώτατος ἔσοιτο.
>
> What do I deserve to suffer or pay, because I did not lead a quiet life, but neglecting the things that the masses care for, making money, estate management, generalships, public speeches, and the other offices and clubs and political factions that exist in the city . . . I tried to persuade each of you not to take care of your affairs before yourself, in order to be as good and wise as possible. (36b-c)

Here Socrates sums up how little he cared for the interests of the average Athenian and distances himself from *hoi polloi*, who then condemn him to execution. But in this sarcastic defense he reveals what he considered to be the main preoccupations of most citizens—military commands and political wrangling, as well as personal estate management, the type of mundane obsessions that philosophers shun. The first thing on his list, however, is *chrêmatismos*.

They called it "the art of making money." Also referred to as *chrêmatistikê*, by the classical period *chrêmatismos* had developed into a technical term with a special name for its practitioners—*chrêmatistai* (sing. *chrêmatistês*), "moneymakers." *Chrêmatistikê* was apparently so commonplace in the daily life of Athenians during Plato's time that it earned a prominent position alongside the military and political pursuits that have made Athens so famous to this day.

This book is about how ancient Athenians practiced the art of making money: the methods they employed in the quest for profit; their strategies for accumulating wealth; the process whereby they made decisions in business and estate management; and their motivation for choosing among the economic options at their disposal. At first glance such questions might appear simple or straightforward to the point of seeming agonizingly boring. But far from being dull they are in fact highly controversial, caught up in a complex web of some of the most contentious debates in the study of the ancient economy. Although these topics have been central to the field for decades, scholars are still sharply divided over Athenians' and other ancient Greeks' approach to their economic affairs.

One example from Xenophon's *Poroi* will suffice to illustrate how radically divergent scholars' interpretations of ancient Greek moneymaking strategies can be. While recommending that the *polis* expand its involvement in the mines at Laureion to increase its revenues, Xenophon provides important details about the nature of the economy of fourth-century BCE Athens. He describes how individuals switch between fields of production in response to fluctuations in the prices of various goods:

> ὅταν πολλοὶ χαλκοτύποι γένωνται, ἀξίων γενομένων τῶν χαλκευτικῶν ἔργων, καταλύονται οἱ χαλκοτύποι, καὶ οἱ σιδηρεῖς γε ὡσαύτως· καὶ ὅταν γε πολὺς σῖτος καὶ οἶνος γένηται, ἀξίων ὄντων τῶν καρπῶν, ἀλυσιτελεῖς αἱ γεωργίαι γίγνονται, ὥστε πολλοὶ ἀφέμενοι τοῦ τὴν γῆν ἐργάζεσθαι ἐπ' ἐμπορίας καὶ καπηλείας καὶ τοκισμοὺς τρέπονται.

> Whenever there are many bronzesmiths and bronze products become cheap, bronzesmiths are ruined, and likewise for blacksmiths; and whenever there is a great deal of wheat and wine, and the produce becomes cheap, farming becomes unprofitable, so that many people, removing themselves from working the land, turn to maritime trade, retailing, and lending at interest.[1]

Xenophon's words convey unparalleled insights into the operation of the economic system and the behavior of the individuals within it, which can be

1. Xenophon, *Poroi* 4.6.

explained in terms of mainstream modern (neoclassical) economic theory. When the market is flooded with a given item there is a drop in its price; this in turn causes people to cease manufacturing that product and enter into something more lucrative. Xenophon perhaps even implies that these producers are comparing the relative profitability of different goods and deciding how to make money on that basis. In short, market considerations (prices, profits, and losses) are the sole motivating factors Xenophon discusses, and the economy seems to be performing according to the basic laws of supply and demand in markets, as many scholars have argued.[2]

One could easily say that the individuals Xenophon depicts were pursuing their interests in an economically rational manner, motivated primarily by gain and following the patterns of entry and exit in modern economic theory.[3] Economic rationality, in its simplest form, is when someone evaluates a variety of investment alternatives and chooses to enter the field that will maximize income or profit; the Greeks in Xenophon's mind could be interpreted as behaving in precisely this way as part of their decisions in response to price changes. As Polanyi observes, supply and demand result from the aggregate effects of large numbers of individuals acting in an economically rational manner.[4]

But Xenophon's words have also been read quite differently. Gauthier, for example, considers this passage to be "essential pour saisir l'absence de mentalité économique (au sens modern) des anciens Grecs."[5] How can a matter-of-fact statement that can be explained in such basic modern economic terms also simultaneously be said to reveal "the absence of an economic mentality in the modern sense among ancient Greeks?"[6] Gauthier's perspective, which is embodied in his use of the technical term *mentalité*, is based on an established theoretical position that has been held in varying degrees by many scholars of economic history for over half a century.

The notion of *mentalité*, that past societies did not share the same mental outlook as people in the modern West, was promulgated by one of the most

2. Austin and Vidal-Naquet 1977, 318n4; Bresson 2000, 294, and 2016a, 432; Figueira 2012, 681–82; Harris and Lewis 2016, 2–3.

3. See McCloskey 1996, for entry and exit in neoclassical economics, motivated by economically rational choice for profit.

4. Polanyi 1977, 125–26.

5. Gauthier 1976, 120.

6. Gauthier partly bases his claim on the idea that "Le marché . . . était d'abord et essentiellement le marché local. Et certes cela sonne étrangement aux oreilles des modernes, pour qui le marché est élastique" (129). But Athens was connected to the larger Aegean and Mediterranean economy, so the supply of goods at Athens was affected by not just a local market; moreover, market elasticity (and inelasticity) is a complex problem and very much a modern phenomenon as well, for which see Jones 2014, 63–65.

influential schools of twentieth-century historiography, the French *Annalistes*.[7] Guided by anthropology and especially the central methodological principle of cultural relativism, which posits that different cultures behave and think in unique ways, proponents of *mentalité* (or mentality) emphasize the particularism of past societies and object to the imposition of modern categories of analysis onto the premodern world.[8] Mentality provided generations of historians studying all periods with the framework and vocabulary to articulate the distinctive conceptual and cognitive features that defined other cultures' understanding of reality.

It was Moses Finley who was most responsible for importing the ideas of mentality and cultural specificity into ancient economic history. This approach was in line with a broad spectrum of theories, including economic anthropology, Max Weber's Protestant ethic, peasant studies, and Marxism, which all opposed retrojecting economic rationality onto the ancients alongside the use of methodological individualism, an analytical focus that is based on the modern Western notion of the self. Fundamental to modernization theories and the history of capitalism is the assumption that economic rationality, the self-interested maximization of profit and wealth, was an unprecedented development, unique to the modern mind and the emergence of the individual as part of the processes that created industrial capitalism. Finley was on the cutting edge, therefore, in bringing ancient history up to date with the latest theoretical advances in the wider fields of anthropology and history.

Some of the most arresting and captivating statements ever made in the field regard the Athenians' and other Greeks' particular *mentalité*. Scholars in turn argued for a "profoundly unproductive mentality";[9] a "non-economic mentality";[10] a "non-economic" or "non-productive mentality," and "mental habits" which inhibited a "productive spirit";[11] a "non-market mentality."[12] Moreover, rationality became explicitly intertwined with mentality: "The Athenians lacked the mentality appropriate to modern conceptions of 'rational economic man.' They did not develop accounting techniques capable of calculating comparative rates of profit."[13] Those who portrayed the behavior

7. For a discussion, see Arnold 2000; Ginzburg 1980; Burke 2015.

8. See, e.g., Darnton 1999, who identifies the object of his inquiry as an "alien mentality" (262).

9. Millett 1983, 44.

10. Gauthier 1976, 129–30, followed Finley's interpretation of a noneconomic mentality, and believed that the notion of the "juste prix," among other things, constituted a departure from a "mentalité économique."

11. Austin and Vidal-Naquet 1977, 11, 15, 113.

12. Meikle 2002, 248–49, contrasts "ancient behavior and mentality and modern market behavior and mentality."

13. Millett 1991, 165; see also at 71–80, and 189 for further statements on ancient Greeks' nonproductive mentality.

and mental universe of ancient Greeks in modern terms were seen as doing violence to the past.

Mentalité was an explanation so brilliant, so powerful, and so simple, that it seemed to account for much of the undeniable contrast between ancient and modern economies. There must have been *something* different about how the ancient Greeks conceptualized their economic affairs, whether in their culture or cosmology, that distinguished their behavior and mental universe from that of modern economic actors. Finley's contributions brought about a revolution in ancient economic history. His research incorporated new perspectives from the social sciences and humanities outside of classics; his critiques were so incisive and compelling that they first transformed and later dominated the discourse of the entire field.

At the same time, however, a number of scholars countered with considerable evidence that ancient Greeks actually behaved in an economically rational manner. Wesley Thompson went straight to the heart of the matter, arguing that classical Athenians exhibited a mentality that was not contrary to modern economic sensibilities, but rather could be described by the terms "entrepreneurship" and "investment."[14] Cohen's study of Athenian banking suggested a similar interpretation—that the Athenians engaged in more sophisticated economic behavior than the Finley school acknowledged.[15] This point of view was supported by Rathbone's book on economic rationalism in Roman Egypt,[16] as well as Burke's article on the disembedding of the fourth-century Athenian economy.[17] Harris contended that "one had to be a canny *homo oeconomicus* to achieve success as a *homo politicus*," and that "economic rationality was not incompatible with the pursuit of status and honor."[18] Morris also made an intriguing case for economic rationality on theoretical grounds.[19] The most direct treatment of economic rationality in ancient Greece, however, belongs to Christesen, who took a close look at evidence from the Laureion mining industry and concluded that fourth-century Athenians carried out silver smelting in a way that maximized their profits.[20]

In the wake of such arguments, an increasing number of scholars have accepted the idea that ancient Greeks behaved in an economically rational manner, and that a wide range of modern economic principles and theory can

14. Thompson 1978, 1982.
15. Cohen 1992.
16. Rathbone 1991.
17. Burke 1992.
18. Harris 2002, 85–86.
19. Morris 2002.
20. Christesen 2003.

be applied to ancient societies.[21] In particular, New Institutional Economics (NIE) has taken the field by storm, championed by the editors of *The Cambridge Economic History of the Greco-Roman World* as the preferred approach for future ancient economic history, and built upon the assumption of economic rationality.[22] Throughout his massive two-volume work, Bresson demonstrates the efficacy of NIE;[23] he strongly opposes the view that the Greeks lacked rationality,[24] invoking the idea of mentality to conclude that ancient Greeks and Romans were profit-oriented in their economic strategies.[25] Many now support the position that Greeks aimed for the economically rational maximization of wealth or income,[26] and some have explicitly addressed economic rationality with respect to institutional development in ancient Greece.[27] In short, a "new orthodoxy" has replaced the Finley school, employing the methods of NIE with much success, emphasizing growth, progress, and rationality.

But the pendulum has swung so far back in the other direction that amid the flood of recent work a number of scholars are now objecting to NIE precisely because economic rationality lies at its behavioral foundations. Boldizzoni has delivered a passionate and incisive critique of NIE, especially because it imposes rationality upon premodern societies.[28] As Thonemann notes in his *Times Literary Supplement* review of Peter Temin's *The Roman Market Economy*,[29] it has not been proven that ancient individuals behaved in an economically rational manner, which makes it difficult to accept that a market economy was operating in antiquity; from this perspective, he says, the Finley thesis is still attractive in many ways. Rosivach raises an important consideration, whether assuming economic rationality among ancient Greeks comes at the cost of recognizing their cultural distinctiveness.[30] Even scholars who argue for self-interested profit-seeking behavior like Christ are unwilling to declare definitively that Athenian behavior could be described as economically rational.[31] Vlassopoulos sums up his hesitation to endorse some elements of Ober's

21. See, e.g., Jones 2014.
22. Morris, Saller, and Scheidel 2007. For economic rationality as the basis of individual behavioral assumptions in NIE (though with modifications), see North 1990, 17–26. For a more nuanced view, however, see Lewis 2018.
23. Bresson 2007–2008.
24. Bresson 2016a, 11, 22–27, 436.
25. Bresson 2016a, 376.
26. Acton 2014; Bresson and Bresson 2004; Jansen 2007; Tridimas 2013; Föllinger 2016; Tzochev 2016; O'Halloran 2018.
27. Ober 2009, 2010, 2015; Lyttkens 2013.
28. Boldizzoni 2011.
29. Thonemann 2013.
30. Rosivach 2014, 188.
31. Christ 2006, 145n4.

The Rise and Fall of Classical Greece in similar terms: "If there is value in a social science approach to ancient history (and I am personally deeply sceptical about it, for reasons that there is no space to explore here), this will have to be proved through careful analysis."[32] Ober's book utilizes rational choice theory as one of its core models for ancient Greek behavior. Similar criticisms of Alain Bresson's *The Making of the Ancient Greek Economy* were recently voiced by Wang,[33] who rejects economic rationality as being too narrow, and advocates a more culturally sensitive focus that "dispels the imagination of an isolated, threatened *homo economicus* who constantly lives in a state of hostility and rivalry."[34] Especially problematic is the theoretical underpinning of *homo oeconomicus*: the modern notion of the self and its associated heuristic approach, methodological individualism.[35] Wang instead proposes a "cultural analysis."[36]

These and other scholars have expressed reservations about economic rationality, and for good reason—they are advancing powerful, firmly grounded criticisms that cannot be ignored. The models of the NIE school are reminiscent of the theories of a universal human nature that originated during the Enlightenment, which anthropologists and cultural historians railed against for much of the twentieth century.[37] Heeding the call of anthropologists such as Geertz, who argued forcefully and convincingly against the whitewashed, pasteurized, Enlightenment-based view of a shared human nature, many historians have tried to capture the distinctiveness of the ancient Greek economy, eschewing rationality and seeking to uncover how Greek culture shaped the economic behavior of its people.[38]

It is clear that uncritically assuming economic rationality oversimplifies a more complex reality, but does that mean it should be discarded altogether? The statements on economic rationality are contradictory enough to make one's head spin. It is an issue fraught with controversy for more than a century.[39]

32. Vlassopoulos, in *BMCR* 2016.03.04.

33. Wang, in *BMCR* 2016.07.35.

34. Wang 2018, 52.

35. Wang 2018, 5–7.

36. Wang 2018, 4.

37. Cf. Pirngruber 2017, 10, who critiques extreme proponents who posit universally the "rationality of an abstract *homo oeconomicus*, whose motivations and needs/wants are supposed not to have changed throughout the course of history."

38. See especially Geertz 1973.

39. There are numerous critiques of the model of economic rationality, and especially the central assumptions of profit and wealth maximization. Probably the most famous belong to Simon 1955, 1992. More recently, Sen 1977, 1997, expressed further criticisms. Moreover, economic anthropologists and sociologists have also demonstrated problems with the central model of *homo oeconomicus*, for which see, e.g., Bourdieu 2005, 5–7. Nevertheless, these fields have now incorporated economic rationality into their broader theories of human behavior, since scholars have been unable to dispense with the model, which remains at the heart of much economic analysis (see,

For a nonexpert new to the ancient economy there seems to be no consensus. Instead one meets a dizzying array of subtly nuanced and highly qualified opinions at every possible point along the spectrum from enthusiastic acceptance that ancient Greeks behaved in a manner consistent with modern concepts of economic rationality to outright denial. Most scholars fall somewhere in the middle, and for experts this textured nuance is essential for analytical precision. But the ancient economy attracts interest from nonspecialists as well, who consult antiquity to form their theories of big-picture and long-term economic development, and these accounts in turn come back to inform ancient economic history. Marxist-influenced historians, for example, believe that self-interested profit maximization is specific to the individualism of the modern world, where the self has become disembedded from traditional kinship and social structures.[40] These critiques from the wider field of economic history must be addressed if any real progress can be made because methodologically responsible scholars will always look to later periods and the larger debates on the history of capitalism for theoretical and comparative perspectives with which to contextualize the evidence from antiquity.

In short, economic rationality has still not been proven for the ancient economy, so the models and methods that have become the norm in ancient economic history need to be reassessed. For Finley this question encapsulated the main problems in the study of the ancient economy:

> The issue is one of choice. Given that no man, not even Robinson Crusoe, is absolutely free, how free was a Greek or Roman to choose among a range of possible "employments" . . . More precisely, how much weight was attached to what we would call economic factors in the choice, maximization of income, for example, or market calculations? (1973, 43)

In other words, did Greeks and Romans behave in ways that would be considered "rational" according to modern economic theory? Finley recognized

---

e.g., Zafirovski and Levine 1997, 267–68). For the field of economic sociology, see Swedberg and Granovetter 2001. A helpful overview of the criticisms of rational choice theory is voiced by MacDonald 2003, 556. Though I will limit my focus to the central model of rationality, today there are multiple variations that scholars have developed. For extensive discussions of the full complexity of the notion of economic rationality in all its forms, see Hargreaves Heap 1989, and Zouboulakis 2014.

40. Marx declared in the introduction to the *Grundrisse* that the individual was not the same in the premodern world, and that the classical economists Adam Smith and David Ricardo committed a fatal methodological error in retrojecting the modern concept of the individual back onto premodern society: "The more deeply we go back in history, the more the individual, and hence also the producing individual, appear as dependent, as belonging to a greater whole" (Tucker 1978, 222).

economic rationality as being the crux of the matter. For a clear understanding of the performance of the ancient economy, it is absolutely essential for scholars to determine the extent to which ancient individual behavior resembled that of modern actors. The people who drove and in turn responded to price changes in the system Xenophon describes above certainly seem to be motivated primarily by the type of market considerations Finley mentions, which is highly suggestive of economically rational behavior among a large number of people.

But in order to establish definitively whether or not Athenians thought about and treated their economic affairs in a rational way, Finley's emphasis on choice is spot-on. A close analysis of behavior and psychology must be carried out at the level of the economic decision-making process itself. To prove that someone behaved in an economically rational manner, that person would have to be shown to be at least implicitly making a deliberate choice between different economic alternatives, as Dennis Kehoe points out.[41] Evaluating multiple options and selecting one that satisfies the desire for profit is therefore an essential criterion to look for when identifying aspects of economic rationality in ancient behavior. But as Paul Christesen persuasively argues, fourth-century BCE Athenians did have the ability to do comparative assessments of various investments.[42]

Economic rationality was once described by Paul Cartledge as the "will o' the wisp" in the study of the ancient economy,[43] and thus it remains. It is true that a few scholars have directly addressed the issue, but most have only done so indirectly or tangentially by looking at proxies for rational or irrational behavior, and not comprehensive, detailed analyses of individual decision making. But while some have adopted it into their heuristic toolbox and argue vigorously for its inclusion in ancient economic history, others see it as toxic, problematic at best even for the modern world, and unthinkable for premodern societies. Another group thinks it should not even be an object of discussion, that the question is resolved and have forged ahead in new directions. Many are put off by the muddles inherent in the notion of economic rationality itself and steer clear of this thorny issue. This reluctance to explore economic rationality is understandable, since to do so involves descending into a quagmire of methodological problems. Moreover, economic rationality has never been proven for any premodern historical context, and even for such advanced societies as

41. Kehoe 1993, 476, 483–84; 1997, 6–7.

42. Christesen 2003. Among the opportunities for investment were loans, slaves, livestock, cereals, vines, olives, maritime trade, pottery, textile production, mining, retail trade, bathhouses, milling, banking, quarrying, fishing, and others.

43. Cartledge 2002, 21.

Renaissance Florence historians are divided, with some speaking of a "nascent spirit of European capitalism,"[44] and others of a "traditional *mentalité*."[45]

Many scholars insist that the field has moved on, but because the same terms of the great debate of the ancient economy keep popping up, especially with respect to economic rationality, the matter is overdue for a complete reevaluation.[46] Even as some advocate a more holistic, nuanced perspective that incorporates the full range of theoretical contributions, the dichotomous rhetoric of the old debate still persists. Until mentality is dealt with explicitly and systematically through the lens of rationality, objections to modernizing or "formalist" approaches based on social science models will continue to resurface.[47]

With such a wide range of interpretations, the field remains bifurcated on this critical question despite the progress in the study of the rest of the economy overall. The lack of direct engagement with the concept of economic rationality is one of the major obstacles to moving past the polarized debate over the ancient economy. The two threads of rationality and *mentalité* have become intimately and almost inextricably intertwined together and are also nearly impossible to untangle from other issues in the Greek economy.[48] A focused treatment is necessary both to assess the flurry of recent contributions and to fill an important gap in scholarship.

Avoiding the problem just increases confusion since without regular and overt dialogue scholars cannot even agree on what economic rationality is. As Braudel has pointed out, many depart from the standard definition of profit maximization by individuals and apply "rationality" loosely to economic (or even political and social) systems or institutions without acknowledging that such a use of the term becomes entirely subjective once removed from the realm of individual economic behavior, for which it is a well-defined concept. He eloquently argues that the "rationality" that is often imputed to the overall economic system or of institutions "cannot be the same thing as the rational behavior of the individual entrepreneur who seeks the path of maximum profit to himself."[49] Simply put, economic rationality is the maximization of profit or

44. Goldthwaite 2009, 8.

45. Padgett and McLean 2006, 1543–44.

46. As Feinman 2016, 140–41, puts it, in spite of widespread insistence that the old debates between primitivists and modernizers have long since been abandoned, the same issues, such as the rejection of a "market mentality," keep recurring in ancient economic history scholarship.

47. "Formalist" and "substantivist" are terms that were originally coined by Karl Polanyi in his theories of the differences between the modern economy, which is describable by "formal" economic theory (including economic rationality), and premodern economies, which can only be analyzed through "substantivism," an anthropology-based approach to economic behavior.

48. There have been some studies of *mentalité* for the ancient economy, e.g., Andreau, France, and Pittia 2004.

49. Braudel 1982, 576.

wealth by individuals. It is not related to the efficiency or performance of structures external to the individual. For example, the irrationality of political institutions emphasized by the Frankfurt School has nothing to do with economic rationality whatsoever (except insofar as rational action by individuals can create seemingly irrational or inefficient outcomes at the collective level) since economic rationality per se only refers to individual behavior. As Jon Elster once put it, "Individual rationality leads to collective disaster."[50] Rationality also does not concern the desired aims of economic action but only the means to attaining these ends—one can pursue "irrational" goals but still behave in an economically rational manner.[51]

Since John Stuart Mill, economics has considered rational behavior to be, in its most basic form, maximizing return or wealth in the market,[52] but in response to myriad critiques that people are not solely motivated by monetary gain in their daily lives, scholars have developed the inclusive notion of utility, which more accurately reflects the full spectrum of goals an individual might desire.[53] Rational choice in economics today is merely "the 'sensible apportioning of means to ends' . . . the pursuit of profit, defined broadly."[54] Sensibly apportioning one's means to one's desired ends naturally includes a process of comparison and choice: "According to [his] preferences, the individual assesses the various alternatives at his disposal, he weighs up the pros and cons, the costs and benefits of the alternatives against each other and finally chooses that (those) alternative(s) which come(s) closest to his preferences or which promise(s) to bring about the maximum net benefit."[55] Whatever one's ends may be (profit, knowledge, companionship, etc.), as long as someone is acting in the way that best attains them, he or she is said to be maximizing utility.[56]

Utility is extremely difficult to observe in a concrete sense, however, and impossible to quantify. It is too nebulous to serve as an index of rationality alone since it is highly susceptible to subjective interpretation. Furthermore, focusing only on utility would simply bypass the question of whether or not

50. Braudel 1982, 467. Also see Elster 1989, 126: "There are innumerable examples in social life of [the] perverse tendency of individual rationality to generate collective disaster."

51. McCloskey 1996, 143; Kirchgässner 2008, 12.

52. See Persky 1995.

53. For extensive discussions of the full complexity of the notion of economic rationality in all its forms, see Hargreaves Heap 1989, and Zouboulakis 2014.

54. McCloskey 1996, 143.

55. Kirchgässner 2008, 12.

56. Polanyi 1957b, 245–46, defines rational action as follows: "The manner in which the logic of rational action produces formal economics . . . rational action is here defined as choice of means in relation to ends. Means are anything appropriate to serve the end. . . . Thus 'rational' does not refer either to ends or to means, but rather to the relating of means to ends . . . whatever the end, it is rational to choose one's means accordingly."

ancient Greeks behaved like modern individuals, because the maximization of profit or wealth has been the single element that has been extolled as the quintessence of modern economic behavior in the modern industrial capitalist system.[57] Maximizing return, on the other hand, can be measured quantitatively, and therefore functions as an effective heuristic device to explore the problem of rationality, as has been argued by Grassby.[58] Combined with the ability to compare the relative profitability of different investment options, profit maximization is a useful measure of rationality which is well-defined, objective, and easily observable.[59]

But one must proceed with caution—as the critics rightly note, cultural specificity needs to be fully integrated into any assessment of ancient economic behavior because pure rationality is not an accurate depiction of reality, and economists themselves have long recognized that rationality is an insufficient account of economic behavior when pushed to the extreme. Herbert Simon famously pointed out the information and time limitations on the economic decision-making process to highlight the imperfections in rational behavior, and argued for "bounded rationality" in which individuals "satisfice" rather than maximize.[60] Behavioral economists argue that the psychology of decision-making is heavily influenced by irrationality, especially emotional and instinctive impulses.[61] Thaler has performed experiments in laboratory settings in which mental accounting practices, consumer choices, feelings of self-control, and fairness all exhibit "quasi-rational" inconsistencies with neoclassical rational choice theory.[62] Shiller illustrates the effects of emotions on economic choices within the context of speculative bubbles, where artificial and unsustainable price increases balloon from excessive entry into specific markets because of the emotional envy of those who have been recently successful.[63] Therefore, irrationality and emotions need to be integrated to encompass the complexity of economic behavior holistically. Simon's model of "bounded rationality" and Hargreaves Heap's "expressive rationality," which incorporates nonmonetary considerations, have been embraced by a number of economic

57. Profit and wealth maximization are at the crux of the disagreements over rationality in the premodern world, for which see Morley 2007, 8–9, and Christesen 2003, 33–39.

58. Grassby 1995, 4: "The concept of profit maximization, despite its limited application in real life, has a simplicity and directness which social and cultural explanations lack. It is easy to verify by self-analysis."

59. Acton 2014 also uses profit maximization as his main heuristic device. For the limits of profit maximization as an explanation for human behavior, see e.g., Amemiya 2005.

60. See, e.g., Simon 1955, 1992.

61. See, e.g., Kahneman and Tversky 1979.

62. Thaler 1991.

63. Shiller 2000.

historians to account for the full intricacies of human behavior embodied by utility.[64] Similar challenges to the basic paradigm of profit maximization appear in game theory, economic anthropology and sociology, and peasant studies, which all complement purely gain-oriented behavior with the variety of influences within the elaborate fabric of cultural and social contexts. Nevertheless, without some parameters such a wide-ranging discussion would quickly lose cohesion—so keeping these perspectives in mind, a sustained analytical focus on profit and wealth maximization is necessary.[65]

Only a concentrated examination of the full range of available evidence can address this issue sufficiently, so I will draw from as much source material as possible for accounts of how ancient Athenians managed their businesses and estates, especially oratory, philosophy, and epigraphical documents of the classical period. Each of these materials presents its own problems for interpretation. For example, philosophers have been used extensively for ancient Greek economic history, but many of the most illuminating pieces of evidence have been overlooked. Furthermore, the testimony of philosophers must be taken with a grain of salt. When Socrates above depicts a stark contrast between what he himself and most other Athenians (*hoi polloi*) did with their time, the first two activities he mentions are making money and estate management. As far as the economy is concerned, philosophers' personal opinions cannot be considered to be representative of general attitudes or patterns of behavior in ancient Greece. Philosophers had moralizing agendas and tried to change *hoi polloi* to conform to their own values, and the masses clearly did not listen. Relying only on philosophers' prescriptive views distorts our impression of the economy through the veil of their atypical value judgments. Herein lies a vital methodological lesson. The moralizing prescriptions of philosophers should be kept distinct from the descriptive statements they make about how most other people behaved, which are a more accurate reflection of everyday reality.

Therefore, the big-picture observations and universalizing theories that philosophers express must be accompanied by a comprehensive and in-depth analysis of the real-life economic decisions of individuals that are attested in other texts. Only by exploring the complete range of behavior at every layer of generality and specificity will we be able to draw meaningful conclusions. Biographies, inscriptions, oratory, and poetry all contain important evidence for individual moneymaking practices. Moreover, these sources of course

64. See, e.g., Christesen 2003, 32; Engen 2010, 31–32.

65. Game theory also assumes economic rationality and employs some of the most formalistic versions of the models. See Von Neumann and Morgenstern 1944, who did the first comprehensive work on game theory. For a lucid account of this field, see Davis 2012.

have their own biases and agendas that make them challenging to interpret. The Attic orators have been employed extensively in the study of the ancient economy, but the full potential for illuminating the economic decision-making process of the actors preserved in their speeches has not been realized. These accounts need to be unpacked and analyzed with a microscope at the finest-grained level of detail possible. Although there is a significant amount of fabrication in these speeches, it is unlikely that someone would try to convince a court on the basis of unbelievable or improbable principles of behavior;[66] therefore, I will approach these accounts as exemplifying the types of economic motivations and strategies that the Athenians would consider to be credible. It is true that numbers are especially unreliable, but without alternative figures on which to base a conjecture, it is also dangerous to assert substitute estimates based on assumptions from modern averages without the full knowledge of the state of an industry or the level of supply and demand of a given product at a certain time. Inscriptions are also often fragmentary but when supplemented by their broader historical context they preserve crucial details about the economic decisions of ancient Greek individuals.

These sources are inherently more representative of the rich rather than the poor, but there are also signs of social mobility and the emergence of nouveaux riches that reveal economic strategies among the lower classes as well. Moreover, our examples are skewed mainly toward classical Athens, but other *poleis* will appear and provide important evidence from the archaic to the Hellenistic periods, much of which corroborates the impression from fifth- and fourth-century Athenian sources. Archaic poets were not trying to do economic history, but nevertheless it is possible to glean insights about the actions of the citizens within their communities and the social consequences of the self-interested pursuit of wealth among a large percentage of the citizens of a *polis*. Similar patterns of behavior can indeed be observed throughout the ancient Greek world more broadly.

Finally, if economically rational behavior is to serve properly as an analytical category, it needs to be examined within the Greeks' particular cultural and institutional context. For culture, special attention must be paid to how they framed their discussions of economic decisions and motivations.[67] Values governing the acquisition of wealth, as well as the terms in which they expressed their approach to economic affairs will need to be prominent. Moreover, I will explore how individuals responded to market realities by navigating

66. Cf. Cohen 1992, 26–27.
67. For the importance of framing, see Günther 2014.

and manipulating the institutional context in which they lived; here the costs of nonmarket opportunities and arrangements that could be made in lieu of resorting to legal measures, as emphasized by Coase for example, will also be an important focus.[68]

I will begin with the Athenians' own notion of *chrêmatistikê*, the art of making money. Though the term *chrêmata* has its roots in wealth more generally and predates the invention of coinage, *chrêmatistikê* and its synonym *chrêmatismos* are not attested before the monetization of the Greek world, so I will adhere to the translation "making money." The title of this book is therefore pointed and specific—to view economic phenomena through the lens of ancient Greek cultural conceptualization.

But we must also break free of insular discussions among experts in ancient history to address larger debates in economic history and the long-term development of capitalism. Thus, the focus will be maintained on economic rationality and the behaviors that are associated with modern capitalism, especially the continuous reinvestment of profit for the purpose of maximizing income and wealth. The sustained, intentional accumulation of capital for its own sake is expressed by Marx's distinction between money being used to buy commodities in order to make further money as an end in itself in the form of increased exchange value (M-C-M), as opposed to just acquiring additional commodities for their use value and therefore not primarily aiming at profit (C-M-C).[69]

Furthermore, how did the Athenians' institutions shape their moneymaking practices? Can they even be investigated as discrete individuals separate from social structures as assumed by methodological individualism? How was *chrêmatistikê* carried out in an economy embedded in their own particular cultural and social practices? What opportunities (or obstacles) for profit seeking did the institution of slavery offer that differed from those of modern capitalism based on free wage labor? Also, without firms or corporate institutions, moneymaking took place within the institutional bounds of the *oikos*, so *chrêmatistikê* must be examined within the context of traditional estate management, *oikonomia*. In what ways did Athenians balance the utility-maximizing aims of households with the profit-maximizing goals of businesses when the latter were part of the former?[70]

68. Coase 1937 and 1960.

69. Money being used to buy commodities for the sake of making further money (M-C-M), i.e., for their exchange value, is the more advanced behavior that Marx attributes to modern capitalism, rather than commodities being created to acquire money merely as a means to acquire new commodities for their use value (C-M-C), which is the more primitive behavior in Marx's view. See *Das Kapital*, vol. 1, ch. 3.

70. Schefold 2011.

What emerges is a rich, textured account of the complexity of cultural, financial, political, psychological, and social factors that affected individual behavior in ancient Athens. I will begin in chapter 1 with the conceptual framework that structured Athenians' discussions of economic behavior within their notional categories of *chrêmatistikê* and *oikonomia*. Furthermore, alongside profit and wealth maximization, emotions and irrationality will feature prominently, as will philosophers' theories of the mind in which they described the psychological impulses that directed the economic decision-making process of Athenian individuals.

This overview of the big-picture conceptual framework will then be followed by a close examination of the best preserved individual case studies of Athenian estate management in chapters 2 and 3, which are devoted to diversified and specialized estates, respectively. The focus of chapter 4 will be the analysis of the economic decision-making process at the finest level of detail possible, in the well attested (or plausibly fabricated) behaviors and motivations that can be unpacked in the actual transactions that occurred in the sphere of maritime trade (*emporia*). Finally I will then branch out in chapter 5 to compare patterns of economic behavior in the ancient Greek world beyond Athens. Cultural values governing the acquisition of wealth and the place of the individual in society will be explored in depth, as will the Greeks' cosmology, especially their beliefs about the origins of humanity, their overall view of the universe, and the supernatural forces that governed their approach to their economic affairs.

CHAPTER 1

Hunger in Their Souls

Profit and Wealth Maximization in Athenian Thought

Introduction: Aristotle on *Chrêmatistikê*

Aristotle opens his discussion of the state (*polis*) in book 1 of the *Politics* with a systematic examination of its smallest fundamental building block, the citizen household (*oikia*). He devotes considerable attention to individual estate management, *oikonomia*, and lists its most important components: the relationship between husband and wife, father and child, master and slave, and the art of making money (*chrêmatistikê*).[1] Initially this last item might appear to be peripheral or out of place. But soon it becomes clear why *chrêmatistikê* looms so large in his mind—he thinks it is central to the estate management of the typical citizen. It was such a salient, prominent feature of daily life that it was complicating the way he and others conceptualized *oikonomia*.

Aristotle believed *chrêmatistikê* was transforming economic reality, and his account suddenly becomes animated as he dives into a digression to explore it in depth. Human creativity and innovation allowed people to break the limits imposed by nature, *physis*, on the accumulation of wealth.[2] Natural economic success was restricted to what the earth could sustain, but with the art of moneymaking, *chrêmatistikê*, the bounds of one's wealth were now unlimited: χρηματιστικήν, δι' ἣν οὐδὲν δοκεῖ πέρας εἶναι πλούτου καὶ κτήσεως, "Moneymaking, through which there seems to be no end of wealth and acquisition" (Aristotle, *Politics* 1.9.1, 1256b40–1257a1).

1. *Politics* 1.3.3, 1253b5–14.

2. See Meikle 1995a, 43–67, and Von Reden 2003, 184–87, for in-depth analyses of this passage. Polanyi 1957a describes Aristotle as "discovering the economy" in this discussion. For Aristotle's treatment of *chrêmatistikê* in the *Politics*, see Austin and Vidal-Naquet 1977, 362–68. Meikle 1996 shows that Aristotle's view of *chrêmatistikê* is largely negative, and there is a moralizing tone in this and other passages concerned with moneymaking and business. In order to become the target of Aristotle's moral censures, such behavior must have been very widespread. For Aristotle's economic analysis in the *Politics* and the *Nicomachean Ethics*, which is unique in the extant literature from ancient Greece, see Finley 1970, 3–25.

He was particularly fascinated with the new types of moneymaking that the invention of coinage created for trade and moneylending. His pace seems to quicken as he tries to articulate the essence of this achievement of human culture:

> εὐλογώτατα μισεῖται ἡ ὀβολοστατικὴ διὰ τὸ ἀπ' αὐτοῦ τοῦ νομίσματος εἶναι τὴν κτῆσιν καὶ οὐκ ἐφ' ὅπερ ἐπορίσθη. μεταβολῆς γὰρ ἐγένετο χάριν, ὁ δὲ τόκος αὐτὸ ποιεῖ πλέον ὅθεν καὶ τοὔνομα τοῦτ' εἴληφεν: ὅμοια γὰρ τὰ τικτόμενα τοῖς γεννῶσιν αὐτά ἐστιν, ὁ δὲ τόκος γίνεται νόμισμα ἐκ νομίσματος: ὥστε καὶ μάλιστα παρὰ φύσιν οὗτος τῶν χρηματισμῶν ἐστιν.

> Usury is laudably hated because it is the acquisition of money from itself, and not for what it was invented. For it arose for the sake of exchange, but interest makes it increase, whence it has received this name: for the offspring themselves are similar to the parents, and the interest is money arising from money, such that it is also the type of moneymaking most contrary to nature. (1.10.4–5, 1258b3–9)

With coinage, people were taking advantage of opportunities for making profit that were qualitatively different from those they had previously had at their disposal. One example is *obolostatikê*, technically a kind of small-time moneylending characterized by high interest rates or quick turnover with rapid velocity of transactions, but here probably referring to usury in general.[3] The term also likely elicited images of even more imaginative (or insidious) interest schemes in Aristotle's (and his audience's) mind, as Strepsiades in Aristophanes' *Clouds* depicts the *obolostatai* charging interest upon unpaid interest, τόκοι τόκων (1155–56). No wonder Aristotle says such usurers are hated—they have taken the possibilities of coinage a step further beyond nature, as they are not just making money from money, but levying additional interest upon the interest itself—that is, compound interest. The frenetic pace at which the usurer chases down borrowers to collect interest overdue on earlier interest could certainly be perceived as violating the laws of nature.

Retail trade (*kapêlikon* or *kapêlikê*) was also capable of producing novel mechanisms for generating profit when combined with coined money: πορισθέντος οὖν ἤδη νομίσματος ἐκ τῆς ἀναγκαίας ἀλλαγῆς θάτερον εἶδος τῆς

3. As argued by Millett 1991, 182–86.

χρηματιστικῆς ἐγένετο, τὸ καπηλικόν, τὸ μὲν πρῶτον ἁπλῶς ἴσως γινόμενον, εἶτα δι' ἐμπειρίας ἤδη τεχνικώτερον, πόθεν καὶ πῶς μεταβαλλόμενον πλεῖστον ποιήσει κέρδος, "And so with coinage now invented from necessary exchange, the other form of moneymaking appeared, retail trade, which was simple at first, but then through experience it became more technical, from which sources and how one will make the most profit by transacting."[4] Aristotle's words here imply a great deal and can be unpacked to reveal significant insights about the behavior he was observing in the economy around him. Through "experience" or "experimentation" (ἐμπειρίας) in their day-to-day exchange transactions (μεταβαλλόμενον), traders in the field of *kapêlikê* were refining their methods and making them "more technical." In Aristotle's eyes, coinage and human ingenuity permitted the limitless accumulation of money to an extent that was truly unprecedented.

This last term (τεχνικώτερον) elucidates the dynamic process Aristotle describes; moneymaking in trade and commerce was becoming increasingly advanced over time as a result of human innovation. He says that *chrêmatistikê* is associated with "experience and art," ἐμπειρίας τινὸς καὶ τέχνης (*Politics* 1.9.1), and he was not alone in this view. *Chrêmatistikê* is also referred to as a *technê*, "art," in Plato's dialogues (*Gorgias* 451d–452e), an *epistêmê*, "science" (*Euthydemus* 289a), and an *epitêdeuma*, "pursuit" (*Euthydemus* 307a). The line between *technai* and *epistêmai* was often blurred in Athenian thought, but this range of labels illustrates that *chrêmatistikê* was sufficiently developed to a point that it was an easily recognizable craft with a definite goal. Therefore, through their experience in the transactions they were conducting, these people were making the art of moneymaking more sophisticated.

Most importantly, the purpose of this experimentation was to figure out how to realize the greatest profit (πλεῖστον κέρδος). Greeks were honing their craft and improving their technical skill in the field of *chrêmatistikê* because they were seeking to maximize their returns:

> καὶ ἄπειρος δὴ οὗτος ὁ πλοῦτος, ὁ ἀπὸ ταύτης τῆς χρηματιστικῆς . . . τέλος δὲ ὁ τοιοῦτος πλοῦτος καὶ χρημάτων κτῆσις . . . διὸ τῇ μὲν φαίνεται ἀναγκαῖον εἶναι παντὸς πλούτου πέρας, ἐπὶ δὲ τῶν γινομένων ὁρῶμεν συμβαῖνον τοὐναντίον· πάντες γὰρ εἰς ἄπειρον αὔξουσιν οἱ χρηματιζόμενοι τὸ νόμισμα.

4. Aristotle, *Politics* 1.9.8–9, 1257b1–5.

> Indeed this wealth has no limit, which comes from this type of moneymaking . . . and the end is wealth of this kind and the acquisition of money . . . on the one hand it seems necessary that there be a limit for all wealth, but on the other we see the opposite occurring in actual deeds; for everyone engaged in moneymaking will increase his money without limit.[5]

The conclusion from this statement is that these individuals were maximizing not only their profits, but their overall wealth as well. Moreover, Aristotle says that the ultimate end (*telos*) of this kind of moneymaking is the acquisition of wealth for its own sake, using money to make money (M-C-M, not C-M-C). So the purpose of this *chrêmatistikê* was to continuously increase wealth without limit. These Greeks responded to the new opportunities arising from the invention of coinage with creativity, to elevate their gains to levels previously impossible, beyond the limits permitted by nature alone. Not only does this behavior resemble the profit and wealth maximization that is the cornerstone of economic rationality in modern economic theory, but also the continuous reinvestment into additional production often cited as the defining characteristic of modern capitalistic enterprise.

"Everyone engaged in moneymaking will increase his money without limit" is a strong claim, however, which must be unpacked. To say that "everyone" achieves the endless accumulation of money is obviously an exaggeration, though it may nonetheless reflect a desire that was common enough to be a general rule of behavior in Aristotle's mind. But more significantly, it is not entirely clear if Aristotle restricts this comment to trade alone or jumps to make a broader observation. The πάντες in this passage may refer to everyone within "this type of moneymaking" or everyone engaged in *chrêmatistikê* overall. The limiting nature of ταύτης undoubtedly applies to the first couple of sentences and would very naturally fit with the passage's attention on trade. I myself have argued that retail traders in fourth-century BCE Athens sought to maximize their profits in an economically rational manner.[6] But Aristotle may have slipped here away from just *kapêlikê* to make a grandiose claim about all *chrêmatistai*. So just how widespread was this kind of behavior? Did it extend beyond retail trade and moneylending? Also, did it only exist in Athens?

First, based on the larger context of Aristotle's exploration of *chrêmatistikê*, it does not seem to be entirely marginal since it falls within his analysis of the

5. Aristotle, *Politics* 1.9.13–14, 1257b24–35.
6. Leese 2017b.

fundamental aspects of estate management of the typical Greek citizen, the smallest constituent element of the *polis*. If the *oikonomia* of citizens were not affected by the profit and wealth maximizing of the market, why would he allow it to distract him from his focus on administering the members of a household and the disposition of property? *Obolostatikê* was certainly practiced by a tiny minority in the city, but Aristotle would not indulge in such a lengthy overall excursus for the sake of a few exceptional individuals. The centrality of *chrêmatistikê* to the daily life of the citizen base of the *polis* seems to be a main idea emerging from his discussion. This pattern is so prevalent that it intruded into his theoretical treatment of the citizen household.

To be called an art, *chrêmatistikê* had to be common enough to be observable, and it was both producing new techniques for profit seeking in trade and moneylending, and also expanding into spheres of life not traditionally associated with wealth alone. Plato and Aristotle both felt anxiety that *chrêmatistikê* was spreading—cause for alarm because it was not just confined to highly specialized commercial trades but was threatening to undermine the cohesion of the citizen body itself. In the *Republic*, Plato's Socrates describes at length how moneymaking has subsumed a multitude of other arts, which are now all practiced for the sake of making money (397e). He asks the question, "Is someone a moneymaker or a shepherd?" (345c), because the aims of other arts have been muddled by their contact with *chrêmatistikê*; doctors (342d), shepherds (345d), and soldiers (397e) alike all acted as *chrêmatistai* in seeking riches from their arts as opposed to the inherent point of their *technai*, which was to provide essential services for the common good. He even goes so far as to declare that all craftsmen were moneymakers by nature (434b). Aristotle likewise says that people have found ways to transform other arts into a means of seeking profit. Warfare and medicine have been warped by *chrêmatistikê*, like many other arts, as their original purpose has been diverted to the creation of wealth: οἱ δὲ πάσας ποιοῦσι χρηματιστικάς, ὡς τοῦτο τέλος ὄν, πρὸς δὲ τὸ τέλος ἅπαντα δέον ἀπαντᾶν.[7] Sophistry is presented by both Plato and Aristotle as nothing more than *chrêmatistikê* under the guise of teaching rhetoric and wisdom.[8] Though not profit-generating by nature, these *technai* had been subverted and their main end, *telos*, redirected toward money itself.

Chrêmatistikê was an art unlike any other—it could encroach upon and even swallow seemingly unrelated *technai* and *epistêmai*. This unique ability emanated from the very nature of money. To Aristotle, *chrêmatistikê* was per-

7. *Politics* 1.9.17–18 (1258a10–14). See Meikle 1995a, 70–79.
8. Plato, *Sophist* 226a; Aristotle, *Sophistici Elenchi*. 165a 22, 171b 28.

haps even more intricately intertwined with other *technai*, since it could not stand on its own, but must be attached to another such as *kapêlikê*.[9] The impression from Aristotle and Plato is one of a growing, dynamic force that was spilling over beyond its own bounds and engulfing other pursuits as well. At the conceptual level also, this overlap between arts indicates that their boundaries and definitions were not static but subject to manipulation and distorted by human practice. This notional fluidity mirrors that of the money itself.

Oikonomia as *Chrêmatistikê*

Chrêmatistikê was so broad and its behavior so pervasive in the life of the *polis* that it seems to have conceptually penetrated into the everyday *oikonomia* of citizens more generally. Aristotle himself has difficulty separating the two. In the *Politics*, he expends a great deal of energy on finding the precise distinction between *chrêmatistikê* and the art of household management, *oikonomikê*. First he classifies *chrêmatistikê* as belonging to the art of acquisition (*ktêtikê*), which is itself subsidiary to household management (1.4.1, 1253b23–24). He follows with a declaration that the two cannot be the same thing, since *chrêmatistikê* is for acquisition and *oikonomikê* is for use: ὅτι μὲν οὖν οὐχ ἡ αὐτὴ ἡ οἰκονομικὴ τῇ χρηματιστικῇ, δῆλον τῆς μὲν γὰρ τὸ πορίσασθαι, τῆς δὲ τὸ χρήσασθαι· τίς γὰρ ἔσται ἡ χρησομένη τοῖς κατὰ τὴν οἰκίαν παρὰ τὴν οἰκονομικήν, "And so it is clear that household management is not the same thing as moneymaking, since the work of the latter is to provide and that of the former to use; for what will be the art that uses the things throughout the house, unless it is household management?" (1.8.2, 1256a10–13). Thus, *chrêmatistikê* and *oikonomikê* are qualitatively dissimilar in this statement, both in their ends and in their means, the former being concerned with acquisition, and the latter with use or disposition.

But the more he looks into it, the less certain Aristotle is of the difference between the two arts, or which aspects of *oikonomia* could be excluded from *chrêmatistikê*: "The moneymaker has to find where money and property are to be procured, and there are many sorts of wealth, including husbandry, and the care and provision of food—are these part of moneymaking or different arts?" (*Politics* 1.8.3). Eventually he settles upon a distinction that is highly nuanced, but still somewhat avoids the issue: there is a type of acquisition that is part of *oikonomia* and is natural because it has a limit, while *chrêmatistikê* is specifi-

9. Meikle 1995a, 79.

cally concerned with the accumulation of unlimited amounts of money, which, as a product of human culture, can burst any limits imposed by nature.

In the end he is not able to separate the two concepts entirely or even maintain his own neat division between use and acquisition. Later in the *Politics*, he says that a man's *oikonomia* is to acquire (*ktasthai*) wealth and a woman's is to protect (*phylattein*) it: οἰκονομία ἑτέρα ἀνδρὸς καὶ γυναικός· τοῦ μὲν γὰρ κτᾶσθαι τῆς δὲ φυλάττειν ἔργον ἐστίν (3.2.10, 1277b23–25). Here, in stating that there are different types of *oikonomia* appropriate to men and women, Aristotle's categorization changes based on the context, because he now attributes provision and acquisition (which he reserved for *chrêmatistikê* above) to a man's *oikonomia*, and reserves protection and use for women. Furthermore, in the *Nicomachean Ethics*, where he discusses the types of giving and receiving that characterize prodigality and liberality, he says that getting wealth and protecting it (*phylakê*) are modes of acquisition (*ktêsis*), not use: χρῆσις δ' εἶναι δοκεῖ χρημάτων δαπάνη καὶ δόσις· ἡ δὲ λῆψις καὶ ἡ φυλακὴ κτῆσις μᾶλλον (4.1.7, 1120a8–9). Here he associates protection with acquisition, whereas he had distinguished between them in his allocation of the elements of men's and women's *oikonomia* at *Politics* 3.2.10. So although Aristotle does define *oikonomia* and *chrêmatistikê*, they are not fixed but shift according to their context.[10]

His mind struggles to pinpoint the precise nature of *chrêmatistikê*, and for good reason—neither he nor the Greeks of his time seem to have been entirely certain to what extent *chrêmatistikê* and *oikonomia* were separate arts or actually the same thing: πότερον δὲ μέρος αὐτῆς ἐστί τι ἢ ἕτερον εἶδος, ἔχει διαμφισβήτησιν, "It is debated if *chrêmatistikê* is a part of *oikonomia* or if the two are different arts" (1.8.2, 1256a13–14). As he remarks earlier, δοκεῖ τοῖς μὲν εἶναι οἰκονομία, τοῖς δὲ μέγιστον μέρος αὐτῆς, "To some it seems to be *oikonomia* itself, while to others it seems to be the greatest part of it" (1.3.3, 1253b12–14). It was because of this lack of agreement over the nature of *oikonomia* and *chrêmatistikê* that Aristotle felt compelled to investigate their relationship in the first place (ὅπως δ' ἔχει, θεωρητέον). So *chrêmatistikê* had so thoroughly pervaded household management that people were not really sure where the one art ended and the other began, and Aristotle was no exception.

Indeed, Aristotle's stark prescriptive demarcation between use and acquisi-

10. Earlier he states that retail trade is not a natural part of *chrêmatistikê* because it aims at the provision of more than what is sufficient (1.9.4, 1257a18–20), an ever-increasing accumulation of wealth, whereas simple exchange for one's needs does by nature belong to *chrêmatistikê*. Later in the same passage, however, he says that *metablêtikê* to secure necessities is not a type of *chrêmatistikê* (1.9.6–7, 1257a29–30), so it seems that he is having a very difficult time clearly distinguishing between the various terms he is employing in this discussion.

tion was not followed by many people of his time, who simply treated *oikonomikê* as *chrêmatistikê*—they ran their households for profit:

> δοκεῖ τισι τοῦτ᾽ εἶναι τῆς οἰκονομικῆς ἔργον, καὶ διατελοῦσιν ἢ σῴζειν οἰόμενοι δεῖν ἢ αὔξειν τὴν τοῦ νομίσματος οὐσίαν εἰς ἄπειρον. αἴτιον δὲ ταύτης τῆς διαθέσεως τὸ σπουδάζειν περὶ τὸ ζῆν, ἀλλὰ μὴ τὸ εὖ ζῆν· εἰς ἄπειρον οὖν ἐκείνης τῆς ἐπιθυμίας οὔσης, καὶ τῶν ποιητικῶν ἀπείρων ἐπιθυμοῦσιν. ὅσοι δὲ καὶ τοῦ εὖ ζῆν ἐπιβάλλονται τὸ πρὸς τὰς ἀπολαύσεις τὰς σωματικὰς ζητοῦσιν, ὥστ᾽ ἐπεὶ καὶ τοῦτ᾽ ἐν τῇ κτήσει φαίνεται ὑπάρχειν, πᾶσα ἡ διατριβὴ περὶ τὸν χρηματισμόν ἐστι.
>
> It seems to some that this (increase) is the purpose of estate management, and they persevere in thinking that it is necessary for them either to save or increase their property (in the form) of money to an unlimited extent. And the reason for this disposition is their zeal for living but not for living well. And so, with that desire being for unlimited increase, so also they desire unlimited productive means. But even those people who do desire to live well seek this in respect to the pleasures of the body, so that when even this seems to exist in acquisition, all their time is spent in moneymaking. (*Politics*, 1.9.15–16, 1257b38–1258a7)

Thus, rather than observing his conceptual and terminological division between household management and moneymaking, these individuals designed their estates to make as much money as possible.

The phrase "to an unlimited extent" (*eis apeiron*) is of the utmost importance because here Aristotle reveals that it was not just in marginal trades that people were maximizing profit or wealth. They were also using their estate management to pursue these goals, driven by the unbounded desire for gain. The details of the approach these individuals take are also significant. The alternatives "save or increase" were complementary methods of augmenting wealth by protecting against loss on the one hand and seeking higher returns on the other. Moreover, he states this desire was aimed at not just consumption, but also at the "unlimited productive means," which implies another twofold process in which mental activity is directed toward both the ends and the means necessary for the further generation of wealth. The distinction between means and ends, as well as the continuous reinvestment of profit in mechanisms that endlessly create additional money are fundamental to wealth maximization in modern economic theory. Those who spent "all their time" in *chrêmatismos* as part of their overall estate management therefore employed methods that are all in line with the behaviors that achieve the maximization of wealth. Finally, they are described in such specific detail that they seem to be a category of individuals widespread enough that Aristotle has gained personal familiarity with their methods.

Such a conclusion is consistent with Aristotle's ideas elsewhere, where it seems that the obsession with wealth was not restricted only to the more recently invented coinage-based arts, but was an objective of *oikonomia* more broadly. As he declares in the opening lines of the *Nicomachean Ethics*, "Of the many arts and sciences there are also many ends . . . that of estate management is wealth," πολλῶν δὲ πράξεων οὐσῶν καὶ τεχνῶν καὶ ἐπιστημῶν πολλὰ γίνεται καὶ τὰ τέλη: ἰατρικῆς μὲν γὰρ ὑγίεια, ναυπηγικῆς δὲ πλοῖον, στρατηγικῆς δὲ νίκη, οἰκονομικῆς δὲ πλοῦτος (1.3). This statement certainly does not refer only to moneylending and trade, but rather suggests that Greeks in general were using the art of household management as a means of pursuing the end of wealth (*ploutos*).[11]

Chrêmatistikê and *oikonomia* were so closely associated with each other that they were sometimes interchangeable. Akin to Aristotle's conflation of the two notions above is Plato's comment in the *Republic* that young men only learn philosophy in the time before they take up household management and moneymaking (*oikonomia* and *chrêmatismos*) as adults, seeming to equate the two as young men's primary occupation after reaching adulthood (*Republic* 498a). Moreover, the individualistic quality of this economic activity in *oikonomia* is further underscored by Plato's prescriptions for the guardians in his ideal city, who should be soldiers only, not moneymakers; if they live like normal farmers they will turn into *oikonomoi*. The context of this passage is a diatribe against private gain, and *oikonomia* is seen primarily a means of pursuing personal economic profit over the interests of the community at large, for the purpose of *chrêmatistikê* (*Republic* 415e–417a). Therefore, Plato (or his Socrates) also used the term *oikonomia* synonymously with *chrêmatistikê* and *chrêmatismos*.

Even agriculture had been conceptually absorbed into the larger notion of *chrêmatistikê*. Agriculture was so intimately linked with profit that farming and animal husbandry are the first fields that Aristotle mentions in his enumeration of the different varieties of moneymaking:

> ἔστι δὲ χρηματιστικῆς μέρη χρήσιμα: τὸ περὶ τὰ κτήματα ἔμπειρον εἶναι, ποῖα λυσιτελέστατα καὶ ποῦ καὶ πῶς, οἷον ἵππων κτῆσις ποία τις ἢ βοῶν

11. Balot 2001, 39, agrees that Aristotle believed it was not just traders engaging in unnatural *kapêlikê*, but also citizen householders who tried to maximize their wealth.

ἢ προβάτων, ὁμοίως δὲ καὶ τῶν λοιπῶν ζῴων· δεῖ γὰρ ἔμπειρον εἶναι πρὸς ἄλληλά τε τούτων τίνα λυσιτελέστατα, καὶ ποῖα ἐν ποίοις τόποις. ἄλλα γὰρ ἐν ἄλλαις εὐθηνεῖ χώραις, εἶτα περὶ γεωργίας, καὶ ταύτης ἤδη ψιλῆς τε καὶ πεφυτευμένης, καὶ μελιττουργίας, καὶ τῶν ἄλλων ζῴων τῶν πλωτῶν ἢ πτηνῶν, ἀφ' ὅσων ἔστι τυγχάνειν βοηθείας.[12]

These are the useful branches of moneymaking: the practical experience with possessions, what sorts are most profitable and where and how, such as what sort of acquisition of horses or cows or sheep, and likewise for the rest of animals (for it is necessary to be experienced in which of these are most profitable in respect to one another, and what kinds are most profitable in which places, for different animals thrive in different places). The next branch concerns farming, and of this there are cereals and trees, and also bee-keeping, and of however many other animals, either swimming or flying, from which it is possible to make a living.

Here agriculture and animal husbandry are presented as types of *chrêmatistikê* and Aristotle sums them up immediately afterward as, "These are the divisions and first parts of moneymaking in its most proper form" (τῆς μὲν οὖν οἰκειοτάτης χρηματιστικῆς ταῦτα μόρια καὶ πρῶτα).[13] The first and most natural types of property that come to Aristotle's mind when listing the practically useful branches of *chrêmatistikê* are livestock and agricultural production.

His use of the superlative "most profitable" (λυσιτελέστατα) twice in this short passage is even more significant, however, as an explicit, unambiguous declaration that people were using agriculture and animal husbandry to maximize their profits. Therefore, agriculture clearly fell under the larger category of *chrêmatistikê* in Aristotle's mind, and it was not only in retail trade and moneylending where Greeks aimed at ever-increasing gain.

Indeed, Aristotle laments that the currency and degree of sophistication that agricultural treatises had gained by his time, such as those by Charetides of Paros and Apollodorus of Lemnos, had not yet inspired similar works for other sorts of moneymaking activities.[14] The agricultural and estate management pamphlets that appeared by the classical period demonstrate the scientific approach Greeks took to farming and *oikonomia*. In the late fifth to the fourth century, Antisthenes was said by Xenophon in the *Memorabilia* to be an *oiko*-

12. *Politics* 1.11.1–2, 1258b12–21.
13. *Politics* 1.11.2–3, 1258b22–23.
14. *Politics* 1.11.7, 1258b–1259a.

nomos who was extremely successful to the point of making himself a general;[15] though this is uncertain, it is known that he wrote on household management: Περὶ ἐπιτρόπου ἢ περὶ τοῦ πείθεσθαι (*On the Manager or on Obedience*), as well as the oddly titled Περὶ νίκης οἰκονομικός (*On Victory: An Economic Work*).[16] Androtion was the author of a pamphlet called "Farming Matters" (Γεωργικά),[17] and Xenophon along with many others was writing manuals on how to make money in agriculture at this time. At least fifty Greek treatises were published on various subjects in agriculture and *oikonomia* in the classical and Hellenistic world, which were followed by such successors in the Roman world as Cato, Columella, and Varro.[18]

Already in the archaic period, Hesiod set out a calendar in the *Works and Days* whereby to make optimal use of the agricultural cycle and slave productivity throughout the seasons of the year. The encouragement Hesiod gives a peasant to maximize his and his slaves' output is "so that you may buy the farm of others, and another not buy yours."[19] Xenophon and pseudo-Aristotle in their works on *oikonomia* both advocate the systematic, orderly management of estates to increase the efficiency and productivity of labor, and to secure as great profit as possible.[20] By properly training one's wife, slave overseer (*epitropos*), and housekeeper (*tamia*), one can control income and spending.[21] Limiting expenditures and keeping careful accounts allows one to make agriculture a profitable trade.

Xenophon's main agenda in the *Oeconomicus*, largely placed in the mouth of the dialogue's main character, the country gentleman Ischomachus, is to show how to become an "awesome" or "clever" *chrêmatistês* by practicing farming (Xenophon, *Oeconomicus* 2.18). In the dialogue, he argues that agriculture can be as lucrative as any other activity and also provide additional nonmonetary rewards that the so-called banausic trades cannot. But although Xenophon emphasizes the physical, military, political, and social benefits of becoming a gentleman farmer, his advice to enter agriculture is mainly designed to persuade his audience of the financial potential and ease of farming. As Pomeroy states,

15. Xenophon, *Memorabilia* 3.4. He is said to "understand nothing except for amassing money" (ἐπιστάμενόν τε ἄλλο οὐδὲν ἢ χρήματα συλλέγειν), and the associated traits ascribed to him are summed up by Socrates as being those of a "good estate manager" (ἀγαθὸς οἰκονόμος).

16. Diogenes Laertius 6.16. For Antisthenes see Davies 1971, 39 (#1194); Chandezon 2011, 99–100.

17. Davies 1971, 33.

18. See Varro, *De Re Rustica* praefatio, for an extensive list of Greek, Hellenistic, and early Roman agronomists. Columella also provides a list at his own, *De Re Rustica* 1.1.7–14.

19. Hesiod, *Works and Days* 341.

20. Both works advocate the efficient division of labor along gender lines, in addition to methods of slave management to maximize productivity.

21. For slave *epitropoi* and management of estates, see Carlsen 2002; Chandezon 2011.

"According to the *Oeconomicus*, profit is the chief goal of estate management,"[22] and Edward Harris agrees: "Ischomachos certainly ran his household in an 'entrepreneurial spirit,' with an eye to *kerdos*."[23] Indeed, this interpretation is well supported, as the focus on increasing wealth is repeated throughout. The term *kerdos* appears a number of times in the dialogue, indicating that much of the discussion centers on what brings profit.[24] The verb *auxanô*, "grow" or "increase," occurs frequently as well,[25] and this in particular reveals the central interest in the dialogue: how to enlarge one's estate.[26] Therefore, just as Aristotle observed for *oikonomia* in general, Xenophon recommends agriculture as an effective way of making money in the *Oeconomicus*.

Xenophon's advice comes at the level of the highest management, in the choices of production to be made with the estate's money, as well as the selection and training of the rest of the staff. A strict division of labor by gender is outlined to maximize the productivity of both the outdoor and the indoor household operations. The wife, the male slave overseer (*epitropos*), and the female slave housekeeper (*tamia*), are all part of the management of the profitable *oikos* unit which Xenophon envisions. By convincing his wife that the household is also her property, the male estate owner enlists her as an equally productive partner in the ownership and administration of the estate, as opposed to being a wasteful consumer of the *oikos*' property.[27] With his wife having an equal stake in the operation of the household, she was the most trusted partner, keeping the accounts, and tracking expenses and income. Likewise, since the male slave overseer and female slave housekeeper were also invested with a large amount of responsibility,[28] Xenophon advocates giving them a similar stake in the management of the estate and ensuring their loyalty by offering a share of the profits for their successful efforts: καὶ πῶς, ἐγὼ ἔφην, πρὸς τῶν θεῶν εὔνοιαν ἔχειν σοὶ καὶ τοῖς σοῖς διδάσκεις ὅντινα ἂν βούλῃ; εὐεργετῶν νὴ Δί', ἔφη ὁ Ἰσχόμαχος, ὅταν τινὸς ἀγαθοῦ οἱ θεοὶ ἀφθονίαν διδῶσιν ἡμῖν.[29]

22. Pomeroy 1994, 51–52.

23. Harris 2002, 84.

24. *Kerdos* appears at, e.g., 2.18, 3.8, 8.12, 12.15–16, 14.8, 14.10. The opposite, *zêmia*, loss, also appears frequently, as the consequence for not following Socrates' and Ischomachus' advice: 1.7, 1.8–9, 2.18, 8.21, 9.14, 12.19. The juxtaposition between profit and loss as the consequences of hard work or laziness also figures prominently in Hesiod's advice in the *Works and Days*.

25. E.g., at 1.4, 1.6, 1.16, 2.1, 3.10, 3.15, 5.1, 6.4, 7.16, 7.43, 9.12, 11.8, 11.13.

26. Figueira 2012, 677. Pomeroy 1994, 61, also notes the importance of *periousia*, "surplus," in the dialogue, which again emphasizes the aim of growth and profit.

27. Xenophon, *Oeconomicus* 7.11–16.

28. For the training of the *epitropos*, see Carlsen 2002, 116.

29. Xenophon, *Oeconomicus* 12.6–7. He repeats this idea of providing a share of the household's success for his housekeeper in 9.12. Varro, *De Re Rustica* 1.17.5, also advocates giving rewards to

His advice is corroborated by Pseudo-Aristotle, who says that a *telos*, including better clothing, treatment, praise, and eventually emancipation must be set before slaves to encourage their productivity.[30] By watching over everything in the household, and personally being present in all operations, the master of the *oikos* can ensure the maximum profitability of his estate, reducing waste while increasing the collaborative desires of his partners in management, his wife and slaves.

In his account of agriculture's profitability, Xenophon clearly demonstrates how specializing in farming could be used to make money. Ischomachus' father in the *Oeconomicus* is described as a "property flipper" who buys unproductive estates for the purpose of fixing them up and reselling them at a profit:[31]

> τοῖς γε μέντοι ἐπιμελεῖσθαι δυναμένοις καὶ συντεταμένως γεωργοῦσιν ἀνυτικωτάτην χρημάτισιν ἀπὸ γεωργίας καὶ αὐτὸς ἐπετήδευσε καὶ ἐμὲ ἐδίδαξεν ὁ πατήρ. οὐδέποτε γὰρ εἴα χῶρον ἐξειργασμένον ὠνεῖσθαι . . . τοὺς μὲν γὰρ ἐξειργασμένους ἔφη καὶ πολλοῦ ἀργυρίου γίγνεσθαι καὶ ἐπίδοσιν οὐκ ἔχειν . . . οὐδὲν οὖν ἔχει πλείονα ἐπίδοσιν ἢ χῶρος ἐξ ἀργοῦ πάμφορος γιγνόμενος. εὖ γὰρ ἴσθι, ἔφη, ὦ Σώκρατες, ὅτι τῆς ἀρχαίας τιμῆς πολλοὺς πολλαπλασίου χώρους ἀξίους ἡμεῖς ἤδη ἐποιήσαμεν . . . ἐπιθυμῆσαι ἔφη τοιούτου χώρου ὅπως ἔχοι ὅ τι ποιοίη ἅμα καὶ ὠφελούμενος ἥδοιτο. καὶ ἐγὼ μέντοι ἀκούσας τοῦτο ἠρόμην αὐτόν: πότερα δέ, ὦ Ἰσχόμαχε, ὁπόσους ἐξειργάσατο χώρους ὁ πατὴρ πάντας ἐκέκτητο ἢ καὶ ἀπεδίδοτο, εἰ πολὺ ἀργύριον εὑρίσκοι; καὶ ἀπεδίδοτο νὴ Δί', ἔφη ὁ Ἰσχόμαχος: ἀλλὰ ἄλλον τοι εὐθὺς ἀντεωνεῖτο, ἀργὸν δέ, διὰ τὴν φιλεργίαν.

> "From farming comes the quickest way of making money for those who are able to be careful and who put their all into farming, as my father taught me and also practiced himself. For he never allowed me to buy a piece of land that was well-worked. . . . For he said that those plots which were well-worked cost a lot of money and were incapable of improvement. . . . Therefore nothing is capable of more improvement than a land which becomes all-productive from a state of neglect. For know well, Socrates, that we have already made farms worth many times their origi-

slave managers: praefectos alacriores faciendum praemiis dandaque opera ut habeant peculium et coniunctas conservas, e quibus habeant filios.

30. *Oikonomika* 1.5.6.

31. Xenophon, *Oeconomicus* 20.22–26.

> nal price. . . . He said that he desired such a farm so that he might have something to do and to have pleasure while he was making profit. For as it seems to me, Socrates," he said, "my father was the Athenian who loved farming the most." And I, upon hearing this asked him: "Did your father keep all the farms he improved, Ischomachus, or did he sell them, if he could get a lot of money?" "He sold them, of course," said Ischomachus, "but he would straightaway buy another, and an unworked one, because of his love of labor."

Here Xenophon lays out how one could apply estate management principles to making money. By constantly being on the lookout for future opportunities to mobilize his capital productively, Ischomachus' father takes a systematic approach to *chrêmatistikê* in agriculture, identifying and purchasing neglected properties and "flipping" them at a profit. In other words, Ischomachus' father was in farming for M-C-M, not C-M-C—he sought the monetary value he earned selling these new farms, and then immediately converted the profits into new properties with significant growth potential to keep his wealth constantly producing additional return.[32] As with the traders Aristotle discussed above, this continuous reinvestment into further productivity is of the utmost importance, because it shows that agriculture could be practiced for the same profit and wealth maximization that is characteristic of modern capitalist enterprise.

The Good Moneymaker: A Character Sketch

Chrêmatistikê was so prevalent that by the classical period an entire class of individuals called *chrêmatistai*, "moneymakers," had emerged in Athens, and likely beyond as well. There were so many people committed to making money that Plato's Socrates even posits that "lovers of profit" were one of the three main types of human being, alongside lovers of wisdom and victory (*Republic* 581c). These people were devoted primarily to accumulating wealth because they believed that it was the greatest good (Plato, *Gorgias* 452a–c), and the most extreme moneymakers were overly fond of their wealth in the same way that poets feel about their poems and fathers for their children, which made them hard to be around because they praised nothing but wealth (Plato, *Rep*. 330b–c). *Chrêmatistai* find no value in honor or learning except to the extent they can

32. See the introduction chapter for a definition of these terms.

be used for the end of producing money (*Republic* 581d). Because the context of these passages is not restricted to Athens alone, the implication may be that "lovers of profit" were a general class of human being that existed in the ancient Greek world more broadly.

As with all *technai* and *epistêmai*, *chrêmatistikê* had a given set of skills associated with it, and Plato illustrates the qualities that were necessary to be a successful moneymaker. In the *Republic*, Socrates describes in depth a certain personality type, "the oligarchic man," who exhibits the characteristics of a good *chrêmatistês*:[33]

> ταπεινωθεὶς ὑπὸ πενίας πρὸς χρηματισμὸν τραπόμενος γλίσχρως καὶ κατὰ σμικρὸν φειδόμενος καὶ ἐργαζόμενος χρήματα συλλέγεται. ἆρ' οὐκ οἴει τὸν τοιοῦτον τότε εἰς μὲν τὸν θρόνον ἐκεῖνον τὸ ἐπιθυμητικόν τε καὶ φιλοχρήματον ἐγκαθίζειν καὶ μέγαν βασιλέα ποιεῖν ἐν ἑαυτῷ. . . . Τὸ δέ γε οἶμαι λογιστικόν τε καὶ θυμοειδὲς χαμαὶ ἔνθεν καὶ ἔνθεν παρακαθίσας ὑπ' ἐκείνῳ καὶ καταδουλωσάμενος, τὸ μὲν οὐδὲν ἄλλο ἐᾷ λογίζεσθαι οὐδὲ σκοπεῖν ἀλλ' ἢ ὁπόθεν ἐξ ἐλαττόνων χρημάτων πλείω ἔσται, τὸ δὲ αὖ θαυμάζειν καὶ τιμᾶν μηδὲν ἄλλο ἢ πλοῦτόν τε καὶ πλουσίους, καὶ φιλοτιμεῖσθαι μηδ' ἐφ' ἑνὶ ἄλλῳ ἢ ἐπὶ χρημάτων κτήσει καὶ ἐάν τι ἄλλο εἰς τοῦτο φέρῃ.
>
> Brought low by poverty and turning greedily to making money, by being sparing and hardworking, little by little he accumulates wealth. Do you not think that such a man then has set the appetitive and moneymaking parts of his mind on a throne, and has made it an autocrat within himself? . . . And I think that having set down on the ground and beaten down into slavery under wealth the calculating and passionate parts of his brain, the one he does not allow either to calculate or consider anything other than from where more money will be made from less, and the other in turn he does not allow to wonder at or honor anything other than wealth and wealthy people, and to be proud of nothing other than the acquisition of wealth, and if something else leads to this. (*Republic* 553c–d)

This vivid account provides fascinating insight into Plato's theory of the mind and the mental activities required to be a profitable moneymaker. He dedicates the calculative and spirited processes of his mind entirely to *chrêmatistikê*, and

33. Plato, *Republic* 553c–554b.

allows them to do nothing else. Plato depicts this as an active deliberate choice (ἐᾷ), of favoring one type of pleasure and expending one's full energy on attaining it. This man "enslaves" (δουλούμενος) all the desires besides those associated with acquiring money, deeming them frivolous or useless (ματαίους); he prizes wealth above all else (χρήματα περὶ πλείστου ποιεῖσθαι), and only engages in activities that are purely productive; any sort of extraneous consumption is irrelevant and worthless (τὰς ἀναγκαίους ἐπιθυμίας μόνον τῶν παρ' αὑτῷ ἀποπιμπλάς. τὰ δὲ ἄλλα ἀναλώματα μὴ παρεχόμενος).

Most relevant is the sole object this man permits the calculative and spirited portions of his brain to pursue: "from where more money will be made from less." Plato emphasizes that through working hard (*ergatês, ergazomenos*) and being sparing (*pheidolos, pheidomenos*), one can amass wealth continuously. But this can solely be accomplished by subordinating all desires to that of making money, and indulging only those that are absolutely necessary. Furthermore, he focuses incessantly on how to make a "profit from everything," as this unwavering dedication to making money requires constant calculation and consideration. No wonder *chrêmatistikê* is conceptualized as subsuming other arts—to be entirely focused on accumulating money one must be flexible, open to any possible means of making profit.

Such detailed descriptions of *chrêmatistai* and their character are rare in the ancient Greek sources, and although Plato was presenting this person as a stereotype of the extreme form of what he called the "oligarchic" man, nevertheless, this behavior may have been widespread in ancient Greece. Plato was certainly familiar enough with the qualities and methods needed for *chrêmatismos* that he can provide a vivid account of their frame of mind and motivation.[34] Indeed, he seems to have such intimate knowledge of the psychology of moneymaking individuals based on his own personal experiences, and expects that his audience would have encountered these behaviors in their own lives. Obviously most people in ancient Greece would not fit the exact description of the oligarchic man, but enough people shared these characteristics to be regarded as a recognizable personality type. Indeed, to Plato, it was not just the oligarchic man who submitted to pains and labors to increase his wealth, but people engaged in *chrêmatismos* more broadly; anyone who practiced the art of moneymaking denied himself pleasure and chose to undergo the toils (*epipona*) inherent in that lifestyle in order to achieve the goal of acquiring wealth (*Rep.* 357c). The "illiberal" (*aneleutherios*) man was defined by Aristotle as any-

34. As Leese 2017b argues, there was a widespread awareness of *kapêloi* business tactics among fourth-century Athenians, so Plato's knowledge should not come as a surprise.

one who is more eager than he ought to be for money (*N.E.* 4.1.3). And just like anger and honor, many people were unrestrained (*akrateis*) in their pursuit of gain (*N.E.* 7.1.7). Both philosophers therefore attributed the qualities of Plato's oligarchic man to *chrêmatistai* in general.

Like Plato, Aristotle also notes that moneymakers were not *akrateis* with respect to all pleasures. On the contrary, they intently and carefully controlled every other desire, specifically those that were bad for *chrêmatismos* because they interfered with the acquisition of money (*N.E.* 7.12.4). Their focus was on gain first and foremost, and as Plato puts it, they enslave (*doulousthai*) other desires as useless.[35] Aristotle uses the same metaphor of master and slave to illustrate how the rational element of the brain *rules* the irrational portions (*Politics* 1.5.6). Plato likewise envisioned the *psychê* as being composed of rational and irrational elements, and in this passage he describes in detail "the oligarchic man" who gives privileged place to the appetitive (ἐπιθυμητικόν) part of the brain, which he equates with the money-loving region (φιλοχρήματον), and enslaves the spirited (θυμοειδὲς) and calculating (λογιστικόν) elements. Therefore, Aristotle identifies the same traits that Plato assigned to the "oligarchic" man, and says that they were shared by good *chrêmatistai*.

Aristotle defines *technai* as "rational qualities concerned with making" (*N.E.* 6.5.1–4, 1140a), which means that he would have considered the art of *chrêmatistikê* to be the rational application of the mental faculties to the pursuit of money. In his theory of the mind, he pays a great deal of attention to the rule of the rational parts of the brain over the irrational and includes an elaborate explanation of how the process of "deliberative choice" (*proairesis*) is the rational exertion of logic over pleasures in the *Nicomachean* and *Eudemian Ethics*. Engaging in *chrêmatistikê* as a *technê*, therefore, necessarily involves deliberate rational choice (*proairesis*). Controlling the desirous and irrational portions of the brain was the job of the rational element, according to Aristotle. It was an exercise of rationality and deliberative choice to reflect upon one's desires and to decide intentionally to indulge or deny them. Aristotle portrays *enkrateia*, self-restraint, as being whenever someone rationally decides to control his desire (*epithumia*): ἐγκρατεύεται δ' ὅταν πράττῃ παρὰ τὴν ἐπιθυμίαν κατὰ τὸν λογισμόν (*E.E.* 2.7.3, 1223a37–38). Plato depicts the exact same conflict between the calculating or rational (*logistikon*), and irrational and appetitive (*alogiston te kai epithumêtikon*) regions of the *psychê* (4.439d–441a). Likewise, he also states that the rational or calculative portion of the mind should be the

35. Plato elaborates on this idea at *Republic* 558d–559c.

element that rules the other (441e), so he sees rationality as being used to suppress desires that were contrary to moneymaking.

It is not just rational choice that is depicted in these accounts, however, but something even more intriguing. Indeed, Plato's description of a *chrêmatistês* who intently, rationally, and soberly focuses on maximizing his wealth is even reminiscent of the approach to moneymaking that Max Weber argued was quintessential to the Protestant ethic and the "spirit of modern capitalism":

> The concept spirit of capitalism is here used in this specific sense. It is the spirit of modern capitalism . . . the *summum bonum* of this ethic, the earning of more and more money, combined with the strict avoidance of all spontaneous enjoyment of life, is above all completely devoid of any eudaemonistic, not to say hedonistic, admixture.[36]

These characteristics of Max Weber's spirit of modern capitalism and the endless accumulation of profit resemble Plato's and Aristotle's sketches of ancient moneymakers. Like Weber's Protestant capitalists, the *chrêmatistai* attested in fourth-century Athenian philosophical works denied themselves all but the most necessary indulgences, and were likewise dedicated to the relentless earning of more and more money. Such uncannily similar descriptions by Weber, Plato, and Aristotle are too close to be coincidental; rather, it seems that the same traits were indispensable for the long-term maximization of profits and wealth in both ancient Athens and the modern world.

Some businesspeople in ancient Greece therefore behaved in a manner that echoes Max Weber's famed Protestant ethic and spirit of modern capitalism, perhaps the most extreme theoretical model posited as uniquely defining the economic behavior of the modern Western world. And there is further evidence in Plato that suggests such behavior was actually fairly common:[37]

> Τὴν μὲν ὑπ' ἔρωτος πλούτου πάντα χρόνον ἄσχολον ποιοῦντος τῶν ἄλλων ἐπιμελεῖσθαι πλὴν τῶν ἰδίων κτημάτων, ἐξ ὧν κρεμαμένη πᾶσα ψυχὴ πολίτου παντὸς οὐκ ἄν ποτε δύναιτο τῶν ἄλλων ἐπιμέλειαν ἴσχειν πλὴν τοῦ καθ' ἡμέραν κέρδους· καὶ ὅτι μὲν πρὸς τοῦτο φέρει μάθημα ἢ καὶ ἐπιτήδευμα, ἰδίᾳ πᾶς μανθάνειν τε καὶ ἀσκεῖν ἑτοιμότατός ἐστιν, τῶν δὲ ἄλλων καταγελᾷ. . . . ἀλλὰ διὰ τὴν τοῦ χρυσοῦ τε καὶ

36. Weber 2009, 24–25.
37. Plato, *Laws* 831c–832b.

> ἀργύρου ἀπληστίαν πᾶσαν μὲν τέχνην καὶ μηχανήν, καλλίω τε καὶ ἀσχημονεστέραν, ἐθέλειν ὑπομένειν πάντα ἄνδρα, εἰ μέλλει πλούσιος ἔσεσθαι . . . οἷς γε ἀνάγκη διὰ βίου πεινῶσιν τὴν ψυχὴν ἀεὶ τὴν αὑτῶν διεξελθεῖν. . . . Αὕτη μὲν δή . . . μία, ἡ διὰ βίου ἄπληστος ζήτησις, παρέχουσα ἄσχολον ἕκαστον.
>
> Because of the lust for wealth that allows no leisure time to care for anything at all besides one's own personal property, upon which the soul of every citizen hangs, and is not ever able to have care for anything else except for day-to-day profit. And whatever learning or pursuit leads to this, every man is most ready to learn and to practice for himself; and everything else he laughs at in scorn. . . . Because of the insatiability of [the desire for] gold and silver, every man is willing to undergo every art and mechanism, whether noble or shameful, if he is going to become rich. . . . For these people it is necessary to spend their lives with hunger always in their own souls. . . . This one lifelong insatiable pursuit, deprives each man of any leisure.

In this passage, Plato rails against the selfish lust for wealth (*erôs ploutou*) that causes citizens to disregard the collective good and focus only on their own economic gains. Without leisure time (*ascholon*) to help the *polis*, the entire soul (*pasa psychê*) of every citizen (*politou pantos*) hangs upon his personal fortune, and he spends his time thinking only of his daily profits. Every person (*pas*) is dedicated to learning new arts to undertake any means of making money, however unholy or shameless, and to employing every art and device (*technên kai mêchanên*) that can make him richer. He then commits to the disciplined lifestyle (*askein*) that is necessary for *chrêmatistikê* and laughs at (*katagela*) everything else that does not contribute to this goal. Plato may be exaggerating in many ways, especially when he says that every person, and more specifically every citizen, lives purely for his own material benefit. Grumpiness aside, however, these views are not at all unrepresentative of how Plato felt about the masses in general. While in seeking to indulge their desires the people in this passage differ from the attitude of the Protestant ethic and the good *chrêmatistês* (as exemplified in the behavior of the oligarchic man) toward pleasures, nevertheless they share many of the same characteristics.

Moreover, if some ancient Greek individuals were driven by a "hunger in their souls" to acquire wealth, and were directed toward this goal alone, they bear an even more important resemblance to the peculiarities of Weber's spirit of modern capitalism. Weber further elaborates that "[money] is thought of so purely as an end in itself, that from the point of view of the happiness of, or utility to, the single individual, it appears entirely transcendental and absolutely irrational."[38] Aristotle and Plato likewise believed it was irrational for ancient Greek lovers of money to be driven solely to acquire wealth and nothing else. Weber here again echoes the same estimation of this behavior that was expressed by ancient Greek philosophers. They also believed that it was largely an irrational urge that compelled people to accumulate wealth insatiably, so the effects of the Protestant ethic, in motivating endless accumulation, were also identified by ancient Greeks, except that the latter were driven by different, though still irrational, reasons.

Finally, both Weber's Protestant ethic and Plato's account of ancient Greek *chrêmatistai* highlight the long-term devotion to accumulating wealth. As Plato states in the passage from the *Laws*, ancient Greeks could be committed to making money on more than just an occasional basis, but rather adopt an entire lifestyle dedicated to amassing wealth. In his account of the oligarchical man, his emphasis is on the lifelong acquisition of money: κατὰ σμικρὸν φειδόμενος καὶ ἐργαζόμενος χρήματα συλλέγεται, "By being sparing and hardworking, he accumulates money little by little." What he seems to be describing here is the sustained maximization of wealth throughout one's lifetime.

This observation of Plato is not an aberration but is supported by direct parallels with Aristotle's description of methods to maximize profit and wealth above. First, Plato says these individuals spend their entire time making money (*panta chronon*), which mirrors exactly Aristotle's statement above about those who devote "all their time" to *chrêmatistikê*. Next, both authors recognize the distinction between the means as opposed to ends—Plato's point about *chrêmatistai* mobilizing every art and device (*technên kai mêchanên*) to the goal of becoming rich is mirrored by Aristotle's declaration that such individuals "desire unlimited productive means" for the end of creating unlimited wealth. Plato's "insatiability" (*aplêstian* and *aplêstos*), is expressed by the "boundless" (*apeiron*) acquisition of Aristotle. In short, maximization is emphasized by each author, as are the elements that are necessary for achieving it.

Frugality and Calculation

Frugality, precision, controlling expenditures, being industrious, and avoiding excessive consumption on pleasure are not just advocated in theory, but

38. Weber 2009, 25.

also in the actual practice of *oikonomia*. Pseudo-Aristotle echoes Ischomachus' sentiments about minimizing women's spending on cosmetics and personal adornment.[39] Cato, in his *De Agri Cultura*, also emphasizes the importance of frugality for growth, identifying extravagant consumption as being detrimental to profitability; he likewise suggests keeping detailed, separate accounts for cash and all the different agricultural products on the estate.[40] Some individuals really did take this systematic approach to their own household management. Pericles, for example, is said to have had such concern for preventing waste that he arranged the affairs of his entire estate[41] with a view to making accurate records: τὸν πατρῷον καὶ δίκαιον πλοῦτον . . . συνέταξεν εἰς οἰκονομίαν ἣν ᾤετο ῥᾴστην καὶ ἀκριβεστάτην εἶναι, "He ordered his ancestral and legal wealth in the manner of household management which he thought easiest and most precise" (Plutarch, *Pericles* 16.3).[42] He was so meticulous in limiting the expenditures of his own family, even, that he came to be despised by them for this reason: οὐχ ἡδὺς ἦν ἐνηλίκοις παισὶν οὐδὲ γυναιξὶ δαψιλὴς χορηγός, ἀλλ᾽ ἐμέμφοντο τὴν ἐφήμερον ταύτην καὶ συνηγμένην εἰς τὸ ἀκριβέστατον δαπάνην, οὐδενός, οἷον ἐν οἰκίᾳ μεγάλῃ καὶ πράγμασιν ἀφθόνοις, περιρρέοντος, ἀλλὰ παντὸς μὲν ἀναλώματος, παντὸς δὲ λήμματος δι᾽ ἀριθμοῦ καὶ μέτρου βαδίζοντος, "He was not a pleasant leader among his sons, nor a generous one among his female relatives, but they reproached his daily spending, which was restricted to the most exacting point, with no surplus as in a great house and prosperous conditions, but with every expense and every income going through arithmetic and measurement" (16.4). What is significant about this passage and Plutarch's focus on wealth in Pericles' *oikonomia*, is that the control of consumption and expenditure are characteristic of a household using methods similar to those of a firm aiming at growth.

The great precision, expressed in the superlative ἀκριβεστάτην, with which

39. Pseudo-Aristotle, *Oikonomika* 1.5.3.

40. Cato on frugality being necessary for profitability: "Scito idem agrum quod hominem, quamvis quaestuosus siet, si sumptuosus erit, relinqui non multum" (*De Agri Cultura* 1.1.6). For separate accounts: "Ea cognita aequo animo sint, quae reliqua opera sint curare uti perficiantur: rationes putare argentariam, frumentariam, pabuli causa quae parata sunt; rationem vinariam, oleariam, quid venierit, quid exactum siet, quid reliquum siet, quid siet quod veneat: quae satis accipiunda sint, satis accipiantur: reliqua quae sint uti conpareant. Siquid desit in annum, uti paretur: quae supersint, ut veneant" (*De Agri Cultura* 1.2.5–6).

41. Very little is known about Pericles' property, for which see Davies 1971, 459–60. Thucydides 2.13.1 states that he had farms (*agroi*) and houses (*oikiai*), and as Davies notes, this accords with what we know from Plato, that his sons became *hippeis* (*Meno* 94b), and that he sold his produce (*karpoi*) in the agora (Plutarch, *Pericles* 16.3), all pointing to agriculture as the basis for his wealth.

42. Plutarch's source for this account of Pericles' estate management is unknown. Stadter 1989, 197–99, notes that Theopompus, Theophrastus, and Stesimbrotus have all been suggested as Plutarch's source, and that a comedy or a Socratic dialogue could also be Plutarch's source.

he kept accounts of every transaction is noteworthy in this instance, as was the help he enlisted from his slave overseer, Euangelos: ὁ δὲ πᾶσαν αὐτοῦ τὴν τοιαύτην συνέχων ἀκρίβειαν εἷς ἦν οἰκέτης, Εὐάγγελος, ὡς ἕτερος οὐδεὶς εὖ πεφυκὼς ἢ κατεσκευασμένος ὑπὸ τοῦ Περικλέους πρὸς οἰκονομίαν, "And there was one slave, Euangelos, holding together all his precision of this kind like no one else, whether by nature or trained by Pericles for household management" (16.5). Euangelos is said to have used so much precision, ἀκρίβειαν, in his administration that he even closely tracked daily expenditures (ἐφήμερον δαπάνην). Such meticulous control by the overseer corroborates Plutarch's comment that Pericles arranged his estate management however would be ῥᾴστην, "easiest," to allow him to focus on politics. By appointing a slave overseer for his entire estate, Pericles was not being negligent, but rather was concerned with ensuring its growth both through managing the accounts and regulating the spending of his family. Xenophon and Pseudo-Aristotle advocate tracking monthly and annual expenditures,[43] and Hypereides depicts Athenogenes as requiring the slave managers of his three perfumeries to submit accounts for him to inspect every month.[44] The most famous banker in ancient Greece, Pasion, kept very accurate books,[45] as did his son Apollodorus in the accounts of the expenses incurred during his trierarchy.[46] So although Euangelos may be depicted as extreme, he nevertheless follows the same practices recommended in agronomic manuals and attested for other Athenian households.

This is not to say that all ancient Greeks used full, extensive systems of written accounting like modern business, monitoring their production and expenditures entirely in cash balances. Recently, Stephen Johnstone has argued that Greek farms could have operated in the absence of written accounting, and that produce could be apportioned into monthly and annual containers, which per se constituted the method of accounting.[47] This practice of accounting as physical separation and "containerization" is an intriguing suggestion, and perhaps sheds some light upon how ancient Greeks could have managed their produce and consumption over the year without meticulously detailed books. But this does not mean that there was no actual monetary calculation involved; Xenophon says that Ischomachus set aside the goods "calculated" (*apolelogismena*) to last for certain amounts of time (9.8), which is consistent with some sort of prior planning rather than just an ad hoc piling up and dividing up of the

43. Xenophon, *Oeconomicus* 7.36, 9.8; Pseudo-Aristotle, *Oikonomika* 1.6.6.
44. Hypereides, *Against Athenogenes* 4.19.
45. Dem. 49.5, 52.3–6.
46. Dem. 50.30.
47. Johnstone 2011, 71–77. His argument is based on Xenophon, *Oeconomicus* 7.36, which perhaps, and 9.8 which certainly, describe the physical separation of goods into containers.

goods. Some households may have practiced the accounting that Johnstone has proposed, but Pomeroy is correct that written records were used in Ischomachus' house.[48] Moreover, other households from ancient Greece are said to have maintained written accounts as well.[49] Nonetheless, as seen in Pericles' and Ischomachus' control over expenditures,[50] it matters little whether accounting was done in physical or written form; in either case, consumption is restricted so as not to deplete the profitability of the household.

But could Athenians make the arithmetical calculations necessary to determine what investments would maximize income? In Plato, calculation (*logistikê*) is called a *technê* (*Charmides* 165e), and numerical reckoning (*arithmêtikê*) is also referred to as a *technê* in the *Gorgias* (453e), so it seems that calculating in numbers was sufficiently developed by the classical period to be seen as a skill with its own sophistication. In the *Republic* he devotes a great deal of attention to *logistikê*, in which he ultimately argues that the calculating portion of the mind should be what directs human action, in its decision-making (439d–441e). Likewise, as he states in his description of the oligarchical man, the calculating portion of the brain can be devoted to nothing more than the accumulation of wealth. He specifically mentions calculations being performed solely for the purpose of making money, "from where more money will be made from less." This statement is a clear link between calculation and maximizing profit. Since Plato is presenting an "ideal type" of the money-hungry man in this discussion, it seems that he is drawing upon real-world examples from his own life in Athens,[51] so to Plato, at least, the person who devotes his calculating energies entirely to *chrêmatistikê* was a very real phenomenon. The application of this calculation in Plato's account, therefore, is explicitly stated

48. See, e.g., Xenophon, *Oeconomicus* 9.10, which Johnstone notes refers only to items which were used occasionally. This precision may be somewhat overstated, since other items could be accounted for in writing as well (as Pomeroy 1994 notes), and Xenophon is not being absolutely explicit in limiting the written list only to such occasional items. Rather, he may have emphasized the written list in this section only to show that written lists could be used not *only* for foodstuffs and money, but also for other household items as well.

49. The household in Lysias 32 used written accounts (32.7, 22, 25–26), and it seems that Demosthenes' father also kept detailed accounts to be able to list his property and its monetary value in such specific terms, and to calculate the profits from each of his workshops. Other examples of written accounts include Dem. 56.1, Dem. 25.60–61, Dem. 52.6, Isocrates 17.20 and 22–34. In Ps.-Arist. *Oik.*, 1.6.6, the *epitropos* does the monthly and yearly accounts. For a discussion of accounting in estate management, see Chandezon 2011, 108–17.

50. Ischomachus advocates controlling expenditures at 7.36 and 9.8 clearly as part of the overall argument that consumption can be kept at a minimum and tracked to allow for the profitability and growth of the household.

51. The individual he describes is presented by him as being the son of a general or other high-ranking individual whose wealth has been ruined by sycophants (553b), a situation which is as fourth-century Athenian as one could imagine.

to be the persistent accumulation of money, and the long-term maximization of profit and wealth.

It is unlikely that such calculations would have required modern techniques, but were rather based on many combined lifetimes of experience. Knowing the type of risk that voyages were subject to would have been acquired over the course of a career and could be handed down across generations either directly, or indirectly through slaves. Christesen has shown that relative levels of risk and profitability were well-established in rates of interest for different types of investments.[52] These rates of interest seem to have developed as the result of long years of accumulated knowledge from the experiences of countless traders in countless transactions. Although lenders and borrowers could negotiate any interest rate (*tokos*) they wanted,[53] there was a universal sense that the riskier the venture, the higher the rate should be. In Demosthenes' speech *Against Lacritus*, the language of the contract in question clearly demonstrates an awareness of the greater risk which came with sailing too late in the season, and the *tokos* is increased to account for this extra danger for the lender.[54]

Even rough calculations could give a sufficient idea of whether or not a field might be more profitable than another. Dairy farmers, for example, are said to have been able to compare the returns they could receive from cow versus goat milk. In addition to his statements in the *Politics* cited above, Aristotle provides further insight on this issue in his *Historia Animalium*, where he says that pastoralists had a good sense of the yields from different animals' cheese: "Shepherds say there is more cheese in cow's than goat's milk—from an amphora (nine gallons) of goats' milk they can get nineteen cheeses at an obol apiece, and from the same amount of cow's milk, thirty."[55] Such a comparison is, indeed, characteristic of an individual who evaluates the relative merits of different investments purely on their profitability (λυσιτελέστατα), and then makes a decision on the basis of potential gain. In Aristophanes, Dicaeopolis does some quick calculations while he waits for the rest of the *ekklêsia* to arrive in *Acharnians*,[56] and the *Clouds* opens with Strepsiades doing his household accounts, calculating the interest on his debts.[57] Theophrastus' Stupid

52. Christesen 2003, 50–53.

53. For interest rates at Athens, see Cohen 1989, 207–23; Millett 1991, 95–108. See Cohen 1992, 44–46, for a discussion of the Greek term *tokos*, which he prefers to translate as "yield" rather than "interest." The distinction between the two translations is of great interest for both Greek and English concepts of return on such investments, but is largely inconsequential for the purposes of my analysis in this study.

54. Dem. 35.10.

55. Aristotle, *Historia Animalium* 3.20, 522a30–32.

56. *Acharnians* 31.

57. *Clouds* 12–22.

Man in *Characters* needs to ask others if his arithmetic is correct, suggesting that Greeks in general should be able to check their own accounting.[58] In each of these three situations, the verb *logizomai* is used for the act of calculation, revealing a widespread practice that was described in the same terms by Greek authors as different as Aristophanes and Theophrastus.

In ancient Greece, the invention of coined money would have provided the commensurability needed to determine how profitable different sorts of production could be relative to each other, with prices available for the entry and operations costs of potential investment options. Aristotle discusses these advantages, permitting all goods to be compared according to a single, objective standard.[59] As he states in the *Politics* cited above, for effective *chrêmatistikê*, owners must know how lucrative certain types of property are in different situations, which suggests that Greeks did have the ability to compare their likely gains. But he also says one must be "experienced in which [properties] are profitable in respect to one another"; thus, the calculation of potential returns was also a matter of experience. Whether this assessment was made using accounting, experience, trial and error, or some combination of the three, the Greeks were able to articulate the importance of making such determinations. Michele Faraguna has demonstrated that temple accounts contain the most basic, fundamental details which allow for comparisons of profit, and has argued that ancient Greeks would have been able to use simple accounting procedures, combined with the abacus, to calculate gain effectively.[60] Some scholars have concluded that ancient Greeks and Romans exhibit signs of economic rationality in their accounting practices.[61] Calculation is attested within discussions of estate property in ancient Greek households (e.g., Lysias 32.21–22 and 24), and so it is likely that ancient Greeks used a combination of all the means at their disposal to determine profitability. As a technological innovation, coined money greatly facilitated the potential to acquire and maximize wealth.

Calculating gain and loss is said to have been central in day-to-day eco-

58. Theophrastus, *Characters* 14.2.

59. *Nicomachean Ethics* 5.5.8–16, 1133a7–1133b16. For a lengthy discussion of this passage, see Meikle 1995a, 21–42, who argues that money does not provide true commensurability, a point which Johnstone 2011, 47–48, also emphasizes. Nevertheless, Aristotle's point is correct: money provides functional, practical commensurability, which is much more difficult in its absence. Weber 2009, 6; Schaps 2004; and Seaford 2004 likewise all emphasize the unprecedented possibilities for calculation created by the invention of money because of the facilitated commensurability between different goods, which would have made it much easier to compare the profits and costs associated with options in the economic decision-making process.

60. Faraguna 2008.

61. See, e.g., Bresson and Bresson 2004, 98; Rathbone 1991. For the difficulties of determining rationality through accounting practices, however, see Andreau and Maucourant 1999; and Kehoe 1993.

nomic decisions on estates. In Xenophon's *Memorabilia*, Socrates describes the thought process of the ἀγαθὸς οἰκονόμος as being focused on profit on the one hand (λυσιτελές τε καὶ κερδαλέον), and loss on the other (ἀλυσιτελές τε καὶ ζημιῶδες).[62] As Xenophon states elsewhere in his own voice, οἱ μὲν ἀγροὺς κεκτημένοι πάντες ἔχοιεν ἂν εἰπεῖν ὁπόσα ζεύγη ἀρκεῖ εἰς τὸ χωρίον καὶ ὁπόσοι ἐργάται: ἢν δ' ἐπὶ πλέον τῶν ἱκανῶν ἐμβάλλῃ τις, ζημίαν λογίζονται, "All who own farms could say how many yokes and how many workers are enough for their plot of land. And if someone adds more than is sufficient, they calculate it as loss" (*Poroi* 4.5).[63] The last two words of this quote, ζημίαν λογίζονται, suggest that "calculation" of loss was an integral part of *oikonomia*, and Xenophon extends this behavior to "all who own farms." Moreover, far from just another indication that many Greeks were trying to run their agricultural properties for profit, this passage provides evidence for even more sophisticated economic insights. To say that they realize that adding additional livestock or slaves will result in loss is a recognition of diminishing marginal returns.[64] Though simple, this understanding of the optimal level of capital on a piece of property was based upon, and driven by, their inclination to assess profit and loss.

Some people even gained a reputation for being calculating, or at least were described so in court speeches as a rhetorical tactic. The speaker of Lysias 7, *On the Olive Stump*, for example, tries to downplay his opponents' charges that he was just such an individual: ἐγὼ τοίνυν, ὦ βουλή, ἐν μὲν τῷ τέως χρόνῳ, ὅσοι με φάσκοιεν δεινὸν εἶναι καὶ ἀκριβῆ καὶ οὐδὲν ἂν εἰκῇ καὶ ἀλογίστως ποιῆσαι, ἠγανάκτουν ἄν, ἡγούμενος μᾶλλον λέγεσθαι <ἢ> ὥς μοι προσῆκε, "Well then, Boule, I would have been upset in the past, at whoever would say that I am clever, precise, and doing nothing at random or without calculation, thinking that it was spoken beyond what was fitting for me" (12). "Clever, precise, and doing nothing at random or without calculation" is how his opponents try to depict him; ironically, the manner in which he (or Lysias) addresses this charge proves his opponents right. In his argument against the likelihood that he would have cut the olive tree down for monetary gain, he actually proves himself to be just as calculating, precise, and clever as his opponents claim. This defense argument is a clear example of a profit versus risk calculation, where the speaker argues that it would not have been reasonable for him to remove the stump when the potential money he could have made would have been so far outweighed by the risk, the death penalty: πῶς ἂν ἐτόλμησα τοσούτων μεμισθωμένων καὶ ἁπάντων συνειδότων ἀφανίσαι τὸν σηκὸν βραχέος μὲν

62. Xen., *Mem.* 3.4.11.
63. See Gauthier 1976, 119–20, for a discussion of this passage.
64. For the economic concept of diminishing marginal returns, see Blaug 1997, 75–84.

κέρδους ἕνεκα, προθεσμίας δὲ οὐδεμιᾶς οὔσης τῷ κινδύνῳ, "How could I have dared with so many people renting the land, and everyone knowing that I had removed the stump for the sake of small profit, and there being no statute of limitations for the risk?" (17). The terms which the speaker focuses on the most in this argument are "profit" (*kerdos* 12, 13) and "risk" (*kindunos* 14, 15, 17), all part of an *eikos* argument to show that no one would risk so much for so little gain (presumably the land used to grow cereals). The argument's success depends on the jury agreeing that such unreasonable behavior been extremely unlikely. The speaker clearly thinks that this type of profit-risk measurement will be effective in convincing his audience whether or not the action in question was believable.

Excessive calculation (*mikrologia*) was seen by Theophrastus as an extreme character trait in the world of fourth-century Athens (*Characters* 10). This person calculates (*logizetai*) monetary return and loss in all situations, including those that are inappropriate. Moreover, he also is excessively sparing (*pheidolia*), particularly with money, and so shares this trait with the model moneymakers as depicted by Aristotle and Plato above. Theophrastus' interest in such personality types was likely inspired by his teacher, Aristotle, who likewise thinks any extreme characteristics could be a flaw, and himself devotes attention to overly precise calculation, in his discussion of "stinginess": ἡ γὰρ ἀκριβολογία μικροπρεπές. καὶ πῶς κάλλιστον καὶ πρεπωδέστατον, σκέψαιτ' ἂν μᾶλλον ἢ πόσου καὶ πῶς ἐλαχίστου (*N.E.* 4.2.8–9). He brings up this topic to emphasize that in spending on the state or one's friends, when one should be generous, *akribologia* (precise calculation) is the opposite of *megaloprepeia* (magnanimity)—it is *mikroprepês*, or stingy. Just like Theophrastus, Aristotle identifies monetary expenditures as the type of activity that is associated with calculation, and there must have been many people who would have gone to extraordinary lengths to determine how cheaply something could be done.

Here Aristotle reveals his prescriptive attitudes toward economic behavior and simultaneously describes the patterns he observed in Greeks around him; some were acting in ways Aristotle disapproved, and therefore offer important complementary evidence to his own prescriptions on how they should act. The prescriptive nature of Aristotle's comment, that being excessively calculating was less appropriate for interactions between friends than in other contexts, reveals the underlying reality—people did practice *akribologia* in their daily lives, some even among their own friends. The corollary of this is that in dealings with people who were not friends, as in impersonal market transactions, such fine calculation was not only acceptable, but probably the norm. Moreover, the implication of these personality stereotypes is that there was a normal level of calculation that they observed around them every day which these exceeded.

So calculation was not seen to be a bad thing per se. Aristotle declares that people were said to be prudent (φρονίμους) when they calculate well (*logisontai*) to attain a particular end (*N.E.* 6.5.2). Among those called φρονίμους is Pericles, partly because of his ability to see what was good for himself in his own *oikonomia* (*N.E.* 6.5.5). By contrast, spacey philosophers like Thales are said to be wise (*sophos*) but not prudent, because although they can discern the mysteries of the universe, they cannot manage their own affairs effectively (*N.E.* 6.7.5–6, 1141b3–10). There was a big difference between the behavior of typical Greeks and that of oddball philosophers when it came to calculating for one's advantage. Therefore, the right amount of calculation was considered to be a virtue, so the Athenians saw monetary calculation to be a common and laudable practice, and certainly widespread enough to merit a considerable amount of attention in philosophical writings.

Risk, Safety, and Profit in Economic Decision-Making

Furthermore, as seen in the risk-profit calculation used by the speaker of Lysias 7, the terms risk, safety, and profit are fundamental in Greek thought and deliberation within the decision-making process itself. The debate over the Sicilian expedition in Thucydides is heavily framed in terms of risk, safety, potential gain, and calculation terminology also recurs throughout. Ancient Greeks frequently conceptualized their economic decisions in terms of risk and profit, much like modern businesspeople. Aristotle, for example, demonstrates his own awareness of the relationship between risk and profit in his discussion of the difference between exchange-based (*metablêtikê*) moneymaking trades:[65]

> τῆς μὲν οὖν οἰκειοτάτης χρηματιστικῆς ταῦτα μόρια καὶ πρῶτα, τῆς δὲ μεταβλητικῆς μέγιστον μὲν ἐμπορία (καὶ ταύτης μέρη τρία, ναυκληρία φορτηγία παράστασις· διαφέρει δὲ τούτων ἕτερα ἑτέρων τῷ τὰ μὲν ἀσφαλέστερα εἶναι, τὰ δὲ πλείω πορίζειν τὴν ἐπικαρπίαν).
>
> These then are the branches and first parts of wealth getting in its most proper sense. Of the kind that deals with exchange, the largest branch is commerce of exchange (of which there are three subsections: ship own-

65. Aristotle, *Politics* 1.11.3, 1258b20–24.

> ing, transport, and marketing:[66] these differ from each other in the fact that some are safer and others bring more return).

Safety (*asphaleia*) and return (*epikarpia*) are the first considerations that come to Aristotle's mind in distinguishing between the relative advantages and drawbacks of each of these forms of moneymaking, which suggests that they were also central in the minds of Greeks deciding whether to choose potential investment options. "Safety" further reveals the conceptual framework of Greek economic thought, as another way they framed what modern scholars would call risk. As the opposite of risk, safety is a positive expression of the same negative idea embodied in the term *kindunos*.

Indeed, when one turns from these general, theoretical accounts of aggregate behavior to examples of real-life individuals and their actual economic decision-making process, this same concern for profit balanced by an awareness of risk becomes apparent.[67] In one of the only depictions of an ancient Greek evaluating alternative moneymaking opportunities, he does *not* select the option that will bring him the most money possible. When faced with the choice of taking over the management of his father's more lucrative bank or less profitable shield factory, Apollodorus picked the latter:[68]

> νέμονται τὴν τράπεζαν καὶ τὸ ἀσπιδοπηγεῖον, καὶ λαβὼν αἵρεσιν Ἀπολλόδωρος αἱρεῖται τὸ ἀσπιδοπηγεῖον ἀντὶ τῆς τραπέζης . . . οὔτε γὰρ ἡ πρόσοδος ἦν πλείων, ἀλλ᾽ ἐλάττων (τὸ μὲν γὰρ τάλαντον, ἡ δ᾽ ἑκατὸν μνᾶς ἔφερεν) . . . διόπερ σωφρονῶν εἵλετο τὸ ἀσπιδοπηγεῖον οὗτος· τὸ μὲν γὰρ κτῆμ᾽ ἀκίνδυνόν ἐστιν, ἡ δ᾽ ἐργασία προσόδους ἔχουσ᾽ ἐπικινδύνους ἀπὸ χρημάτων ἀλλοτρίων.

> They divided up the bank and the shield factory, and Apollodorus having the choice selected the shield factory instead of the bank . . . and not because the income was not greater, but less, the factory brought in a talent, while the bank brought in 100 *minae* . . . for this reason he wisely

66. The exact sense of *parastasis* seems to be "display or exposure for sale" (LSJ), or "offering for sale" (Saunders 1995), but I have used Apostle and Gerson's "marketing," in the sense of putting up for sale in the market (1986).

67. By using the term "risk" I am not suggesting that the ancient Greeks had consciously developed the distinction between "uncertainty" and "risk" as in modern economic thought. Nevertheless, they do seem to have had some notion of risk, which was variable with respect to different economic investments. For an interesting discussion of the ways in which Greeks dealt with risk through the use of curses and other magical and religious means, see Eidinow 2007.

68. For the life of Apollodorus, see Trevett 1992.

> chose the shield factory: because it was a risk-free possession, whereas the bank was an operation holding risk-laden revenues from the money of others. (Dem. 36.11)

Here, in his deliberation between two economic alternatives, Apollodorus preferred the factory with less return because it also carried lower risk, which according to Demosthenes was the determining factor. So although the bank earned 66 percent more revenue each year, Apollodorus decided to go with the shield factory since it was "risk-free." Although risk-free is an exaggeration, it effectively illustrates the contrast between the investment options and the criteria whereby Apollodorus made his choice. This situation is highly reminiscent of Kahneman and Tversky's "Prospect Theory" in which the guarantee of lesser return is seen to be more attractive than an uncertain greater return.[69] Therefore, Apollodorus' decision is made in the same manner as modern individuals observed in behavioral economics experiments.

Moreover, when compared to actual modern business practice, it seems that Apollodorus' attention to risk and safety of return is perfectly in line with the advice of successful investors in the modern world. In *The Intelligent Investor*, Benjamin Graham opens his first chapter with a distinction between "investment" and "speculation": "An investment operation is one which, upon thorough analysis, promises safety of principal and an adequate return. Operations not meeting these requirements are speculative."[70] Demosthenes' evaluation of Apollodorus' choice as "wise" is based on exactly the same criteria that are emphasized by Graham: safety and return. Risk (*kindunos*), and not the highest possible return, is the decisive consideration which Demosthenes attributes to Apollodorus' choice of the shield factory, so he seems to be articulating an idea very similar to that of modern investment theorists.[71]

Both Apollodorus' decision and the terms Demosthenes uses to describe it are significant; they demonstrate that they themselves and their audience understood the importance of weighing risk against profit in choosing investments. Nor was Demosthenes alone among ancient Greeks in expressing this concern for risk when assessing the profits of potential investments; ancient Greek literature contains plenty of evidence of a similar balancing of risk and profit in the comparison of investment options. Risk and profit are the central considerations in many of the discussions of economic decisions made

69. Kahneman and Tversky 1979.

70. Graham 2003, 18.

71. For a similar awareness of the high risks associated with highly profitable investments in the Roman world, see Frier 1980, 21–24.

by ancient Greeks, who therefore seem to have evaluated economic choices in these exact terms.

Indeed, examples of profit-risk calculations are extant even from the earliest Greek literature. Hesiod warns his brother Perses against hazarding his entire livelihood on the high seas, in case the desire to seek profit should seize him: "Leave the greater part behind, and put the lesser portion on board" (*Works and Days* 690).[72] Seeking *kerdos* on the sea[73] is acceptable only if you risk the lesser part of your possessions and keep the majority of your goods safe on land. This may be advice imparted by Hesiod's father, who, escaping poverty, sought his fortune in being a maritime trader and eventually was able to purchase a piece of land for himself in Boeotia. Though he needed to risk it all on the high seas before, his success made it such that his sons could seek their livelihoods in less dangerous pursuits like agriculture. Their father made enough money in maritime trade to retire comfortably and ensure his sons did not need to engage in the same sort of hazardous profit-seeking behavior.

Athenians like the author of the pseudo-Aristotelian *Oikonomika* agree with Hesiod, saying that more property should be productive than idle, but that not all property should be risked at once.[74] Here, we can see the same concern for gain and productivity, but with a careful eye turned toward safety. Hypereides, in the speech *In Defense of Euxenippos*,[75] also shows how prominently risk factored in decisions on whether or not to pursue a particular investment when he mentions the dangers in the field of mining: ὅταν γὰρ ᾖι φοβερὸν τὸ κτᾶσθαι καὶ φείδεσθαι, τίς βουλήσεται κινδυνεύειν, "When there is fear in acquisition and saving, who will want to take the risk?" (37). Thus, fear and safety were central considerations in decisions of what types of investment to acquire, with the increased risk (*kindunos*) to profits. Socrates, in Plato's *Gorgias*, makes the conceptual link between risk and return explicit in his discussion of maritime traders. He asks why sailors choose such a dangerous trade, and the answer is simple: τίς γὰρ βούλεται πλεῖν τε καὶ κινδυνεύειν καὶ πράγματ' ἔχειν; ἀλλ' ἐκεῖνο οἶμαι οὗ ἕνεκα πλέουσιν, πλουτεῖν· πλούτου γὰρ ἕνεκα πλέουσιν, "For who wants to sail and take risks and engage in business? I think that this is the reason they sail: to be rich. They sail for the sake of wealth" (467d). These sailors are moneymakers (*chrêmatismon, chrêmatizomenoi*), and they willingly run risks (*kinduneuein*) because they want to be rich (*ploutein*). Doing business

72. ἀλλὰ πλέω λείπειν, τὰ δὲ μείονα φορτίζεσθαι.

73. Hesiod, *Works and Days* 632.

74. καὶ πλείω τὰ κάρπιμα εἶναι τῶν ἀκάρπων, καὶ τὰς ἐργασίας οὕτω νενεμῆσθαι ὅπως μὴ ἅμα κινδυνεύσωσιν ἅπασαι (Ps.-Arist. *Oikonomika* 1.6.2).

75. See Whitehead 2000, 256.

is here equated with taking risk, and the purpose of undergoing this danger is to become rich; enduring risk is therefore the means by which someone accumulates wealth. Risk and profit were intimately linked in Greek discussions of economic matters.

The comparative estimation of risk and profit can be seen in Xenophon's attempts to convince his liturgical class audience to support his idea for the creation of a capital fund (*aphormê*) to invest in the transformation of the Athenian public economy:[76]

> κτῆσιν δὲ ἀπ' οὐδενὸς ἂν οὕτω καλὴν κτήσαιντο ὥσπερ ἀφ' οὗ ἂν προτελέσωσιν εἰς τὴν ἀφορμήν· ᾧ μὲν γὰρ ἂν δέκα μναῖ εἰσφορὰ γένηται, ὥσπερ ναυτικόν, σχεδὸν ἐπίπεμπτον αὐτῷ γίγνεται, τριώβολον τῆς ἡμέρας λαμβάνοντι· ᾧ δέ γ' ἂν πέντε μναῖ, πλέον ἢ ἐπίτριτον. οἱ δέ γε πλεῖστοι Ἀθηναίων πλείονα λήψονται κατ' ἐνιαυτὸν ἢ ὅσα ἂν εἰσενέγκωσιν. οἱ γὰρ μνᾶν προτελέσαντες ἐγγὺς δυοῖν μναῖν πρόσοδον ἕξουσι, καὶ ταῦτα ἐν πόλει, ὃ δοκεῖ τῶν ἀνθρωπίνων ἀσφαλέστατόν τε καὶ πολυχρονιώτατον εἶναι.
>
> But from nothing else could they acquire so fine an investment as from whatever they advance to the *aphormê*. For whoever contributes ten *minae* will get almost a fifth in return, just as in nautical loans, when he receives his daily *triobolon*. Whoever contributes five *minae* will receive in return almost a third. And most of the Athenians will receive more than they contribute each year. For those advancing one *mina* will receive a return of almost two *minae*, and these in the *polis*, which seems to be the safest and most long-lasting of human institutions.

Xenophon's words in this passage of the *Poroi* are a window into the thought process of Athenians who were deciding between different ways of mobilizing their money for productive activities.[77] Xenophon thinks his Athenian audience would have been persuaded by the comparison between the returns from the *aphormê* and those of profitable investments. His first strategy in trying to convince his audience to support the *aphormê* is to depict its return (more than 33 percent) as approximating that of bottomry loans,[78] which were some of the

76. Xenophon, *Poroi* 3.9–10. For a discussion of this passage, see Gauthier 1976, 93–96; Jansen 2007, 338–52.

77. Jansen 2007, and Cartledge 1997, 166, and notes to Xenophon 1977, both think that Xenophon's proposals in the *Poroi* are evidence of an economically rational approach.

78. See Millett 1991, 104–5, 184–85, for interest rates on maritime loans.

riskiest but also most rewarding investments in ancient Greece. Profit was not Xenophon's only selling point, however, as at the end of this passage he says that this return was provided by the *polis*, the safest (*asphalestaton*) and longest-lasting of all human institutions. Thus, risk reduction seems to be just as important as profit in his audience's mind. Contributing to the *aphormê* is not only as profitable as bottomry loans, but it also carries none of the risk, precisely what made the shield factory so much more attractive to Apollodorus than the bank. By presenting the *aphormê* as a safe alternative to bottomry loans, Xenophon reveals that his audience would have found a low-risk, high-profit investment more attractive than one which carried greater hazards. Safety and risk both feature prominently in many of his discussions of investment options: οἷόν τε δὴ οὕτως καὶ ἰδιώτας συνισταμένους καὶ κοινουμένους τὴν τύχην ἀσφαλέστερον κινδυνεύειν, "Indeed, it is also possible for private individuals in this way to take risks more safely, by coming together and sharing their luck."[79] The terms he uses, "risk," "safety," and "sharing luck," clearly illustrate the conceptual link between these notions that recur together in ancient Athenian descriptions of moneymaking activities.

Safety can also be seen as a central factor in the thought process about how to commit one's money in Lysias' fragmentary speech *Against Aeschines* 4: οἱ ἐν τῷ Πειραιεῖ διάκεινται ὥστε πολὺ ἀσφαλέστερον εἶναι δοκεῖν εἰς τὸν Ἀδρίαν πλεῖν ἢ τούτῳ συμβάλλειν, "Those in the Piraeus are so disposed as to think that it is safer to sail into the Adriatic than to lend to this guy." Here the speaker jokes that through not paying back his loans, "which he considered more his own than his inherited patrimony," Aeschines' credit had become so bad that moneylenders in the Piraeus think it is riskier to lend to him than to sail in a distant and dangerous sea. This is a hilarious exaggeration by use of an extreme example, but nonetheless one which depicts the lenders comparing the pitfalls of two different economic activities. Once again, alongside the potential profitability of lending to this person, safety (*asphaleia*) is a central concern, which means that Lysias, Xenophon, and Aristotle all used the exact same terminology when evaluating the likely risks of an economic decision, and expected their audiences to understand their assessments in precisely these terms as well.

But risk was also considered a necessary component of moneymaking. As Aristotle states in the *Eudemian Ethics*, people do not choose to be healthy or happy, but "to make money and take risks in order to be happy," οὐθεὶς ὑγιαίνειν προαιρεῖται, ἀλλὰ περιπατεῖν ἢ καθῆσθαι τοῦ ὑγιαίνειν ἕνεκεν, οὐδ' εὐδαιμονεῖν, ἀλλὰ χρηματίζεσθαι ἢ κινδυνεύειν τοῦ εὐδαιμονεῖν ἕνεκα (2.10.7,

79. *Poroi* 4.32.

1226a9–12). In this specific context, Aristotle seems to be using the two terms synonymously, which is similar to the sense in which Hypereides employed the term *kinduneuein* in the passage quoted above. If "taking risks" was often used simply as another way of saying "making money" in ancient Greece, then risk was considered an integral part of conducting business. This is the exact point Hesiod is making when he tells Perses to be wary of the dangers of seaborne commerce if he desires to make profit.

The Insatiable Hunger for Wealth

Antisthenes in Xenophon's *Symposium* says that many individuals engaged in moneymaking behavior to such an extent that they were willing to undergo any risk (*kindunos*) in order to amass more wealth:

> Ὅτι νομίζω, ὦ ἄνδρες, τοὺς ἀνθρώπους οὐκ ἐν τῷ οἴκῳ τὸν πλοῦτον καὶ τὴν πενίαν ἔχειν ἀλλ' ἐν ταῖς ψυχαῖς. ὁρῶ γὰρ πολλοὺς μὲν ἰδιώτας, οἳ πάνυ πολλὰ ἔχοντες χρήματα οὕτω πένεσθαι ἡγοῦνται ὥστε πάντα μὲν πόνον, πάντα δὲ κίνδυνον ὑποδύονται, ἐφ' ᾧ πλείω κτήσονται.
>
> I think, gentlemen, that people have wealth and poverty not in their houses, but in their souls. For I see that many private individuals, who are altogether very rich, think they are so poor that they undergo every labor, every risk, in order to acquire more wealth.[80]

This statement adds further support to the conclusion that Greeks did, in fact, consider risk when pursuing their profits, and also suggests that they accepted it as an inevitable part of the moneymaking process. Combined with the rest of the evidence outlined above, this confirms that wealthy Greeks would make comparisons of the relative levels of return and risk in their decisions regarding potential investments.

More intriguing, however, is the observation that even the very rich can *feel* poor. Antisthenes draws the contrast between the objective reality and these individuals' subjective understanding of their situation. They are poor not in their houses, but in their souls. What Antisthenes is describing is a psychological urge to fill a perceived lack of wealth, not a real one. The perspective of these wealthy individuals is distorted to the point that they believe they are poor. This

80. Xenophon, *Symposium* 4.34–35.

emptiness is unable to be filled with the wealth they already have, and so they try to acquire more. He identifies the *psychê* as the source of these feelings. As seen in the passage from *Laws* cited above, Plato provides similar imagery for this endless yearning for wealth, which he refers to as a "hunger in their souls" (πεινῶσιν τὴν ψυχὴν), that drives an "insatiable quest" for wealth (8.832a). Plato therefore echoes Antisthenes' sentiment in two important respects. This desire to make money is impossible to satisfy, an uncontrollable emotional drive located deep in the *psychê*—a hunger that cannot be filled.

The impulse to accumulate endlessly was not tied to an objective baseline, or just to secure one's livelihood. On the contrary, this lust for wealth drove some people who were already rich to undergo difficulties to acquire more even when it was not necessary for their welfare. Because these individuals *believe* they are poor, they are driven by an insatiable hunger or longing, a psychological impulse to acquire ever-increasing levels of wealth; they are willing to endure every type of toil and risk what they already have in the hopes of attaining more.

The hunger for riches went far beyond the need to supply one's daily necessities; rather, it was unlimited. In the *Poroi*, Xenophon says that while one can have too much furniture, the demand for money never drops: καὶ γὰρ δὴ ἔπιπλα μέν, ἐπειδὰν ἱκανά τις κτήσηται τῇ οἰκίᾳ, οὐ μάλα ἔτι προσωνοῦνται· ἀργύριον δὲ οὐδείς πω οὕτω πολὺ ἐκτήσατο ὥστε μηκέτι προσδεῖσθαι, "As for furniture, whenever someone acquires enough for his house, he does not buy more. But money, on the other hand, no one yet has acquired so much that he still does not desire more" (*Poroi* 4.7). Aristophanes in *Ploutos* depicts two characters telling the god Ploutos that people can have enough of love, baked goods, music, honor, war, ambition, and lentil soup, but no one can have enough wealth:[81]

σοῦ δ' ἐγένετ' οὐδεὶς μεστὸς οὐδεπώποτε.
ἀλλ' ἢν τάλαντά τις λάβῃ τριακαίδεκα,
πολὺ μᾶλλον ἐπιθυμεῖ λαβεῖν ἑκκαίδεκα·
κἂν ταῦθ' ἀνύσηται, τετταράκοντα βούλεται,
ἤ φησιν οὐκ εἶναι βιωτὸν τὸν βίον.

No one is ever full of you,
but if someone gets thirteen talents,
he much more desires to get sixteen,

81. Aristophanes, *Ploutos* 187–97.

> and if he procures these for himself, he wants forty,
> or he says that his life is unlivable. (193–97)

Ploutos therefore was special, in that it was not subject to the same constraints that governed other goods, but had no limit to its accumulation. Solon, in lines alternatively attributed to Theognis, agrees, saying that those who possess the most wealth only want more: οἳ γὰρ νῦν ἡμῶν πλεῖστον ἔχουσι βίον, διπλάσιον σπεύδουσι. τίς ἂν κορέσειεν ἅπαντας, "For those of us who now have the greatest wealth yearn for twice as much; who could satisfy them all?"[82]

Plato addresses this problem of uncontrolled wealth acquisition throughout his corpus. In the *Laws*, he says that the majority of people disregard good repute and moderate gain, and instead seek wealth voraciously:

> σμικρὸν γένος ἀνθρώπων . . . ὅταν ἐξῇ χρήματα λαβεῖν πολλά, νήφει καὶ πρότερον αἱρεῖται τοῦ πολλοῦ τὸ τοῦ μέτρου ἐχόμενον· τὰ δὲ τῶν ἀνθρώπων πλήθη πᾶν τοὐναντίον ἔχει τούτοις, δεόμενά τε ἀμέτρως δεῖται καὶ ἐξὸν κερδαίνειν τὰ μέτρια ἀπλήστως αἱρεῖται κερδαίνειν.

> Small is the class of men . . . who, whenever they are able to take much wealth, are sober, and choose what is moderate rather than what is more. The majority of people are completely contrary to these men; when they desire, they desire without measure, and when it is possible to make moderate profit, they choose to profit insatiably.[83]

The majority of humanity is driven to make as much profit as they can, even when it is considered more proper to accumulate moderately. Therefore, the eager maximization of profit and wealth are what Plato identifies as being an aim of many people in his world.[84] Nor should it be shocking that this is the case. In the *Republic*, he thinks it is reasonable to suppose that an entire city's population would overstep the boundaries of what is necessary and seek unlimited gain (373d).

To Plato, money and wealth are central to satisfying other desires, and he is consistent in saying that most people are driven to indulge and even maximize their pleasures insatiably (*Republic* 586c). As noted above, in his theory of the

82. Theognis 226–28; West, Solon F 13, 72–74.
83. Plato, *Laws* 918c–d.
84. As Föllinger 2016, 61, puts it, "According to Plato, the desire to maximize one's own benefit is a central characteristic of human beings" (Bei Platon ist der Wunsch, den eigenen Nutzen zu maximieren, ein zentraler Zug des Menschen).

mind (or soul), Plato describes the human *psychê* as consisting of three main parts: a rational element that calculates (*logistikon*), an irrational, or spirited portion (*thumoeides*), and the third, another irrational part which he refers to as the *epithumêtikon*, "appetitive" portion, which seeks food, drink, and sexual pleasure (*Republic* 440a).

Most significantly, he gives another name to this appetitive region, the "money-loving" part of the mind, because "it is through money that these desires are especially achieved" (*Republic* 580e–581a). Food, drink, and sex, therefore, some of the most basic wants in the human mind, are best achieved through money, according to Plato, which was so central to realizing corporal pleasures that he renamed the lustful portion of the brain the "money-loving" part:

> ἆρ᾽ οὖν καὶ τὴν ἡδονὴν αὐτοῦ καὶ φιλίαν εἰ φαῖμεν εἶναι τοῦ κέρδους, μάλιστ᾽ ἂν εἰς ἓν κεφάλαιον ἀπερειδοίμεθα τῷ λόγῳ, ὥστε τι ἡμῖν αὐτοῖς δηλοῦν, ὁπότε τοῦτο τῆς ψυχῆς τὸ μέρος λέγοιμεν, καὶ καλοῦντες αὐτὸ φιλοχρήματον καὶ φιλοκερδὲς ὀρθῶς ἂν καλοῖμεν;
>
> And so, if we should say that its pleasure and love were for profit, would it not be best to fix upon one heading in our analysis, so that it is clear to us whenever we refer to this part of the soul, and would we not be right to call it the money- and profit-loving part?[85]

Plato therefore labeled one of the main regions of the Greek *psychê* the "money- and profit-loving part." It was not just people on the margins of society who had this portion of the brain; it was seen as being an integral part of the mind for Greeks in general. Central within the *psychê*, such a prominent position is not consistent with an interpretation that the desire for profit was exceptional or rare in that society.

But Aristotle takes the description of these mental processes a step further—he says that the act of desiring applied not just to the pleasure itself, but also to the means of creating the money to attain such pleasure (*epithumousin*), namely, the means necessary to produce the desired ends (*Politics* 1.9.15–16, 1257b38–1258a9). In saying that Greeks desired the productive means, Aristotle demonstrates that he understands the distinction between means and ends central to economic rationality in a way that simply saying that they desired pleasure as an end does not. But he also states in the same passage that they

85. *Republic* 581a.

sought boundless wealth (*apeiron*) as an end as well, so he considers the desire as extending toward maximizing both the end of wealth and the means to producing that end.

In the passage cited above, Aristotle is aware of the importance of the means-to-ends relationship in his use of the term *proaireisthai*, "choose deliberately": people do not choose to be healthy or happy, but "to make money and take risks in order to be happy" (*Eudemian Ethics*, 2.10.7, 1226a9–12). The distinction between the ends and the means of attaining them is critical in this situation, because modern economic theory restricts the scope of rationality not to the ends one desires, but rather to the means employed to attaining those ends. Similarly Aristotle here describes the object of deliberate choice (*proairesis*) as the decision to undertake risks for the purpose of making money, which is the means to the greater end of being happy. Aristotle's theory of behavior with respect to this means-to-ends relationship therefore presupposes rational choice in a way that resembles modern economic rationality.

Conclusions

In their theories of the mind and human psychology, therefore, Xenophon, Plato, and Aristotle all locate the love for money deep in the *psychê*; although they were certainly referring to Athenians, they do not explicitly restrict their observations to citizens of that city alone, and their statements certainly seem to carry an air of universal trends across the Greek world. Moreover, archaic poets likewise emphasized a fundamental mental drive to accumulate wealth, and ascribed similar behavior to the people of their own times and places, both within Athens and in other *poleis*. The combined weight of these authors' testimony is of the utmost importance. They are all consistent in asserting that even some of the richest Greeks, who already had more money than they needed, still sought to increase their wealth immeasurably.

From the archaic period through the fourth century, ancient Greeks' desires to make money and to accumulate as much wealth as possible are well attested.[86] Aristotle's use of the superlative πλεῖστον κέρδος summing up those who attempt to realize the "greatest profit" and the phrase "everyone engaged in moneymaking will increase his money without limit" (εἰς ἄπειρον αὔξουσιν) are unequivocal attestations of the drive to maximize profit and wealth. His

86. See Seaford 2004, 157–62, for further discussion and examples of other archaic and classical Greek statements about the desire for money as a universal aim.

conclusion that there is "no end of wealth and acquisition" strongly suggests that some had not just attempted to maximize their wealth but had actually achieved this goal.

The lust for money was therefore insatiable, ever-expanding, and increasing without limit. Plato's explanation for this phenomenon is that there was an entire money- or profit-loving region of the Greek mind. Furthermore, both Plato and Aristotle state that moneymakers would resort to any means in their quest to make profit from any source (ἀπὸ παντὸς, πόθεν καὶ πῶς), and were willing to learn any new *technê* or *epitêdeuma* to maximize profits. Money was the ultimate goal for these individuals who are depicted as deliberating about the best means of achieving the end of making profit, which is the main characteristic of the economically rational decision-making process.[87] They dedicate all their time to finding ways to increase their gains, and pursue boundless accumulation. It is significant that both philosophers emphasize these same basic issues that are so central to economic rationality. They consistently echo modern economic theory in their selection of the most important behavioral elements, the nature of those traits, and the outcome of those patterns as being the maximization of wealth.

Moneymaking innovations ruptured the bounds that nature set to all other goods. Experimentation and creativity made the art of *chrêmatistikê* more technical (*technikôteron*), sophisticated enough that individuals engaged in moneymaking could expand their wealth on an ever-increasing basis. Greeks are also described as choosing among alternatives and switching their production based on prices and profitability, comparing the potential return of investment options and ultimately deciding on whatever was most lucrative. At the conceptual level, *chrêmatistikê* had become broad enough that it even engulfed traditional estate management; it had subsumed a wide range of occupations into its larger category, and transformed the purpose of other arts to the end of making money. Most significantly, rather than just being characteristic of an isolated class of exceptional individuals, it had even penetrated estate management and agriculture, the traditional lifestyle of citizens of the *polis*.

These behavioral patterns are sufficiently reminiscent of an economically rational approach to making money, as described by modern economic theory, to justify an in-depth analysis of individual business and estate management strategies. So to what extent is the impression gleaned from poets and philosophers above reflected in actual case studies of Athenian economic behavior?

87. Indeed, the willingness to profit from everything, from every source, is also depicted in Xenophon's *Poroi* (see introduction chapter) where people in general react to price fluctuations with changes in supply and demand: they move to whatever activities will bring them more money.

Are these patterns restricted to a few aberrant examples, just an Athenian phenomenon, or were they widespread throughout the Greek world? I will now turn to case studies of ancient Athenian economic decision-making to see how the principles of profit, risk, and safety, as discussed in the sources above, actually guided the moneymaking strategies of real-life individuals. Starting with big-picture *oikonomia* on diversified estates, I will then turn to estates that specialized in one type of production, and then end with maritime trade, where Greeks from *poleis* other than Athens will feature prominently.

CHAPTER 2

Making Money in the *Oikos*

Strategies for Diversification and Profit

The first chapter explored discussions of moneymaking strategies using a top-down approach at the theoretical level. But to see how these ideas and theories actually played out on the ground we must look at the attested economic decision-making process and choices made by Athenian individuals in their estate management, where *chrêmatistikê* and *oikonomia* come together. To do so, I will examine the moneymaking strategies both at the level of estate management overall and in the finer details of the administration of individual business enterprises when available. Athenian estates feature most prominently because of the restricted nature of our sources, but I will also demonstrate that similar patterns of behavior can be seen in other Greek *poleis*.

Diversified estates constitute some of our best-preserved case studies of *oikonomia*. Is there evidence that Athenians tried to balance or negotiate the utility-maximizing aims of the household with the profit-maximizing aims of the firm? Does it seem that they favored one over the other? I will analyze their patterns of diversification, how they chose to spend their profits, their motives for acquiring new properties, and strategies to manage risk and maximize profit. To have an objective frame of reference by which to assess ancient Athenians' motives for diversifying their estates, it will be useful to compare their actions to models of peasant risk aversion on the one hand, and the ways modern corporations diversify to reduce risk on the other.[1] Moreover, in order

1. The noncapitalist peasant subsistence model was first articulated by Chayanov 1966, from whom the field of peasant economic studies has emerged. For the anti-surplus, safety-first, peasant subsistence model, sometimes referred to as the "moral economy" of the peasant, see, e.g., Wolf 1966; Hodges 1988, 11; Scott 1976. See, e.g., Gallant 1991, 7–10, for the application of risk-minimizing peasant subsistence models to ancient Greece, which are, of course, perfectly appropriate for those who actually did resemble modern peasants. For the limits of the peasant model, and its applicability to wealthy individuals, see Horden and Purcell 2000, 271–78. Wood 1988 provides a lengthy discussion of many of the issues in labeling ancient Greeks as "peasants."

to determine if estate owners were committed to ever-increasing productivity and profitability, it will be necessary to distinguish between short-term profit and long-term wealth maximization. To do so, I will examine the total proportion of estates that were dedicated to consumptive and productive purposes. Furthermore, the practice of tax evasion and liturgy avoidance are also useful indicators of long-term wealth-maximizing strategies. It seems that many Athenians and other Greeks made the decision to invest in wealth that was invisible (*aphanês*) to the *polis* to allow them to avoid serving liturgies and paying taxes that would restrict the long-term growth of their estates.

Estate inventories in the Attic orators and the Attic Stelai are often treated as static entities, with the result that their dynamism is downplayed. End of life choices were often different from those during the prime of one's life, at the height of one's career. Consequently the life cycle is a very important factor for understanding ancient Greek business and estate owners' economic behavior and investment choices. I will piece together the estate management strategies as best I can by focusing on the choices individuals made with their money, with the most probable reconstruction of their initial estate's composition and then unpacking each individual's subsequent decision-making process. Because a number of scholars have already conducted detailed examinations of the profits and costs of various workshops and properties, I will restrict my analysis to the motives that guided economic decisions at the level of overall estate management—why owners chose to acquire specific properties, and how they preferred to spend their profits.[2]

Timarchus' Father Arizelos: A Strategy of Short- and Long-Term Profit

The estate of Timarchus' father, Arizelos, is one of the best known from ancient Greece, and provides a window into the economic decision-making process of an estate owner. It is detailed in Aeschines' speech *Against Timarchus* which centers on the reprehensible actions of the son, but also preserves a great deal of evidence about his father's moneymaking activities and estate management strategies. Arizelos was the owner of a diversified estate who seems to have managed his property largely with the aim to maintain and increase the profit-

2. My analysis will therefore be at a different level from those scholars who have focused on the nitty-gritty details of factory operations in their efforts to reconstruct the most probable rates of profit based on the assumption that the figures reported by the Greeks themselves are unreliable. I am not entirely rejecting ancient figures as implausible, but am also recognizing the more likely calculations made by scholars who have delved into the details; I will use the full range of the attested and reconstructed rates of profit as maxima and minima.

ability of his holdings in the long term. To show how Timarchus squandered his inheritance, Aeschines lists its contents in depth:

> τούτῳ γὰρ κατέλιπεν ὁ πατὴρ οὐσίαν, ἀφ' ἧς ἕτερος μὲν κἂν ἐλητούργει, οὗτος δὲ οὐδ' αὑτῷ διαφυλάξαι ἐδυνήθη: οἰκίαν μὲν ὄπισθεν τῆς πόλεως, ἐσχατιὰν δὲ Σφηττοῖ, Ἀλωπεκῆσι δ' ἕτερον χωρίον, χωρὶς δὲ οἰκέτας δημιουργοὺς τῆς σκυτοτομικῆς τέχνης ἐννέα ἢ δέκα, ὧν ἕκαστος τούτῳ δύ' ὀβολοὺς ἀποφορὰν ἔφερε τῆς ἡμέρας, ὁ δ' ἡγεμὼν τοῦ ἐργαστηρίου τριώβολον: ἔτι δὲ πρὸς τούτοις γυναῖκα ἀμόργινα ἐπισταμένην ἐργάζεσθαι καὶ ἔργα λεπτὰ εἰς τὴν ἀγορὰν ἐκφέρουσαν, καὶ ἄνδρα ποικιλτήν, καὶ ὀφείλοντάς τινας αὐτῷ ἀργύριον, καὶ ἔπιπλα.
>
> For his father left to him property from which another man could have served liturgies, but Timarchus could not even preserve it for himself. There was a house behind the Acropolis, a plot of land at Sphettos,[3] another at Alopeke, as well as nine or ten slave manufacturers of the shoemaking trade, each of whom paid an *apophora* of two obols per day, and the manager of the workshop three obols daily. And still in addition to these, he left a woman who was skilled in working in flax from Amorgos, producing fine goods for the market, a man working in embroidery, some individuals owing money to him and furniture.[4]

As Aeschines says, Arizelos left enough money for Timarchus to serve liturgies. In addition to slave manufacturers producing goods for the market, land, and houses, he also had a great deal of money on loan (1.99–100), at least half a talent's worth that is known,[5] which Timarchus apparently collected (1.100); moreover, the large amount of *aphanês*,[6] or invisible wealth, in loans is said explicitly to have come from properties he had sold:

3. There is no clear way to distinguish qualitatively between the *eschatia* (marginal, fringe land) at Sphettos and the other plots of land, the *choria*, owned by Arizelos. See Jameson 2002, for an in-depth discussion of the distinction. See Lambert 1997, for the wide range in prices of *eschatiai* sold in the *rationes centesimarum*, some of which were extremely expensive, up to four talents, and so cannot be considered to be "marginal" or inferior land.

4. Aeschines 1.97.

5. Aeschines 1.100 does not specify the number of borrowers Arizelos had, but only that it was to more than one person (τισιν). The nature of *aphanês* wealth makes it impossible to guess its full extent. It is not clear how much of his wealth loans constituted, but the loan of a half talent to Metagenes of Sphettus (1.100) suggests that the total may have been substantial, and he is said to have lent to a number of people.

6. The Athenians distinguished *aphanês*, invisible, property in the form of cash, loans, slaves, and other moveable goods from *phanera*, visible assets in land and houses. For *aphanês* and *phanera ousia*, see Gabrielsen 1986, 99–114; Gabrielsen 1994, 53–60; Cohen 1992, 191–207.

ὡς τοίνυν ἐκέκτητο ὁ πατὴρ αὐτοῦ ἀργύριον οὐκ ὀλίγον, ὃ οὗτος ἠφάνικε, τοῦθ' ὑμῖν ἐπιδείξω. φοβηθεὶς γὰρ τὰς λητουργίας ἀπέδοτο ἃ ἦν αὐτῷ κτήματα ἄνευ τῶν ἀρτίως εἰρημένων, χωρίον Κηφισιᾶσιν, ἕτερον Ἀμφιτροπῆσιν, ἐργαστήρια δύο ἐν τοῖς ἀργυρείοις, ἓν μὲν ἐν Αὐλῶνι, ἕτερον δ' ἐπὶ Θρασύλλῳ.

And that his father owned a large amount of money, which Timarchus has hidden, I will demonstrate to you. For Arizelos, fearing liturgies, sold what possessions he had aside from those just mentioned: a plot of land at Kephisia, another at Amphitrope, and two workshops in the silver mining regions, one at Aulon, and another near [the tomb of][7] Thrasyllos. (1.101)

In this earlier stage of estate composition, Arizelos had also previously owned two additional plots of land and two silver ore processing workshops in the Laureion silver mining district,[8] which Aeschines mentioned he had sold and transformed into loans (1.99–100).[9] Arizelos is explicitly said by Aeschines to have made the decision to invest in mining (1.105), so he himself was apparently responsible for the acquisition of much, if not all the productive property in his estate at his death.[10] Thus, Arizelos owned a diversified estate, with agriculture, loans, manufacturing, and mining activities all represented.

According to the peasant models frequently applied to ancient Greece, the most obvious explanation for this diversity is simple: the minimization of risk. Having four scattered plots of land would have allowed him to avoid the

7. This detail is from the translation of Adams 1919.

8. These *ergastêria* were most certainly silver ore processing workshops, probably washeries, which are well-known from the archaeological, epigraphical, and literary record. In Demosthenes *Against Pantaenetus*, the lawsuit concerned a loan against the security of an *ergastêrion* and thirty slaves (37.4), worth altogether three talents and two thousand drachmas (37.50).

9. The potential size of the loans can perhaps be suggested by the values of ore washing workshops known from the literary and epigraphical record: Pantaenetus' workshop was worth three and a third talents (Dem. 37.50); the workshops known from *horos* inscriptions were worth at least 1,400 drachmas (Finley 1985, #90), and two talents (Finley 1985, #88), on the understanding that hypothecation could yield about half the property's actual value, as in the case of Pantaenetus. Thus, the sale of each workshop could have yielded anywhere between a quarter of a talent and two talents. Therefore, the loans could have been in the order of several talents, perhaps even composing the majority of the estate's value.

10. Some of the wealth may have belonged to Timarchus' uncle, whose property Arizelos was said to have been administering (1.102), but it certainly would have been difficult for Timarchus to have been able to steal his uncle's property to the point Aeschines depicts: that the latter was receiving state assistance as a disabled pauper. Such payments were only possible after a *dokimasia*, a scrutiny which doubtless would have inquired about the loss of his property. For the *dokimasia* of disabled citizens (*adynatoi*) in Athens, see Todd 1993, 115n13, 301.

devastation of a flood or bad harvest,[11] and by supplementing his agricultural holdings with mining properties and loans, he was able to protect himself even further against a disaster in any one of these fields. Moreover, his slave manufacturers would have been able to bring in a reliable return throughout the year to offset the agricultural properties' decline in productivity during the winter. This was a diverse variety of investments, each of which was vulnerable to different types of dangers, which protected his estate from being completely wiped out by a single disaster or fluctuation in market prices. Though it is unclear whether or not he would have farmed his own plots of land or if they were rented out to tenants, his slave craftspeople and mining properties would have brought in a steady stream of cash, as would his loans, if they were for interest. Such diversification would have shielded Arizelos from the devastating market fluctuations described by Xenophon in the *Poroi* (see introduction chapter). At first glance, therefore, Arizelos' property list in isolation seems to conform to patterns of risk-reducing diversification.

Looking more closely at Arizelos' decision-making process, however, it seems that he did not diversify his estate properties to avoid risk, but rather made his acquisitions primarily with an eye to profit. First, as Aeschines says, he purchased the mining *ergastêria*, workshops, in the Laureion region, and after he owned them for a certain time, he had made enough money to raise himself up into the liturgical class. Before owning these *ergastêria*, Arizelos was not concerned with being charged to serve liturgies, but after making a hefty return, he eventually so feared he would become liable to liturgical obligations that he sold these properties.

Along with these mining *ergastêria* he also liquidated two plots of land, which yields further insights into his estate management goals. This was not a risk-reducing action, since Arizelos lost the risk-minimizing benefits of the scattered land plots he sold, selling his farthest-flung holdings at Kephisia and Amphitrope near Sounion, and concentrating his agricultural activities onto fewer plots of land closer to the city. He also exited from mining, leaving an estate composed of a less diverse variety of investments, and riskier overall.

Therefore, risk avoidance cannot be assumed for Arizelos' economic decision-making process, and profit was the primary motivation for his initial decision to invest in these *ergastêria*. Because he only began to fear liturgies after their acquisition, it seems that these *ergastêria* helped Arizelos to increase

11. Fragmentation of landholdings was the rule in Athens, which may have been for risk minimization, but also perhaps resulted from the windfall acquisition of land plots that were fragmented from sale and partible inheritance, for which see Davies 1981, 52–55; Osborne 1985, 47–52, 62–63; Foxhall 2002.

his wealth substantially, and that his ownership of these properties made it more likely that he be selected to serve. The implication is that these were not only lucrative assets but visibly profitable enough to attract the attention of the Athenian *polis*.

Profit was what apparently drove Arizelos to acquire these *ergastêria* in the first place; he operated them for a long enough period to permit sustained growth and increase his coffers as much as possible. Indeed, Arizelos' desire for further gain and continued growth for his estate can be seen most clearly in the very motivation for selling the mining *ergastêria*: φοβηθεὶς γὰρ τὰς λητουργίας, "because he feared liturgies." Having made so much money from his mining properties, he is said to have sold these properties and not his other holdings of land and slaves, because they were the most conspicuously profitable assets he owned.[12] He invested in silver ore processing, then exited once he had made as much money as he could without facing the heavy demands of liturgies, whereupon he transformed these assets into *aphanês*, hidden, form by lending the proceeds, according to Aeschines. The insistence with which he collected the only loan about which anything is known, half a talent to Metagenes, suggests that his moneylending was not friendly but a matter of business.[13] His other decisions, to enter the field of silver ore processing, profit as much as possible, then liquidate these properties to avoid liturgies and continue to profit from the estate, are a strong sign of a profit-seeking inclination, so these loans were likely for interest. Nor would this be a surprise; although Aeschines omits the exact details of their nature, Nausicrates' and Xenopeithes' moneylending fortune of almost ninety talents (38.20) was not described by Demosthenes as having been for interest (he simply uses the neutral term for loans, *chrea*, at 38.7–9), nor were Pasion's loans still outstanding at his death (36.5), but these fortunes most certainly consisted of interest-bearing loans, geared for profit. Another indication that these loans hinted at by Aeschines were not likely just friendly is that Aeschines would have been able to disparage Timarchus' squandering of his father's fortune as being even more despicable if he mentioned that it was partially invested in *eranos* loans. On the contrary, the profit-oriented decision making of Arizelos is much more consistent with a move to moneylending at interest, though he may have also lent on *eranos*. In any case, the strategies Arizelos employed were directed at sustaining continued growth.

---

12. The large number of citizens making fortunes in the Laureion mining district, combined with the mechanisms for democratic participation at Athens itself would have meant that information about profitable enterprises in southern Attica would have been prominent in the discussions of wealth at Athens itself. Arizelos was wise to liquidate these mining properties to avoid liturgies.

13. Metagenes was apparently repaying the loan in installments, since he had originally owed thirty *minae*, but still owed seven *minae* at the time of Arizelos' death (1.100).

Not that Arizelos was simply aiming at profit in his economic decision-making process, but he appears to have been trying to maximize wealth overall. His property acquisition follows a pattern of seizing what he perceived to be lucrative opportunities in a timely manner as they arose.[14] As Finley has argued, such windfall acquisition characterized much ancient investment practice.[15] Given the imperfect information networks in antiquity, the chance arrival of news by word of mouth was often the rule, and long-term material success could depend upon snatching up profitable opportunities at the right time.[16] Therefore, the diversity of Arizelos' holdings may be a sign of a gain-oriented, acquisitive strategy, in which he purchased different types of property in the hope of bringing in extra cash from a variety of ventures. Profit certainly motivated his purchase of the silver ore washeries, and his liquidation of these properties allowed for continued long-term growth.

The evidence indicates that Arizelos was continuously trying to reinvest his money into additional productive purposes instead of just spending it on consumption, unlike Timarchus who squandered the property. Although a percentage is impossible to determine without specific figures, it seems that *all* the assets listed by Aeschines, aside from the furniture and part of the house, were productive.[17] The slave manufacturers were extremely profitable, and even if he was only receiving the minimum return from his shoe workshop (see below), he still would have been bringing in a steady sum from products in high demand. His two other productive slaves, who were explicitly said to be making specialized textiles of fine quality for the market, εἰς τὴν ἀγοράν (1.97), were certainly chosen and kept for their profitability. Indeed, even ordinary textiles were sold for substantial sums,[18] and specialized garments of Amorgos flax and embroidered items of finer quality would have brought an even higher price.[19]

14. The opportunism in ancient Greeks' acquisition of productive property is emphasized strongly by Foxhall 2007.

15. Finley 1973, 117–22; Millett 1991, 166, agrees.

16. Osborne 1988, 291, argues that the circulation of news about opportunities for leases was often restricted to inside groups.

17. Kazakévich 2008, 372, notes that the slave manufacturers probably worked in the city residence. The parallels for this are quite common: at least some of Demosthenes' father's slave workers lived and worked in his residence (see below), and Komon in Demosthenes 48 owned two houses, each of which housed a slave workshop, including his own residence. Choosing to place one's slave workshops in one's house was a way to avoid the costs of renting out a separate space. As seen in Olynthus, many houses were completely filled with productive spaces, for which see Cahill 2002.

18. Ordinary cloaks sold for up to 20 drachmas apiece, with lower quality garments roughly half the price. See Amemiya 2007, 70–71. For the profits that could be made from textile production, see Xenophon, *Memorabilia* 2.7.

19. An interesting illustration of the potential returns from such fine woven goods can be seen in Pausanias' comment at 7.21.14 that most of the women of Roman Patrae, who outnumbered the men two to one and needed to support themselves, made a living weaving fine flaxen dresses and hair nets.

Moreover, his workshops in the Laureion region were major cash-generating properties whose acquisition eventually raised him into the liturgical class, and it was only at the point that he was going to lose significant sums to liturgies that he curtailed his *phanera ousia*, and transformed this wealth into *aphanês* form as loans.

Thus, Arizelos concentrated his wealth into as many different profit-generating properties as he could. But did he actually try to maximize his profits? For this question the running of the shoe workshop is of great interest. A key piece of evidence appears when Aeschines mentions the daily rate owed by each slave, two obols per working slave (nine or ten of them), and three obols per day from the *hêgemôn*,[20] "manager," probably also a slave himself.[21] In the most despotic scenario, Arizelos would have required his slaves to pay him a daily rate and also all the profits. However, if this were the case, it would be odd for Aeschines to mention the daily rate, and as in other examples from the Attic orators, he probably would have just presented the total returns of the workshop which accrued on an annual basis.[22] The more likely scenario is that the slaves paid Timarchus' father a flat rate *per diem* (*apophora*), and that either the *hêgemôn* kept the surplus or split it with Arizelos.[23] Since those Greeks who advocated profit sharing with slave managers did so with an eye to increasing productivity and gains, Arizelos' use of the *apophora* is consistent with a long-term income-maximizing strategy. Having a productive and interested manager would ensure effective management of a single lucrative property while allowing the master to engage in other acts. Arizelos was, after all, also a landowner, a moneylender, was active in the mines, and had other market-producing slaves. To be sure, Arizelos jumped on profitable opportunities, and made the decisions on what to acquire and what to sell primarily with an eye for higher return. At this level, Arizelos was not invested primarily in the management of one piece of property, but rather in the entry and exit into different fields based on monetary gain; this behavior fits well into the model of modern economically rational individuals

20. Aeschines 1.97.

21. Aeschines calls this daily payment *apophora*, the payment that often absentee slave managers paid to their masters, for which see Harpocration, ἀποφορά; Andocides 1.38; Old Oligarch (Pseudo-Xenophon), *Ath. Pol.* 1.11. See also Kazakévich 2008, 352–56; Cohen 1992, 93–94; Garlan 1988, 69–73; Lauffer 1979, 67–71, 106–10, 175–76; Fisher 2008, 124–27; Davies 2007, 354–55.

22. Cf. Demosthenes' father's workshops in Dem. 27.9, and Apollodorus' shield factory and bank in Dem. 36.11–12, where the total annual proceeds are listed as a single lump sum.

23. Xenophon, *Oeconomicus* 12.6 of course advocated sharing profits with slave managers to maximize profit and productivity; this incentive-based profit sharing is also consistent with Pseudo-Aristotle's advice to reward slaves with manumission as a *telos*, goal, to increase productivity (*Oikonomika* 1.5.6).

who compare the profitability of different investments and make their choices on that basis.

The figures that Aeschines gives for the income from the shoe workshop show that Arizelos was earning an impressive rate of profit from the workshop in any case. Nine or ten workers paying 2 obols, led by a slave manager who paid 3 obols per day would make between 21 and 23 obols per day, amounting to between 1,277.5 and 1,400 drachmas per year, between a fifth and a quarter of a talent in silver per year. After factoring in the replacement costs for the slaves themselves, Thompson calculates that the workshop would have brought in at least 15 to 19 percent of its value in earnings each year.[24] This is close to the rates of return for maritime loans, so he would have been securing a steady and sizable income from the workshop even if he only received the fixed, *per diem* rate.[25]

That Arizelos was receiving such large profits from this steady, reliable source was simply smart business. In *The Intelligent Investor*, Benjamin Graham recommends that investors place between a quarter and three-quarters of their property in stocks, which can reasonably be expected to provide a steady, long-term return of 6 percent per year.[26] By comparison, Arizelos' profits look very desirable. Although Thompson's estimates do not include additional costs, they should be regarded as approximate minima, since he calculates the rate of return based on the highest attested price for manufacturing slaves known from ancient Greece. If the value of his shoemakers was somewhat less, as is probable (the average slave in the Attic Stelai cost less than half of the slaves Thompson uses),[27] then the relative profits of the workshop would have been even greater. Since the margin of error of Thompson's calculations would offset additional, unconsidered costs, Arizelos' shoe workshop may have even approached one of those "special situations" in investment, as Graham refers to them: "which over many years could be counted on to bring a nice annual return of 20% or better."[28] His profit-sharing scheme would have ensured the workshop's continued productivity by giving his slaves an incentive to work hard, produce

24. Thompson 1978, 408.

25. Cohen 1992, 93, agrees that this was a fixed rate.

26. Graham 2003, 89–91. See also Zweigg 2003, 85.

27. See Pritchett and Pippin 1956, 276.

28. Graham 2003, 32. Early modern factory profits provide a valuable comparison, for which see Braudel 1982, 343: one producing calicoes in Mulhouse made about 25 percent profit in 1770, but dropped down to 8.5 percent in 1784; a paper mill at Vidalon-lès-Annonay, whose profits stayed at or below 10 percent from 1772–1800; a cotton mill at Augsburg brought 15.4 percent between 1769 and 1781; a silk manufactory in Crefeld whose profits varied between 2.5 and 17.25 percent in the five-year period of 1793–1797. In mid-fourteenth-century Florence, the wool manufactory of Antonio di Lando degli Albizzi averaged 22 percent annually from 1346 to 1350, and that of Francesco Del Bene averaged 11.7 percent from 1355 to 1370 (Goldthwaite 2009, 272).

the best products, and minimize costs, just as is advocated by ancient Greek writers of estate management treatises. And so, Arizelos' shoe workshop was likely designed to maximize its earnings, and his decision to keep it after he liquidated other properties demonstrates that he did, indeed, enjoy its revenue in the long term, which is suggestive of a profit-maximizing approach to his estate management overall.

Whether Arizelos was actually maximizing his gains in the administration of his estate is impossible to determine with absolute certainty, but his choices all align with the goal of increasing his wealth both in the short and the long term. He operated his shoe workshop at a high rate of profit, and also employed the majority of his property in productive purposes. He then apparently decided to invest the profits from agriculture and slave manufacturing into mining *ergastêria* to make money. Once these made him wealthy enough that he suspected he might be considered for liturgies, he did not invest in social status and honor by celebrating his state obligations,[29] but rather opted for long-term continuous economic growth by liquidating productive visible assets and transforming them into *aphanês* loans. His profit-oriented decisions with respect to acquiring and selling his mining *ergastêria*, and the further growth he achieved by avoiding liturgies, are all consistent with a long-term strategy to maximize his wealth.

All the choices Arizelos is depicted as making are directed at profit. His investment in mining was a calculated move to make money, as was the decision to exit this field as soon as he had reaped from it all he could. He certainly displayed a profit-oriented attitude in his moves both to enter and exit mining activities. He entered to maximize the returns on his principal, and then he exited after he was afraid that his gains from these properties were reaching the point that he would then be called upon to serve liturgies. He liquidated his most conspicuously profitable assets, while simultaneously deciding to keep his lucrative shoe workshop and slave textile manufactures, and invested the proceeds in loans, which could not be detected by the *polis*. And so he made a series of deliberate choices to increase his estate by acquiring new, profit-generating properties when he had the money, and then transformed them into invisible form to permit further long-term growth.

Arizelos maintained a diversified estate, which was riskier than when he started but still well-balanced between his various holdings. He kept some

29. For the limits of *philotimia* as a motivation for liturgy performance, see Cohen 1992, 198–201, who shows that it was only after they had tried to avoid liturgies and were forced to serve them against their will that many champions of *philotimia* then exploited them for the social esteem that they brought. For liturgy avoidance in classical Athens, see Christ 2006, 143–200.

of his lower-risk assets, while liquidating others and reinvesting them into higher-risk loans. He started from a safely diversified estate portfolio, and then chose the right mix of properties to allow him to continue to enjoy, and increase, his profits in the long run. The move from lower- to higher-risk property shows that profit, not the avoidance of risk, primarily characterized his decision-making process. But although risk reduction is not explicitly stated as a motivation in Aeschines' account, this does not mean Arizelos was oblivious to it. He had a safe balance of properties at first, and far from just throwing all his money into dangerous but high-yield maritime loans, he decided to keep some land and the slaves when he converted his other property into loans.

Therefore, Arizelos was said to have permitted the long-term maximization of his wealth and profit by avoiding liturgies. He also kept a balanced estate that was productive but not entirely concentrated in high-risk holdings. As far as profit maximization is concerned, he seems to have run his shoe workshop to make as much money as it could, and he certainly squeezed the most return possible from his mining properties; afterward he selected the precise mixture of properties to avoid liturgies and enable long-term growth, with a significant amount of wealth mobilized for profit in riskier ventures while still maintaining safer holdings to ensure the stability of his estate and high rates of steady cash income.

Demosthenes the Elder: Profitable Choices for Long-Term Growth

The famous orator Demosthenes' father (of the same name) is our next case study. His estate is described in detail in the speeches Demosthenes delivered to try to recover his inheritance from its guardians, speeches 27–29, *Against Aphobus 1–3*. Demosthenes the Elder's estate is one of the best-preserved from classical Greece, but also one of the most frustrating to interpret, as it is filled with uncertainties, ambiguities, and rhetorical manipulation. I will restrict my discussion to the general patterns of his economic decisions and overall moneymaking strategies since so many scholars have performed in-depth quantitative analyses based on the specific figures preserved and there are limits to what can be said for certain.[30] Nevertheless, Demosthenes the Elder's decision-making process exhibits many of the same strategies employed by Arizelos, so

30. There are a number of problematic issues I have no space to address. For detailed discussions of Demosthenes' estate and its interpretive difficulties, see Davies 1971, 113–39; De Ste. Croix 1953; Finley 1973, 116–17; Millett 1991, 163–71; Thompson 1982, 68–71; 1978, 410–11; Harris 2002, 81–82; Amemiya 2007, 31–34; Acton 2014, 254–70.

he also may be argued to have been aiming to maximize his profit and wealth in the long term.

His economic choices can be reconstructed through Demosthenes' narrative. Not only did he consistently invest his money in highly productive assets, but he also kept his money in *aphanês* form, which apparently allowed him to avoid liturgies and permit uninterrupted growth throughout his lifetime. His estate consisted primarily of two slave workshops and loans, and is listed in detail by Demosthenes:

> ὁ γὰρ πατὴρ . . . κατέλιπεν δύ' ἐργαστήρια, τέχνης οὐ μικρᾶς ἑκάτερον, μαχαιροποιοὺς μὲν τριάκοντα καὶ δύ' ἢ τρεῖς, ἀνὰ πέντε μνᾶς καὶ ἕξ, τοὺς δ' οὐκ ἐλάττονος ἢ τριῶν μνῶν ἀξίους, ἀφ' ὧν τριάκοντα μνᾶς ἀτελεῖς ἐλάμβανεν τοῦ ἐνιαυτοῦ τὴν πρόσοδον, κλινοποιοὺς δ' εἴκοσι τὸν ἀριθμόν, τετταράκοντα μνῶν ὑποκειμένους, οἳ δώδεκα μνᾶς ἀτελεῖς αὐτῷ προσέφερον.
>
> For my father left me two workshops each of significant production: thirty-two or thirty-three sword makers, some worth more than five or six *minae*, and the rest not less than three *minae* apiece, from whom he received thirty *minae* in net profit each year; and twenty couch makers, security for a forty *minae* loan, who yielded him a net profit twelve *minae* per year. (Dem. 27.9)

The sword factory certainly predated the couch factory, and probably constituted the original source for the rest of his wealth.[31] This factory was managed by a slave, Milyas, an *epitropos* who administered (διῴκησεν) everything (27.19), was perhaps also given a share of the profits as an incentive to maximize the factory's productivity, and was manumitted in Demosthenes the Elder's will (29.26).[32] Demosthenes the Elder did not take a detached approach

31. Plutarch, *Demosthenes* 4, citing a contemporary source, Theopompus, says that he was referred to by his contemporaries as the "sword-maker," suggesting that this was how he made his wealth originally. This factory was also the largest property he owned, and it is much less likely that he acquired it via his other assets (loans) than vice versa.

32. Demosthenes the Elder must have had an accurate idea of the profitability of his workshops, because it seems that he himself enjoyed the profits, rather than only receiving a fixed wage or *apophora*. Thompson 1982, 68–71, has argued convincingly (against Francotte 1900, 12; and Bolkestein 1958, 63) that since Demosthenes himself bore the losses and therefore the risk from his factories, his father was receiving the profits from the factory and was not leaving all the profits to his overseer, Milyas. Cohen 1992, 93, following Francotte and Bolkestein, claims that Milyas would have paid a fixed fee and kept all the profits, but cites no evidence for this. Acton 2014, 255, also argues for an *apophora*, but this is based on Demosthenes' figures for the later profits of the depleted workshop which may be oversimplifications for the sake of the jurors. At Dem. 27.22, the

to his factory management as a *rentier*, but was closely involved in its operation and in the acquisition of materials, selling materials when it was more advantageous than stockpiling them (27.32), and therefore preferring to mobilize them productively rather than letting them sit unproductive.[33] The fact that he did not simply allow his materials to lie idle, but sold them if there was a good opportunity, demonstrates that he was actively considering the relative costs and benefits of storing materials for future production as opposed to selling them when he had an interested buyer during favorable market circumstances or was not currently using them for productive purposes.

Moreover, this sword factory seems to have been housed in (or on the property of) his residence, allowing close supervision of its operations, *epimeleia*, as advocated in Xenophon's *Oeconomicus*.[34] Installing a slave manager, Milyas, in charge of the *machaira* workshop shows that Demosthenes' father did not simply sit back casually and allow it to be mismanaged, but chose to ensure that it was being run as effectively as possible. Milyas indeed managed this factory well, since it was highly lucrative, bringing in thirty *minae* of *ateleis*, "net," return, beyond the costs of the maintenance and operations. This profit rate was about 16 percent of the slaves' value per year.[35] Therefore, as with Arizelos, Demosthenes the Elder's factory approached Graham's "special situations."[36]

Rather than expanding this holding further, he decided to reinvest its profits into other forms, possibly to avoid diminishing marginal returns, or perhaps

guardians claim Milyas took the profits, but the loss was all Demosthenes', as Thompson rightly points out.

33. It is clear that Demosthenes the Elder kept books for the running of the estate (27.49), and it seems that he worked closely with Milyas, as both kept records (Milyas kept accounts at 27.19) and were actively involved in the finances of the workshops. The guardians' mismanagement illustrates by contrast Demosthenes senior's effective *epimeleia*. For Xenophon, *epimeleia* was one of the indispensible traits of a successful *oikonomos*, saying that on-site presence, "the master's eye" was the most important factor in determining whether an estate would operate at a profit or at a loss.

34. Dem. 27.24 says that the couch makers for sure were in the house οἴκοι, and then says they were taken out of the house ἐκ τῆς οἰκίας. As Finley 1985 [1951], 67, states, the *machaira* workshop was probably also located in the house since no workshop is mentioned. MacDowell 2009 agrees. Factory materials are also said to have been sold "out of the house" by the guardians (27.32), and if the materials were in the house, the factories probably were as well.

35. The capital value of the *machaira* workshop must be subtracted from the total which Demosthenes gives for all the "productive" assets at 27.10 (4 T, 5,000 dr.), which also includes the value of the couch-making workshop and the talent lent at 12 percent interest, making its total capital value 3 talents, 1,000 drachmas, producing 30 minae per year, or 15.8 percent annual return. See also Davies 1971, 127; Amemiya 2007, 33; and Osborne 2004, 272 on the factory profits, who all agree that 16 percent is approximately correct for the net profit rates of this factory. Osborne 2004, 272, notes that the sword factory slaves would have been worth about 450 drachmas on average and brought in 90 drachmas net per year, making them able to repay their own cost within five years.

36. Acton 2014, 265, distrusts Demosthenes' figures and argues that the profit rate is too high, since Demosthenes must have omitted expenses. Nevertheless even his revised figure of 9 percent annual return, which can be considered a minimum, would surpass the typical ideal rates of profit as discussed by Graham.

because increasing the size of the factory further would have attracted attention to its success and made him liable for liturgies (see below).[37] Since the sword factory was most likely the basis for the rest of Demosthenes the Elder's acquisitions, it seems that he decided to invest the profits from this factory in loans. The couch factory, for example, was seized as security for a nonfriendly loan of 40 *minae*. This property was so profitable for Demosthenes the Elder, yielding up to 30 percent net (*ateleis*) profit on his initial investment, that it must be considered that he intentionally made this loan for the purpose of acquiring the factory;[38] he was also able to use the materials he already had for his *machaira* factory for couch making (27.31), and kept it all within his house. Demosthenes the Elder therefore invested his sword factory profits into a higher risk form, loans, which in the case of the couch factory actually yielded him a more lucrative asset after the borrower had defaulted. He purposefully made the decision to lend this money in a productive venture on the security of a profit-generating piece of property.

Indeed, moneylending appears to have been Demosthenes the Elder's preferred investment with the profits from the sword factory, and this activity seems to have been generating high returns. The rest of the loans outstanding at the time of his death are listed by Demosthenes as follows:

> ἀργυρίου δ᾽ εἰς τάλαντον ἐπὶ δραχμῇ δεδανεισμένου, οὗ τόκος ἐγίγνετο τοῦ ἐνιαυτοῦ ἑκάστου πλεῖν ἢ ἑπτὰ μναῖ . . . ναυτικὰ δ᾽ ἑβδομήκοντα μνᾶς, ἔκδοσιν παρὰ Ξούθῳ, τετρακοσίας δὲ καὶ δισχιλίας ἐπὶ τῇ τραπέζῃ

37. Thompson 1978, 410, suggests that Demosthenes the Elder sought to diversify because of the limited market for knives and swords, and went into the couch-making field to enable him to do double duty with his ivory supplies. Indeed, since he bought his ivory supplies in bulk and also sold such factory materials when it was advantageous, he may have known the owner of the couch factory as a customer for ivory, and perhaps agreed to lend against the security of the couch factory because he knew he could use the ivory for both factories and could therefore profit nicely from this opportunity in case of default. He may have agreed to make the loan in the first place *because* it could land him this factory, which he could integrate so easily into his present productive operations. This is all highly speculative, but is worth considering nonetheless.

38. Davies 1971, 127–29, says that the couch factory yielded under 20 percent net profit because its value was greater than 40 *minae* and other things also were used as security for the loan: "30 percent is 'extraordinarily high.'" Amemiya 2007, 33, agrees that the slaves' value was higher, adding the valid point that security was normally twice the value of the loan making 15 percent profit for the couch factory by value. Therefore, the slaves yielded between 15 and 20 percent, but as a return on his initial investment, Demosthenes the Elder was bringing in 30 percent profit on this property, for whom 12 *minae* clear profit actually was around 30 percent since his initial investment was only 40 *minae*. As Osborne 2004, 272, notes, at the price Demosthenes the Elder paid, 200 drachmas each, the couch makers would have been able to pay themselves off in just over three years at 60 drachmas net annually. Although low, the estimates of Acton 2014, 264–65, based on the arguments of Harris 1988, 362–63, for the higher value of the slaves relative to the amount pledged on them as security, are useful minima, and reveal that at the very least the couch workshop would have brought in the 5 percent return advocated as the normal ideal by modern investors.

τῇ Πασίωνος, ἑξακοσίας δ' ἐπὶ τῇ Πυλάδου, παρὰ Δημομέλει δὲ τῷ Δήμωνος υἱεῖ χιλίας καὶ ἑξακοσίας, κατὰ διακοσίας δὲ καὶ τριακοσίας ὁμοῦ τι τάλαντον διακεχρημένον.

And he had a talent of silver lent out at the rate of a drachma (per month), the interest from which came to more than seven *minae* per year . . . and seventy *minae* in maritime loans, a bottomry loan with Xouthos, and also 2,400 drachmas in the bank of Pasion, and six hundred in that of Pylades, and 1,600 drachmas with Demomeles the son of Demon, and about a talent altogether lent out in sums of two hundred and three hundred drachmas. (Dem. 27.9–11)

Therefore, Demosthenes the Elder made the decision to invest his sword workshop's profits in loans—he did not keep them idle or invest them in land. The choice to be a moneylender was important because it also allowed him to continually reinvest his wealth in a productive form while hiding it from liturgies. He invested his profits in a higher-risk form for greater return, showing that like Arizelos he made profit-oriented and not risk-minimizing choices. In addition to the productive 40 *minae* loan that resulted in the couch factory, at least 7,000 drachmas were mobilized in high-yield (20 to 30 percent interest) bottomry loans,[39] and possibly the rest of the 4,600 drachmas of sums listed immediately afterward, though these may have been just bank deposits. Another talent was lent at 12 percent annual interest, making all his loans productive and yielding at least 12 percent with the exception of another talent perhaps lent at interest.

This last item, a talent κατὰ διακοσίας δὲ καὶ τριακοσίας ὁμοῦ τι τάλαντον διακεχρημένον, is normally assumed to be interest-free *eranos* loans,[40] an inter-

39. The slave workshops, the 7,000 drachmas lent on bottomry and the talent lent at 12 percent interest must all be considered productive, as should the factory materials. As far as the bank deposits are concerned, it is unknown how much they received in interest per year but since they were considered to be loans to bankers, they seem to have yielded some sort of interest payments. Interest from bank deposits is a matter of debate, for which see Bogaert 1968, 345–51; Millett 1991, 238–41. Cohen 1992, 111–15, and Shipton 1997, 415–16, provide good evidence that bank deposits did indeed yield interest. Further evidence that bank deposits yielded interest can be seen in the fact that they were considered to be loans (Cohen 1992, 114–16). It is likely, however, that these sums were not simple deposits but were actually engaged in maritime loans. In the text, the previously listed possessions at home (*oikoi*) are stated in the *men* clause, while these items all fall into a *de* clause introduced by the word *nautika*, which is followed by the 70 *minae* deposit with Xouthos, and then in rapid succession the rest of the sums *epi* or *para* certain other individuals in the dative case. Therefore, since the sums all fall in the *de* half of a *men-de* construction, each listed in rapid succession, they are likely to be all *nautika*, though they may also be bank deposits. Therefore, since it is most likely that these sums secured some sort of interest, either as deposits or maritime loans, they should be considered productive. See Cohen 1992, 115.

40. See, e.g., Foxhall 2007, 43; and Millett 1991, 168, who initially lists this sum as being per-

pretation that has stirred up far less debate than it should. There is very little in the term διακεχρημένον that implies anything at all about interest or the lack thereof. Διαχράομαι in the sense of loaning money actually seems to be a *hapax legomenon*, for which the LSJ provides the innocuous definition of "to be lent out to different persons," and redirects the reader to the seemingly otherwise unattested form of διακίχρημι, for which only this passage is cited. Χράω, the root verb, is sometimes used of lending in a friendly way, as seen in the contrast Aristotle draws between *chrêsis* (friendly lending) and *daneismos* (lending for interest) at *Eudemian Ethics* 5.2.13, 1131a. But it can also be used as a synonym for δανείζω, to lend at interest, meaning that there is ambiguity in the term *chrênai*.[41] Thus, it is entirely uncertain exactly what sort of loans these entailed, so it cannot simply be assumed that they consisted of interest-free *eranos* loans.

I find it difficult to believe that this talent was lent on *eranos* loans, because, as Millett shows,[42] such loans were a point of pride, an important responsibility for any good citizen, and Demosthenes would have secured the goodwill of the jury by emphasizing their *eranos* nature. But he does not do that. Rather, he uses the ambiguous term *diakichrênai*. Why such ambiguity in this passage when he is so explicit, precise, and calculating in his discussions of interest in the rest of the speech? If this talent were lent on friendly terms, in *eranos*, why would Demosthenes not celebrate this fact to depict even more effectively his guardians' squandering of the estate as despicable? Why does Demosthenes not say they were *eranos* loans when he mentions *eranos* loans in a different context in the same speech (25)? Theophrastus' "Alazon," braggart, boasts of his five talents of *eranos* loans.[43] I am inclined to think that these were interest-bearing loans whose true nature was deliberately obfuscated by the speaker to ingratiate himself to the jury by presenting his father as less profit-seeking than he actually was (lest he seem to be one of the *obolostatai*).

Some have interpreted the combination of interest-free *eranos* loans with lending at interest as a sign of an economically irrational attitude,[44] but this is to ignore the importance of social capital and the building of networks of trust, which may have been instrumental in securing long-term economic opportunities and security. As Foxhall argues, the medium- and long-term benefits of

haps lent out "(interest-free ?)," but then states unequivocally that they were "interest-free *eranos* loans" (170). This interpretation is also shared by Amemiya 2007, 32; and Shipton 1997, 416n129, who says "'loaned free of interest' is my translation of *diakechrêmenon*, a word which appears to imply a lending transaction without charge."

41. See Millett 1991, 28–30.

42. Millett 1991, 153–59.

43. *Characters* 23.5–6; cf. the selfish man, *Authadês*, who is negatively depicted as grumbling about making *eranos* loans (*Characters* 15.7).

44. See, e.g., Millett 1991, 170–71.

eranos loans within the highly socialized fabric of the ancient Greek economy could be productive in very important ways;[45] they would still be investments in social capital.[46] And so, engaging in *eranos* loans should not be judged as economically "irrational," but rather as one of the many transactions costs necessary to do business in the uncertain, inchoate market economy of ancient Greece. In an embedded economy, social expenditures are needed to remain a viable, active member of social networks.

It may be that Demosthenes was exploiting the ambiguity in the term *diakichrênai* to obscure the interest-bearing nature of his father's small-time lending.[47] For someone so acutely aware of the effects that moneylending at interest could have on a jury's perception, why would he list these sums so quickly and give them such cursory treatment if they would have helped his case, especially when he is so precisely calculating in his discussion of interest in other places? He does not mention the interest rate of the certain maritime loan or the probable ones. Millett has suggested that Demosthenes may be lying in this passage, or obscuring the truth.[48] Demosthenes could have been intentionally exploiting the ambiguity in the term *chrênai* to present his father more favorably than as a high-interest moneylender, a deliberate obfuscation of his father's interest-bearing lending on a small scale. Demosthenes was aware of how odious the moneylender Nicobulus might be perceived to be, and wrote an elaborate defense of his trade in the speech he wrote for him (Dem. 37.52–54); likewise, he emphasizes the despicable nature of Stephanus' moneylending with a vivid depiction of his exploitation even of kin, and the clear use of the word *tokizein*, which unequivocally means to lend at interest. He probably

45. Foxhall 2007, 48–49.

46. For social capital see Bourdieu 2001.

47. Cohen 1992, 121n43, citing a parallel at Dem. 28.4, argues that this talent was lent at interest, saying that the preposition *kata* followed by a drachma amount refers to the interest rate, and that the figures 200 and 300 refer to interest rates of 20 and 30 percent on an unknown number of loans which made up the talent *diakechrêmenon*. Cohen's interpretation is intriguing, but the parallel he cites is for the payment of *eisphorai*, and his confidence that this *kata* refers to interest is somewhat ungrounded. It seems more likely that κατὰ διακοσίας δὲ καὶ τριακοσίας here is referring to amounts loaned (Pearson 1972, 116, agrees). A parallel for borrowers of sums at 200 and 300 drachma intervals are also attested at the Temple of Nemesis at Rhamnous in the fifth century and Delos in the fourth century; there is another parallel for the use of κατά with amounts of loans rather than interest rates in Aristotle, *Nicomachean Ethics* 4.1.40, where he discusses *tokistai*, high-interest money lenders who loan "small amounts of money at high rates of interest": κατὰ μικρὰ ἐπὶ πολλῶι. Κατά refers to the amounts and ἐπί refers to the interest rate (as elsewhere in this speech at 27.9, 17, and 23). This parallel implies high interest rates in these small loans, and may be a sign that Demosthenes the Elder was engaged in not only lending of large amounts, but also small-time, high-interest loans, classing him among the most disdained types of moneylenders. Small-time lending at high interest was particularly odious (see Schaps 2004, 185–86; Millett 1991, 179–88), and would find little sympathy with a jury.

48. Millett 1991, 157.

feared that the court would perceive his father as one of the hated *obolostatai* discussed in chapter 1. The deposits with bankers or bottomry may have likewise been glossed over quickly in order to downplay his father's appearance as a moneylender for profit. And so, Demosthenes does not actually lie here, but being so keenly aware of the jury's view of moneylenders, it seems that he has craftily covered up his father's moneylending for profit by taking advantage of the ambiguity inherent in the term *diakichrênai*.

Moreover, to ingratiate himself to the jury even further, he offers many allowances to his guardians—he lowers the interest owed from the dowry to make himself seem less greedy (27.17), he allows the guardians half the profits from his father's factory when they should owe the full amount (27.18), and then again says he is reckoning small interest on unpaid profits (35), and concedes some expenses for maintenance (34) and *eisphorai* (37). He clearly is trying to present himself as less greedy, and therefore more gracious, to the jury, with these allowances in this speech. The very manner in which Demosthenes argues, so vocally reducing the amounts he is owed, shows that he is finely calculating the way the jury will respond to his arguments. On the one hand he is trying to maximize his return by including as much property (and profit) as he can, but he also makes a *captatio benevolentiae* by trying to appear as if he is being more moderate in his demands, which increases his standing with the jury and therefore his chances of winning. This is a well-deliberated strategy to maximize the amount he could receive from the suit by not appearing excessively greedy or calculating like an odious moneylender. The citizens clearly resented *obolostatai*-type characters for their relentless pursuit of profit, likely based on their own personal familiarity of suffering at the hands of individuals who would take their quest for wealth to extreme levels.[49]

Another reason why I am inclined to interpret the passage above as a clever misrepresentation by Demosthenes to cover the full extent of his father's lending at interest is that he also seems to have engaged in significant rhetorical manipulation also to obscure the fact that his father was hiding his money from liturgies. Many scholars have argued that Demosthenes the Elder kept so much of his money in *aphanês*, invisible form to avoid liturgies,[50] suggesting an over-

49. Athenian citizens had extensive personal everyday experience of price-gouging and being manipulated in market transactions, for which see Leese 2017b.

50. Korver 1942, 21–22, notes that Demosthenes the Elder possessed only *aphanês*, invisible, wealth. Davies 1971, 128–29, following De Ste. Croix 1953, 55n105, suggests that he kept much of his wealth in *aphanês* form to avoid liturgies since there is no evidence of his having served any, a conclusion with which Cohen 1992, 200–201n64, and Engen 2011, 99–100, agree. Moreover, it may be that he took some of this *aphanês* wealth and converted it into cash and factory materials to provide for his family after he died. Thus, it may be that his portfolio consisted of a much higher percentage of risky loans during his life than leading up to his death. Indeed, besides the house, its

all approach similar to that of Arizelos, which Badian describes as a "careful investment to avoid tax collectors."[51]

In the most natural place to list the liturgies his father had performed, at the end of the speeches, he does not do so, but instead appeals to the jury based on his characterization of his guardians. This is even odder given the fact that he so readily boasts about the voluntary liturgies he himself performed later on in life.[52] Demosthenes does not emphasize his father's liturgies even in contexts in which it would have been absolutely essential, and rather makes extremely oblique references to his estate's liturgical services. He notes that his estate was τριηραρχεῖν εἰθισμένος καὶ μεγάλας εἰσφορὰς εἰσφέρειν, "accustomed to performing the trierarchy and to making large *eisphorai*" (Dem. 27.64), but this need not refer to anything more than the trierarchic *symmory* in which his guardians enrolled his estate (27.7), the liturgy they forced him to serve in order to be able to bring his suit (28.16–17), and the *eisphorai* which they themselves said that they paid from his estate (27.37). He goes on to say that his father left him sufficient property to pay *eisphorai* (27.66), and "to be successor for you of the liturgies in his place" (ἐμὲ δ' ὑμῖν διάδοχον ἀνθ' αὑτοῦ τῶν λῃτουργιῶν ἐσόμενον 28.19), but does not mention these *eisphorai* when he lists the public services his family has served. His phrasing of this last statement is particularly careful and ambiguous to avoid a strict lie, as he does not say that his father had performed the liturgies, just that he himself was going to. Indeed, the phrase ἀνθ' αὑτοῦ could even be translated as "instead of himself." When given the opportunity to show that his maternal grandfather, Gylon, did not owe money to the state treasury, he mentions that his uncle by marriage, Demochares, did not conceal his property out of fear of being forced to repay Gylon's public debts, but completed *chorêgiai* and trierarchies (28.3). In the same passage, when it would then be natural to draw attention to the liturgies his own father served, he does not list any, but instead says cryptically: αὐτὸς ὁ πατὴρ τήν τ' ἄλλην οὐσίαν καὶ τέτταρα τάλαντα καὶ τρισχιλίας φανερὰς ἐποίησεν, "He made the rest of his property and the four talents three

furnishings, and the sword factory, there is no *phanera ousia* in his estate besides the couch factory, which had been obtained from a loan of 4,000 drachmas. Thus, a loan of two-thirds of a talent was transformed into a productive workshop, and combined with the talent at 12 percent interest, and the 7,000 drachmas in bottomry, as well as the talent lent of unknown nature, along with the 4,600 drachmas in the banks (which may have been lent for bottomry loans as well), it seems that prior to the couch factory, Demosthenes the Elder's estate consisted of 27,600 drachmas of loans, 33 percent of his entire estate. Therefore, it seems that his preference in the end of his life was to move a higher and higher percentage of his wealth into interest-bearing loans. The fact that he acquired the couch factory may have been by accident, or it may have also been an opportunity which he decided he could not pass up since it yielded such high profits.

51. Badian 2000, 14.

52. See Christ 1990, 156n41.

thousand drachmae *phanera.*" Not a hint about the liturgies performed by his father, but only a half-hearted claim that he made his entire fortune "visible," which is strictly not correct, because it was only made visible when his guardians had registered his estate with the *polis* for tax purposes. Therefore he did not actually reveal his property, but kept it hidden, only to be exposed in case of a lawsuit. This corroborates Aphobus' charges that Demosthenes' father would not allow the estate to be leased, because of the risks of revealing its full amount to the *dêmos* (28.2, 28.7). He does not say that he should receive a favorable ruling because his father *had* performed liturgies, but because he himself would "want to serve liturgies" in return for the *charis* he had received from the jury in the restoration of his estate (28.24). Aphobus, on the other hand, would not be willing to carry out liturgies on behalf of the property which he denies having received, but would rather want to hide it (*apokrupsesthai*) to seem that he had been acquitted justly.

In other words, Demosthenes here has transferred from his father to his guardians the "hiding" of wealth which his father committed and which he himself was trying to deemphasize for the jury, in a brilliant rhetorical turn. Indeed, he charges his guardians with concealing (ἀφανιζόντων) his money in 27.44, and then uses the same participle for Aphobus twice in quick repetition in 27.48, with the participle for stealing sandwiched between for emphasis (ἠφανικότα . . . κλέπτοντα . . . ἠφανικότα). In the second speech, he again repeats the same verb in 28.10, saying they had all hidden the will (ἠφανίκατε), and in 28.12 that Aphobus himself had hidden the slaves (ἠφάνικεν). He also says that Aphobus hid his money in 29.37 (ἀφανεῖς πεποίηκας), and again at 29.43 (ἠφάνιζεν). Thus, Demosthenes turns the guardians' charges indicting his father against them, highlighting their own wealth-hiding: my father did not conceal his wealth, but revealed it himself—it is *you* who are hiding my wealth! The repetition of "hiding" terms in these speeches shows just how prominently they loomed in Demosthenes' mind while he was planning his defense, and the fact that he is so fully intent on disproving his father's wealth-hiding may reveal a very defensive, and possibly guilty, sentiment on the part of Demosthenes. His obsession with focusing on his guardians' wealth-hiding here would then be a clever projection of his father's crime onto his enemies, a brilliant distortion of the facts of the case to serve his immediate purpose

Since the loans were *aphanês*, the decision to invest in this form was more rational for Demosthenes the Elder than in any sort of *phanera ousia*, which would have increased the risk of being called upon to serve liturgies. Whether engaged in cash generation or invested in social capital, these loans were employed for productive purposes;[53] the decision to invest not in land but in loans demonstrates a desire to mobilize his profits productively without subjecting them to public demands. Even holding money in cash form would have been more rational than to invest in land for a liturgy avoider.[54] Hiding wealth in loans provided him both with the short-term profits of interest payments, and with the ability to maximize his profits and wealth for uninterrupted long-term growth.

The shrewdness of his money hiding is illustrated by the fact that his estate had grown many times beyond the typical level of liturgical class fortunes out of the sight of the *dêmos*. Therefore, like Arizelos, who built up his fortune through *phanera ousia*, and then liquidated much of it in order to evade liturgy payments and to allow further growth, Demosthenes' father seems to have likewise attempted to permit the unimpeded augmentation of his estate by ensuring that it would never be subject to liturgies. In his liturgy avoidance, Demosthenes the Elder's true attitude toward moneymaking and wealth maximization is revealed. He preferred to run the risks of being caught for liturgy avoidance to enable the continued growth of his moneymaking property, which is entirely suggestive of a long-term wealth maximizing strategy.

This interpretation is further supported by the high proportion of his estate

53. As Bourdieu 2001 argues, the social returns from such nonmarket behaviors as friendly loans can and should be seen as investments in different types of capital, including social capital. Therefore they may have been seen as productive in the sense that they would bring a return in the future, though the form of this return would not be as certain or easily quantifiable as an interest payment in cash.

54. The amounts of cash and materials for the factory are probably not an accurate representation of the amounts which Demosthenes' father typically kept on hand, since they represent the state of affairs at the time of his death. Like Diodotus who left five talents of cash with his brother before leaving on a campaign from which he would not return (Lysias 32.4–15), Demosthenes' father seems to have arranged his affairs in anticipation of his own death, and so the large amounts of cash and factory materials may have been acquired by him in order to ensure the smooth running of the factory under the guardians after his death. Millett 1991, 169, refers to this sum as one which was "hoarded in [his] house," a sign of economically irrational behavior. However, this sum of cash may have been specially prepared by Demosthenes the Elder to take care of his family in anticipation of his own death and is therefore not to be taken as an indication of how he would normally have used his money during his life. On the contrary, this was a special situation in which he seems to have stockpiled cash and productive materials in advance to ensure the productivity of the workshops for his young son. He may have even repurposed some sort of productive property, perhaps loans at interest, in order to secure this large sum of cash for his family, and this may have normally been invested in profit-generating enterprises as part of his standard moneymaking practice. As yet another example of the types of arrangements that could be made by an estate owner at the end of his life, fathers normally tried to set aside their daughters' dowries before their deaths, for which see Cox 1998, 119n53, who cites numerous examples, including the arrangements made by Demosthenes the Elder and Diodotus: Lysias 19.14–15, 32.6; Dem. 27.5, 28.15–16, 29.43; 40.6–7, 20–22, 56–57; 41.3, 6, 26, 29; 45.66; 59.7–8; Plutarch, *Alcibiades* 8.1–5; [Andocides] 4.13; Isoc. 16.31.

engaged in cash production; the vast majority of Demosthenes the Elder's wealth was concentrated in productive capital of some sort. The 6,000 drachma loan at 12 percent, the 7,000 drachmas in bottomry, the 4,600 in bank deposits or bottomry, 4,000 drachmas of capital in the couch factory, the 19,000 drachmas of value in the *machaira* factory, the 15,000 drachmas of factory materials, and the 1,500 drachmas for the half of the house engaged in craft production comes to a total of 57,100 drachmas out of a total of 82,600, or 69 percent of his wealth engaged in cash production. If the uncertain talent out on loan is included, as is likely, 63,100 drachmas, or 76 percent would be engaged in cash generation. Moreover, this figure would be an underestimate if the 8,000 drachmas in cash had been intentionally set aside by Demosthenes' father in anticipation of his own death, and had previously been invested in loans or some other sort of productive property. Indeed much of his wealth was hidden. In this scenario, up to 71,100 drachmas out of 82,600 would have been productively engaged, or 86 percent. Indeed, the only property that can certainly be interpreted as unproductive is the 10,000 drachmas worth of jewels, furniture, and handmaidens, *therapainai*, much of which was part of Demosthenes' mother's dowry, and probably also half of the house's value, 1,500 drachmas.

The pattern of Demosthenes' father's economic decisions is clear—he chose not to use his profits from the *machaira* factory to buy land or mining properties, but for moneylending purposes, so he certainly wished to maintain his gains from factories and loans over the long term. He enjoyed high rates of return on his properties, up to 16 percent from the sword factory, 30 percent from the couch factory, and between 12 and 30 percent on his loans. Rather than leaving his sword factory profits idle, he reinvested them in a higher-risk form—loans—which simultaneously allowed him to sustain his productive factory, and also to mobilize those profits in generating additional returns over the long term. These *aphanês* loans enabled investment at high rates of interest while also ensuring that its growth was uninhibited by liturgies, which is in itself a strategy aimed at long-term maximization of wealth.

Ciron: A Diversified Estate Geared toward Long-Term Growth

Our next case study is the focus of Isaeus 8, *On the Estate of Ciron*. Ciron's estate consisted of an expensive agricultural plot at Phlya worth 1 talent, a house in the city worth 2,000 drachmae and rented out to a tenant, and his own personal residence in the city worth 1,300 drachmae.[55] He also had wage-earning slaves,

55. For Ciron, see Davies 1971, 312–16 (8443). His estate is listed at Isaeus 8.35.

and not a few (οὐκ ὀλίγα) loans out on interest.[56] Ciron combined large agricultural possessions with slaves bringing in a steady income of cash throughout the year, in addition to loans at interest.

The emphasis which the speaker of Isaeus 8 places on the loans at interest (8 and 37), describing them as οὐκ ὀλίγα, indicates that they were substantial. Though their value is unknown, the size of the dowry which he provided for his first daughter, 25 *minae* or almost a half-talent (8), followed by a second dowry of 1,000 drachmas for her second marriage, indicates that he had a large amount of cash at his disposal, or at least the ability to generate a great deal of liquidity very quickly, even though the dowry was partly made up of clothing and jewelry (8). Dowries typically amounted to about 10 percent of a Greek's overall wealth,[57] so Ciron's fortune was likely much greater than just his *phanera ousia*, and his *aphanês* wealth may have constituted the majority of his estate.

Overall, Ciron's economic decisions seem to be characterized by a concern with mobilizing his assets for productive income generation, and perhaps even long-term growth. First, rather than indulging in consumption, he dedicated the more expensive residence he owned in the city to productive purposes by renting it out, living in the poorer one himself. He likely even used his personal residence for productive activities, since it seems to have housed his cash-generating slaves, as seen in other estates.[58] Although his use of the *agros* is uncertain, it was located in the fertile deme of Phlya and probably grew food for his household, and he may have sold surplus produce for market exchange as well. Thus, Ciron likely employed the full extent of the assets he owned in productive purposes to maintain a steady stream of income. Though diversified between slave manufacturers, interest-bearing loans, and the rented house, his estate-management choices exhibit an interest in generating cash income from each property.

Moreover, the fact that he paid a dowry of twenty-five *minae* for his daughter to marry Nausimenes, the son of Nausikydes,[59] a successful miller who raised himself into the liturgical class, indicates that he may have been trying to establish a long-term marriage alliance with this entrepreneur's son to combine the two families' fortunes. This amounts to more than a quarter of his attested property, a significant investment in his daughter's marriage.[60] The size of the

56. The loans are said to have been for interest at 8.35: ἀφ' ὧν ἐκεῖνος τόκους ἐλάμβανε.

57. Based on the available figures, for which see Cox 1998, 118; Schaps 1979, 99.

58. E.g., Dem. 48, Dem. 27–28.

59. Xen., *Mem.* 2.7.6; Aristophanes, *Ecclesiazusae* 426; Plato, *Gorgias* 487c; Davies 1971, 315. See Leese 2017a, who argues that many marriage alliances were sought after specifically toward increasing personal material wealth and economic security.

60. This is the largest proportion of an overall estate given as dowry known from the ancient Greek world, for which see the amounts listed at Cox 1998, 117–18.

dowry perhaps reveals a desire to add further security to his household by uniting his with that of the successful miller Nausikydes. This choice certainly is consistent with a desire to invest in profitable opportunities, both within and outside of the market.

Furthermore, Ciron may have been trying to avoid liturgies, since he is not known to have served any, even though his property approached the level at which one might be called upon to serve.[61] The dowry he gave with his daughter is indeed suggestive of a much larger estate, as it is the dowry that constitutes by far the highest percentage of someone's known wealth in ancient Greek history.[62] In the absence of other sources, this large dowry most likely came from the substantial amount of loans at interest. Since the dowry did not make up all his liquid wealth (there being large additional sums lent out) Ciron's total wealth did in fact approach, and probably even surpassed the minimum level for liturgical service.[63] Therefore, it is likely that Ciron was practicing liturgy avoidance, a conclusion entirely consistent with the considerable sums of liquid assets he held, and the fact that his *phanera ousia* sat comfortably enough below the minimum levels with some allowance made for money in loans and large dowries. Ciron chose to invest a large amount of his wealth in interest-bearing loans at the end of his life, and not into land, allowing him to profit doubly through making money and avoiding state demands. In conclusion, Ciron exhibits behavior similar to that of Arizelos and Demosthenes' father: a concern with long-term profitability and perhaps also uninterrupted growth through liturgy avoidance.

Unfortunately, it is impossible to determine if he was maximizing his profits, but he certainly seems to have been interested in cash-generating assets, and employed the full extent of his property in productive purposes. Moreover, the fact that he held much of his cash in interest-bearing loans at the time of his death shows that he was still invested in high-risk, high-profit activity throughout his entire lifetime in order to increase his estate, and was interested in profitable acquisition, not risk avoidance. The decision to invest in loans and not in further *phanera ousia* is therefore perhaps suggestive of a strategy similar to that of Arizelos, the avoidance of public demands by concentrating wealth in *aphanês* form. Finally, he pursued a profitable marriage alliance, further evidence for an interest in ensuring the growth and security of his estate. In the

61. Davies 1971, 312–16.

62. Cox 1998, 117–18.

63. Modern scholars note that this seems to have been about three talents (Davies 1971, xxiii–xxiv), though there was no absolute fixed minimum, the most relatively wealthy being selected as liturgists based on the known values of their wealth.

end, Ciron possessed a balanced mix of high- and low-risk assets, allowing for a steady return, and perhaps even wealth maximization, over the long run.

Stratocles: A Balanced Estate of High- and Low-Risk Properties

Stratocles' estate is preserved in Isaeus 11, *On the Estate of Hagnias*, a speech that recounts the disputes among members of the famous Buselid family who are squabbling to inherit this fortune.[64] In the narrative, the wealth of Stratocles himself is enumerated: at his death he owned land at Thria worth 2.5 talents, a house at Melite worth 3,000 drachmas, and another at Eleusis worth 500 drachmas; he leased out the land at a rate of 12 *minae* per year (8 percent), and the houses at 3 *minae* per year (8.6 percent), bringing in 15 *minae*, or a quarter of a talent each year in cash. He also had 4,000 drachmas lent out at 18 percent interest, yielding another 720 drachmas annually. This property altogether was worth 22,500 drachmas (3 T, 4,500 dr.), and produced 2,220 drachmas in cash per year, or just under 10 percent. Almost another talent's worth (5,800 dr.) was in cash, furniture, sheep, and agricultural produce (11.43), suggesting that he was able to do quite well on his property with sizable liquidity and profits. He also extended interest-free *eranos* loans amounting to 1,000 drachmas (11.43).

Thus, out of his 4 talents and 5,300 drachmas,[65] at least 3 talents, 4,500 drachmas was engaged in producing cash income. This is at least 76.8 percent of his overall estate generating cash, and perhaps more than this, since he also owned sheep and other property. He clearly preferred to put a high proportion of his wealth to productive use. Much of his money, two-thirds of a talent, was lent out at 18 percent annually, a very high interest rate yielding large profits. Overall he achieved a steady return from his properties with his estate balanced between low-risk landed property and higher-risk loans.[66] Graham's ideal portfolio, as seen above, averaged about 6 percent profit per year, and Stratocles' estate certainly meets those conditions, so much of his property brought in the sorts of profits that would make a modern investor happy.

64. For the property of Stratocles and the rest of the known wealth of his family the Buselids, see Davies 1971, 87–88.

65. The speaker tries to sum his property up at 5 talents, 3,000 dr. (Isaeus 11.42), but the numbers do not add up to this amount. Rather, it seems that he was including the 15 *minae* rent paid by the houses and land as well as the 20 *minae* of annual revenue from these properties added to the 720 drachmas from the loans. Including rents and interest as part of the estate's value once is shameless enough, let alone to include the rent payments twice in the value of the estate!

66. Thompson 1978, 406–7.

Moreover, Stratocles administered the estate of his wife's brother, Theophon, his daughter's husband, for nine years after Theophon died (Isaeus 11.41), an opportunity so lucrative that Stratocles is said to have increased his own personal fortune from below the level of liturgical payments to being worth five and a half talents.[67] To add to his property so significantly in such a short period of time is an indication that he saw the administration of this estate as an opportunity to achieve substantial growth.[68]

Furthermore, like Ciron, Arizelos, and Demosthenes' father, Stratocles is not known to have served any liturgies,[69] and since his *phanera ousia* was sitting right about at the three-talent liturgical lower general threshold, it may be that he kept his landed property at that level in order to avoid liturgies. He did, indeed, invest in *aphanês* loans after the administration of Theophon's estate, choosing loans over additional acquisitions in land, so perhaps he was also trying to obscure the extent of his profits from this orphan's estate. Like Ciron he made the decision to keep much of his wealth at the end of his life not in land, but in loans.

Therefore, based on the available evidence, it seems that Stratocles was effectively maximizing the long-term profitability of his estate. The vast majority of his assets were engaged in cash production,[70] at rates that surpass even those of modern investment portfolios. He balanced low-risk properties that still brought in impressive returns with higher-risk loans that yielded substantial profits, right up to the end of his life. He could have even purposefully targeted Theophon's estate in arranging his daughter's marriage, and then profited handsomely from administering the estate, so much that he entered the levels of wealth attested for members of the liturgical class. He perhaps even hid the full extent of his riches from the *polis* to avoid liturgies—he certainly owned additional property whose value is unknown. All these factors, combined with the fact that he was still investing his wealth in high-risk, high-profit loans at the time he died, are highly suggestive of a strategy to maintain growth and maximize wealth in the long run. Long-term growth and profitability certainly characterize Stratocles' decision-making process and moneymaking strategies.

67. Isaeus 11.42.

68. Such dramatic profits from estate administration are attested elsewhere: an estate worth three and a half talents was increased to over six talents in a period of six years by the administrator of the estate (Dem. 27.58).

69. Davies 1971, 77.

70. The 4,900 drachmas of agricultural produce and other items shows that the agricultural plots were also used productively.

Euktemon: The Acquisition of Cash-Generating Enterprises

Like that of Demosthenes' father, Euktemon's estate in Isaeus 6, *On the Estate of Philoctemon* presents difficulties for determining profit maximization and risk management, but his diversification also seems to follow the pattern of profit-oriented property acquisition. He owned a farm at Athmonon worth 75 *minae*, a bathhouse in the Serangeion in the Piraeus valued at 30 *minae*, a house in Athens of 45 *minae*, goats with a goatherd worth 13 *minae*, two pairs of mules at 13.5 *minae*, and an unspecified number of slaves producing crafts for the market (Isaeus 6.33). In addition, he also owned two *synoikiai*, apartment buildings, which would have been profitable enough simply rented out,[71] but they also apparently served as brothels, one in the Kerameikos wine district run by a former prostitute, and another in the Piraeus operated by a freedwoman (19), perhaps also an ex-prostitute. Brothel-keeping was considered one of the most shameful investments one could make so Euktemon did not let scruples stand in the way of profits.[72]

His diversified estate is most likely the result of timely opportunistic acquisition since the types of income-producing properties that he owned are indeed consistent with a strategy of seizing profitable opportunities as they arose. The slaves are explicitly described as producing goods for the *agora*, so he had an interest in maintaining steady cash income as well. The bathhouse in the Serangeion in the Piraeus was likewise probably aimed at securing monetary returns,[73] and along with the slaves and *synoikiai*/brothels, this acquisition indicates a desire to expand beyond agricultural investments.

Furthermore, the locations of the brothels are highly suggestive of a well-considered investment in terms of providing a service which would have been in high demand in those areas and targeting a specific type of consumer frequenting those areas. The Piraeus was full of foreign and native sailors who would be at sea for long periods of time, as well as metic (resident foreigner) traders who lived in the port area for business purposes. Moreover, the wine-selling district near the Kerameikos may have also been selected as the site of a

71. Frier 1980, 21–23, citing Aulus Gellius, *Attic Nights* 15.1.1–3, discusses the high risks and high profits that were understood to be associated with large urban multiple resident dwellings in Rome.

72. Theophrastus, *Characters* 6.5, describes brothel keeping along with tax farming and inn keeping as the most shameful professions one could have and Aristotle, *Nicomachean Ethics* 4.1.40 agrees. See Millett 1991, 179–82. For a recent comprehensive overview of Athenian attitudes toward prostitution, see Cohen 2015, 25–44.

73. For explicit references to the profits generated from a *balaneion*, bathhouse, see Isaeus 5.28–29. The fact that Euktemon's bathhouse was purchased by the banker Aristolochos suggests that it was a profitable investment.

brothel for similar reasons. Thus, the choice of prostitution as an enterprise in these two locations should be seen as an intentional strategy of making money based on providing a high-demand service to a target consumer base in a well-chosen location.[74] Even if Euktemon only drew money from these *synoikiai* as a rentier, their prime locations made them calculated investments aimed at profiting from a specific target market group.

The percentage of Euktemon's property that was productive was very high. Unfortunately, there is no account of his nonproductive property besides, perhaps, his 45 *minae* house. However, of his known property, at least 75 percent (the 75 *minae* farm, the 13 *minae* goat herd, the 13.5 *minae* pair of mules, and the 30 *minae* bathhouse) was productive in some sense, under the assumption that the house was not. Moreover, this is probably a vast underestimate, since the value of the two *synoikiai*/brothels and the slaves making crafts for the market were not listed and therefore could not be included in this calculation. The *synoikiai*/brothels themselves must have been worth at least as much as his personal residence,[75] which would bring the total to 83 percent productive (221.5/266.5 *minae*), if they were both worth 45 *minae* apiece. Since this figure does not even include the craft-producing slaves, it could even be higher than this, though the slaves' value may be offset by nonproductive property of some sort. Although precise quantification is impossible, the general impression provided by these rough calculations is that Euktemon followed a pattern of acquiring and maintaining as many productive properties as possible.[76] The evidence indicates that he was interested in continuous financial gain and growth in the administration of his estate, though definitive conclusions cannot be attained as far as strict profit maximization is concerned.

Euktemon therefore owned a balanced mix of *synoikiai*/brothels, land, a bathhouse, livestock, and slaves producing goods for the market. Diversification by acquiring cash-generating opportunities as they arose seems to have characterized his choices, much like many of the other individuals examined thus far. As with Ciron and Stratocles, few of Euktemon's assets were purely consumptive, and most were producing long-term profitability.

---

74. The decision to appoint a former prostitute as manager over the other prostitutes indicates that Euktemon wanted this establishment run well. For methods of profit maximization among brothel owners and managers, see the strategies of Nicarete in Demosthenes, *Against Neaira* (59.18–19).

75. These properties may have constituted an even higher percentage of his overall wealth. Pasion owned a *synoikia* worth 100 *minae* (Dem. 45.28), and at least one other worth perhaps 26 *minae* (53.13).

76. His decisions at the end of his life to liquidate his properties at the behest of a freedwoman former prostitute should not be taken as evidence for his economic decision-making during the rest of his life, but are said by the speaker of the speech to have been influenced by his senility.

Adeimantos' Estate: Craft Production and Cash Crops

Adeimantos was one of the Athenians who was prosecuted for participating in the so-called *Hermokopidai* incident, the mutilation of the Herms that occurred before the Sicilian Expedition during the Peloponnesian War, in which Alcibiades was also implicated.[77] As a result, Adeimantos' property was confiscated and sold at auction, with the composition of his estate listed on the inscriptions that preserve the property sales associated with this incident, the Attic Stelai. Like Euktemon, Stratocles, and Ciron, Adeimantos also owned a balanced estate of high-risk and lower-risk properties, and his diversification again is most consistent with a profit-oriented strategy of pursuing promising opportunities as they became available. Adeimantos' estate consisted of plots of land at Xypetnaion and Kudimachos, the latter of which produced crops for sure, a slave manufacturer of spits, and an unknown number of slave shoemakers. Aristarchos apparently managed his own workshop because unlike the other shoemaker included he is given his own column with shoemaking items listed under his name.[78] At first glance, Adeimantos' pattern of property acquisition was to supplement agricultural holdings with slave manufacturers producing goods for the market.

The shoe workshop reveals a cash-generating interest on the part of the owner. Athens' population produced constant demand for shoes, and he installed a slave manager at the head of the shoe workshop. Because Aristarchos' shoe workshop was listed in his own name,[79] he certainly enjoyed some sort of prestige in his position of authority, and he may have been awarded with finan cial incentives to operate the workshop at high productivity and profitability.

What is most interesting about Adeimantos' wealth, however, is the fact that he was an Athenian citizen who made the choice to acquire a substantial wine-producing estate on the island of Thasos.[80] This property was a signifi-

77. Adeimantos' name is listed in Andocides *On the Mysteries* 16 along with the other individuals charged.

78. Attic Stelai, VI, 17–61, 116–17 (Pritchett 1953, 270–73); Foxhall 2007, 44–45. The workshop is said to have been the property "of Aristarchos," whose name is in the genitive: ἐκ τῶν Ἀριστάρχο τοῦ σκυτοτ[όμο] (line 32).

79. Cohen 2002, 103, notes the importance of this observation.

80. Acquisition of foreign properties is well-attested for Athenian citizens: see, e.g., Oionias, who owned 81 talents of land in Euboea, the largest landed holdings known from the ancient Greek world, and Axiochos in the Attic Stelai, and Xen., *Mem.* 4.3.1. Apparently Athenians had been so eager to snatch up land in the territories of their subject allies during the fifth century that the practice was explicitly forbidden in the Stele of Aristoteles. For the acquisition of allied land by Athenians during the fifth-century empire, see Moreno 2011. For a general introduction to the Stele of Aristoteles and the Athenians' imperial (or nonimperial) ambitions during the fourth century, see Cargill 1981.

cant moneymaking enterprise specializing in the famed high-quality wine of that island,[81] and contained 590 amphoras and 3 *choes* of Thasian wine.[82] Although the sale price of the wine is lost, prices are preserved elsewhere for Thasian wine of one drachma per *chous*, which will allow estimates to be made.[83] If it is correct that an Athenian amphora (the likely unit of measurement in the Attic Stelai) was roughly a *metrêtês* (12 *choes*), Adeimantos' wine could have been sold for as much as 7,083 drachmas, or well over a talent. Such a large amount of good quality wine for export is clear evidence of a market-oriented productive venture, and it appears that Adeimantos used his Thasian wine production specifically as a way to make money, to supplement his earnings on his other properties.

Indeed, vineyards took a great deal of intensive care in order to be successful,[84] and an operation of this scale must have been acquired for the express purpose of generating profit from cash crops grown for market sale. Just as he did for his shoe workshop, Adeimantos also seems to have installed a slave manager for this property, Aristomachos,[85] who is listed along with the rest of the property on Thasos. The presence of this individual suggests that Adeimantos wanted this vineyard to be run properly. As far as the size of the Thasian wine farm relative to the estate as a whole, according to Foxhall's extrapolations for the total value of his properties from the rent they produced, 1,632 dr. 4 ob. (lines 116–17), his entire estate would have been worth approximately three and a half talents if rented out at 8 percent.[86] If this is the case, then the wine operation in Thasos would have made up a huge proportion of his total property, so although he owned a diversified estate, he also concentrated a great deal of his wealth into this highly lucrative venture.

Therefore, the vast majority of Adeimantos' property was engaged in cash production for the market, the bulk of which was invested in this market-oriented wine farm. Moreover, Adeimantos seems to have been maximizing his returns from the plot of land itself, as evidenced by the large amount of oak and pine wood which was sold from his estate along with a few *pithoi* for 1,800 drachmas, over a quarter of a talent. As Foxhall notes, selling this wood is a sign

81. Foxhall 2007, 40, 81.

82. Attic Stelai VI, 60–61 (Pritchett 1953); Fornara 1983, 175n12. For Thasos' wine, see Salviat 1986; Brun 2004, 94.

83. According to the prices in Boardman 1988, 29; Lang 1956 and 1976, 55–81. This price is about half that of Chian wine, but more than Attic (Amemiya 2007, 69, lists some more wine prices).

84. Burford 1993, 133–35.

85. Attic Stelai VI, 54–55 (Pritchett 1953).

86. Foxhall 2007, 40. The rent rates in the Attic Stelai seem to have been from the property leased out by the *polêtai* during the auction process.

of exploiting his properties to their fullest, and suggests that Adeimantos was expanding his vineyard into previously uncultivated land in a quest for further productive capacity.

This extremely specialized farm on Thasos, which apparently grew only wine, was an income-generating property first and foremost, most likely acquired purposefully as a profitable opportunity. Since he was an Athenian citizen, he probably purchased this wine farm after his other assets, including the shoe workshop producing goods for the market. In conclusion, Adeimantos' diversification shows no signs of being motivated by an aversion to risk, but rather was the result of a profit-oriented strategy of purchasing cash-generating investments one at a time—his estate was probably lower risk before he acquired the vineyard on Thasos, indicating a desire to move into a higher return and riskier property.[87] Nevertheless, though most of his wealth was risked on this wine farm, he still ended up balancing safer properties, in the slave manufacturers and other agricultural plots, with this higher-risk vineyard geared for profit.

General Patterns of Diversification in Ancient Greece

The quest for profit best explains the acquisitive pattern seen in the sources of individual properties being added to estates in a piecemeal manner. In these diversified estates, many of the different properties are small in size, which suggests that these ventures were probably the result of windfall purchase in which the owners jumped on potentially profitable assets as they became available, for the purpose of making money. This rapid seizure of opportunities as a model for ancient Greek economic behavior has also been proposed by Lin Foxhall, who states that: "Opportunities to acquire wealth-generating resources were seized as and when they appeared. These rich households aimed to maximize

87. Wine production was risky because of climatic fluctuations affecting yield, and combined with the necessarily high labor inputs, was an ideal choice for large landowners trying to produce a profitable cash crop (Sallares 1991, 297; Foxhall 2007, 81). Wine production indeed was extremely profitable in the ancient economy. Cato (*De Agri Cultura* 1.1.7) says that a vineyard is the first choice in agricultural production if the land is amenable (de omnibus agris optimoque loco iugera agri centum, vinea est prima, si vino bono et multo est, secundo loco hortus inriguus, tertio salictum, quarto oletum, quinto pratum, sexto campus frumentarius, septimo silva caedua, octavo arbustum, nono glandaria silva), and Columella's demonstration of the profitability of vineyards has attracted a great deal of attention from ancient historians. Finley 1973, 117, calls Columella's implied profits of 34 percent "nonsense"; Duncan-Jones 1982, 33–59, nevertheless agrees with Cato's opinion that vines were more profitable than other crops, and calculates that 7–10 percent was the likely profit from viticulture.

the opportunities for accumulating wealth over the long-term,"[88] and that "rich Athenians (and, perhaps, most wealthy Greeks) were opportunistic in their approach to acquiring economic 'enterprises' and resources . . . risks were most certainly taken in hopes of great profits by the rich who could afford to do so."[89] This model is not only consistent with modern notions of economic rationality, but also with Finley's theory of the windfall nature of ancient property acquisition, which the evidence I have analyzed in this chapter corroborates. Demosthenes the Elder invested in loans as the opportunity arose, and received not only interest, but also his highly profitable couch factory; Arizelos decided to invest in mining *ergastêria* when the chance presented itself and made enough money to rival the fortunes of those in the liturgical class; Adeimantos similarly came into ownership of his export-oriented wine farm at Thasos.

Seizing opportunities in a timely manner among the wealthy of ancient Greece is well-attested in the short-term rental of properties by men of substance to supplement their already sizable holdings through the quick acquisition of productive assets. At Hellenistic Delos, for example, the majority of lessees of temple estates were wealthy citizens of Delos, who leased estates as part of their personal moneymaking and wealth management strategies.[90] Wealthy families were so eager in their rush to secure these lucrative sacred leases that rent prices were driven higher and higher over the years as a result of leasing to the highest bidder.[91] For Attica, Osborne has shown that very rich men competed fiercely to snatch up even small plots of land, and this phenomenon was not restricted to Athens and Delos only, but is also attested at such smaller *poleis* as Thespiai, for example.[92] There was no shortage of demand for land by wealthy lessees, and the motivation to lease such estates seems to have been the quick profits that could be raised.

The leasing of orphans' estates was also a desirable opportunity, as attested by the numerous preserved *horoi* (mortgage stones) in which large amounts

88. Foxhall 2007, 47.

89. Foxhall 2007, 52.

90. Osborne 1988, 299–304.

91. See Reger 1994, 218–19. The leases at Delos underwent rapid increase to the point that lessees became indebted to the temple when they could not pay their leases. Some even borrowed just before, simultaneously with, or during the course of their leases, suggesting that they were investing this borrowed cash in profitable agriculture or animal husbandry. These were not low-risk leases. The profits they brought drove their prices up at an astronomical rate. They were lucrative opportunities seized upon at the moment they became available in a region that was poor in agricultural land. This shows an eagerness to invest in profitable enterprise, especially by the wealthy.

92. Osborne 1988, 291–92. Pernin 2014 shows how widespread leases were even in the most remote rural *poleis* and villages, so these leasing patterns characterized the Greek world in general by the Hellenistic period.

of property were offered up on mortgage on a spur-of-the-moment basis.[93] Administering orphans' estates could be very profitable—Demosthenes says that estates are known to have been doubled or even trebled by their guardians (Dem. 27.64). These opportunities would appear irregularly, so the impetus to act at the right time would have been of great importance, and many seem to have immediately seized the chance to acquire these investments, pledging their own property to do so. The speed with which high sums were mobilized on landed holdings can be seen in the large values of property that were able to be mortgaged, over a talent in some cases.[94]

Cases in which agricultural land was quickly snatched up in large quantities can be seen in the multiple talents individuals paid for some plots when the chance arose in the fourth-century Athenian inscriptions known as the *rationes centesimarum* (accounts of one-hundredths), an extensive list of land transactions.[95] In short, individuals were prepared to jump at these plots, and they very quickly made the decision to mortgage large amounts of their property so as not to let these purchases (or leases) slip away. And so, a quick response and a good information network could be essential in guaranteeing that one could capitalize on lucrative opportunities before others got them. Some estate owners even seem to have been on the lookout for *nonmarket* possibilities to increase their wealth, as in Stratocles' marriage alliance with Theophon which provided him with an extra estate from which to profit and raise himself up to the liturgical class, and Ciron's marriage alliance with the wealthy miller Nausimenes.

Rather than investing further capital into already existing holdings to increase productivity, expansion into alternative fields may have been the easiest, most effective way for ancient Greek entrepreneurs to mobilize their money into additional income-generating enterprise. The ease with which one could invest small amounts of capital in a new field, and then decide based on its profitability either to abandon this new enterprise or to commit additional funds for increased growth, can be seen with slave manufacturers. Entry was very

93. For the leasing of orphans' estates, see Finley 1985 [1951], 38–44; Osborne 1988, 308–10, 313–19; 2002, 121; Thür 2010; Cudjoe 2010; Leese 2016–2017. Orphans' estates were some of the best chances for windfall gain when they arose, and perfectly exemplify the drive for timely acquisition of profitable opportunities. Nor were orphans' estates rare or of negligible value—up to 40 percent of the property in Athens' *timêma*, property assessment, of 6,000 talents was in the hands of orphans and heiresses as dowry (Lambert 1997, 257). For the Athenian *timêma* in 378/7, see Polybius 2.62.7, and Philochorus *FGrHist* 328, F 46. See Harding 2008, 146–47.

94. See, e.g., Finley 1985 [1951], 133. Contrary to the claims of Finley 1985 [1951], 114–17, that classical Athenians had no concept of collateral, mortgaging property as collateral did exist, for which see Isager and Hansen 1975, 154–56; Thompson 1978, 404–5; Harris 2008 and 2013a.

95. Lewis 1973; Andreyev 1974; Lambert 1997. There is some debate as to whether these inscriptions record leases or sales.

simple and low risk, as a single slave could be purchased to enter into a new field of production, and further expansion could also be accomplished through low-risk incremental additions of a few slaves at a time.[96] The presence of a single flax worker and an embroiderer alongside the workshop of shoemakers in Arizelos' estate certainly fits this pattern. He may have acquired these slaves as a way of gauging the potential profits of entry into a different field of manufacture, and these two slaves represent the beginning stages of his expansion into another trade. The slave woman is explicitly said to have been making fine goods for the market, and so it may be that Arizelos wanted to increase his profits by entering a new field of manufacture and testing the market before committing a larger sum and augmenting the operation. In this case, entry was as easy as buying a slave or two along with some materials. Indeed, such an approach would have enabled an evaluation of the profitability of a field of production without needing to perform complex theoretical calculations and then risking one's entire livelihood based on such guesswork.

Columella advocates experimentation for maximizing the profitability of a farm,[97] and this is precisely the way in which Bresson and Bresson argue that ancient Greeks achieved their own economically rational profit maximization.[98] But experimentation is also central to the strategies of modern economic firms as well, especially when deciding on the best combinations for profitability: "The problem becomes one of finding the best mixture of activities, which is much more complicated than merely ranking gross margins. In fact, in such a situation there is generally no way of analyzing the best solution. Even today one basically has to adopt 'trial and error.'"[99] Modern firms still have difficulty maximizing profits with the availability of complex accounting, procedures and detailed market information.[100] Not just sophisticated bookkeeping, but experimentation and trial and error remain the necessary methods to achieve optimal profits even in business today.

The expansion into closely related or "by-product" fields is one of the most

---

96. Indeed, as Thompson 1982, 74, has argued, the low capital costs of starting up a new enterprise made the incremental, experimental entry into new fields of production very easy. See Acton 2016 for the low capital costs of expanding into new fields of manufacture in ancient Greece. For a clear explanation of the economic concepts of entry and exit, see McCloskey 1996, 126–42.

97. Columella 1.4.5.

98. Bresson and Bresson 2004, 101–11.

99. Macve 1985, 250. North 1990, 79, agrees: "Maximizing activity by the firm results from learning by doing."

100. Even modern firms have difficulties in achieving true profit maximization. Markides 1995, 102–3, shows that many firms from the 1960s to the 1980s were investing in suboptimal investment portfolios, meaning that they were *non*-profit-maximizing (his emphasis); but also that even profit-maximizing firms overinvested in diversification in the 1960s "because the capital market provided them with wrong signals and incentives."

widespread diversification strategies in modern business, and the acquisition of the couch factory by Demosthenes the Elder could certainly be interpreted in similar terms since it allowed him to serve double-duty with the productive materials he already used for the *machairai*.[101] Moreover, as Osborne points out, manufacturing slaves could be used as surplus agricultural laborers on land plots in times of peak labor demands, as a way of maximizing their productivity for multiple ventures.[102] Skilled slaves could also be leased out to other business owners, which would offset the risks of trying to enter another field. Therefore, the need for experimentation is characteristic of both the modern and ancient economy, and many of the individuals explored in this chapter were likely employing strategies similar to those of modern firms in their search for increased profitability as they sought to expand their productive wealth.

The passage I have just quoted by Macve raises another important issue in our analysis: diversification is an important strategy to achieve profit maximization by modern corporations. As Markides states, "If a firm is profit-maximizing, it should diversify up to its optimal limit (assuming it knows what this is), and then stop, otherwise its profitability and market value will suffer."[103] Graham insists upon diversification as a central characteristic of successful portfolio policy.[104] In modern business, diversifying is often necessary for profit maximization in the long term.

This corporate model demonstrates that diversification is not automatically a sign of the safety-first risk aversion traditionally attributed to a peasant mentality, but can also be a way to maximize profits, as part of economically rational moneymaking strategies. Moreover, since the estates preserved from ancient Greece are exclusively the property of the wealthy, it would be a serious methodological problem to assume that rich estate owners pursued the same economic strategies as peasants living at the subsistence level. Thus, wealthy estate owners' diversification in ancient Greece may have actually been more akin to long-term profit-maximizing strategies of modern corporations than to the risk-minimizing tendencies of peasant-based economic models.

The desire to maximize profits is certainly suggested by the high rates of return that are attested for some of the properties belonging to ancient Athenian diversified estates. As discussed above, the profit rates secured by Arizelos' shoe workshop, Demosthenes the Elder's couch and *machaira* work-

101. For the process of diversification into by-product or related fields, and the most effective means of doing so, see Chandler 1990, 41–43.

102. See Osborne 2004, for the use of slave manufacturers to offset periods of low productivity in the agricultural off-season.

103. Markides 1995, 102.

104. Graham 2003, 88–91.

shops, Stratocles' rental properties and loans, all fall within the levels advocated by modern investment experts. Some even surpass the expected returns that a reasonable investor could expect and approach the "special situations" that occur, bringing outstanding profits of close to 20 percent a year. The fact that Arizelos and Demosthenes the Elder kept their highly profitable factories intact until their deaths indicates that they enjoyed high returns from relatively safe operations for a substantial portion of their lifetimes, so it may be concluded that they were maximizing their profits in the long run with the operation of these properties.

Furthermore, the full extent or vast majority of the diversified estates in this chapter was invested in profitable purposes rather than consumption,[105] which is suggestive of a desire to maximize not just profit, but also *wealth* in the long term. Almost all these estate owners exhibit a long-term commitment to profitable enterprises while also avoiding excessive consumptive expenditures, as their estates consisted predominantly, and almost entirely, of productive assets. The overwhelming predominance of productive property in these estates, is also a sign that their owners designed them for profit in a manner akin to modern business, which should be expected since the household was the structure for all business, and ancient Greeks saw a growing, increasing *oikos* as the ideal.

Probably the best evidence for a desire to make as much money as possible from an estate in the long term, however, is liturgy avoidance. A number of the estate owners studied in this chapter certainly or likely engaged in tax evasion and liturgy avoidance by liquidating conspicuously profitable visible assets and reinvesting them into *aphanês* wealth which could not be detected by the *polis*. Hiding wealth allowed for continued profitability, and as such constituted an important strategy of estate management for those individuals who wanted to dodge the fortune-diminishing effects of liturgies. The desire of many of the individuals explored in this chapter to avoid liturgies and ensure the potential for long-term growth in their estates points to an attitude which was unequivocally acquisitive, and oriented toward maximizing wealth up to the end of their lives.

Loans would have been riskier investments, but the increased hazards were more than offset by the fact that *aphanês* wealth permitted high rates of growth while eliminating the more dangerous risk of being called to serve

105. The estate owners such as Demosthenes the Elder and Arizelos who kept their factories in their houses are part of a well-established pattern in the literature, including Komon from Demosthenes 48 *Against Olympiodoros*, who owned two houses, including his private residence, both of which housed slave workshops. In Olynthus, the archaeological record reveals many houses that were completely filled with productive space. The full use of potential house space for production is consistent with a profit-maximizing strategy.

liturgies. Liturgy avoidance was also a way to manage risk, by decreasing the chance that one's estate would be depleted by state demands. Investing in *aphanês* wealth to evade liturgies and permit further growth was an important reason for diversification, and although it was certainly motivated by the desire to avoid liturgies, it was not a risk-averse strategy. Rather, it was a calculated choice to *manage* risk—investing in higher-yield *aphanês* wealth, though less secure than land, also significantly reduced the danger of being called to serve liturgies, which would have devastated the profitability and long-term growth potential of these estates.

It is true that not all Athenians would have wanted to avoid taxes or liturgies. Apollodorus, the speaker of Lysias 21 *On the Charge of Taking Bribes*, and others not only performed liturgies but spent more than was required. The social capital and *philotimia* they received from these very public and visible expenditures was clearly more valuable to them than the money they spent. But these individuals are probably more representative of what Thorstein Veblen would call the leisure class than some of the cases I have discussed in this chapter. For the leisure class, spending large amounts of money in conspicuous consumption (and even waste) is essential for their expression of membership in the social and economic elite; as I have argued elsewhere, such expenditures could reap enormous rewards.[106]

But for those who were not yet members of the leisure class and especially those who were *aspiring* to join, avoiding taxes and liturgies would have been one of the most effective means of sustaining the growth needed to attain that status. Others simply did not want to pay taxes, a pattern that is also attested in the Greek world outside of Athens. Pseudo-Aristotle, for example, details the persistent efforts of Syracusans to avoid the taxation imposed upon them by the tyrant Dionysius in the early fourth century BCE, in which they tried to keep one step ahead of Dionysius' taxation policies by continuously changing their investments to whatever was untaxed.[107] In an inscription from second-century BCE Priene, exemptions from taxation and liturgies were major incentives for purchasing the priesthood of Dionysos Phleos: the more the winning bidder paid for the priesthood, the higher tax exemptions he received—the winner paid two drachmas more than the amount of the largest tax exemption (12,002 drachmas), suggesting that he had outbid the next highest person by a single drachma, and that there had been a competitive auction.[108]

Overall this pattern of seeking wealth over the social returns from public

106. Leese 2017a.
107. *Oikonomika* 2.2.20.
108. Arnaoutoglou 1998, 138–39.

demands reflects behavior not only in Athens but in the larger Greek world as well. Speaking of Greeks in general, Aristotle corroborates the impression seen in Athens, Syracuse, and Priene, that most people would rather have money than the honor from public services: οἱ γὰρ πολλοὶ μᾶλλον ὀρέγονται τοῦ κέρδους ἢ τῆς τιμῆς, "For the masses grasp at profit rather than honor."[109] People of different classes had different preferences—whereas the higher leisure class might welcome the honor, others would prefer the money. Therefore, far from being merely an Athenian phenomenon, evasion of taxes and liturgies is widely attested in multiple Greek *poleis*, a strategy that is part of the general patterns to maximize wealth attested from the archaic to the Hellenistic period.

Conclusions

Diversification in ancient Athenian estate management followed a few basic principles: in every case of a diversified fortune from ancient Athens, lower-risk properties bringing a steady return were combined with more risky investments yielding higher profit.[110] Peasant models of risk minimization and corporate diversification strategies to reduce risk are extremely useful frames of reference to evaluate Athenian moneymaking decisions, but none of the ancient individuals for whom we have any sort of extensive evidence fit either of these models perfectly. The economic decision-making process of these estate owners reveals that instead of simply risk management, diversification often seems to have been the result of the timely windfall acquisition of profitable investments as they became available in a world of limited information about, and access to, gainful opportunities. There is no explicit evidence of any of these individuals diversifying specifically to reduce risk like modern corporations. Nor do these estate owners fit models of risk-averse peasants. Profit, rather than risk minimization, is the predominant motivation for the acquisition of new properties in these diversified estates. Indeed, the only discernible pattern shared by these individuals is that their economic decisions were primarily ori-

109. *Politics* 6.4.3, 1318b17.

110. Thompson 1978, 406–7, noted this pattern, referring to the "balanced portfolios" of ancient Greek estate owners. Millett 1991, 166, has objected that these estates are more of a random mishmash of properties acquired in a manner that is "irrational" according to modern economic theory. The structural imperfections of the ancient Greek market economy, however, with asymmetries of information and the absence of centralized property registers, made windfall acquisition the rule for ancient property acquisition, because of the result of irregular, unpredictable receipt of information about profitable opportunities by word of mouth. Structural imperfections and information problems, however, do not make individuals' actions irrational—these individuals behaved rationally in response to the specific structural imperfections of their economic system.

ented toward the acquisition of additional lucrative enterprises. Diversification therefore was often an unintentional by-product of an overall profit-oriented strategy of making money. It was also facilitated by the institution of slavery, which allowed for incremental expansion and experimentation into new fields.

Arizelos certainly, and others likely, made their choices with an eye to maximizing their wealth over the course of their lives as *oikonomoi*. Not only did the majority of the fortunes discussed in this chapter consist of mainly productive, rather than consumptive, assets, but most of their properties or businesses were also highly profitable. Most of the possessions on these estates would make a modern investor happy, and although the attested rates of return may be exaggerated, the overall pattern of long-term growth and acquisition is unmistakable. The choices these estate owners made were oriented toward increased profitability in the long run. Many even continuously reinvested their profits into additional enterprises, which demonstrates a clear strategy to maximize productivity over the course of their careers. Moreover, the fact that many estate owners were reinvesting the returns from their lower-risk properties into higher-risk and higher-yielding loans at the end of their lives suggests that they were attempting to maximize their wealth even up to the point of their deaths. Finally, the trends of liturgy avoidance and tax evasion are themselves clear signs of a desire to maximize wealth over the long term, and the evidence from Hellenistic Delos and fourth-century Syracuse indicates that these behaviors were not restricted to Athens alone but were found across the Greek world.

CHAPTER 3

Moneymaking Strategies on Specialized Estates

Introduction: All Your Eggs in One Basket

In 1885, in a speech to business students at Curry Commercial College in Pittsburgh, steel tycoon Andrew Carnegie famously advocated a policy not of diversification, but of uncompromising specialization: "Put all your eggs in one basket and then watch that basket. Do not scatter your shot. . . . The great successes of life are made by concentration." For Carnegie, specialization, not diversification, was the secret to maximizing profits.

In this chapter, I will argue that some of the best evidence for long-term profit- and wealth-maximizing strategies in ancient Athens can be seen in the Carnegies of that time. These were the individuals who specialized in one field for the majority of their lives and made such tremendous fortunes that their exploits are still preserved to this day. By specializing in a single highly lucrative industry in the long term, a number of "business tycoons" were able to emerge and achieve for themselves and their families wealth, status, honor, power, and eternal fame. The most abundant evidence for Athenians who concentrated their wealth into a single lucrative field in the long term can be seen in silver mining, banking, and moneylending, so I will focus primarily on these activities. Some of the most fantastic fortunes in ancient Athens were created by specializing in one industry; these individuals employed such effective strategies to maximize wealth in the long run that the news about their success spurred others to emulate them.[1]

This extreme concentration came at a price, however. Market fluctuations, warfare, and sketchy business practices stymied many in their efforts to maintain their prosperity, and the vast majority of fortunes that were able to persist across multiple generations were able to do so largely because their owners

1. As Shipton 2000 demonstrates, even poorer Athenians were able to invest in the mines, and seem to have done so (see below).

eventually transformed some of their assets into other forms. There are many examples of specialized estate owners diversifying, which helped to secure their fortunes against loss. Nevertheless, the properties that specialized estate owners chose to acquire as part of their diversification were still very profitable and often quite risky, revealing that they simultaneously chose to manage their risks while still trying to maximize their profits and wealth.

Nicias, Kallias, and Long-Term Profit Maximization in Silver Mining

In Aeschylus' *Persians*, when Persian Queen Atossa asks if the Athenians have enough wealth in their houses to carry on a war against the Great King, the chorus replied: "They have a fountain of silver; a treasure chest in the earth."[2] There was a silver rush in southern Attica during the classical period. The volume of silver mined and coined was immense,[3] as were the private fortunes made in this highly profitable industry. The wealth from this fountain of silver did, indeed, make it into the households of many Athenians, as Atossa asked. Thus, it should be no surprise that some of the best examples of long-term wealth maximization in ancient Greece belong to the individuals who specialized in this lucrative industry.

Nicias, who is best known for his tragic downfall in Thucydides' riveting account of the Sicilian Expedition, is one such individual. The tremendous amount of wealth attested for Nicias in the Laureion mines, 100 talents,[4] was probably built upon the efforts of his father, Nikeratos, who left a fortune large enough for his three sons to be liturgical class members. It is not known exactly what sort of properties Nikeratos possessed, but the best guess from the available evidence is that he elevated his family into the Athenian elite through a lifetime of silver mining, and enriched them to such an extent that he laid the foundations whereby Nicias was eventually able to possess his fortune of 100 talents.

Nicias himself followed a strategy of long-term specialization in the profitable silver mines of Laureion, as he owned very little real estate,[5] and his wealth consisted almost entirely of mining property.[6] His fortune seems to have collapsed to the point that his son Nikeratos (II) left a fortune of only 14 talents at

2. *Persians*, 237–38.

3. For recent estimates, see Kroll 2009.

4. Lysias, 19.47.

5. Kron 1996, 216, says he also owned a house and land worth 10,000 drachmas, but this may have been only acquired to be dedicated to Delian Apollo (Plutarch, *Nicias* 3.6). Plutarch's account of Nicias is heavily grounded in contemporary sources, for which see Titchener 1988.

6. Plutarch, *Nicias* 4.2.

his own death.[7] As Davies argues, the most likely reason for such a precipitous decline was the drop in the values of mining properties following the Spartan fortification of Deceleia,[8] which would explain Nicias' desire for peace during the Peloponnesian War. Therefore, his wealth was apparently so completely concentrated in mining operations that after the Peloponnesian War his estate lost more than 85 percent of its total worth.[9]

Indeed, Plutarch says that Nicias' mining interests were risky, but also very lucrative,[10] and Nicias must have had intimate knowledge of the high risks and returns involved in focusing his moneymaking activities in silver mining. This concerted effort at concentrating all his wealth in the Laureion mines for his entire life is suggestive of a strategy of long-term maximization. He specialized in one of the most profitable activities known from ancient Greece and built a tremendous fortune from his lifelong exploitation of the mines. Moreover, his descendants seem to have realized how profitable mining could be and held on to the family properties in the Laureion mining region, and after Nikeratos II died, his own son Nikeratos III stayed in mining and eventually attained the position of *tamias stratiotikôn*, treasurer of the military fund, regaining his family's social standing and wealth through his own long-term investment in the silver industry.[11]

In one of his strategies to maximize the income he could receive from his mines, Nicias apparently made a well-considered productive investment when he purchased a skilled slave for the price of one talent to supervise his operations.[12] This overseer is the most expensive slave whose purchase price is preserved from classical Greece, and must have been well-known as a successful miner if Nicias spent such a tremendous sum on him. The scale of this investment suggests that Nicias considered this slave manager to be important for helping to secure the greatest possible gains from his mining operations.

In addition to his high-risk and high-return exploitation of the mines themselves, Nicias also possessed an enormous number of slave workers, 1,000 at least, whom he leased out to Sosias the Thracian at the rate of one obol per day apiece.[13]

---

7. Lysias 19.47–48.

8. Davies 1971, 405–6. This also seems to have been the reason for the collapse of Kallias' mining fortune (see below).

9. An alternative explanation is that his descendants hid their fortune from the *polis*, which is also a wealth-maximizing strategy, as I argued in chapter 2.

10. *Nicias*, 4.2.

11. For Nikeratos II and III, see Davies 1971, 405–6.

12. Xen., *Mem*. 2.5.2.

13. Xenophon, *Poroi* 4.14. According to Mussche 1998, 45, an inscription reading "SOSIA latom[ia]" dating to the late fifth or early fourth century in a Thorikos quarry might refer to this

Νικίας ποτὲ ὁ Νικηράτου ἐκτήσατο ἐν τοῖς ἀργυρείοις χιλίους ἀνθρώπους, οὓς ἐκεῖνος Σωσίᾳ τῷ Θρᾳκὶ ἐξεμίσθωσεν, ἐφ' ᾧ ὀβολὸν μὲν ἀτελῆ ἑκάστου τῆς ἡμέρας ἀποδιδόναι, τὸν δ' ἀριθμὸν ἴσους ἀεὶ παρέχειν. ἐγένετο δὲ καὶ Ἱππονίκῳ ἑξακόσια ἀνδράποδα κατὰ τὸν αὐτὸν τρόπον τοῦτον ἐκδεδομένα, ἃ προσέφερε μνᾶν ἀτελῆ τῆς ἡμέρας, Φιλημονίδῃ δὲ τριακόσια.

Once Nicias owned a thousand slaves in the silver mines whom he leased out to Sosias the Thracian, for which Sosias paid one obol net profit for each slave per day, and always returned an equal number. And Hipponikos had six hundred slaves leased out in the same manner, which brought him a mina in net profit each day, and Philemonides had three hundred.[14]

These slaves, who would have been worth 30 talents in total at 200 drachmas each,[15] brought in a total of 10 talents of cash per year, one-third their overall value. This was a highly profitable investment, then, that could also remain steadily productive regardless of his luck in his own mining ventures; they could simply be redirected to where others needed them, and for a reliable return.

It seems that this enterprise was so successful that Nicias kept expanding his army of slave workers. Xenophon says that everyone who possessed such slaves would constantly add to their numbers, reinvesting their proceeds back into acquiring new productive slaves: καὶ νῦν δὲ οἱ κεκτημένοι ἐν τοῖς μετάλλοις ἀνδράποδα οὐδεὶς τοῦ πλήθους ἀφαιρεῖ, ἀλλ' ἀεὶ προσκτᾶται ὁπόσα ἂν πλεῖστα δύνηται, "And now no one of those who own slaves in the mines decreases their number, but always acquires in addition as many as he is able."[16] Nicias, indeed, with his 1,000 slaves, would be the sort of mining slave owner that Xenophon said always added to their numbers. The most logical explanation based on the evidence is that he was converting his monetary gains from mining into the growth of his productive slave army. Increasing this workforce by continuously reinvesting his profits into additional productive enterprise is indicative of an income-maximizing attitude over the long term.

Nicias' investment in these slaves is not only an example of ever-increasing

Sosias. It is not clear whether or not he was a slave entrepreneur or foreman, as Lauffer 1956, 11, thinks. Austin and Vidal-Naquet 1977, 319n9, note that Sosias may have been a metic and that his role is unclear. See Lauffer 1956, 77–81, for an in-depth discussion on Sosias.

14. Xenophon, *Poroi* 4.14–15.

15. This is only slightly higher than the average price of slaves sold in the Attic Stelai, 175–200 drachmas apiece, for which see Pritchett and Pippin 1956, 276.

16. Xenophon, *Poroi* 4.4.

productive capacity, but also an effective means of diversification as a result of the initial specialization in mining and subsequent attempts to expand. Nicias could either choose to commit his entire slave workforce to his own prospecting ventures, or lease them out, a strategy to maximize the labor of the slaves when they were not being used in his own mines,[17] and which simultaneously enabled profit maximization and risk reduction through diversification. Nicias' slave armies also provided an effective hedge against risk, just as Baptist has argued for slave owners in the US cotton South.[18] They could be used as security to repay loans, or sold off individually, providing remarkable flexibility to allow Nicias to use them to the optimal advantage. He could work them in his own mines, lease them out for the mines of others when his own operations were not running at full capacity, or he could liquidate them little by little, which gave him the ability to adjust his profits and costs with great precision. These slaves could be moved back into his own mines if he struck it big, incrementally downsized to offset costs, or leased out for profit to capitalize on the risks taken by other prospectors in need of labor.

Furthermore, the low price of their rent and the large number of slaves suggests that Nicias may have been trying to secure a local monopoly on rented labor by employing so many and renting them out at this rate. Monopolies were not unheard of in ancient Greece; for example Rosivach has argued that long-term local monopolies existed for the animal breeders who supplied victims to certain sanctuaries,[19] and it seems that many individuals recognized monopolies' potential to make huge profits. Aristotle mentions two monopolies in particular, one in oil pressing equipment by the philosopher Thales, and another in iron by an unnamed Syracusan man:[20]

17. The maximization of labor productivity and efficiency are all advocated by Hesiod, Xenophon, and pseudo-Xenophon. Labor maximization can perhaps be seen in the prostitutes who served as textile weavers at the same time in Bau Z in the Kerameikos, for which see Knigge 2005. The maximization of labor is seen as an important component of economically rational strategies for nineteenth-century American farmers, for which see Bruegel 2006, 537.

18. Baptist 2012.

19. Rosivach 1994, 102–3. Monopolies secured through the help of the state or for the state itself are also well-attested for ancient Greece, for which see Gabrielsen 2011, 216–50. Some examples of monopolies include the case in which Byzantium sold the right to change money to a single bank (pseudo-Aristotle, *Oikonomika* 2.2.3), and the state-owned monopoly on lead from the Laureion mines proposed by Pythocles of Athens (pseudo-Aristotle, *Oikonomika* 2.2.36).

20. *Para* is used in this passage for this deposit, and perhaps means that this man was a banker. See Cohen 1992, 122–23, for *para* used for deposits with bankers. It is used at Dem. 27.11 for 70 *minae* deposited for maritime loans with Xouthus, and Demomeles, and also for a deposit left with the banker Eumathes in Isaeus, fr. 18.

ἐν Σικελίᾳ δέ τις τεθέντος παρ᾽ αὐτῷ νομίσματος συνεπρίατο πάντα τὸν σίδηρον ἐκ τῶν σιδηρείων, μετὰ δὲ ταῦτα ὡς ἀφίκοντο ἐκ τῶν ἐμπορίων οἱ ἔμποροι, ἐπώλει μόνος, οὐ πολλὴν ποιήσας ὑπερβολὴν τῆς τιμῆς: ἀλλ᾽ ὅμως ἐπὶ τοῖς πεντήκοντα ταλάντοις ἐπέλαβεν ἑκατόν. τοῦτο μὲν οὖν Διονύσιος αἰσθόμενος τὰ μὲν χρήματα ἐκέλευσεν ἐκκομίσασθαι, μὴ μέντοι γε ἔτι μένειν ἐν Συρακούσαις, ὡς πόρους εὑρίσκοντα τοῖς αὑτοῦ πράγμασιν ἀσυμφόρους: τὸ μέντοι ὅραμα Θάλεω καὶ τοῦτο ταὐτόν ἐστιν: ἀμφότεροι γὰρ ἑαυτοῖς ἐτέχνασαν γενέσθαι μονοπωλίαν.

A certain man in Sicily, when some money had been deposited with him, bought up all the iron from the iron mines, and afterward when sea traders arrived from their voyages, he alone was selling, but without making too great an increase on the price. Nevertheless, he made a hundred talents on his original fifty. And so, when Dionysios heard this, he ordered him to take his money away, and certainly not to stay in Syracuse, since he was discovering ways and means that were detrimental to his own affairs. This spectacle was the same as that of Thales, for both men had devised a way to secure a monopoly for themselves. (Aristotle, *Politics* 1.11.11–12)

The story of Thales may be apocryphal, though the ironic motivation for securing his monopoly may have been invented *post factum* to better suit his status as a philosopher. As for the Syracusan man, on the other hand, there is no reason to disbelieve its truth, and there should be little surprise that Aristotle calls the attempt to establish monopolies a universal principle of business,[21] since this Syracusan made 200 percent profit, 100 talents, on his 50 talent investment. Thus, securing timely (if only temporary) monopolies was known to have occurred in ancient Greece.

Unfortunately, it is not certain if Nicias was trying to build up a local monopoly in the supply of slave labor, but the fact that he owned so many slaves whom he rented out suggests that he had cornered a significant share of this market. Moreover, Hipponikos' army of 600 slaves, and Philemonides' of 300, both show that the rental of slaves in the Laureion region was profitable enough to be emulated on a mass scale, in which one could choke out competition through large quantity and low prices, and perhaps secure a steady stream

21. ἔστι δ᾽, ὥσπερ εἴπομεν, καθόλου τὸ τοιοῦτον χρηματιστικόν, ἐάν τις δύνηται μονοπωλίαν αὑτῷ κατασκευάζειν, "And this is a general sort of thing in moneymaking, as we have said, if someone is able to secure a monopoly for himself" (Aristotle, *Politics* 1.11.10).

of cash through monopolizing local markets for labor. Flooding the market with cheap slave workers would have had the effect of deflating prices for labor, and driving out competitors, especially small-time slave and free wage earners. Therefore, grabbing a large share of the market would have enabled these wealthiest slave owners to achieve oligopoly or local monopolies.

The net return on these slaves would have been tremendous. Even at the rate of an obol net profit per day,[22] each of these slaves would have brought in 60 drachmas per year, about a third of their original purchase price.[23] If they brought in a net profit of 30 to 33 percent of their capital value per year, these slaves were extremely profitable investments, and could pay for themselves within a period of three years.[24] These rates of return are well above even what Benjamin Graham considers "special situations," those long-term investments that yield 20 percent annually, and they should probably be considered exaggerated somewhat.[25] Nevertheless, the fact that Nicias invested so much of his money in these slaves, 33 talents' worth if they were 200 drachmas apiece, demonstrates a clear intention to commit a high proportion of his overall wealth to profit-generating slaves.

These slaves would have amounted to one-third of his entire fortune invested in producing steady returns that would have simultaneously also amounted to diversification. Compared to prospecting in mines, this army of slaves would have been a less risky means of guaranteeing continuous profits from a more reliable source. Slaves were certainly not a risk-free investment, particularly those who worked in the brutal conditions of the mines, who would be liable to run away or get sick and die, and his slave army may have been among the 20,000 slaves that Thucydides says escaped to the Spartans after the fortification of Deceleia in 413.[26] But because their contract stipulated that Sosias return the same number of slaves to Nicias at the end of each day, their agreement offset some of the hazards inherent in owning mining slaves. Less dependent on chance than prospecting, while also producing gains regardless of Nicias' fortunes in his own mining operations, this slave workforce in effect helped Nicias diversify to reduce risk while still maintaining high rates of return. Thus, these slaves can be seen as a long-term profit-maximizing investment that

22. The obol per day was said by Xenophon to be net profit, ἀτελής (Xen., *Poroi* 4.14–15). This is also how Demosthenes' father's profits from his factories are described (Dem. 27.9).

23. The best evidence for the price of the average slave in Athens, which was around 175–200 drachmas, can be gleaned from the Attic Stelai, for which see Pritchett and Pippin 1956, 276.

24. Osborne 1995, 34, agrees.

25. As argued by Acton 2014, 261.

26. As Davies 1971, 406, also believes. See Thucydides 7.27.5 for the flight of slaves after the fortification of Deceleia.

could repay themselves in only a few years and yield large amounts of cash on a regular basis. Nicias was able to maximize his gains in the long run while still offsetting his risk in his approach to his mining operations, his leasing of slaves, and his estate management overall.

Nicias' mining properties and slaves were so extensive that he was probably expanding their operation continuously to secure increasingly greater profits. And so, Nicias and his heirs represent an almost certain example of individuals choosing to enter and remain within an extremely lucrative field which enabled them to enjoy huge returns over the long run. The choice to stick with mining indicates a strategy of consistently sustaining the economic activity that would bring in the highest possible yield throughout their lifetimes. The concentration of wealth by Nicias in the mines and their subsequent decline in value reveals an all-in approach to estate management, which his heirs tried to continue after his death.

Another fantastically wealthy miner was Kallias II, son of Hipponikos. He was called *Lakkoploutos*, "pit-wealthy," supposedly because he had gotten rich from discovering a cache of Persian gold in a pit following the battle of Marathon.[27] The *phthonos* (jealousy) in this story is unmistakable, however, and it was probably made up by elite rivals who were envious of his wealth: Kallias was πλουσιώτατος ὢν Ἀθηναίων (the richest of the Athenians),[28] so much so that centuries later Plutarch still called him "Kallias the Rich."[29] Indeed, the aristocratic bias against him and the true origins of his fortune are summarized succinctly by Cornelius Nepos: "Non tam generosus quam pecuniosus qui magnas pecunias ex metallis fecerat" (He was not so much well-born as he was rich, since he made his huge fortune from the mines).[30] He is said to have been worth over 200 talents,[31] and was so successful throughout his career of mining operations that his son Hipponikos was also himself described as "omnium Graeca lingua loquentium ditissimus" (the wealthiest of all who spoke in the Greek language).[32] Therefore, the nickname, *Lakkoploutos*, must actually refer to the mines that made Kallias rich, not the discovery of Persian gold, which

27. Plutarch, *Aristides* 5.6. For this family's wealth, see Davies 1971, 260–61. That Kallias I, son of Phaenippus and grandfather of Kallias II, is said to have been the only person who was willing to buy Peisistratus' property when he was banished from Athens (Herodotus 6.121), shows that the family had money even before the mines, enough perhaps to enable horse breeding during the sixth century (Herodotus 6.122).

28. Plutarch, *Aristides* 25.4.

29. τὸν πλούσιον, *Pericles* 24.5.

30. *Cimon* 1.3.

31. Lysias 19.48.

32. Nepos, *Alcibiades* 2.1; Hipponikos is also described as the "wealthiest of the Greeks" in Andocides 1.130, and Isocrates 16.31.

was probably a false etymology invented out of *phthonos*. The detail about his wealth being from the silver industry and not from a noble lineage is significant: Kallias' fortune was self-made from silver prospecting over the course of his lifetime.

The evidence is sparse, to be sure, but the implications seem clear: mining provided extraordinary wealth for Kallias and his son Hipponikos, and both concentrated their moneymaking energies in this industry in the long run because it was so profitable. Becoming the richest person in the Greek world by one's own efforts is not an achievement to be dismissed lightly, and the family's ability to become so wealthy and famous from mining was probably the result of a concerted, long-term effort to build and maintain this fortune. As noted above, Hipponikos himself may have also vied with Nicias in an attempt to secure a local monopoly on slave labor.[33] Hipponikos' own son Kallias III was believed to be quite rich when he inherited his estate, but at his death in 387 was found to have been worth only two talents,[34] and was forced to play the part of the "begging priest" later on in life.[35] He owned property in the Laureion mining region at Nape in 367/6,[36] but otherwise his family's mining wealth seems to have disappeared. As for the collapse of the family fortune, the only plausible explanation in the absence of any other evidence seems to be that their mining properties dropped precipitously in value following the Spartan occupation of Deceleia in 413.[37]

Therefore, Kallias and his son Hipponikos concentrated all or a majority of their wealth into the mines at Laureion and they both pursued the profits from silver for their entire lives.[38] This seems to be good evidence for a strategy to maximize wealth in the long run, though the precise manner in which they ran their estates will never be known. Both father and son were perceptive enough to take advantage of lucrative opportunities for investment in the Laureion region. Hipponikos' accumulation of his own six-hundred-slave army also probably demonstrates a desire to reinvest the profits from mining continuously in further productive enterprise, slaves who could equally mine for the

33. As Xenophon, *Poroi* 4.15, says, he also had an army of 600 slaves whom he rented out in the Laureion mining region.

34. Lysias 19.48.

35. Aristotle, *Rhetoric* 3.2.10, 1405a19–20.

36. Crosby and Young 1941.

37. Davies 1971, 261. The devastation of the Laureion mining operations in the Peloponnesian War is well-documented. The Laureion mining region seems to have become almost entirely unused, with very little to no evidence for mining from the late fifth century down into the second quarter of the fourth century (for which see Mussche 1998, 62–64, on Thorikos, the major mining town in the Laureion district, where the evidence for mining at the end of the fifth and beginning of the fourth century is almost absent).

38. Kron 1996, 171–72, agrees.

master or be leased out for cash.[39] The choice to augment his slave holdings on a continual basis reveals a strategy that is simultaneously oriented toward ever-expanding profits as well as flexibility, as was also seen in the case of Nicias.

In conclusion, Nicias' and Kallias' families seem to have made and lost their fortunes by focusing their moneymaking activities in the silver mining industry. Long-term specialization in this field was practiced by each family for multiple successive generations, to the point that their wealth seems to have collapsed after the Peloponnesian War due to their excessive concentration in this one industry. Likewise, even their diversification into the supply of slave labor also suffered the same consequences of excessive specialization in the Laureion mining district. Moreover, the decision to sustain a strategy of concentration in this single extraordinarily profitable industry for multiple generations even after such a devastating collapse is further indicative of an attempt at long-term wealth maximization within these families. Nicias also made an expensive investment in an expert slave manager of his mining operations in order to ensure the highest returns possible.

It is also possible that Nicias' and Hipponikos' decision to acquire vast numbers of slaves to work in the mines was part of attempts to actualize the advantages of economies of scale, in which all aspects of the productive process are subsumed under a single owner's control.[40] Indeed, these slaves were probably purchased by these estate owners to work in their own mining properties. Their owners' flexibility and desire to maximize the returns on their slaves' labor seems to have led them to expand these holdings continuously over a long period of time. Increasing the number of these slaves would have simultaneously reduced risk by means of diversification while also maintaining the high rates of profit that they are attested as producing. This effective strategy would have doubtless continued successfully had the Peloponnesian War not been renewed and the Spartans not fortified Deceleia.

Finally, they may have been trying to secure local monopolies on the labor supply market in their respective regions, which would demonstrate yet another layer of motivation to invest in these slaves. Perhaps their goal in continuously reinvesting their surpluses into the acquisition of new slaves was to establish

39. It would have been extremely difficult to acquire such a large number of slaves at a single moment, and therefore these large slave armies are most likely the result of a long process of continuously expanding their numbers. Xenophon's testimony that this continuous expansion is the pattern for mining slave owners is good evidence that Nicias, Hipponikos, and Philemonides were gradually adding to the numbers of their slaves over time and not acquiring them all at once.

40. Obviously they would not have been informed by theory, but through practice they may have recognized the general benefits and principles. For a definition and lengthy discussion of the advantages of economies of scale, see North 1986, 175–76; Chandler 1990, 17–31.

monopolies on slave labor, in which case these slave armies provide intriguing insight into some of the business strategies otherwise lost from ancient Greece. The desire to constantly mobilize profits in additional productive property certainly seems to be evidence for a long-term intent to maximize returns. This impression also supported by the rates of profit that these slaves would have brought, as well as the reduction of risk that would have resulted. Based on the available evidence it is safe to conclude that the long-term maximization of wealth was the most likely goal of each of these estate owners.

The Silver Rush in Fourth-Century BCE Athens

Since news would have spread so quickly in Athens,[41] the successes of such individuals as Kallias and Nicias would have inspired others to try to strike it rich in the mines as well. In the 350s, Xenophon describes the mines at Laureion as inexhaustible, and mentions that more and more individuals were being drawn to them every day.[42] The archaeological record suggests an explosion in activity in southern Attica during the mid-fourth century, when a large number of new mining and processing installations were built,[43] and even remote regions like the deme of Atene which had previously been sparsely populated came under intensive cultivation.[44]

In its psychological impetus, this silver rush can be compared to modern gold rushes, and even the scramble to invest in the stock market in the early twentieth century and the housing market in more recent years. In the modern world, such a phenomenon of mass entry into a field motivated by the desire to emulate the successes of others is referred to as "irrational exuberance" since it is based on the (in hindsight) unrealistic expectation that one will be able to succeed in a field at a time just after news of such impressive fortunes has circulated among the public, when it is becoming flooded with investors and prices have begun to balloon to unnatural and unsustainable levels.[45] To an individual unversed in economic theory trying to get the most return for his drachma, however, the successes of others in the mining industry would have been reliable information for the field's potential profitability. Even those who do know

41. Ober 2008.
42. *Poroi* 4.2–6.
43. For the increase in archaeological sites in the fourth century in the Laureion region, see, e.g., Lohmann 1993; Goette 2000; Jones 1982; Kakovogiannis 1982; Young 1956.
44. Lohmann 1993.
45. Shiller 2000.

economics will try to beat the market,[46] and the huge speculative bubbles that are known from the early modern to the present day, the tulip bubble in Amsterdam, the South Sea Company stock bubble, and American stock market and housing bubbles, are all comparable to the silver rush in classical Athens, in which large numbers of investors entered a field to strike it rich, many of whom eventually saw their fortunes collapse.

Indeed the huge fortunes that became public knowledge do seem to have motivated many others to enter mining; silver prospecting was open even to non-elites since only a small capital investment was required. Kirsty Shipton's extensive study of the individuals engaged in mining shows that the possibility of prospecting was open to a large section of the Athenian population, many of whom were attracted by the relatively low prices of mine leases, as seen in the *polêtai* records.[47] The majority of the attested mine lessees are not known to be members of the liturgical class and should be considered to be of the lower or middle wealth strata. Therefore, the Athenian silver rush, based as it was on the desire to strike it rich following the example of others, was likely driven by the same psychological forces that create modern speculative bubbles.

Vast fortunes are attested in the high-risk field of mining by a number of Athenians. Euthykrates, for example, is rumored to have made 60 talents from mining.[48] Another man, Diphilos, apparently accumulated at least 160 talents from mining, more than the property of Nicias.[49] Even more astounding is the Epikrates who amassed 600 talents from mining![50] Many families seem to have joined the ranks of the liturgical class through their mining efforts, so the silver ore of Laureion provided a major source of social mobility in classical Athens. Though some of these figures might be exaggerations, nonetheless they are comparable to the fortunes owned by Kallias and Nicias and in any case communicate the scale at which Athenians *perceived* mining to be so profitable. With just the public share of the great silver strike of 483 in Attica, a formidable fleet of triremes could be built. Silver mining profits were massive, and as Xenophon reveals, there was no sign that the gains were slowing down in the mid-fourth century, at least. Rather, increased expansion and exploitation characterized the workings of the Laureion mines in the fourth century.

Nor was it only in Attica that huge mining fortunes were made. The legend-

46. See Graham 2003, for frequent reference to individuals who try to "beat the market" in the contemporary US.

47. Shipton 2000.

48. Hypereides, *Euxenippus* 4.34; Kron 1996, 203.

49. [Plutarch], *Lives of the Ten Orators* 843d4–e1.

50. Harpokration, s.v. *Epikrates*. As Davies 1971, 182, demonstrates, this is likely the same man who made 300 talents from an unregistered mine (see below in this section).

ary wealth of archaic Siphnos was derived from its own silver mines,[51] which were exhausted before the classical period. The mainland mines owned by Thasos brought in 200 to 300 talents of public revenue every year, not including what private individuals were getting.[52] The profitability of these mines was maintained into the late fifth century at least,[53] and it is most likely that the private wealth made from just these mines far exceeded the 200 talents a year that went into the public coffers.

Although conclusions from the figures in the evidence from the *polêtai* lists may be used only with great caution, Errietta Bissa has illustrated a number of general patterns in the exploitation of the mines and the ownership of mining properties that agree with the observations on the balancing of risk and profit made above—the poorer classes seem to have concentrated in prospecting, whereas the elite were more likely to invest their wealth in land, ore washeries, and cupellation furnaces rather than just in mining alone.[54] The reason for this is clear, since the processing and service properties preferred by the elite all required large capital costs, whereas prospectors could buy tools and mining concessions relatively cheaply, and could rent housing, slaves, and the services of ore-processing workshops. Many of the richest therefore provided food, shelter, ore-processing facilities, cupellation, and slaves to the poorer individuals who were doing the actual mining. This was indeed a less risky approach, as Bissa shows, since the odds of profiting from the prospectors who certainly needed food, shelter, and slaves were better than the chances of a single mine being productive. Therefore, many wealthy individuals preferred to choose the lower risk but still steady profits from providing services to miners.

Perhaps another risk-reducing measure can be seen in the fact that, as Hypereides states, many of the wealthiest investors pooled their fortunes in the most highly productive mines, sharing the risk and proceeds.[55] Other mine owners seem to have spread their attention between different mines, such as Thrasylochus of Anagyrous, who in 367 leased one for 1,550 dr., more than a quarter of a talent, and another for 150 drachmas.[56] The variation in price was apparently based on a mine's known productivity, meaning Thrasylochus chose

51. Herodotus 3.57.

52. Herodotus 6.46.

53. Thuc. 4.105.

54. Bissa 2008. This is in line with the conclusions reached by Lohmann 1993 on olive cultivation in fourth-century Atene expanding to cater to miners in Laureion. For other patterns of land exploitation and leasing in the Laureion region, see Osborne 1985, 111–226.

55. Hypereides, *Euxenippus* 4.35 ὃ ἠργάζετο μὲν ἤ[δ]η τρία ἔτη, μετεῖχον δ' αὐτοῦ οἱ πλουσ[ιώ]τατοι σχεδόν τι τῶν ἐν τῇ πόλει. As Xenophon, *Poroi* 4.28–29 states, sticking with older, proven mines was a way to avoid the risks of complete loss that might come with an entirely new cutting.

56. Shipton 2000, 97 (tables 1.4 and 1.6).

to invest in one high-risk and one low-risk mine, balancing his risk through putting most of his money into a sure return, while at the same time also risking a small portion in exploring a mine with less certainty of return, but greater potential rewards.

Nevertheless, although many must have tried to balance or minimize their risk in their mining operations, the primary motivation to invest in the silver mining industry must have been profit, first and foremost. Since there is no indication that silver mining per se brought honor and respectability, it must be concluded that monetary return was the primary motivation for entering this field. Moreover, for a time during the fourth century at least it seems that mining properties were exempt from liturgies in Athens, which would have provided even more extraordinary opportunities for individual estate growth.[57] The wealth made from mining could bring social status, but devoting oneself to mining was probably not an end in itself. A single property in the mining region would have been perceived as being able to yield much greater profits than renting out a house or agricultural land, as suggested by the actions of Arizelos (see chapter 2). Demostratus, whose family owned one such smelting oven in the Laureion region, exemplifies how specializing in one specific stage in the silver production process could raise a family out of obscurity into the liturgical class.[58] If a single smelting oven could enrich a family to the point where they could afford to perform liturgies, it would also be able to supplement an elite citizen's wealth handsomely as well. Indeed, as the low number of ore-processing facilities relative to mines and mine lessees demonstrates, each ore washery and smelting furnace would have served a large number of mines, and so would have been able to guarantee a relatively steady supply of customers for their services, amounting to a reliable stream of profits.

Concerning the actual ore-processing operations, Paul Christesen has identified profit-maximizing techniques in the smelting residue of silver ore of the Laureion region. He begins with Conophagos' detailed chemical analysis of the lead-silver content of the Laureion ore and the costs associated with removing the silver, in which melting uncrushed ore would only yield 9 drachmas per ton, whereas the same ton of precrushed ore would bring 32 drachmas.[59] Thus the efficiency of ore washeries, in which ore was crushed down to grains the size of one millimeter, was a sign that Athenian miners had succeeded in maximizing the profit which they could yield from their ore. Moreover, the high lead content of the slag from the Laureion region is a sign that cupellation

57. Dem. 42.18.
58. Davies 1971, 139 (#3623).
59. Christesen 2003, 44–45, citing Conophagos 1980.

furnaces were being operated with the least amount of fuel possible, and in the firewood-bare southern regions of Attica, saving money on fuel would have resulted in greater profits than burning the extra fuel needed to squeeze every last drop of silver out of the ore. Thoroughly crushing the ore before smelting would have dramatically reduced the quantity of costly fuel needed to run the fires, so much so that the savings would have more than covered the costs for maintaining such installations and the slaves who operated them. Therefore, innovations in the techniques of ore processing and cupellation resulted in the maximization of return from the silver ore.[60]

Furthermore, although many individuals tempered their quest for profit with a concern for risk, mining also attracted some of the most reckless and opportunistic individuals in all of Greek history. The aforementioned Epikrates who was decried by Lycurgus is probably to be identified with the Epikrates of Pallene, who was charged with boring his own mine beyond its legal confines and may have amassed 300 talents in three years from this mine alone.[61] A certain Euthykrates seems to have made much of his 60 talents from illegal prospecting in an unregistered mine.[62] The speaker of Demosthenes 42, *Against Phaenippus*, was another miner who profited a great deal from an unregistered mine and was heavily fined as a result—for huge losses.[63] He says that he accumulated a huge fortune in mining, and apparently raised himself into the liturgical class through long-term specialization in

60. Innovations to increase efficiency and profits are unmistakable in the archaeological evidence of ore washeries from Laureion. From earlier examples in the early fifth century BCE that may have consisted only of a slanted stone floor (Mussche 1998, 51; see also preliminary reports by Spitaels 1978, and Mussche 1990), to the most common fourth-century rectangular model, to the round, helicoidal ore washery found at Dimoulaki, innovation abounded in ore washery design. The familiar rectangular model was designed not only to sort lead-heavy from lighter stone quickly and continuously, but even to recycle water in the water-starved region of southern Attica. As Mussche 1994, 214, states, after the highest-quality ores were mined in the Late Helladic period at Thorikos, trial and error was central to the innovation process of ore concentration; mining only became profitable again after the concentration (ore-crushing) process was discovered.

61. Hypereides, *Euxenippus* 4.35. The fragmentary nature of this passage makes it impossible to determine if Epikrates made the three hundred talents or if the "richest men" who had a stake in the mine made the 300 talents from it: φήναντος γὰρ Λυσάνδρου τὸ Ἐπικράτους μέταλλον τοῦ Παλληνέως ἐντὸς τῶν μέτρων τετμημένον, ὃ ἠργάζετο μὲν ἤ[δ]η τρία ἔτη, μετεῖχον δ᾽ αὐτοῦ οἱ πλουσ[ιώ]τατοι σχεδόν τι τῶν ἐν τῇ πόλει, ὁ δὲ Λ[ύσα]νδρος ὑπισχνεῖτ[ο τρι]ακόσια τάλαντα εἰσ[πράξει]ν τῇ πόλει τ[οσαῦτα] γὰρ εἰληφέναι α[ὐτοὺς ἐ]κ τοῦ μετάλλου. The α[ὐτοὺς that the editors have reconstructed at the end of this passage, referring to the antecedent οἱ πλουσ[ιώ]τατοι could also be read as α[ὐτὸν, meaning that Epikrates was the man who had actually made the 300 talents from the mine. Therefore, it is possible that the 300 talent sum indicated by Lysander would have been the penalty for Epikrates alone and that he actually made these 300 talents, since Epikrates was the only one named as being indicted. The entire sum itself may also be a fabrication, but there are no alternative figures to work with.

62. Hypereides 4.34; Davies 1971, 192.

63. Dem. 42.3. Other individuals who are known to have engaged in illegal mining include Nausicles in Hypereides 4.34, and Davies 1971, inv. # 10552 and 14384.

extremely high-risk mining activities.[64] Others are also said to have made their money from unregistered mines.[65]

These illegal miners, with the massive fortunes they are accused of making, are probably some of the best examples of profit-maximizing individuals, in that they decided to disregard social sanction and legal prohibitions in order to extract as much money for themselves as possible. The hazards of being caught in illegal mining were enormous.[66] Those who were willing to go to such lengths, including jeopardizing their citizenship, to secure wealth, clearly possessed a mentality that was profit-seeking first and foremost. Though it was risky, these individuals clearly believed that concentrating in mining would maximize their wealth, which they valued above their reputations and the collective interests of the larger citizen body.

These individuals are, to be certain, extreme examples, but their actions reveal unequivocally that the desire to maximize wealth does characterize the behavior of some ancient Athenians. The actions of those who broke the law are often the best preserved behavior in the sources, but this is not to say that their drive for profit was exceptional. Rather, they provide a window into the intentions of law-abiding citizens who invested in the mines as well, who were certainly far more common. Others involved in silver mining were probably also trying to make as much money as they could; these law-breaking individuals, then, represent the most extreme manifestation of a broader behavioral pattern, one end of a spectrum of profit-maximizing silver miners, most of whom acted legally. Indeed, as I will argue in the next chapter on maritime traders, it is often in the deals gone wrong that the best evidence for ancient Greek moneymaking strategies has been preserved, and although most Athenians would not break the law and risk their citizenship to strike it rich, the actions of those who were willing to do so illustrate the aims of Athenian miners overall: to accumulate as much wealth as possible.

To conclude, it seems that Kallias, his son Hipponikos, Nicias, and many of the other miners who made tremendous fortunes from the silver at Laureion were likely seeking to maximize their profit and wealth in the long term. Though the details about the exact methods with which they actually ran their operations will never be known, the aggregate evidence of high risk takers who concentrated all their wealth into the silver mines fits the criteria for *homines oeconomici* who recognize that a specific field is more profitable than others

64. See a discussion of this man in Osborne 2002, 123.

65. Hypereides 4.34.

66. See, e.g., the fines imposed on the speaker of Demosthenes, *Against Phaenippus*, and the prosecutions for illegal miners in Hypereides, *In Defense of Euxenippus*.

and put all their efforts and money into it to maximize their return. Moreover, even those who had an eye to risk management still seem to have been trying to maximize the gains they could achieve from their decision to enter this highly lucrative field.

Because many of these individuals stuck with mining for their entire lives, they were concerned with long-term growth rather than just striking it rich and investing in land and retiring comfortably. Indeed, Nicias and Kallias at least were so devoted to specializing in the mines that the Spartan occupation of Deceleia apparently wiped out the vast majority of their fortunes. They did not decide to buy land and live in ease once they made a sufficient amount of money, but even seem to have been deliberately expanding their mining operations on a continual basis until their fortunes collapsed. They kept their eggs in one basket and watched that basket, which allowed them to capitalize on the extraordinary profits from the silver industry throughout their lives, an approach aimed at maximizing their wealth, but which ultimately also left it vulnerable to decimation.

Lysias' Father Kephalos: Manufacturing, Wartime Profiteering, and an Economy of Scale?

The economic choices of the Syracusan Kephalos, father of the orator Lysias, provide important evidence for strategies to maximize wealth on a long-term basis in the field of manufacturing.[67] In Aristophanes' *Peace*, the various characters demonstrate a clear awareness of the strong contrast between the economic opportunities available during peace and wartime,[68] and Kephalos seems to have understood the extraordinary possibilities for profit amid the military conflicts of his age. He moved to Athens and founded a massive shield factory during the fifty-year period of Athenian imperialism, the *Pentêkontaetia*, and therefore made the decision to mass-produce a critical product when its demand was at its peak for the largest market in the Greek world.

Kephalos was persuaded to move to Athens by Pericles as his *xenos*, guest-friend, but he may have also been motivated by the unusually promising chance to maximize his profits and wealth by capitalizing on the high demand for shields during the zenith of the Athenian Empire, when he could expect to do a lot of uninterrupted business. He was already rich when he left Syracuse,[69] and

67. Davies 1971, 587–90.
68. See the discussion by Harris and Lewis 2016, 1–2.
69. [Plutarch], *Vitae Decem Oratorum* 835c.

remained in Athens for thirty years.[70] He eventually integrated into the highest segments of Athenian society,[71] even becoming a paradigm for the rich man in Plato's *Republic*,[72] in which he describes himself as being a "moneymaker" (χρηματιστής) of moderate success; not living up to his grandfather's achievements, who multiplied his fortune "many times over" (πολλάκις), but surpassing his father who decreased his patrimony. Kephalos says that he increased his own inheritance, and was content with leaving it a little greater for his sons (330b). His modesty as a *chrêmatistês*, however, may be a Platonic invention, since his purpose in the dialogue is to articulate how money is seen as being useful to a wealthy old man on the verge of death (330d–331b). Since Plato's agenda in this work includes an attack on immoderate wealth maximization, it can perhaps be assumed that he is exaggerating Kephalos' humility about his moneymaking abilities. Indeed, the family's fortune is attested as reaching 70 talents before 404/3, making Lysias the richest metic, resident foreigner, in Athens.[73]

Whether he left Syracuse for the purpose of seizing this economic opportunity, or was forced out as an exile,[74] Kephalos made the choice to build up a shield factory in Athens which eventually employed up to 120 slave craftspeople.[75] The decision to produce shields, a much-needed product at a time of unprecedented demand within the largest market in Greece, resulted in steady and sizable returns.[76] Therefore, whatever his reasons for initially coming to Athens, the only reasonable explanation for why Kephalos set up such a huge shield factory was that he was trying to secure maximum profits over the course of his career. This factory lasted another thirty years until his death, whereupon he handed it over to his sons.

Lysias and his brother still maintained the shield workshop after their father's death, so both Kephalos and his sons were interested in the continued operation and growth of this factory. Staying in the family business was a good strategy for his sons to pursue their own long-term economic success. Since Lysias and his brother were metics, they were barred from owning land at Athens, and therefore maintaining the already successful shield factory was probably the wisest decision they could make from a profit or wealth-maximizing

70. Lys. 12.4.
71. Dion. Hal., *Lysias* 1.
72. 328c–331d.
73. *P.Oxy.* 13, 1606, lines 30–155.
74. [Plutarch], *Vitae Decem Oratorum* 835c.
75. Lysias 12.19.
76. Davies 1971, 588, argues convincingly that Kephalos must have arrived in Athens no later than 451 BCE and died about 421.

perspective. Though they could have liquidated the property and reinvested it in other forms, the opportunity cost of doing so would have been the loss of this lucrative enterprise. Why should they risk their fortune by speculating in less certain ventures? Because they kept such a large factory intact, it had probably achieved the optimal size and operational efficiency needed to ensure continuous profitability. Choosing to stick with the factory also would have provided them with financial stability. Because brothers in ancient Greece often chose not to share an inherited family business, Kephalos' sons certainly would have discussed how best to mobilize their wealth after their father's death and in light of the limited opportunities available to them as metics, keeping this shield factory operating at maximum capacity would have probably been the most lucrative option they could choose.

It is unclear how many of the brothers' 120 total slaves confiscated by the Thirty Tyrants were actually employed in the factory (Lys. 12.19), but since no other major property is mentioned in the speech, it seems certain that the vast majority of the slaves were involved in the shield factory. Lysias states that the Thirty Tyrants went to the factory to make a list of the slaves (12.8), and does not mention slaves being listed at any other location. Therefore, it appears that the factory was where most of his slaves were located—indeed these shield manufacturers were so numerous that they needed to be enumerated on paper. Even if each slave was worth as much as Demosthenes' father's most expensive slaves, 6 *minae* apiece (Dem. 27.9), then the maximum value of the slaves in Kephalos' factory would have amounted to 12 talents (72,000 drachmas), which is far below the total of 70 talents attested in *P.Oxy.* 13, 1606. Therefore, there may have been other property in the family aside from the shield factory, and this additional wealth is likely what allowed Lysias to aid the *polis* in the revolution of 403 by contributing money, shields, and the maintenance for three hundred men after his workshop was confiscated by the Thirty.[77]

But even if it did not make up all of Kephalos' property, the size of the workshop is far larger than any other attested from ancient Greece, so it cannot have been of insignificant value. Lysias' failure to mention any other items of comparable worth confiscated by the Thirty Tyrants strongly suggests that the shield factory was the only noteworthy conspicuous component of the family's wealth. Since he was still contributing shields even after this confiscation, he may have owned additional shield workshops elsewhere, perhaps at Syracuse, his home city, which like Athens was one of the most populous *poleis* in the Greek world, ruled over a large empire, and therefore also had extremely high

77. [Plutarch], *Vitae Decem Oratorum* 835–36.

demand. He may have simply also had another stockpile elsewhere. Whatever the case, and further speculation is fruitless, his shield production operations may have been even more extensive than what is mentioned in the sources. Therefore, shield manufacturing was almost certainly Kephalos' primary (and preferred) moneymaking activity.

Furthermore, Lysias' father may have even attempted to establish an economy of scale to capitalize on the advantages of increased production and market share. In the absence of other certain productive property, the five talents worth of cash confiscated by the Thirty may be an indication of how profitable the factory could be.[78] Such considerable liquidity suggests that the brothers were enjoying steady and sizable profits, which are in turn a sign that the factory was still being run successfully. With a workshop of this size, it is probable that some sort of specialization in workers' tasks was used to increase efficiency. Here it may be useful to turn to the most extensive discussion of division of labor in ancient Greece: the paradigmatic city shoe workshop, which Xenophon describes in the *Cyropedia*. As he illustrates, a workshop as small as four could implement an effective division of labor in order to expand productivity and improve quality:

> ἐν μὲν γὰρ ταῖς μικραῖς πόλεσιν οἱ αὐτοὶ ποιουσι κλίνην, θύραν, ἄροτρον, τράπεζαν, πολλάκις δ' ὁ αὐτὸς οὗτος καὶ οἰκοδομεῖ, καὶ ἀγαπᾷ ἢν καὶ οὕτως ἱκανοὺς αὐτὸν τρέφειν ἐργοδότας λαμβάνῃ· ἀδύνατον οὖν πολλὰ τεχνώμενον ἄνθρωπον πάντα καλῶς ποιεῖν. ἐν δὲ ταῖς μεγάλαις πόλεσι διὰ τὸ πολλοὺς ἑκάστου δεῖσθαι ἀρκεῖ καὶ μία ἑκάστῳ τέχνη εἰς τὸ τρέφεσθαι· πολλάκις δὲ οὐδ' ὅλη μία· ἀλλ' ὑποδήματα ποιεῖ ὁ μὲν ἀνδρεῖα, ὁ δὲ γυναικεῖα· ἔστι δὲ ἔνθα καὶ ὑποδήματα ὁ μὲν νευρορραφῶν μόνον τρέφεται, ὁ δὲ σχίζων, ὁ δὲ χιτῶνας μόνον συντέμνων, ὁ δέ γε τούτων οὐδὲν ποιῶν ἀλλὰ συντιθείς.
>
> For in small towns the same men make couches, doors, plows, and tables, and this same man also builds houses, and is happy if in this way he gets enough work to sustain himself. And so, it is impossible for the jack of all trades to do everything well. But in large cities, on the other hand, because many people demand each thing, one trade alone is sufficient for each man to live, and often not even a trade in its entirety. But one man makes men's shoes, and another, women's. And there are places where one makes a living just by stitching the threads of shoes, while

78. Lysias 12.19.

> another does only the cutting, another only trims the top coverings, and still another makes none of these parts but only fastens them together. And so, the man spending his time in the most specific work will also necessarily do this thing in the best manner.[79]

In this passage Xenophon provides a valuable glimpse into the highly developed specialization of labor that existed in some of the large cities in ancient Greece, and the increased quality and efficiency that could come from such a division of labor within a single workshop.[80] Although there are no details about the operations in Kephalos' shield factory, because Xenophon describes how a shoe workshop of only four employees could employ the effective labor specialization that is typical of operations in large cities, it is reasonable to suppose that a similar or even more extensive division of labor was implemented in Kephalos' much larger shield factory.

Although not approaching the large size of early Industrial Revolution woolen factories in the late eighteenth century, which employed up to 8,000 workers at a time,[81] Kephalos' factory was certainly substantial. Adam Smith's famous discussion of a late eighteenth-century pin factory at the beginning of his *Wealth of Nations* is an appropriate comparandum to examine. His observations on the undeniable advantages of task specialization in this pin factory show how productivity could be expanded with a division of labor even with a workforce as small as ten, increasing output almost exponentially.[82] Therefore, the principles of the division of labor within a fourth-century BCE shoe factory (chapter 2) that Xenophon depicts could have easily been applied to a factory the size of Kephalos'. With up to one hundred and twenty workers, the benefits of achieving a division of labor with the large number of laborers could have even reached those of an economy of scale. Indeed, as the largest factory known from the ancient Greek world, if any operation can be said to have approached the benefits of economy of scale, it would certainly be Kephalos'.

It is impossible to determine whether Kephalos or his sons achieved true maximization, but the size of the workshop certainly demonstrates a desire to grow and expand—the volume of the production can be deduced from the seven hundred shields that had been confiscated at the factory by the Thirty Tyrants (12.19). This is a considerable amount of capital to keep in storage, two and a third talents' worth at the price of shields attested from early third-

79. Xenophon, *Cyropedia* 8.2.5.
80. My overall reading of this passage agrees with that of Figueira 2012, 670–71.
81. Braudel 1982, 330.
82. *Wealth of Nations*, book 1.1.3.

century Teos.[83] The size of this stockpile is indicative of a strategy to overproduce on a large scale in anticipation of future sale, especially in case of a sudden military or political crisis, rather than just making shields to order. This stockpile of shields, along with the large number of slaves involved in their production, is consistent with a yet another strategy—that Kephalos or his sons had been pursuing a policy of continuous expansion, as was the case with Nicias' and Hipponikos' enormous workforces of slaves-for-hire. Unfortunately details are lacking, but it is likely that Lysias' father expanded his business over a long period of time in an attempt to maximize his profits by grabbing the largest share he could in the most important market for shields in the Greek world at the time of peak demand. Much of this is speculative, but nevertheless the evidence is all consistent with a well-executed strategy to maximize returns.

At the very least, it seems safe to conclude that Kephalos' shield factory is a good example of specializing in a specific field to secure long-term growth and profit, as well as the continued maintenance of a profitable business beyond a single generation. This was clearly an extensive operation that was the result of a sustained commitment to grow and control as much of the market as possible. The large stock of shields on hand points in the same direction. It would have been important to have a large enough supply so that if there were a sudden rush to buy shields because of a military or political crisis, the factory would have enough to weather the initial demand and give the slaves time to make more shields. Many Athenians would have already owned shields, so this number may have also been made available for sale to foreigners. To have 700 shields stockpiled and over 100 slaves ready to build more is indicative of a desire to be able to cash in at times of increased demand, and to maintain one's reputation as a reliable shield supplier in case the need suddenly arose.

Bankers: High-Risk Specialization and Attempts to Diversify

Euboulos of Bithynia was a fourth-century BCE banker who managed to make himself a tyrant over the cities of Assos and Aterneus, which he ruled first by himself, and then jointly with his slave and fellow banker Hermias.[84] It is not clear exactly how banking enabled these men to become tyrants, but it seems

83. *SEG*³ 958, line 31, quoted by Davies 1971, 435 (citing Pritchett and Pippin 1956, 307), preserves the price of 20 drachmas per shield, which is the best indication of shield prices at this time. Seven hundred shields at 20 drachmas amounts to 14,000 drachmas, or two and one-third talents.

84. For Hermias, see Strabo 13.1.57; and Didymos, *On Demosthenes* col. 4, ll. 66–69–col. 5, 1–10, citing Theopompos, *On Philip* book 6. For detailed, up-to-date commentary, see Harding 2006, 124–62.

that it provided the means for upward mobility by which both Euboulos and Hermias achieved their magnificent station.[85] Obviously these tyrants are extreme outliers, but those who specialized in banking certainly created some of the greatest fortunes known from ancient Greece.

Pasion the banker is perhaps the most famous Athenian businessman,[86] and can provide detailed evidence for moneymaking strategies in a well-documented establishment. Although it is unknown how much capital Pasion started with when he took over the bank from his own masters, by the time of his death it seems that he had amassed an impressive fortune, consisting of 50 talents of outstanding loans, probably at interest, and 20 talents of landed property.[87] However, of the fifty talents, eleven were actually borrowed by Pasion from the bank deposits against the security of his landed property and lent out at interest,[88] meaning that he had 39 talents of his own out on loan, and eleven taken from bank deposits.[89]

---

85. As argued by Fisher 2008, 123–24, who also rightly points out that the claims that Hermias was a non-Greek eunuch may have been nothing but character denigration. The fact that he was a philosopher whose niece Aristotle wed, and he also competed at the Panhellenic Games, suggests that he may have actually been Greek. Other scholars also believe that Hermias was Greek for other reasons, for which see Harding 2006, 126.

86. For this banker's career, see Cohen 1992; and Trevett 1992. A full chronological survey of Pasion's bank and evidence for its operations during the life of his son Apollodorus can be found at Isager and Hansen 1975, 177–91 and 225–26. There is no evidence for the bank's functioning after the death of Apollodorus.

87. Dem. 36.5.

88. Dem. 36.6. The ἔγγειος οὐσία in 36.5 seems to be the γῆ and συνοικίαι in 36.6 against which Pasion borrowed the eleven talents from the bank. Davies 1971, 431, also agrees that this is what his ἔγγειος οὐσία consisted of, pointing out that Pasion is known to have owned land in at least three demes (Dem. 50.8). Cohen 1992, 130–34, argues that the ἔγγειος οὐσία refers to loans at landed interest rates in contrast with *nautika*. However, there is no evidence for these landed loans, and the existence of multiple *synoikiai* (36.6), along with landed property in at least three demes, seems to be what the ἔγγειος οὐσία is referring to. Moreover, that the ἔγγειος οὐσία excludes the ἀργύριον out on loan is even further reinforced by the πρὸς ταύτηι in the δέ clause, which refers to the feminine antecedent οὐσία: "In addition to this landed property, there was also his own money lent out, more than fifty talents." As Harpokration says in his definition of φανερὰ οὐσία, ἔγγειος οὐσία refers to visible property in contrast with ἀφανὴς οὐσία, which consists of cash and nonlanded assets. Houses and land are summed up as φανερὰ οὐσία in Isaeus 8.35, after which loans are listed separately. Finally, the contrast between ἔγγειος οὐσία on the one hand and money on the other is very marked in Dem. 36.4–6; the former is included in a μέν clause, and the latter in a δέ clause. The examples in which the adjective ἔγγειος is used to refer to loans at landed interest are when it modifies a present or understood τόκος, such as at Dem. 33.3, 34.23; Lysias 32.15. The examples in which it stands by itself modifying οὐσία and clearly refers to landed property include: Dem. 30.30, 35.12; Xenophon *Symposium* 4.31; Plato *Republic* 491d, 546a.

89. Dem. 36.5: ἀργύριον δὲ πρὸς ταύτῃ δεδανεισμένον ἴδιον πλέον ἢ πεντήκοντα τάλαντα. ἐν οὖν τοῖς πεντήκοντα ταλάντοις τούτοις ἀπὸ τῶν παρακαταθηκῶν τῶν τῆς τραπέζης ἕνδεκα τάλαντ' ἐνεργὰ ἦν. It is not precisely clear what distinction was made between Pasion's personal loans and the deposits and loans that belonged to the bank. Apollodorus was only able to collect half of his father's outstanding loans twenty years after his death (see my discussion below in this section), but the bank was able to keep operating nonetheless. Because Pasion was listed as owing eleven talents to the bank deposits (Dem. 45.29), there seems to have been some distinction made

Since the rates of interest at which Pasion lent out his money are unknown, it is possible to make only general observations regarding his moneymaking strategies. Nevertheless, the success of his operations can be seen in the fact that his own fame far eclipsed that of his masters and predecessors, and it should probably be assumed that he increased the total wealth of the bank significantly through his own efforts. He is known to have kept very detailed books,[90] and controlled the income and expenditures of the bank with great precision. For a penniless slave to amass such a large personal fortune, he must have made enormous profits from the bank and his own moneylending activities, most likely acting in some sense to maximize his profits in the long term over the course of his life. It would be odd indeed if he ran his business so meticulously and earned so much money without at least *intending* to maximize his wealth as well.

He then apparently changed his overall moneymaking approach and invested a huge proportion of his profits into landed property, twenty talents' worth, a less risky form than the banking and loans in which he had previously specialized. Some of his known landed, *engeios* wealth (ἔγγειος οὐσία) consisted of *synoikiai*, apartment buildings or multiple residences,[91] one of which was worth 100 *minae*,[92] and another around 2,600 drachmas since it was mortgaged for 1,300 by his son Apollodorus.[93] So his *synoikiai* were probably valued at least 2 talents and possibly more.[94] He also owned at least two farms, one of which Apollodorus mortgaged for 3,000 drachmas,[95] making its worth around a talent. In addition, he may have owned Apollodorus' farm which was devoted to growing figs, olives, vines, and roses, all possibly grown for the market.[96] If it was he and not Apollodorus who purchased these properties, which is consistent with the twenty talents of landed property at his death, the land and real estate he acquired was still productive while also functioning to reduce the overall risk of his estate.

between his personal property and the bank deposits. On the other hand, Apollodorus tries to collect money that Timotheus borrowed "from the bank" (Dem. 49.4), and so he was also apparently responsible for collecting bank debts as well. It is possible that Apollodorus was misrepresenting or distorting the details in his presentation to the jury, but this is entirely uncertain. This is a difficult problem that requires in-depth investigation.

90. Dem. 49.5, 52.3–6.

91. Dem. 36.6.

92. Dem. 45.28. This was left to his wife in his will as part of her very substantial dowry, which also included two talents in loans.

93. Dem. 53.13.

94. Perhaps also the *synoikia* inherited by Apollodorus in Dem. 36.33–35.

95. Dem. 50.13. See Foxhall's observation (2007, 114) that Apollodorus had olives and figs planted on this farm, though whether cash-generating or not is uncertain.

96. Dem. 53.15–16.

Finally, he owned a substantial shield factory, whose value was around 6 talents,[97] and which yielded a full talent per year in profits.[98] This must have been part of the 20 talents listed as *engeios* by Demosthenes, since it surely cannot be part of the 50 talents in loans. The fact that the shield factory brought in a full talent of profit a year shows that it was a very successful enterprise (16 percent annual return), and also suggests that Pasion may have been profit-maximizing its operation, though the specific details are not preserved. Much of this "landed" property, therefore, at least 8 talents between the shield factory and known *synoikiai* alone, was generating significant returns and not just risk-buffering. Nevertheless, the lower risk Pasion achieved by diversifying into these fields is undeniable—though Demosthenes' claim that the shield workshop was free of risk is an exaggeration, he is right that it was certainly less risky than the bank.[99]

We can reconstruct Pasion's decision-making process with a high degree of confidence since he must have come into possession of his land after he became a citizen and had made his banking fortune.[100] Indeed, it is possible to determine the order in which he chose to acquire his various properties, as he seems to have used his banking and lending profits to purchase his shield factory. The shields from this factory then in turn helped him earn his citizenship, which was awarded to him by the *dêmos* largely because of the gift of 1,000 shields that he gave to the state, along with the five trierarchies which he served at his own expense.[101] Based on the prices of shields from Teos in the early third century BCE, 20 drachmas, these shields would have been worth about 3 talents in total,[102] a significant donative to the *polis*. It is not known if Pasion was intentionally trying to gain his citizenship through his benefactions, but nevertheless he seems to have begun purchasing landed property as soon as he was able.

97. Davies 1971, 433–34, estimates the total value at six talents by assuming comparable rates of return to Demosthenes' father's sword factory, and calculates the number of slaves, 60–70, who would have been worth approximately six talents if worth the same as Demosthenes' father's skilled slave workmen. Such estimates are, of course, of limited reliability, but are useful to provide rough, "ballpark" figures nonetheless.

98. Dem. 36.11.

99. Dem. 36.11.

100. On the other hand, it may be that some of these landed properties were acquired by him as a result of defaults on loans, but in any case he chose to hold onto them once they became his. It certainly seems that he was trying to diversify his property with the acquisition of these landed properties, and whether he was looking for security to offset some of his more risky moneylending and banking operations, or just looking to expand into other profitable fields is unknown. The alternative is that perhaps the market for moneylending had reached such a point of saturation that he needed to expand into other fields to avoid the costs of information gathering which would be required to continue to profit from moneylending. He may have reached a point of diminishing marginal returns from moneylending also, though this is just speculation. For an awareness of diminishing marginal returns in ancient Greece, see the discussion in chapter 1.

101. See Dem. 45.85, 59.2.

102. Davies 1971, 435.

Whatever the case, Pasion must have anticipated that there would be tangible benefits to making the gift of 1,000 shields to the *dêmos*. His precise motivation for doing so is unknown, as are the market conditions for the sale of shields at that time, but what can be concluded is that he invested the stockpile of shields he had at his disposal into political capital, and it ended up repaying him in the gift of citizenship and in the new opportunities for investment in land that his inclusion in the *dêmos* brought. This was definitely a productive use of property in the sense that it provided other types of returns than just monetary profit. He did not allow his wealth to lie dormant at a time when it could be invested productively,[103] just as when the general Timotheus approached him time and again to ask for loans. Demosthenes even explicitly says that Pasion preferred to help Timotheus with the expectation that his loan would be repaid both in money and in social and political favors, as well as *charis*, rather than to hold onto an idle surplus of money.[104] Therefore, the opportunity cost of leaving money unproductive was an important consideration in Pasion's investments in political and social capital.

Thus, Pasion seems to have decided to invest in huge amounts of landed property after attaining his citizenship.[105] This choice of turning banking capital into land can certainly be seen as a risk-mitigating measure, intentionally diversifying his wealth in secure investments that were more stable than banking. However, it is also true that his new acquisitions were providing steady income as well.[106] The *synoikiai* and the shield factory were very profitable, and brought in a great deal of dependable revenue on a regular basis; and his cash-generating landed properties supplemented and supported the bank,[107] which remained his primary moneymaking activity of choice. He also may have invested in land because he wanted to guarantee the transmission of his property to his heirs, which was much more difficult to ensure with *aphanês*, invisible, wealth.

Then, while keeping most of his money in the bank and moneylending, he then decided to purchase more stable landed properties, and eventually handed the business over to his own slave and protégé, Phormion, renting it to him for an annual fee so that he could retire and enjoy his newfound citizenship and

103. Pasion's desire to constantly keep his money engaged in productive activities is described by Demosthenes as "philergia," love of working (36.5).

104. Dem. 49.3.

105. It may be that much of this land was seized as security for defaulting loans, as Pasion was listed as owing eleven talents to the bank because Phormion did not have his citizenship to allow him to seize land from a citizen.

106. Shipton 1997, 409–10, also comes to this conclusion.

107. Shipton 1997.

landed property, having risen from a slave to be one of the richest men in Athens. This fortune had been built through the systematic practice of moneylending, which he pursued from the profits he made from the bank for the years up to his citizenship. After he became a citizen, he still concentrated most of his fortune in loans, but he was also able to reinvest many of his gains into more secure land and real estate, which he managed to pass on to his sons, along with their citizenship. Thus, via long-term profit maximizing with the bank, he was able to gain his citizenship and own land, and eventually entrust his business operations to Phormion as a manager. The overall result of his moneymaking successes brought wealth, social standing, and later leisure, respite from his labors, and *kleos* (fame and glory). Pasion went from an extremely high-risk estate during the height of his career to a less precarious balance of properties at the end, the opposite trend seen in the diversified estate owners explored in my last chapter. Overall, he succeeded in maximizing his wealth and utility in the process.

Phormion is less well known than his master, but he owned and operated his own bank after returning Pasion's to his son, Apollodorus, which he had been maintaining after his master's death.[108] He continued to work in the field that had been so profitable for his master, and his own successes are well attested.[109] Unfortunately, few other details survive from the rest of his own economic activity, but his assiduous entrepreneurial spirit can be seen in the fact that he came to own trading ships (πλοῖα), which were detained at one time by the Byzantines.[110] He remained active in both banking and commerce after he was operating on his own, but took a different route from that taken by his master Pasion, becoming directly involved in maritime trade. Like Pasion he expanded his holdings beyond the bank and moneylending to include different types of property, perhaps to diversify to reduce risk.[111] However, merchant ships themselves were not safe investments, since they were always subject to the weather and liable to sink, so his diversification consisted of acquiring additional risky, highly profitable investments. Moreover, since he was likely engaged in maritime lending already, it could be that Phormion was trying to gain control over an even larger share of the trading market by purchasing these ships, and was able to capitalize on the business contacts that he had

108. Dem. 45.64–66; see Davies 1971, 435.

109. Dem. 45.54 and 72.

110. Dem. 45.64.

111. It seems that Phormion (listed as Phormion from Piraeus in *IG* 1^2 1672 [Clinton 2005, 177], lines 62, 212, and 227) also supplied wood to the temple at Eleusis in 329/8, for which see Clinton 2005, 194.

inherited from Pasion in addition to those he had made himself. Perhaps like Nicias' army of slaves, these ships allowed him to expand into another area within a sphere of economic activity already well known to him, one in which he could have made considerable profits given the extensive contacts he had already accumulated.[112]

This expansion into shipping is another example of diversification into related or "by-product" fields, as discussed above in chapter 2. Phormion's knowledge of the field would have made this an informed decision, one in which he could assess its potential profitability from an educated standpoint. From this perspective, there may be something of path dependence in determining the choice he made. Perhaps he ran into diminishing returns to concentrating his money in moneylending and banking, or had reached the limits of his share in this market, and so decided to continue the growth of his money in a promising new direction, a closely related field with which he already was familiar. In any case, if he was diversifying to secure his fortune, he did so with high-risk, high-return investments, which matches the pattern seen above in chapter 2 of diversification by acquiring highly productive properties. Therefore, the reduction of risk in this choice of investment would have lain in the act of diversification itself and not in acquiring assets that were seen as safe per se.

Nor were Pasion and Phormion the only bankers to expand their holdings beyond banking. Blepaios was another rich[113] citizen[114] banker[115] who bought the contract for the *poloi* (poles) and *empolia* (plugs) for the columns of the *Telesterion* at Eleusis.[116] Also, he gave a 20 *minae* productive loan for the purchase of mining concessions (ὠνήν τινα μετάλλων).[117] Thus, he seems to have been engaged in risky loans in banking and in the mines, along with lower-risk but still profitable contracts for temple building. The evidence from the leases of the lands of Apollo at Delos indicates that many individuals in banking tried to diversify their holdings as well, where at least three individuals attested as bankers supplemented their income with other moneymaking

112. Many of the known maritime traders from ancient Greece also engaged in moneylending, for which see my discussion in the next chapter.

113. Alexis in Athenaeus 6.241c, says Blepaios is a rich man, "ploutos."

114. As Cohen 1992, 70n44, states, Blepaios is known to have attended the assembly (Dem. 21.215), and therefore must have been an Athenian citizen.

115. Dem. 21.215; Kirchner 1901, 2876; Bogaert 1968, 81–82.

116. *IG* 2^2 1675, line 32. See Clinton 2008, 149.

117. Dem. 40.52.

enterprise.[118] Diactorides[119] was a banker who also varied his cash-generating activities, having leased temple land and a foundry, both of which were probably profit-oriented investments. Antigonos, son of Charistios, appears to have been a banker,[120] and was one of the best-attested individuals in the temple accounts, also inscribed as a lessee of the landed estate Sosimacheia, as well as a harbor tax collector who became indebted to the temple treasury.[121] He seems to have been focused upon cash-generating opportunities to the point that he ended up overextending himself as a result of the arrears due from the taxes. These actions suggest that he was trying to reap gains from as many different sources as he could, and took such great risks with his money that he pushed himself beyond his means. The competitiveness of the bidding for such leases at Delos, by individuals trying to profit from these opportunities, lends support to the impression that Antigonos was jumping on these investment possibilities as they arose to increase his wealth in whatever way possible.

The overall weight of this evidence indicates that bankers often diversified their holdings by engaging in other types of profitable, cash-producing enterprise in addition to banking. Many of these activities were less risky than banking, but they were also clearly chosen to try to make profit, first and foremost. As with diversified estate owners, the pattern is one of timely acquisition of lucrative opportunities as they became available; the desire to expand into other profitable fields is prominent, and though risk buffering may be the primary motivation for diversification, risk aversion is not evident. Phormion's purchase of merchant ships and Antigonos' tax farming are both examples of additional risky investments bankers made for the purpose of earning cash alongside the bank. The returns from ship owning and tax farming could be substantial, and Antigonos' status as a debtor implies that he also overextended himself and ended up being listed as owing money to the temple.

Other bankers show a similar desire to expand into alternative cash-generating enterprises, but were unable to escape the ruin that resulted from

118. In addition to the two discussed above, Pistes (Kent 1948, #192), who was also a banker, also was the lessee of the Sacred Lake.

119. Kent 1948, #74.

120. Kent 1948, #23; *Inscr. Delos* 455 fr. B line 18, records a contract deposited with this man, suggesting he may have been a banker: see Cohen 1992, 122–23, for *para* used for deposits with bankers.

121. *Inscr. Delos* 442 A 155, D 20.

their initial high-risk specialization.[122] Aristolochos,[123] for example, who had been a successful banker, was also a citizen who owned an unknown amount of land[124] and purchased Euktemon's bathhouse for half a talent in c. 363 BCE.[125] Though perhaps profit-oriented, these assets may represent diversification in order to invest banking revenues into safer form. Aristolochos acquired his land at a time when he already owed money to people, so he was using bank deposits to purchase other investments, land in this case.[126] He therefore seems to have converted banking profits into agriculture and other lower-risk property in an attempt to diversify.

Risk-averse, however, Aristolochos was not. He was apparently so reckless in his economic activity that his bank eventually went under, and he lost all his own property around 349 BCE.[127] He was prosperous initially,[128] but overextended his assets and went bankrupt. Even his land purchases were made on borrowed money, a tenuous base that was ultimately unable to sustain his moneymaking ambitions. He had been a member of the liturgical class, serving several trierarchies jointly with a certain Antidoros of Phaleron, who may have been his business partner in the bank.[129] If this is the case, then Antidoros anticipated or somehow insulated himself from his partner's collapse, as he himself continued to serve as trierarch after Aristolochos lost his fortune. Aristolochos was so devastated by his involvement in high-risk banking that his son was still beset by creditors' lawsuits after his death.

Heracleides was another banker who went bankrupt and was forced to go

122. Hipponikos, son of Kallias II, whom I discussed above in my section on mining, is perhaps described as having owned a bank at Andocides 1.130–31: Ἱππόνικος δὲ ἦν πλουσιώτατος τῶν Ἑλλήνων, τότε μέντοι πάντες ἴστε ὅτι παρὰ τοῖς παιδαρίοις τοῖς μικροτάτοις καὶ τοῖς γυναίοις κληδὼν ἐν ἁπάσῃ τῇ πόλει κατεῖχεν, ὅτι Ἱππόνικος ἐν τῇ οἰκίᾳ ἀλιτήριον τρέφει, ὃς αὐτοῦ τὴν τράπεζαν ἀνατρέπει. If Hipponikos was the wealthiest individual in all of Greece and owned a bank, then this means that he had entered into other moneymaking fields that yielded big profits, and was an even more substantial moneymaker and profit maximizer than argued above in the discussion of Hipponikos and his father Kallias at the beginning of the section on mining.

123. See Davies 1971, 60–61; Bogaert 1968, 72–73.

124. An *agros* is mentioned in Dem. 36.50. The fact that he was a citizen demonstrates that he did not enter banking because he was legally restricted from making other types of investment, but rather because he made the choice to do so, and probably because it was profitable.

125. Isaeus 6.33.

126. ὁρᾷς τὸν Ἀριστόλοκον . . . ποτ᾽ εἶχεν ἀργόν, εἶτά γε νῦν πολλοῖς γὰρ ἐκεῖνος ὀφείλων αὐτὸν ἐκτήσατο (Dem. 36.50). "You see Aristolochos . . . once he owned land, but now many people own it; for he was in debt to many when he acquired it."

127. Dem. 36.50–51, 45.64.

128. Dem. 45.63.

129. See Davies 1971, 35–36 and 60–61. For partners in business sharing liturgies, see Harpocration on *koinonikon*: τάχα δὲ καὶ περὶ τῶν ἑκούσιον κοινωνίαν συνθεμένων ἐμπορίας ἤ τινος ἄλλου, ὧν ἕκαστος οὐκ εἶχε τὸ ὅλον τίμημα τῆς κοινῆς οὐσίας.

into hiding.[130] Likewise, Timodemos and Sosinomos risked their property in banking, and lost it all to creditors when their banks failed.[131] The reason for this is perhaps preserved in a detail about Sosinomos' business practices in Lysias' fragmentary speech *Against Aeschines*. Here, the untrustworthy Aeschines was able to secure a loan from Sosinomos at the crushing rate of 36 percent interest. This was the same Aeschines to whom Lysias says it was "less safe to loan than to sail to the Adriatic." Thus, the increasing recklessness of lending eventually ruined Sosinomos, being engaged as he was in extremely high-risk and high-yield loans to persons of questionable credit. Turning to less reliable borrowers thus seems to have played a major role in the failure of Sosinomos, who like other bankers in ancient Greece were destroyed because of their willingness to lend to progressively riskier customers in an attempt to capitalize on the huge returns available in moneylending.

Banking was a field that attracted individuals eager to maximize their profit and wealth in the long run. While some, such as Pasion, Phormion, Euboulos, and Hermias were very successful, others were less fortunate, and were ruined by their hopes of cashing in on the potential profits to be made in banking and moneylending. Bank failures seem to have been fairly common in ancient Greece, as there are a number of examples preserved in the extant source material. Although Bogaert believed that the numerous bank failures can be blamed on a widespread banking crisis that occurred in fourth-century Athens, Cohen and Shipton disagree.[132] The evidence indicates that these failures were not the result of a single banking crisis, but rather occurred because the field was congenitally fragile by nature. Even banks in the modern world are extremely precarious and prone to collapse. These businessmen were apparently willing to take greater and greater risks, possibly in a market that was dominated by individuals like Pasion, forcing others to advance further and further into the less reliable pool of potential borrowers passed over by more careful bankers. Those engaged in such reckless and high-risk behavior certainly reveal an intent to make as much profit as they could. And those bankers who stayed in the business their entire lives, maintaining their commitment to such lucrative activity as long as possible, made the estate management and business choices they did to maximize their wealth over the course of their moneymaking careers. In conclusion, banking provides some of the clearest evidence for both profit-maximizing behavior in the short run and longer-term wealth maximization.

---

130. Dem. 33.9.

131. Dem. 36.50–51: καὶ τὸν Σωσίνομον καὶ τὸν Τιμόδημον καὶ τοὺς ἄλλους τραπεζίτας, οἵ, ἐπειδὴ διαλύειν ἐδέησεν οἷς ὤφειλον, ἐξέστησαν ἅπαντες τῶν ὄντων, "And Sosinomos and Timodemos and the other bankers, who lost all their possessions when it was necessary to pay back those to whom they owed money." For Timodemos, see Davies 1971, 505.

132. Bogaert 1968, 523; Cohen 1992, 220; Shipton 1997, 409–10.

Diodotus: Specialization in High-Risk, High-Profit Moneylending

As discussed in chapter 1, Aristotle says in his treatment of *chrêmatistikê* in book 1 of the *Politics* that using money to make more money enabled people to increase their profits without limit, to an extent that was contrary to nature. Indeed, moneylending was one of the most lucrative activities in Athens, and it should come as no surprise that some of the best evidence for long-term gain and wealth maximization within a specialized estate can be found in the activities of the merchant who turned to systematic maritime lending: Diodotus from Lysias' speech, *Against Diogeiton*.

Brothers Diodotus and Diogeiton divided up their father's invisible wealth (*aphanês ousia*) and shared the real estate (*phanera ousia*) between them, and Diogeiton asked Diodotus to marry his daughter after the latter had made a fortune in trade (32.4). When Diodotus was called up for military service, he wanted his wife-niece and children to be taken care of in case of his death, so he gave his brother his will along with a deposit (*parakatathêkê*) of 5 talents of silver (32.5), and left his wife 2,000 drachmas and 130 Cyzicene staters (32.6). He also revealed to his brother his fortune of 7 talents and 4,000 drachmas in maritime loans, along with 2,000 drachmas owed to him in the Chersonese (32.6), which apparently yielded interest in the form of grain (32.15, for which see Carey 1989, 217). He also had at least 100 *minae* lent at landed interest (ἐγγείῳ ἐπὶ τόκῳ) and perhaps 2,000 more drachmas in cash or loans (32.15). There was also furniture of great value, but the precise amount is never stated.

It is not clear exactly how much landed property was owned by Diogeiton and Diodotus, but they may have had a house at Collytus, north of the Acropolis (14), one in the Piraeus (8) in which they resided together, and perhaps one more in the city (8). Besides this, there is no evidence at all as to how much landed property was inherited from their father and shared. It was probably not noteworthy, however, since the speaker does not mention anything about its worth explicitly in the extant portions of the speech. On the other hand, he says that if Diogeiton had leased out the nonlanded portions of the estate or transformed its value into land to nourish the children from its income, they would have been as rich as anyone in Athens (23). The implication of this statement is that the land which the family did possess was alone not enough to support the children lavishly, and so must have been minuscule in comparison with the *aphanês* wealth, and consequently never features prominently in the speech.

The fact that Diodotus and Diogeiton jointly owned their parents' *phanera ousia*, coupled with Diogeiton's desire to marry his daughter to his own brother, suggests that the two brothers viewed their estate as a shared asset and were perhaps business partners. Rather than dividing up the estate, they likely tightened their bond through this marriage in order to keep their property together.[133] It was Diodotus' trading wealth that induced Diogeiton to give him his daughter in marriage, which may imply that they kept their business activities separate with their own shares of the *aphanês* wealth, but since Diogeiton also engaged in trade at a later time he had likely also been in the business. In this case, the speaker ascribes Diodotus' wealth to his own efforts, a move that certainly made Diogeiton look even more despicable, in that he was stealing his *brother's* hard-won gains which he had no part in earning.

But giving his daughter to Diogeiton also meant Diodotus did not have to funnel money out of the family in the form of dowry, which is consistent with a shared family business partnership. At the very least, Diogeiton picked up where his brother left off, and sent a cargo worth two talents to the Adriatic (32.25), a hazardous venture.[134] This reveals an unmistakably high-risk, high-reward mentality, to place such a significant percentage of his brother's wealth (approximately one-seventh of Diodotus' property) in a single dangerous deal in the hopes of making a large gain. He was successful in his gamble, which yielded double what he invested, making 2 talents, 100 percent return, in this one transaction. To risk a large sum of money in a single transaction indicates that Diogeiton was interested in making as much money as he could as quickly as possible.

Indeed, it seems that Diogeiton was trying to maximize his profits from his brother's money, since he did not let out the estate or purchase safer, more reliable land with which to support his grandchildren (32.23). He preferred instead to make risky gains on trading transactions to the Adriatic. Thus, by not purchasing land for the support of his orphans or allowing his brother's estate to be leased, he was able to use the liquid cash of his brother on hazardous trading ventures to bring himself large returns. This approach is reminiscent of that of Stratocles in Isaeus 11, who raised himself into the liturgical class through the money he made from administering the estate of Theophon (see chapter 2). Diogeiton was even more greedy, however, since he was taking such a dangerous gamble with his grandchildren's patrimony, whereas Stratocles kept the estate of Theophon intact.

Since Diogeiton was either his brother's partner or picking up where he left off, it seems that the high-risk, high-reward attitude which he took in this trad-

133. Todd 1993, 204–5, agrees that this marriage was probably made to keep the money within the family.

134. As noted in Lysias, *Against Aeschines* 4, sailing to the Adriatic was considered very risky: "Those who dwell in the Piraeus think that it is much safer to sail to the Adriatic than to lend to this guy" (οἱ ἐν τῶι Πειραιεῖ διάκεινται ὥστε πολὺ ἀσφαλέστερον εἶναι δοκεῖν εἰς τὸν Ἀδρίαν πλεῖν ἢ τούτωι συμβάλλειν).

ing venture also characterizes his brother Diodotus' estate management strategies, judging from the fact that he made so much money from maritime trade. From the property listed above, he had 7 talents, 40 *minae* in bottomry loans, 2000 dr. lent in the Chersonese, and 100 *minae* also lent at landed interest; in addition to this, he left 5 talents in cash with his brother, and perhaps also 2,000 drachmas in cash and 130 Cyzicene staters for his daughter. The total of this wealth is 15 talents, not counting the Cyzicene staters, more than half of which, 51 percent, was engaged in maritime loans. The enormous amount of money in commercial loans suggests that maximization of profit was central in Diodotus' mind. None of this money had been invested in land, and a much smaller sum (13 percent) was extended on landed interest, so Diodotus apparently preferred the extremely high rates of return from maritime lending. He certainly made the choice not to acquire additional land or *phanera ousia*, but to concentrate his money solely in the high-risk world of maritime trade and lending.

He did leave five talents in cash as a deposit for his brother; counting this and the money he set aside for his wife in cash, just over a third of his estate was not productively invested at the time of his death.[135] However, as was the case with Demosthenes the Elder (chapter 2), the estate composition left by Diodotus in anticipation of his death cannot be considered typical of his normal practices of investing his wealth during his lifetime. He had been conscripted for military service and had time to arrange his affairs for his family in the case he was killed, leaving the money as a deposit in cash that was explicitly said to be for the care of his family. It had been intentionally set aside at that particular time, so this money was not hoarded unproductively in the house, but was probably taken from some other use and then reallocated to this special purpose.

Thus, the 64 percent of his estate engaged in interest-bearing loans must be considered an absolute minimum for his normal practice in his lifetime. The five talents which he gave to his brother may have been typically lent on additional maritime loans, landed loans, or some other type of productive enterprise. It could have also been acquired through commercial transactions, perhaps recently gained from a trading venture, like the four talents Diogeiton received when his profits had returned from the Adriatic. Therefore, this cash was most likely mobilized in some other type of productive activity during his lifetime, and was certainly not just hoarded because it could not be put to any productive use. Indeed, the ease with which Diogeiton was able to invest two talents in a single cargo load dispels any notion that perhaps Diodotus had

135. Millett 1991, 169–70, has interpreted this cash as being a sign that he either could or would not engage the full extent of his wealth in productive activity.

not been able to find profitable ways to invest this money. The fact that he had two talents invested in landed loans shows that he was keenly aware of a wide variety of opportunities and could easily find a place to put his money to some productive use if he wanted.

Without a full detailed account of his investments during his lifetime, it will be impossible to guess how he would have mobilized the huge amount of cash left as deposit for the care of his family after his death. It might have been invested in further maritime loans, landed loans, or perhaps *phanera ousia*, but this will never be known. In any case, he is explicitly stated to have liquidated these assets for the express purpose of providing for his wife and children, and so the huge sum of unproductive cash left behind after his death cannot be taken as evidence for normal practice throughout his moneymaking career. Rather, the remainder of his wealth, invested productively, should be seen as the typical way in which he preferred to use his money during his lifetime.

Like Nicobulus in Demosthenes 37 *Against Pantaenetus*, who was another maritime trader turned moneylender who invested his profits in a 45 *minae* loan on a mining property, Diodotus seems to have engaged in non-maritime loans precisely in order to keep a large part of his money productive during the sailing off-season. If he had only invested in bottomry loans, there would have been a significant portion of the year in which his money was sitting idle. Therefore, both men were open to other potential opportunities to keep their money in profitable purposes as much as possible.

The money whose use is known suggests that Diodotus would have had this money invested in productive activities. Of the 9 talents and 40 *minae* whose use is known, 79 percent (46,000 drachmas out of 58,000 drachmas) was invested in high-yield, high-risk maritime loans. This figure is probably much closer to the amount of Diodotus' wealth that was employed in profit-generating purposes during his career, though it may have been higher since the 5 talents of cash may have been engaged in productive enterprises, as seen with Diogeiton. Indeed, it was probably invested in higher-risk activity since individuals are most likely to leave their safest assets to their widows and orphans,[136] and he is already known to have left 2 talents of loans at landed interest rates for his family.

Since the portfolio that he passed on to his family was likely to have been the safest form into which it could be transformed, it is probable that his profitably invested wealth was higher than the 64 percent of which the maritime loans at his death actually consisted. Thus, Diodotus seems to have preferred to invest as much of his money in high-risk, high-reward bottomry loans and trading

136. Thompson 1978, 406–7.

ventures as he possibly could during his lifetime. Moreover, since he likely built up his fortune over time through trade and was choosing to invest most of these proceeds into maritime loans, this was probably the strategy which he followed over the course of his business career. In the end, it can be concluded that Diodotus attempted to maximize his wealth on a long-term basis by specializing in high-risk maritime trade and then concentrating his wealth in maritime loans after he had made much of his fortune.

Nor is Diodotus the only individual known to have concentrated his money in loans to such an extent. The huge percentage of loans in Pasion's estate has already been discussed above. Brothers Nausicrates and Xenopeithes left a huge fortune of at least 80 talents (Dem. 38.20), almost all of which was in loans at the time of their deaths.[137] Demosthenes himself seems to have learned from father, and hid his wealth in *aphanês* form, specializing in bottomry loans.[138] He is said to have never owned any *phanera ousia*, [139] and was still apparently one of the wealthiest Athenians,[140] so the full extent of his moneylending must have been substantial. Even more extreme is the immense fortune of the philosopher Zeno, who is reported to have had more than 1,000 talents invested in maritime loans![141] Although this last example is almost certainly a major exaggeration, the overall weight of this evidence is that there were a number of individuals who concentrated their wealth into moneylending at high rates of interest. That such systematic lending is known to have existed in ancient Greece is highly suggestive of a strategy aimed at long-term profit maximization through specializing in high-interest loans. Those individuals who kept their money in loans even up to the time of their deaths seem to have been maximizing their wealth as much as possible to the very end, and some did not even try to transform their wealth into a safer form to help their heirs with more stable property.

Conclusions

In conclusion, the fantastic sums of money made by those individuals who specialized in silver mining, banking, and moneylending, as well as the strategies

137. τὴν οὐσίαν Ξενοπείθης καὶ Ναυσικράτης ἅπασαν χρέα κατέλιπον, καὶ φανερὰν ἐκέκτηντο μικράν τινα, "Xenopeithes and Nausicrates left their entire fortune in loans, and they possessed only a little visible property" (Dem. 38.7). See also Thompson 1978, 405.

138. Cohen 1992, 128. He is said to have kept most of his wealth in bottomry loans (Hypereides, *Against Demosthenes* 4); Plutarch, *Life of Demosthenes* (*Comp*. 3.6). Nevertheless, he did perform some public liturgies (Davies 1971, 136–37), and so was not hiding all his money, at any rate.

139. Deinarchos 1.70.

140. Deinarchos 1.111.

141. Diogenes Laertius 7.13.

they employed, provide compelling evidence for long-term wealth-maximizing strategies in ancient Greece. The estate owners who became wealthy by focusing their moneymaking efforts in these fields for the majority of their careers exhibit behaviors that clearly resemble the patterns outlined by the modern notion of economic rationality. Kallias and Nicias concentrated their wealth in mining and accumulated some of the most impressive fortunes known from Athenian history. Pasion and Phormion continued their heavy investment in banking after they had the freedom to enter other economic activities, and even after they did acquire other types of wealth, they were still reaping huge profits from their banks.

Similarly valuable is the behavior of those who were reckless and blinded by their pursuit of money to break the law and expose themselves to ruin. Those miners who pushed their profit-seeking efforts so far that they were willing to engage in illegal mining, and those bankers who saw their banks fail after they overextended their resources, provide some of the best evidence that exists for high-risk, income-maximizing behavior. Many were ruined in their quest for wealth, but some were successful, and the fortunes that were built from such practices are truly staggering. Though these individuals' behaviors are extreme manifestations of profit-maximizing strategies, they nevertheless yield invaluable insights into what motivated them to break the law: the desire to make as much money as possible.

Further evidence that it was not just the law breakers who tried to maximize their profits and wealth can be seen in the entire classes of nouveaux riches who rose from the lower classes to the political and social elite. The fact that classical Athens saw a large number of individuals emerge from obscurity to join the top levels of the political elite suggests that the drive to maximize profits and wealth was not just confined to a select few, but was rather widespread throughout all levels of society.[142] Theognis deplores the upward mobility of the *kakoi* from as early as the late archaic period in sixth-century Megara, where enough lower-class citizens successfully achieved growth in their fortunes that they drew the ire of contemporary social commentators; this testimony points to patterns that extended beyond the temporal and spatial bounds of classical Athens and were prevalent in the rest of the ancient Greek world. For so many ancient Greek individuals to achieve such impressive economic gains, they must have been engaged in long-term profit- and wealth-maximizing behavior to various degrees. Therefore, it was not only the fabulously wealthy, but also some of the poorer classes who exhibited these behaviors.

---

142. See my discussion of the nouveaux riches in chapter 5.

Moreover, the fact that most of the individuals investigated in this chapter focused their energies in such highly lucrative enterprises for their entire lives, and were even succeeded in the same fields by multiple generations of their heirs, is highly suggestive of long-term wealth maximization. Some, such as Nicias and Hipponikos may have even tried to establish local monopolies in the renting of slave labor to others in the mines. These slave armies were likely first used for their own mining interests, but then were leased out to maximize labor productivity. The renting of slave workers on such a massive scale demonstrates that they also recognized the new opportunities for profit which appeared after the Laureion mines became worked on an increasing scale, which is the same flexibility and eye for opportunity that I argued gave shape to the composition of diversified estates. Xenophon explicitly attributes to these individuals an eagerness to invest in mining on an ever-increasing basis because they were maximizing their returns by doing so. The continuous expansion of these enterprises may also reveal a desire to specialize to the point of controlling the market in a single field. Others, such as Kephalos perhaps even saw the advantages of establishing economies of scale, to secure a large share of the market on individual goods.

Ancient Greeks certainly recognized the benefits of specialization,[143] but when excessive this approach was dangerous, and equally caused the collapse of many fortunes. From this perspective, let us return to the quote by Andrew Carnegie that opened this chapter, in which he advocated concentrating all one's wealth into a single industry to make a fortune. In response to Carnegie's advice to put all your eggs in one basket, Zweig summarizes the realities of the modern economy succinctly: "Of the *Forbes* 400 fortunes from 1982 . . . only 64 of the original members—a measly 16%—were still on the list in 2002." [144] Like these companies that refused to diversify, those money-hungry miners and bankers who lost their fortunes due to their overspecialization in these highly risky fields paid the price for their profit-maximizing strategies. Some, like Archilochos, seem to have tried to diversify in the end, but by then it was too late. Nicias, Kallias, and others lost the majority of their wealth during the Peloponnesian War, not having sufficiently diversified to protect themselves. Davies' theory that these fortunes suffered from the Peloponnesian War is definitely the best explanation for the precipitous decline in many fortunes

143. Plato, *Republic* book 2 opens with a lengthy account of the benefits of specialization of labor, which he sees as the foundation of the *polis* itself. Socrates in Xenophon's *Memorabilia* 2.7 lists a number of individuals who have made large fortunes from specializing in one product.

144. Jason Zweig, commentary on chapter 7 of Benjamin Graham, *The Intelligent Investor*, rev. ed. (New York 2003), 185.

between the fifth and fourth centuries BCE. This would explain why Nicias was so eager to make peace with the Spartans after the death of Cleon—he was losing money while the war was going on amid the annual Spartan invasions, and especially after the fortification of Deceleia. However, evidence for the collapse of fortunes may not actually have always been from overextension in the market or military disasters—they could also be the result of skillful hiding of wealth from the state. Similarly, charges of squandering an estate would have often been directed against people who chose to liquidate assets by putting them in *aphanês* form, as Gabrielsen notes.[145]

The most successful individuals diversified in order to reduce the dangers of their hyperspecialization. Pasion was able to transmit much of his wealth to Apollodorus because he had diversified into landed assets—his moneylending wealth was decimated after his death, as Apollodorus had only managed to collect about half of his father's outstanding loans after twenty years of effort.[146] Those specialized estate owners who did diversify, then, enjoyed their gains in retirement and still passed on much of their fortunes to their heirs.

Even when they did diversify, however, it was almost always into profitable fields: Phormion into maritime trade, Pasion into the shield factory and *synoikiai*, and Nicias and Hipponikos into their slave armies. Even Pasion's land seems to have been producing for the market. It was not risk aversion or avoidance, but rather risk management, that best characterizes the economic decision-making of the individuals I studied in this chapter.[147] In fact, the manner in which they preferred to diversify was into highly lucrative properties.

Like the owners of diversified estates, then, the choices made by wealthy specialized estate owners in this chapter were motivated primarily by profit. Therefore, the same general gain-oriented, risk-balancing strategies were used by both diversified and specialized estate owners. Since the patterns of acquisition were similar, diversification and specialization should be seen as different stages in the same cyclical process in which one could branch out or focus alternately in response to changing market conditions. Overall, if one had to make a broad summary observation based on the similarities in the behavior of these individual case studies, it would be that the quest for profit is the main pattern

145. Gabrielsen 1986, 108.

146. Dem. 36.36.

147. Peasants living near subsistence level, of course, would tell a different story. This is an important point that must be emphasized, since most of the individuals I study here are wealthy. The poorer classes would, of course, be more likely to pursue safety-first, risk-minimizing strategies of production. But as Bresson 2016a, 159, notes, peasant diversification is not irrational, but a rational strategy for limiting uncertainty; McCloskey 1996, 149, agrees, and convincingly argues that peasant strategies really should be considered to be examples of rational behavior within a specific set of ecological constraints.

that best characterizes the economic decision-making and estate-management strategies of Athenian estate owners.

Finally, in the field of trade and moneylending, Diodotus seems to have engaged in high-risk, high-profit-seeking behavior his entire life, starting with trade, and then investing in maritime loans, which dominated his estate composition at the time of his death. It is the concentration of such a large percentage of wealth into such high risk and reward ventures over the course of an entire lifetime that provides the clearest indications of long-term profit and wealth maximization in ancient Greece.

Some of the best evidence for economic choice and business strategies can be found not in estate management, however, but in the realm of maritime trade. Whereas the evidence for profit maximization that I have discussed in these last two chapters is largely indirect, when it comes to the field of commerce, there actually exists direct, unequivocal evidence for profit-maximizing strategies in ancient Athens. Many of the most thoroughly detailed economic transactions from that world are recorded in the private lawsuits arising from disputes over maritime loans and exchange in sea commerce. It is in these deals gone wrong where much of the economic decision-making process and psychological motivation that are invisible in the rest of the extant source material may be found. Merchants and maritime moneylenders were some of the unambiguous examples of profit-maximizing businessmen in antiquity, many of whom came to Athens from other Greek *poleis*; they engaged in some of the riskiest moneymaking activities preserved in the ancient source material, and will be the subject of my next chapter.

CHAPTER 4

Profit, Trust, and Deception in Ancient Greek Maritime Trade

In the *Works and Days*, Hesiod says that sailing was dangerous business, and he assumes that someone would only go to sea for one purpose: profit.[1] He warns his audience against risking their entire livelihood at sea, but says that many people do this nonetheless because "wealth is life for wretched mortals."[2] So who would be so crazy as to gamble their lives at sea? Solon and Theognis provide the answer: those who wanted to escape poverty, and thought that the destitute life was not worth living, would undergo the dangers of maritime trade.[3] As far back as Homer's *Odyssey* merchants are described as being primarily bent on profit, as seen when the Phaeacian youth Euryalos mistakes Odysseus for a sea captain who is "mindful of his outward cargo and with a keen eye out for his return cargo and his greedy profits."[4] In Plato's *Gorgias*, Socrates agrees that no one would endure the risks and hardships of traveling by sea for any other reason than to make money—sailing is nothing but a means to the end of making money and wealth.[5]

As noted above, in Lysias, *Against Diogeiton*, the defendant is said to have earned 100 percent on a trading venture to the Adriatic, having doubled (ἐδιπλασίασεν) his initial investment of two talents (Lysias 32.25). This may be the result of forensic exaggeration, but such a return would not have been impossible, since the Adriatic was known to be a very risky place to sail (Lysias, *Against Aeschines* 4) and gains from such trading ventures would have been

1. *Works and Days* 632.
2. χρήματα γὰρ ψυχὴ πέλεται δειλοῖσι βροτοῖσιν (*Works and Days* 686).
3. Cato the Elder opens his *De Agri Cultura* by describing maritime trade as "dangerous and prone to disaster" (periculosum et calamitosum), and characterizes sea traders as "striving and eager for profit" (strenuum studiosumque rei quaerendae), which is reminiscent of the "eagerness" for wealth attested by Xenophon, Theognis, and other Greek writers (see chapter 5).
4. φόρτου τε μνήμων καὶ ἐπίσκοπος ᾗσιν ὁδαίων | κερδέων θ' ἁρπαλέων (*Odyssey* 8.163–64).
5. *Gorgias* 467d.

on the higher end of the scale.[6] There certainly would have been chances for ancient Greek traders to cash in on particularly fruitful windfall opportunities (see my discussion below). Indeed, the profits from typical ancient Greek trading ventures were at least sufficient to repay the interest on the loans that funded maritime commerce, which were typically set at rates of 20–30 percent, and still have enough left over to justify risking one's life on the sea.[7] Although 100 percent return was probably extraordinary, a single transaction that spanned a few months could repay more than years of operating workshops or lending money.

Some of the best attested moneymaking strategies in ancient Greece are preserved in the maritime court speeches of fourth-century BCE Athens, and in spite of the problems of interpreting these documents, it will be safe to conclude in the end that they contain clear signs of profit-maximizing strategies and economic rationality.[8] Moreover, the traders and moneylenders in these speeches were frequently not from Athens, and therefore provide clear evidence for the behavior of individuals from the Greek world more broadly. Ancient Greek maritime traders were ingenious in their quest for gain, and some even broke contracts and laws to maximize their returns. The political fragmentation of the ancient Greek world created a hazardous trading environment, however, because *poleis* could only effectively enforce contracts within the bounds of their own territories, and the limited mechanisms for verifying information and enforcing agreements enabled opportunistic fortune seekers

6. For ancient Greece, it is not so simple to calculate rates of profit (Hasebroek 1965, 11), but the 100 percent rate of profit by Diogeiton is not entirely unbelievable when compared to attested profits by early modern maritime traders. Braudel 1982, 403–8, and 428–33, says long-distance trade is where the big money was made in the early modern European economy, far more than in industry or agriculture: profits are reported as being 96.12 percent on average for the French India Company from 1725 to 1736; the *Saint-Hilaire* is said to have made 53 percent profit on a single voyage in 1777. Jacob Cornelis Van Neck, one of the first Dutch adventurers to the spice islands of the East Indies was said to have made 400 percent profit on his first voyage in 1599 (Braudel 1984, 212). Grassby 1969, 725–27, shows that while profits for single voyages and even single years for the seventeenth-century British East India Company could be spectacularly high, between 320 percent and even 900 percent(!), the long-term profit rate was much lower when losses were figured in, more like 25 to 30 percent—which, it is interesting to note, is about the level for the rates of interest for ancient Greek maritime loans.

7. Bresson and Bresson 2004, 110, have argued convincingly based on close analysis of case studies of ancient Greek traders, the interest rates one could receive from maritime loans, and the profits traders would receive after paying the necessary taxes, that both traders (*emporoi*) and moneylenders can be seen to be maximizing their profits within individual maritime loan transactions.

8. Hasebroek 1965, 83, says that Greek maritime traders went after the greatest profits they could. He also says that among the true capitalists in ancient Greece were the moneylenders investing their capital in maritime loans (7–9). He restricts the term "capitalist" only to moneylenders, since he considers traders to be from the poor of ancient Greece. Traders turned moneylenders are attested (Dem. 33.4–5, 37.54), however, and it seems that many poorer individuals engaged in trade and made their fortunes thereby.

to engage in deceitful and exploitative behavior.[9] The risks of trade on the open market led many to protect themselves through circles of trust, but even these could be penetrated by clever and unscrupulous individuals.

Demosthenes' exciting account of the trader Zenothemis, sometime between 354 and 340 BCE,[10] vividly portrays the dangers of maritime commerce in the ancient Greek open market. According to the speaker, Demosthenes' uncle Demo, the defendant Zenothemis and his partner, the *nauklêros*[11] Hegestratus,[12] duped multiple moneylenders in Syracuse into advancing sums against a single cargo of grain which they held in their ship. Borrowing multiply on the security of these goods was a clever trick that allowed them to raise an extraordinarily large sum of money (Dem. 32.4–9). They then sent this money away to their home *polis* of Massalia, with the intention of recovering it there after they had sunk the ship and freed themselves from their contractual obligation to repay the loans. It was the perfect scheme.

What they did not expect, however, was that they would be caught while trying to sink the boat. Fellow passengers, awakened by the sound of a drill boring through the hull of the ship in the middle of the night, rushed into the hold and caught Hegestratus with the drill in his hand. Hegestratus managed to make it onto the deck, where he attempted to escape in the lifeboat, but drowned in the process. Zenothemis, though pretending not to be involved, nevertheless tried to complete the plan by convincing the crew to abandon ship. Another passenger, Protus, who was hoping to save his cargo, persuaded the crew with promises of gifts to save the ship, which made it safely to Cephallenia. Zenothemis then tried to prevent the ship from completing its full voyage to Athens, and when he failed in this, he changed tactics and claimed Demo's cargo as his own. Moreover, he was so successful in this false charge that he managed to gain the support of Demo's associate, Protus, who had originally opposed Zenothemis' plot to allow the boat to sink. Without the speed of modern communications, it was only possible to prove the ownership of the grain by sailing to Syracuse and consulting that city's customs records. With the assis-

9. For opportunism in economic transactions, see Williamson 1975, 9–10, 26. Granovetter 2001, 60, provides the following definition of opportunism: "The rational pursuit by economic actors of their own advantage, with all means at their command, including guile and deceit."

10. For the date, see Isager and Hansen 1975, 149. MacDowell 2009, 272, suggests a date sometime in the 340s. For a recent clear overview of this speech, see Thür 2015, 41–42.

11. On the fuzzy distinction ancient Greeks made between *nauklêroi* (ship owners or captains) and *emporoi* (maritime traders), see Finkelstein 1935, 320–36; Reed 2003, 6–14; Hasebroek 1965, 1–8; Isager and Hansen 1975, 64–66. Woolmer 2015, however, provides clarity in his recent treatment of this issue.

12. Cohen 2000, 136, believes Zenothemis was a slave. This is uncertain, as he is described simply as a *hypêretês*, "helper" or "underling." Whether Hegestratus was just the captain or also the shipowner is unknown but in any case he was Zenothemis' associate and boss.

tance of Protus and a group of scoundrels based in the Piraeus who apparently had experience with such schemes, Zenothemis managed to get possession of the grain, and Demo resorted to self-help to seize the cargo.[13] Zenothemis filed a suit against Demo for the cargo, forcing Demo to respond with a *paragraphê* that the suit was inadmissible.[14]

Although it will never be known if the speaker of Demosthenes *Against Zenothemis* was telling the truth, for this study the facts of the case are inconsequential. What really matters are the conditions of the trading world that it portrays, and the plausibility of the accusations. If the behavior of the actors could have been believable to an ancient Greek audience, then the rules of the system that are described by the speaker are probably accurate depictions of reality.

In this chapter I will argue that the actions of men like Zenothemis, while not typical, were common enough to significantly affect the nature of maritime trade in the ancient Greek market. Greek traders lusted after profit to such an extent that many were willing to deceive, cheat, and steal in order to make money, often taking advantage of the information and transportation limitations of the ancient world in which they lived. Such behavior was sufficiently widespread that it created an atmosphere of fear and distrust, causing others to protect themselves by forming circles of trust rather than be exposed to the perils of trade in the open market. Issues of trust and information were so significant, in fact, that opportunities came to be restricted to those with the right personal contacts, a major distortion of the market into personalized networks as opposed to the notion of free trade open to all. These networks were not impenetrable, however. Many profit-seeking individuals were able to access these otherwise unavailable opportunities by exploiting the social pressure that emanated from these relationships. The social obligation that moneylend-

13. For the specific legal process in this case, see Isager and Hansen 1975, 144–47, who identify Zenothemis' suit as a *dikê exoulês*. The exact verb used for the seizure of the goods by Protus is *exagein* (32.17–20), one of many verbs used for legal self-help in Athens, for which see Christ 1998.

14. This is at least how the speaker describes the events; the reality could have been different, but there will never be enough evidence to be able to judge the case based on unbiased accounts. An alternative explanation has been offered by Isager and Hansen 1975, 141–43: if Zenothemis was telling the truth and the cargo really was his by right, then Protus may have been claiming the grain as his own, seeing an opportunity after Hegestratus died in the disaster at sea, which was actually due to a storm and not sabotage by Zenothemis and Hegestratus. If Protus had not picked up a cargo of grain in Syracuse, for which Demo had lent him money (32.14, 20), then claiming the grain formerly owned by Hegestratus, and perhaps even trying to steal the contract (32.28), would allow him to appear as if he were not reneging on his obligations to Demo when he arrived at Athens. This narrative is reconstructed from the few details Demo does mention when summarizing Zenothemis' complaint against Protus (32.27–28). This is a possible alternative narrative, and in either case Protus appears to be an opportunistic scoundrel, breaking agreements for personal profit. For recent treatments of the factual and procedural issues in this case, see Harris 2015; Thür 2015.

ers would have felt to maintain their status as approachable business partners could be manipulated to convince them to make loans they would have otherwise refused. Emotions, therefore, heavily influenced economic decisions.

After first exploring the strategies which maritime traders used to pursue and maximize profitable opportunities, I will then examine the types of measures which moneylenders took to protect themselves. I will finally describe the nature of the economic and social fabric in which traders operated, drawing upon comparative examples to illuminate the ways in which formalistic and substantivist elements could function within the same economic system.

Price Sensitivity, Flexibility, and Versatility in an Uncertain Trading World

One might not expect to find one of the best descriptions of maritime traders' profit-seeking behavior in Xenophon's *Oeconomicus*. Yet, in the midst of the dialogue between Ischomachus and Socrates about how farming could make one a clever *chrêmatistês*, Xenophon's Socrates provides a glimpse into the ways ancient Greek maritime traders identified and secured opportunities for making profits:

> λέγεις . . . τὸν πατέρα φιλογέωργον εἶναι οὐδὲν ἧττον ἢ οἱ ἔμποροι φιλόσιτοί εἰσι. καὶ γὰρ οἱ ἔμποροι διὰ τὸ σφόδρα φιλεῖν τὸν σῖτον, ὅπου ἂν ἀκούσωσι πλεῖστον εἶναι, ἐκεῖσε πλέουσιν ἐπ᾽ αὐτὸν καὶ Αἰγαῖον καὶ Εὔξεινον καὶ Σικελικὸν πόντον περῶντες: ἔπειτα δὲ λαβόντες ὁπόσον δύνανται πλεῖστον ἄγουσιν αὐτὸν διὰ τῆς θαλάττης . . . καὶ ὅταν δεηθῶσιν ἀργυρίου, οὐκ εἰκῇ αὐτὸν ὅπου ἂν τύχωσιν ἀπέβαλον, ἀλλ᾽ ὅπου ἂν ἀκούσωσι τιμᾶσθαί τε μάλιστα τὸν σῖτον καὶ περὶ πλείστου αὐτὸν ποιῶνται οἱ ἄνθρωποι, τούτοις αὐτὸν ἄγοντες παραδιδόασι.
>
> You are saying that your father was no less a lover of farming than merchants are lovers of grain. Indeed, because of their excessive love for grain, wherever they hear it is in the greatest quantity, they sail there for it, crossing even the Aegean, Black, and Sicilian seas. Then, having as much of it as possible, they carry it across the sea and . . . whenever they want money, they do not sell it at random wherever they happen to be, but sell it wherever they hear grain is most expensive, and to the people who value it the most. (*Oeconomicus* 20.27–8)

The four superlatives in this passage perfectly illustrate the maximizing strategies of maritime traders: they go wherever the *most* grain is (and by implication the *lowest* prices), they carry *as much as possible*, they sell it wherever it is *most expensive*, and to people who value it *the most*. Maritime traders want to buy grain wherever the supply is most abundant, since prices would be lower in these places, and do not haphazardly sell their cargo wherever is convenient, but purposely seek out the places where prices are highest, the most lucrative opportunities. The superlatives in this passage suggest that maritime traders were motivated by the same profit-maximizing desires that have been seen in the previous chapters of this study, and are here clearly said to make their choices based on prices to maximize their own gains. The behavior described by Xenophon, which he attributes to all grain merchants, bears a striking relation to the maximizing assumptions of modern economic rationality.

The Mediterranean basin was not a fixed, predictable, static system, and a disaster (war, climate, disease) could turn an exporting region into an importing one, so relative prices were subject to rapid, unpredictable shifts and fluctuations.[15] As the Old Oligarch shows, there could be major variations in the supply and demand of goods in different regions from year to year:

> νόσους τῶν καρπῶν αἵ ἐκ Διός εἰσιν οἱ μὲν κατὰ γῆν κράτιστοι χαλεπῶς φέρουσιν, οἱ δὲ κατὰ θάλατταν ῥᾳδίως. οὐ γὰρ ἅμα πᾶσα γῆ νοσεῖ: ὥστε ἐκ τῆς εὐθενούσης ἀφικνεῖται τοῖς τῆς θαλάττης ἄρχουσιν.
>
> Those strongest on land bear with difficulty the crop diseases that Zeus brings, while those strongest by sea bear them easily. For the entire earth is not sick all at the same time, so that goods from a prosperous land reach those in control of the sea. (pseudo-Xenophon, *Athenaion Politeia*, 2.6)

Variations in harvest could occur from year to year, and could cause supply and demand to be in flux throughout the Mediterranean. With some places producing surpluses at different times while others experienced hardship, relative prices would shift, increasing in afflicted areas, and decreasing in those with an abundance of a certain good.[16] Even a single region suffering or prosper-

15. Horden and Purcell 2000, 152, discuss the interannual variability in wheat yields that are known to have occurred in the Mediterranean. As Osborne 1987, 31–34, shows, annual variations in rainfall throughout the Greek world could be quite drastic, some years receiving three times as much or as little as others.

16. See Rathbone and Von Reden 2015, for a comprehensive overview of variability in grain yields and its effects on prices and profitability. Price fluctuations could be dramatic, doubling or tripling the amount of profit which could be earned at a given time. Prices in 330/29 for barley and wheat more than tripled, being sixteen drachmas a *medimnos* when prices were normally five drachmas (Dem. 34.38–39). The arrival of the Sicilian *kataplous* (grain shipment) in Athens (Dem. 56.9) caused prices to drop in 324/3 (for the date see Isager and Hansen 1975, 209; MacDowell

ing slightly more than usual would provide unforeseen opportunities for the skillful, attentive, and ambitious trader, who could make tremendous fortunes. Therefore intelligent traders would need to adapt to the regional fluctuations in price levels in order to make the most profit.

Special opportunities of this sort include the times in which grain prices in Athens rose to more than triple their normal rate. While most other traders were selling their grain at Athens for sixteen drachmas a *medimnos* in 330/29 (eleven drachmas above the normal rate), the speaker of Demosthenes 34 *Against Phormion* sold his grain at five drachmas a *medimnos*.[17] What this means is that every other trader who did not want to make a public benefaction for the Athenians (as the speaker did in this case), was able to make extraordinary profits, an extra eleven drachmas per *medimnos*! Of course, if prices at supplying regions also increased in conjunction with those in Athens, the returns would have decreased correspondingly, but if prices at the point of supply were similar to those of normal years, each merchant ship carrying entirely grain could make up to 33,000 drachmas, or five and a half talents, of greater profit than on a typical voyage.[18] To put this figure in perspective, at classical Athens three talents was about enough to bring a citizen up to the level of the liturgical class. Therefore, the trader who successfully took advantage of regional changes in relative prices at the right time could make a fortune, and perhaps be set for life, from even a single voyage.

Some ancient Greek traders displayed great versatility in responding to the ever-changing price conditions of the Mediterranean market. For example, the trader Phormion in Demosthenes *Against Phormion* first did not purchase the amount stipulated in his own contract (Dem. 34.7), and finding that prices

2009, 284), and another supply-induced price drop is attested in Dem. 32.25. For the price fluctuations recorded at Delos from the fourth century through the Hellenistic period, see Reger 1994, 289–307; 1997.

17. 34.38–39. Isager and Hansen 1975, 169, identify this crisis as the famine that occurred in 330/29, which they discuss in further detail at 201–2. MacDowell 2009, 279, agrees.

18. This figure is based on the calculations of Casson, who estimates that the typical merchant ship was able to hold about 3,000 *medimnoi*, or 120 tons (Casson 1991, 171–72n23). The best figures for average merchant ship size are supplied by a harbor regulations inscription from third-century BCE Thasos, which describes smaller ships as having a capacity of 80 tons (3,000 talents), while middling vessels carried about 130 tons (5,000 talents). Casson 1991, 183–84 shows that the amounts of grain gifts from merchants to cities in the fourth century BCE also tended to be around 3,000 *medimnoi*, or 120 tons, most likely full shiploads of grain, a figure which corroborates the evidence for average merchant ship size from Thasos. Another ship from the second century is said to have carried 1,500 *metrêtai* of olive oil, which, along with the weight of the jars, comes out to just over 100 tons, right in line with Casson's estimates for grain. The 10,000-*phoros* capacity of the merchant ship set up by the Athenians for defense in the Syracusan harbor before the final naval battle of the Sicilian expedition in 413 is clearly stated by Thucydides to be unusually large. See also Isager and Hansen 1975, 57–59.

were not favorable in the Bosporus due to war, he then made the decision not to load a return cargo according to the agreement, either (Dem. 34.8–9, 22). Similarly, the ship captain Lampis in the same speech capitalized on an opportunity offered by Paerisades in the Bosporus to ship grain duty-free to Athens, but brought it to Acanthus instead (Dem. 34.36–37), breaking the law in order to make greater profits. Finally, around 350,[19] the Phaselite brothers Apollodorus, Artemo, and Lacritus were contractually bound to purchase 3,000 jars of Mendean wine in Mende or Scione, and to carry them thence to the Bosporus (Dem. 35.10), where they were to pick up an unspecified return cargo to convey back to Athens. Upon reaching Mende, however, the brothers Apollodorus and Artemo only picked up 450 jars of Mendean wine, and no other cargo (35.18–20). They did not wish to keep their money inactive, as they lent out in Pontus much of the money they had borrowed, 100 Cyzicene staters (2,800 drachmas),[20] so it may be that their choice to buy only 450 jars of Mendean wine was influenced by market prices. Rather than purchasing the required amount, or sailing to Scione, as the contract would have allowed, they instead decided to lend the money for a trading venture (35.36, the borrower is described as a *nauklêros*), which reveals flexibility and versatility in response to unexpected and unfavorable circumstances.

Therefore, even if it meant breaking a contract or a law, ancient Greek traders adapted to regional conditions and made on-the-spot decisions to alter deals when details on the ground revealed them to be unprofitable. Just as Xenophon describes in the *Oeconomicus* and depicts in the *Poroi* the producers of various crafts who switched fields of production based on the shifting profitability of goods (see introduction chapter), it seems that traders were extremely sensitive to price fluctuations and were able to respond quickly and change their course of action to prevent loss and increase their gains.

Information Networks to Secure the Greatest Profits

In the passage of the *Oeconomicus* quoted above, Xenophon says that merchants go wherever they *hear* (ἀκούω) the best chances for profit are. The use of the verb "hear" perfectly illustrates the realities of ancient Greek maritime

19. For the date, see MacDowell 2009, 262, who thinks it unlikely that the speech predates 355, and that it probably predates 348, when the Macedonians destroyed Olynthus, after which Athenians would not have likely traded with Mende and Scione. Isager and Hansen 1975, 169–70, think the speech dates to sometime before 340.

20. The Cyzicene stater was worth 28 Athenian drachmas in 327 BCE (Dem. 34.23). For the date, see Isager and Hansen 1975, 169.

trade: the only way to know about fruitful opportunities was by word of mouth and written communication. Therefore, creating networks of contacts to share information was necessary to cash in on the most profitable trade possibilities in the Mediterranean. As Meijer and Van Nijf put it: "The success of traders was often dependent on chance and the capacity of an individual to leap at an opportunity."[21] Bang likewise argues that for Roman merchants, it was not just the acquisition of information, but the timeliness of the information that determined how profitable an opportunity could be.[22] If a trader allowed his competitors to beat him to a trade deal, it is likely that the price would both rise at the place of purchase as the supply decreased, and would drop at the place of sale. Therefore, profits would decrease at both the buying and selling ends of a transaction without timely action. Since merchants could only get the highest returns by seizing profitable opportunities before their competitors, securing reliable information and then capitalizing on it quickly was essential for success in this field.

In a well-known passage, the speaker of Demosthenes *Against Dionysodorus*, Dareius,[23] describes how the defendant created information networks with his partners, and thereby shared news about the greatest profits:[24]

> εἶτα πρὸς τὰς καθεστηκυίας τιμὰς ἔπεμπον γράμματα οἱ ἐπιδημοῦντες τοῖς ἀποδημοῦσιν, ἵνα ἐὰν μὲν παρ᾽ ὑμῖν τίμιος ᾖ ὁ σῖτος, δεῦρο αὐτὸν κομίσωσιν, ἐὰν δ᾽ εὐωνότερος γένηται, εἰς ἄλλο τι καταπλεύσωσιν ἐμπόριον.
>
> Then, those remaining at home would send letters regarding the prevailing prices to those [partners] who were abroad, so that if grain became more expensive in your city (Athens), they would bring it here, but if the price dropped, they would sail to some other port. (Dem. 56.8)

Demosthenes' words here closely echo the way Xenophon described maritime traders in the *Oeconomicus*: they try to sell their goods for the highest price possible, and listen for news of the best opportunities. Stationing partners in key ports and then sending out letters about prices to their associates allowed Dionysodorus and his partners to place themselves in the best information

21. Meijer and Van Nijf 1992, 31.

22. Bang 2008, 137–38.

23. His name is preserved in Libanius' hypothesis and in a note at the end of the speech in the earliest medieval manuscript (MacDowell 2009, 284).

24. For the question of this speech's authenticity, see MacDowell 2009, 285 who believes that the speech is, indeed, attributable to Demosthenes.

hubs to alert each other about chances for higher profits (Dem. 56.7–10). In this case, they secured greater profits by selling Egyptian grain at Rhodes rather than Athens, which had seen a price drop after a shipment of grain arrived from Sicily. Without this information, the partners would have been forced to settle for a lower return at Athens. Instead, with partners stationed on both ends of the trade route between Athens and Egypt, they not only ensured that they could capitalize on profitable opportunities as soon as they became available, but also provided the information necessary to choose the best possible option.

Nor are Dionysodorus and his associates the only individuals from ancient Greece known to have placed business partners in key ports at the opposite ends of a trade route. The moneylender Chrysippus had a slave employee or agent[25] working for him in the Bosporus, to whom Phormion was supposed to deliver the letters his master had sent concerning the agreement (Dem. 34.8). This was apparently a situation in which two business partners, here master and slave, strategically stationed themselves at the opposite ends of a major trade route in order to capitalize on chances for profit that might suddenly appear on either end. Similarly, a trader and customer of Pasion's bank left instructions for money at the bank to be paid to his partner when he arrived to claim it at Athens (Dem. 52.3–5).[26] This was doubtless a means for permitting an associate to use the money however he thought advantageous without needing his partner to stay idle or stationary to deliver it personally. Money, as with trading partners, could be stationed wherever it was most useful. If the right opportunity arose, it would be possible for a partner at the other end of a trade route to capitalize on it promptly.

The strategy of using information imbalances to one's advantage may have, in some respects at least, even approached the situation in early modern European trade, in which information networks enabled short-lived monopolies to maximize profits. Braudel discusses how early modern European merchants were able to "evade the free market, to eliminate competition by holding a virtual or actual monopoly, and to keep supply and demand so effectively separated that the terms of trade were entirely dictated by the middleman, who alone knew the state of the market at either end of the long chain."[27] Merchants

25. Evidence for business agents in ancient Greek is problematic at best, for which see Harris 2013b.

26. And so, since Pasion would have given up the deposited sum to the partner, banks were a way for partners to keep money at different ends of the trade routes to allow the other to be able to seize upon opportunities as soon as he reached the other port. Such a technique would have also prevented the loss of this money in shipwrecks while traveling, and also could have served as a safety net in case of loss in a trading venture. Therefore, money was another moving variable that could be manipulated by trading partners to their benefit.

27. Braudel 1982, 416. In Lysias 22, *Against the Grain Dealers*, the Athenian *polis* interceded to

could make extraordinary returns from having exclusive access to a specific item in a given place at a certain time. Such monopolies may have been short-lived, and constantly shifted from place to place, but huge gains were possible in situations where merchants were willing to take risks and exploit a fruitful opportunity. As with Diogeiton, who made 100 percent profit on a trading voyage to the Adriatic, large returns could be made from even a single transaction on an especially dangerous trade route. Given that Greeks were said by Aristotle to have aimed at establishing monopolies as part of their business strategies (Aristotle, *Politics* 1.11.8–12, 1259a5–39), it is not unreasonable to suppose that ancient Greek merchants would have attempted to secure monopolies, even if they were temporary.[28]

Such monopolies could result from the discovery of a new market, for example. Herodotus recounts how the seventh-century BCE trader Colaeus of Samos was blown off course past the pillars of Heracles to Tartessus on the Spanish coast, and was the first Greek trader to reach that place. The reward Colaeus made from discovering this new market was enough to dedicate as a tithe a bowl worth six talents at the Samian Heraion.[29] Sixty talents was the windfall Colaeus made from this one voyage, and Herodotus says that Sostratus profited even more on a single venture. Establishing a quick monopoly at the right time could create an instant fortune.

However profitable they may have been, it is the short-lived nature of such monopolies that needs to be emphasized for ancient Greece. As Hasebroek and Reed have shown, ancient Greek merchant partnerships were very small compared to their early modern counterparts,[30] and Bang has demonstrated that

prevent the control of supply and demand by middlemen who were attempting to profit as much as possible from hoarding grain and forcing customers to pay increased prices. In other words, these retailers were attempting to exercise control over supply and demand in order to be able to gain maximum profits, and the *dêmos* understood what they were up to, and why. For this speech, see Figueira 1986, and Leese 2017b.

28. Hasebroek 1965, 153–58, shows that various *poleis* recognized the benefits of securing monopolies on certain goods, though even those of the state were temporary. For an example of a state monopoly in trade in ancient Greece, see, e.g., the efforts of Cleomenes the governor of Egypt, who affected prices throughout the Mediterranean after he monopolized the export of grain from Egypt (at Dem. 56.7, for which see Isager and Hansen 1975, 205–6). Bissa 2009, 220, shows that Cleomenes' monopoly was only made possible because of a shortage of grain in other *poleis* and because of his extraordinary control over the export of Egyptian grain. For monopolies in conjunction with the state, see Gabrielsen 2011. For monopolies created by the state, see Bissa 2009, 97, 114–15, 229. See Bresson 2008, 237–39 for a discussion of monopoly and monopsony.

29. Herodotus 4.152.

30. Hasebroek 1965, 84, and Reed 2003, 36–38, show that trading partnerships were typically composed of two to three members at most, and those at the higher end of the scale were family members. Merchants' associations were relatively uncommon (Morley 2007, 75–76), and Gabrielsen (2007) shows that they did not perform the same functions as a modern corporation, but were largely for mutual support and the performance of religious ritual.

Roman merchants were not able to take the next step in exerting long-term control over such trading opportunities, an important difference between the ancient and early modern period.[31] Their ability to control markets was negligible in comparison with the great trading companies of early modern Europe, which wielded armies, could use force, had large numbers of personnel, and also commanded the key points on *global* long-distance trade.

Still, ancient Greek traders had some methods for trying to secure short-lived monopolies in specific regions. There is evidence that ancient merchants often frequented the same areas, and became familiar with the demands for different goods in various regions.[32] This impression is borne out by the striking regional patterns in the distribution of Corinthian vessels called *aryballoi* in the archaic period; different iconographic styles were so markedly concentrated in different areas that there seems to be a strong correlation between region and taste.[33] The distribution patterns are highly suggestive of a close relationship between consumer, middleman, and producer, in which the specific styles that were brought to each locale were purposefully transported to these places by merchants who knew what the people in those particular places wanted. Somehow information about tastes was being transmitted to merchants, who in turn bought for these target markets from producers, whom they also apparently informed of the market's demands. Osborne argues convincingly that the styles of much ancient Greek pottery, even in the archaic period, were being marketed for specific regions.[34]

Therefore, merchants still may have been able to control supply, demand, and information on a limited scale, though not to the extent possible in early modern Europe. Indeed, the grain dealers in Lysias 22 *Against the Grain Dealers* were using precisely the same tactics as later European merchant companies to maximize the profit they received from their customers: they manipulated information and hoarded grain to force customers to pay more than they normally would have.[35] Moreover, the merchants' information networks discussed above, establishing business partners at key ports and exploiting

31. Bang 2008, 145, has noted how large commercial entities such as the British and Dutch East India Companies, with their large accumulations of long-term trading capital, were able to absorb market shocks and extend their control over individual markets to an extent not possible for the individual trader or small partnership.

32. Morley 2007, 31.

33. See Shanks 1999, for the evidence for the distribution of these pots, which he helpfully illustrates in pie charts (fig. 4.5).

34. Osborne 1996. Osborne 2007, 285, remarks that Corinthian pottery seems to have been marketed to specific consumers in the archaic period. Cf. Osborne, review of Shanks, *JHS* 121 (2001), 222.

35. Leese 2017b.

profitable opportunities before one's competitors, fit all the criteria discussed for the establishment of monopolies in early modern long-distance trade: "The minimum qualifications for entry to these extremely profitable circuits were: to have sufficient capital and local sources of credit, to be well-informed and well-connected, and to have associates at strategic points along the trade route, who were a party to one's secrets."[36] As seen in the strategies of Dionysodorus, who created networks of information with partners at important ports and attempted to capitalize on profitable opportunities before his competitors, the same principles which were at work in early modern European trade were also used in ancient Greece, though on a lesser scale.

A Race against the Clock: Maximizing Transactions to Maximize Profits

Another way maritime traders could maximize their profits was to increase the number of transactions they could complete per voyage or sailing season. Since sailing speeds were slow in ancient Greece,[37] there would have been a limited number of trading journeys one could make during the safe sailing season of the ancient Mediterranean. As Cohen has observed, both borrowers and lenders would want a quick turnaround so they could receive their profits and then reemploy their money in new ventures as many times as possible.[38] Thus, for an individual concerned with maximizing profit, completing the most transactions possible during that short time would have been an important strategy.

One individual who tried to engage in as many transactions as he could in a single voyage was the ship captain Lampis in Demosthenes *Against Phormion*. He took on an additional load of 1,000 hides in Byzantium on his already overloaded ship, which then sank (34.10). This ship was definitely at capacity, since thirty people died in the wreck, and others, including Lampis, escaped. Lampis' decision to fill his ship to the point that it would sink is a strong indication that he was trying to maximize the number of individual transactions he could make on this single trip, for the purpose of maximizing his profits.

Such a high-risk, high-reward strategy is understandable since ancient

36. Braudel 1982, 416.

37. See Duncan-Jones 1990, 7–29, for sailing speeds during the Roman Empire. Hesiod says that the sailing season is very restricted, only fifty days or so (Hesiod, *Works and Days* 663–65), but the reality was that it was more like six months according to Isager and Hansen 1975, 59; Casson 1991, 100, agrees, and specifies the period from April to October. The most recent book on the ancient sailing season is Beresford 2013.

38. Cohen 1989, 217n48.

Greek maritime loans acted as a form of insurance for the borrower.[39] Since the lender, not the borrower, took on most of the risk in case of a shipwreck,[40] it made sense for a ship owner or captain to pack his ship with as many goods as possible,[41] since he stood to make a maximum profit from such a trip, and with much lower risk than if he had provided all the capital himself.

Other examples of transaction-maximizing strategies are preserved from ancient Greek maritime court cases.[42] In Demosthenes *Against Dionysodorus*, the defendant and his partner Parmeniscus are charged with violating the terms of their contract which stipulated that they borrow money specifically to bring a cargo of grain to Athens from Egypt. The speaker, who was also the plaintiff and their money lender, describes the moneymaking strategies which the defendant and his partner used, selling the grain at Rhodes rather than Athens, and then immediately employing the profits to engage in more transactions: ἐλυσιτέλει πολλῷ μᾶλλον τοῦτ᾽ ἢ δεῦρ᾽ ἐπαναπλεῖν . . . ἐκεῖσε μέν γε ἀεὶ ὡραῖος ὁ πλοῦς, καὶ δὶς ἢ τρὶς ὑπῆρχεν αὐτοῖς ἐργάσασθαι τῷ αὐτῷ ἀργυρίῳ, "This was far more profitable than to sail back here (to Athens). For the sailing trip to that place is always seasonable, and it was possible for them to do business with the same money two or three times."[43] The speaker recognizes that his defaulting borrowers were trying to maximize the number of transactions they could make from a single loan: the shorter sailing distance between Rhodes and Egypt gave the borrowers the opportunity to use the same money two or

39. The debate over the role of maritime loans acting as insurance is well summarized by Engen 2010, 94–95, who sensibly sees them acting simultaneously both as an insurance policy which spread risk, and also a profitable capital investment. Finley 1985, 23, has identified maritime loans as "the earliest type of insurance, and not primarily a form of credit" (141, 252n82), with which his student Millett 1983, 44n17, disagrees. Todd 1993, 337–40, finds De Ste. Croix's interpretation of bottomry as insurance "attractive," and is correct in pointing out that "bottomry" loans only technically apply to cases in which the ship itself (or its cargo) served as security. See also the lengthy discussion of maritime loans in Isager and Hansen 1975, 74–84. The classic work on the subject is still, of course, De Ste. Croix 1974.

40. This is not to say that the ancient Greeks had a highly developed notion of risk as it is understood in modern economic literature and business practice, where spreading risk has created a thriving insurance industry which was absent in ancient Greece. The earliest documents known to have mentioned insurance were written by Genoese merchants beginning in 1343 and 1350, whence it spread to Flanders and Western Europe; and the first book on insurance was written in Portugal in 1488, for which see Franklin 2001, 273–78. Florentine businessmen began using insurance very soon after the Genoese, for which see Goldthwaite 2009, 98–103. For the later development of insurance, see Kindelberger 1984, 184–86.

41. See also Hesiod, *Works and Days* 643–45, who says "the bigger the cargo, the bigger the profit on top of profit": νῆ᾽ ὀλίγην αἰνεῖν, μεγάλῃ δ᾽ ἐνὶ φορτία θέσθαι. μείζων μὲν φόρτος, μεῖζον δ᾽ ἐπὶ κέρδεϊ κέρδος. For the sense of αἰνεῖν in this passage, see West 1978, 318, who lists parallels exclusively of the compound ἐπαινέω, which are numerous, for which he provides the translation "politely decline"; see LSJ ἐπαινέω, for further examples.

42. For the *dikai emporikai*, the ancient Athenian maritime courts, see Cohen 1973; Lanni 2006, 149–74.

43. Dem. 56.29–30.

three times in the same period of time. Not only did they realize greater profits by breaking their contract and selling their grain at Rhodes, but they were also able to gain further by making more transactions, perhaps increasing their returns many times over.

Dionysodorus and Parmeniscus also rented ships while in Rhodes to allow them to make trips to Athens and complete additional transactions without breaking the terms of their contract, while simultaneously freeing themselves from the repayment of their original loan since they could claim that the ship sank (Dem. 56.21–24). The speaker cleverly sees through their ploy, however, and provides a compelling retort that they would not have offered to repay the interest to Rhodes had the ship actually sunk (Dem. 56.32). In any case, it seems that the defendants did, indeed, rent ships to bring additional cargoes to Athens (Dem. 56.25), which demonstrates that these individuals were savvy enough to be able to avoid the technicalities of their outstanding contract while still using the borrowed money for profitable ventures, even if these brought them back to Athens. Why else would they have brought cargo to Athens in rented ships if not to carry out additional business deals?

Indeed, after they broke the terms of their contract, there was no reason for Dionysodorus and Parmeniscus to allow their borrowed money to lie idle. They even re-lent the money they borrowed on further maritime loans while they were also completing additional transactions in order to make more money (Dem. 56.17). This is yet another example of merchants' versatility and adaptability in the face of changing conditions. Not only did these individuals engage in ventures that violated their contract, but they also exploited the opportunity to lend their own borrowed money at the high rates of maritime interest. By doing so, they were able to use the money they borrowed for a second year (Dem. 56.4), receiving much greater profits from breaking their contract and using the money however they wished than they would have by adhering to the terms of the contract. These individuals therefore seem to have cleverly exploited contract loopholes in order to complete as many extra transactions as they could to increase their profits.

Nor were Dionysodorus and Parmeniscus the only traders known to have broken their contract and to have found alternative ways of investing their money rather than letting it lie idle and unproductive. The trader Apollodorus, brother of Lacritus and Artemo in Demosthenes *Against Lacritus*, is said to have lent the money he had borrowed for a commercial deal from Athens to Pontus to a fellow Phaselite ship owner, who was also a friend of his, apparently for another maritime venture (Dem. 35.36).[44] In both of these cases, the

44. Apollodorus is specifically said to have lent the sum of 100 Cyzicene staters. Since the

borrower recognized the opportunity cost of leaving money unproductive, and preferred to put this money to profitable use by lending it to other traders, thereby displaying remarkable resourcefulness and cunning. Ensuring that money was being used productively at all times, and being open to whatever business opportunities might arise, are strategies that indicate that Greek traders were attempting to maximize their profits.

And many of the *emporoi*, maritime traders, known from ancient Greece aimed at not just the short-term maximization of profit, but also the long-term maximization of wealth. The speaker of Demosthenes *Against Apatourios* was a merchant who made so much money from maritime commerce that he was able to stop risking his life and set himself up as a stationary moneylender. He claims he had only moderate means, but it is clear from his actions that he had been able to establish himself as a large-scale moneylender with the profits he had made from a career at sea:

> ἐγὼ γάρ, ὦ ἄνδρες δικασταί, πολὺν ἤδη χρόνον ἐπὶ τῆς ἐργασίας ὢν τῆς κατὰ θάλατταν, μέχρι μέν τινος αὐτὸς ἐκινδύνευον, οὔπω δὲ ἔτη ἐστὶν ἑπτὰ ἀφ᾽ οὗ τὸ μὲν πλεῖν καταλέλυκα, μέτρια δ᾽ ἔχων τούτοις πειρῶμαι ναυτικοῖς[45] ἐργάζεσθαι.

> For I, men of the jury, for a long time now have been engaged in business on the sea, and up to a certain point I personally took part in the dangers, but it is now just under seven years from the time when I gave up sailing and now having moderate wealth I try to do business in these maritime loans. (Dem. 33.4)

This man had accumulated enough wealth over the course of his career as a trader in the long term that he was able to devote himself solely to moneylending; the men to whom he was lending in this speech were known to him from time he had spent at Byzantium (Dem. 33.5), probably fellow merchants with whom he had done business in the past. For these individuals, Apatourios and Parmeno, approached him to seek a loan to cover an earlier obligation (Dem. 33.6), apparently trusting him and knowing that they would in turn be trusted by him to a certain extent.

We also know of merchants who became moneylenders, such as Nicobu-

Cyzicene stater was worth 28 Attic drachmas in 327 BCE (see my discussion above), the best we can say is that the value of this sum in 350 BCE was approximately 2,800 drachmas, just under the 3,000 drachmas that were originally lent to them by the plaintiffs in this case (35.10).

45. τούτοις . . . ναυτικοῖς could refer to either "maritime loans" specifically, or to "nautical men," but in either case a concentration in maritime loans is certainly meant.

lus, who made a loan on a silver ore washery and slaves in Demosthenes *Against Pantaenetus*. He also was a merchant who amassed enough of a fortune to concentrate on moneylending: ὅστις δ' εἴργασται μὲν ὥσπερ ἐγὼ πλέων καὶ κινδυνεύων, εὐπορήσας δὲ μικρῶν ἐδάνεισεν ταῦτα, καὶ χαρίσασθαι βουλόμενος καὶ μὴ λαθεῖν διαρρυὲν αὐτὸν τἀργύριον, "Whoever has done business as I have, sailing and taking risks, and having been a little successful lends these profits, both wanting to do favors and not to lose the money itself as it slips away" (Dem. 37.54). This merchant turned lender also emphasizes the small size of the fortune he has made, but his humility is belied by the fact that he was able to make a 45 *minae* (4,500 drachma) loan to Pantaenetus (37.4), and to hire Demosthenes to write his court speech after the deal had gone awry.

The other metic lenders known from ancient Greece[46] are perhaps the same type of successful merchants who gave up risking their lives on the high seas and turned their attention purely to financial transactions as moneylenders. As the actions of Apollodorus in Demosthenes *Against Lacritus*, and Dionysodorus and Parmeniscus in *Against Dionysodorus* show, however, merchants hardly needed to retire to become lenders themselves, as they lent their own borrowed money to other merchants for commercial ventures. Nicobulus was also still involved in maritime trade while he was lending money on a mining operation, since he went to Pontus after he made the loan and lost almost everything he had on this trading voyage (Dem. 37.6–10). These merchants were constantly in communication with each other, and cooperated to capitalize on opportunities as soon as they became available.

In such a dynamic system, in which merchants were moneylenders and moneylenders merchants, the lines between the two groups became blurred; it seems that, in the desire to engage money in as many transactions as possible at a given moment, the decision to lend or buy was made in response to the dictates of the market at a particular time and place. Merchants probably used moneylending, and even the extension of money they themselves had borrowed to others, as a moneymaking strategy when arriving at a port with few opportunities for profitable purchase or sale. Those who became particularly successful in accumulating profits could then eventually slow down, reduce the number of voyages they made and gradually concentrate their efforts into moneylending. Therefore, the long-term accumulation of wealth may have naturally pushed merchants into the position of moneylenders, who needed to remain stationary in order to attract prospective borrowers and collect their capital.

46. See, e.g., Theodotus *isoletês*, in Dem. 34.44, 35.14; the Chian moneylender in Pontus at Dem. 35.52, though this person may be a trader also; the metic lender in Dem. 33.10.

Crime Does Pay: Breaking Contracts and Laws to Make More Money

There was an even more seditious, and better attested, strategy for maximizing profit by maximizing the number of transactions one could complete on a single voyage or from a single loan: the dangerous practice of borrowing multiply on the security of the same goods, *epidaneisis*. This tactic seems to have been relatively common, as it is described in a number of speeches,[47] and was frequent enough to merit being mentioned in the only maritime loan contract preserved from ancient Greece:[48] ὑποτιθέασι δὲ ταῦτα, οὐκ ὀφείλοντες ἐπὶ τούτοις ἄλλῳ οὐδενὶ οὐδὲν ἀργύριον, οὐδ᾽ ἐπιδανείσονται, "They put down these goods as security, not owing anything on them to anyone else, and not borrowing additionally upon them" (Dem. 35.11). Even though it was *de iure* prohibited, the fact that this clause was included in contracts shows that *epidaneisis* was a *de facto* reality of trade, and we know of only a few cases that were unsuccessful. The method used by partners Zenothemis and Hegestratus, who worked in tandem, each receiving multiple loans against the security of the same goods, is an extreme example of this strategy. They were able to accumulate a great deal of borrowed money, though they planned simply to keep it, rather than to use it to increase the number of transactions they could carry out on a single voyage, which was apparently the goal of most instances of *epidaneisis*.

Some of the most significant insights into the functioning of the economy and the interaction of individuals and institutions in ancient Greece have been made through focusing on criminal or unethical behavior.[49] *Epidaneisis* was

47. See, e.g., Dem. 35.52, 35.21, 32.4–5, 34.7. Isager and Hansen 1975, 161–62, believe that this last example, from Demosthenes *Against Phormion*, was fabricated by the speaker/lender Chrysippus since it is uncertain that the two loans taken on later were for a round trip and consequently may have had lower security requirements, and since the later lenders were the shipowner and a fellow traveler of the ship Phormion was traveling on, and would not have allowed him to put aboard less cargo than they knew he was obligated to load. Though they are correct in pointing out that Lampis did know about the previous loan made to Phormion by Chrysippus (at Dem. 35.9), this is not decisive proof, since Phormion could have lied to these later lenders about the full amount he had already borrowed. Therefore, this must remain a possible, and perhaps even likely, instance of *epidaneisis*. That the speaker made this accusation shows that at the very least the danger was real enough in the minds of the jury, and was known to have been practiced.

48. The authenticity of the contract in Demosthenes 35, *Against Lacritus*, has been disputed in the past, but most scholars today believe it is authentic: MacDowell 2009, 262; Isager and Hansen 1975, 175–76; see Cohen 1989, 214n34, for older bibliography. This contract is a fascinating document, the only one of its kind from classical Greece, and so constitutes a significant source of information on ancient maritime trade. Its structure and terminology very closely resemble other contract details known from the Demosthenic corpus and papyrus contracts from Hellenistic Egypt.

49. See, for example, the work on liturgy avoidance and the consequent prevalence of *aphanês* wealth at Athens. De Ste. Croix 1953; Hasebroek 1965, 88; Gabrielsen 1986; 1994, 53–60; Christ 1990, 157–60; 2006, 143–204; Cohen 1992, 194–201; and Engen 2011, 98–99, all believe liturgy avoidance through investing in *aphanês* wealth was practiced on a large scale, enough to contribute to the expansion of the nonagricultural sectors of the entire Aegean economy (Engen 2011).

widespread enough that the Athenian state took a tough stand in deterring it by executing the son of a general who was found guilty of this practice (Dem. 34.50). Nevertheless, there were limits to how effectively the state could enforce contracts in ancient Greece (see below), and because of the difficulties in monitoring behavior in the market, many traders likely were successful in using *epidaneisis* to maximize the profits they could make on a single voyage.

Epidaneisis is an extraordinary example of the same high-risk, high-reward activity other traders chose to engage in when they entered maritime commerce, and this type of bad behavior provides an unparalleled insight into the economic mentality of maritime traders in ancient Greece. The fact that borrowers would resort to this measure clearly illustrates their desire to maximize the number of transactions they could complete per voyage. Borrowing multiply on the security of the same property is not exceptional to ancient Greece, moreover, but is attested in the modern US as well, for example during the credit-fueled expansion of cotton, the bubble that burst and contributed to the panics of 1837. As Baptist shows, slave owners would borrow additional funds on the security of slaves that were already hypothecated, expecting to make greater profits with the huge (and illegal) injection of liquidity into their pockets.[50] *Epidaneisis* was a clever trick thought up by desperate or unscrupulous borrowers in an attempt to make as much money possible, and the parallels with the modern United States demonstrate that ancient Greeks employed the same tactics and *mentalité* in their pursuit of wealth.

As with the practice of *epidaneisis*, the maritime court speeches contain numerous other examples of individuals who chose to chase profits rather than adhere to contracts or laws. Although not everyone broke the law or contracts, it is equally true that not everyone who did so was caught, and so the bad behavior of these individuals can be used as a reliable guide for the goals and intentions of traders in general, even if the precise strategies pursued by the majority were less extreme than their criminal counterparts. As Dionysodorus and Parmeniscus show above, breaking contracts could provide the borrower with opportunities for profit that would otherwise be lost by sticking to an agreement. They effectively understood and acted upon the opportunity cost of adhering to or breaking the terms of the contract.[51]

Some business partners did more than just violate agreements; they even went so far as to completely turn on their associates to make greater profits.

50. Baptist 2012, 88–89.

51. In addition to Dionysodorus and Parmeniscus above, see also the contract- and law-breaking actions of Zenothemis and Hegestratus in Demosthenes *Against Zenothemis*, and in other speeches, e.g., at Dem. 34.36–37, 35.20, 32; 33.9.

Personal gain is said to have caused partners to flip on each other, or lawsuit opponents to join forces and split the proceeds of their betrayal. In Isaeus' speech *On the Property of Dicaeogenes*, among the colorful characters are a certain Menexenus who agrees to betray his kin in return for personal profit in a side deal made with Dicaeogenes III (Isaeus 5.13); the latter in turn refused to repay a friend and associate of his, an Egyptian named Melas, keeping the money he had borrowed and ruining their relationship (Isaeus 5.40). In Demosthenes *Against Phormion*, the opportunistic Phormion is said to have convinced the ship captain Lampis to switch his testimony and perjure himself in return for a share of the profits (Dem. 34.35, 41, 46). Without Lampis' testimony, the plaintiff had no evidence to secure the verdict he needed to recover his money, which Lampis and Phormion afterward split as a reward for their treachery. The two exploited a contract clause to make a profit together once Lampis, the main witness, ceased to support the plaintiff. Dionysodorus, as discussed above, also flipped on his lender, but in this case, it was to avoid lower profits following a drop in the price of grain when a shipment of Sicilian wheat arrived at the Piraeus (Dem. 56.9). Dionysodorus here displays the price sensitivity and the profit-oriented behavior that so clearly characterized the rest of his actions discussed above.

Perhaps no individual better exemplifies this profit-seeking price sensitivity than Protus, Demo's business associate in Demosthenes *Against Zenothemis*. Protus was initially loyal to Demo, having borrowed money from him for a shipment of grain, and assisted Demo vigorously against Zenothemis who was claiming the grain for himself. Afterward, however, he switched sides, and worked with Zenothemis against Demo:

> ὁ γὰρ Πρῶτος, ἕως μὲν ᾤετο τὸν σῖτον κέρδος ἐλθόντα ποιήσειν, ἀντείχετο τούτου, καὶ μᾶλλον ᾑρεῖτ' αὐτός τε κερδᾶναι καὶ ἡμῖν τὰ δίκαι' ἀποδοῦναι, ἢ κατακοινωνήσας τούτοις τῆς μὲν ὠφελίας τούτους ποιῆσαι μερίτας, ἡμᾶς δ' ἀδικῆσαι: ὡς δὲ δεῦρ' ἥκοντος αὐτοῦ καὶ περὶ ταῦτα πραγματευομένου, ἐπανῆκεν ὁ σῖτος, ἄλλην εὐθέως ἔλαβεν γνώμην.
>
> For Protus, as long as he thought that the grain would make a profit when it came, he clung to it, and chose rather to both profit himself and pay us what we justly deserved rather than join cause with these men . . . but when he had come here and was in business regarding these matters, the price of grain fell, and immediately he changed his mind. (Dem. 32.25)

Thus, a single price fluctuation made Protus flip. Whereas his grain was valuable while prices were high, once they fell he stood to make more by siding with Zenothemis against Demo, having come to an agreement with him in return for a share of the profits. As the main witness against Zenothemis, he was apparently persuaded into switching sides and splitting the proceeds with Zenothemis, which would have been greater (all the returns, principal and gain, being pure profit) than if he had to repay Demo the interest from the lower returns he would have made from the lower price of grain. Protus then escaped the territorial jurisdiction of the Athenian *polis* (32.28), denying Demo the testimony crucial for his case.

Protus' betrayal provides clear evidence for a phenomenon that is paralleled in the modern economy. Douglass North describes how people renege on agreements when it is more profitable to take money and run than to remain on good terms with a partner, a sign of a wealth-maximizing attitude:

> Under what conditions will contracts tend to be self-enforcing? In a wealth-maximizing world, the answer can be stated very simply. Contracts will be self-enforcing when it pays the parties to live up to them—that is . . . the benefits of living up to contracts will exceed the costs. . . . In the context of a wealth-maximizing world, where there are high costs of measurement and no form of enforcement is possible, the gains from cheating and reneging exceed the gains from cooperative behavior. (North 1990, 55)

As North says, in a wealth-maximizing world the wealth maximizer will flip if the returns from reneging are greater.[52] The gains for cheating in this case outweighed the gains from adhering to the contract since the profits from the grain shipment dropped during the time of the dispute. Protus thus seems to have been trying to maximize the profit he could get from a single transaction, even if it meant betraying a business partner. This behavior is precisely what is outlined by game theory in which actors weigh the relative costs and benefits of adhering to or breaking a relationship each time they play a game:

> If the game continues indefinitely, it usually pays the parties to live up to the terms of exchange, because the gains from successive iterations exceed the benefits that could be derived from a single defection,

52. Perhaps Protus was even given the promise of future contacts with these scoundrels in the Piraeus, and so transferred to a rival personal network.

> from "running off with the profits." Note, however, that a game so conceived must be played in perpetuity. If there is an end to the game . . . then indeed the discount rate may enter in to determining whether it is worthwhile to continue to cooperate. The smaller the probability of continuing for another round, the greater must be the payoffs to sustain an equilibrium; also the greater the possibility of short-run gains, the greater must be the payoffs.[53]

In repeated games, the benefits of maintaining a connection are different from those in once-for-all games. It is worthwhile to adhere to agreements if one wants to maintain a viable business relationship in the future. The last time these iterated games are played, however, the rules change, and cheating becomes more common since players know they will not need to have future dealings with the other players. For Protus, it was simply more profitable to renege on his agreement with Demo, and to terminate the relationship. From this perspective, it appears that Protus and others were behaving exactly as the modern individuals studied in game theory: profit-maximizing individuals who act to serve their own personal best interest.

Weak Inter-*Polis* Contract Enforcement: Take the Money and Run

Protus was able to take the money and run because of the limits to international contract enforcement in the ancient Greek world.[54] Danger clouds every transaction when individuals perceive that they can cheat on contracts and escape with the profits. If contracts were self-enforcing, this would not be a problem, but as Douglass North states, the problems of information and enforcement are still very real even to this day:

> Game theory tells us that . . . when the parties acquire perfect information and the game both lasts indefinitely into the future and is played between the same parties, one can reach self-enforcing solutions. But needless to say, these assumptions not only are strong but are simply not observed in the real world. The inevitable conclusion that one arrives at

53. North 1990, 56–57, whose discussion in this section is based upon Axelrod 1984.

54. For the undoubtedly extensive mechanisms for contract enforcement that were enacted by the ancient Greeks, see Harris 2007 and 2020. These measures were mostly effective within the bounds of *poleis* or even inside the confines of the marketplace itself, however. Once someone left the *polis*, the enforcement situation changed drastically. Even in the modern world, state enforcement of contracts has its limits.

> in a wealth-maximizing world is that complex contracting that would allow one to capture the gains from trade in a world of impersonal exchange must be accompanied by some kind of third-party enforcement. (North 1990, 57)

Thus, in a wealth-maximizing world, reneging is profitable when third-party enforcement is unavailable, and, as Protus demonstrates, it seems that cheating in contractual obligations was facilitated by the limited reach of mechanisms for the enforcement of international contracts in ancient Greek maritime trade. Although procedures for enforcement could be powerful *within* a city, as in the case of the death penalty inflicted by the Athenian *polis* on the general's son in *Against Phormion*,[55] when it came to international enforcement of contracts, there was something of a free zone in which individuals could be confident that they could escape punishment.

The *polis* system itself, being a fragmented set of distinct political units, created complications for the stability of international markets, since there were no effective permanent mechanisms for the enforcement of interstate contracts. The very institution of the *polis*, as a political framework, fostered a hazardous international market system, due to each *polis*' limited autonomy. The Greeks themselves recognized the problems with protecting property rights outside of the *polis*, and a number of *poleis* established treaties for the enforcement of contracts with other cities, *symbola* agreements, in which the citizens of both cities had recourse to legal protection in each other's courts. But even with the sophisticated Athenian maritime courts, the *dikai emporikai*, which gave metics access to Athenian judicial procedures and empowered magistrates to use force to protect contracts, there was room for the unscrupulous to escape state enforcement.

As soon as a trader left a city's enforceable territory, he entered a grey area in which he was largely immune to legal action.[56] In short, by leaving a *polis*' terri-

55. Dem. 34.50. The Athenians also threatened capital punishment for residents of Attica shipping grain to ports other than Athens, and for lending money for voyages to any other port (Dem. 34.37, 35.50–51; Lycurgus 1.27). See Cohen 2005, 299; and Todd 1993, 321. Moreover, for *dikai emporikai*, the state directly enforced the law by imprisoning foreigners who could not post bail and convicted defendants until they repaid the damages imposed by the court's judgment (Cohen 2005, 301–2).

56. Lytle 2012 provides evidence for the limits of *polis* enforcement with respect to fishing rights; although fishing in harbors and inland waterways was regulated by the *polis*, the open sea was rather seen to be the common property of all, and *poleis* were not willing or perhaps able to extend their enforcement of fishing rights to the open sea. Morley 2007, 64–70, says enforcement only pertains to within a city's limits. On the limits of international law, see Todd 1993, 329–32, who shows that Athenian legal jurisdiction did apply to the Athenian empire during the fifth century, which was considered an extension of the Athenian *polis*, but beyond that it is difficult to say

tory, one could escape the type of third-party enforcement described by North. As Hasebroek puts it: "Even in time of peace it was easy to avoid payment of legal obligations, for there was no international court in which they could be enforced, and the countless city courts were prejudiced, and unreliable."[57] Many traders in the ancient Greek world seem not to have been resident metics, but rather itinerant *xenoi* (foreigners) who traveled from place to place, making up a community of international wandering merchants.[58] Those whom third-party state enforcement was meant to target were precisely those who were most difficult to track, and the majority of those who were likely to break contracts were also the most mobile, the very people against whom such enforcement would be least effective.

Ancient Greek maritime trade was, to a certain extent, a world of impersonal market exchange (see my discussion of personalistic networks below), but one that had only limited third-party state enforcement. Therefore, through private initiative,[59] the market had expanded beyond the bounds within which it could protect itself. The market system was, in fact, more sophisticated in this respect than the political and legal institutional infrastructure in which it was embedded. In the end, Hasebroek is correct to say that protection for traders was "inadequate,"[60] since the impersonal market, in the form of the actions of ancient Greek traders, had grown beyond the enforceable bounds of the *polis*.

If a trader could only escape *polis* jurisdiction, he could avoid state enforcement and keep the money. In Demosthenes *Against Apatourios*, a single passage describes how two separate individuals tried to escape *polis* enforcement for the contracts in which they were involved:

> οὐ πολλῷ δὲ χρόνῳ μετὰ ταῦτα τῆς τραπέζης ἀνασκευασθείσης, καὶ τοῦ Ἡρακλείδου κατ' ἀρχὰς κεκρυμμένου, ἐπιβουλεύει οὑτοσὶ τούς τε παῖδας ἐκπέμψαι Ἀθήνηθεν καὶ τὴν ναῦν ἐξορμίσαι ἐκ τοῦ λιμένος.

> And not long after these things, when his bank was ruined and Heracleides at first went into hiding, the defendant was planning to send the

that any sort of international enforcement occurred in ancient Greece.

57. Hasebroek 1965, 87. Enforcement and punishment were major problems in ancient Greek *poleis*, which did not have a modern police force, and therefore private individuals often needed to take the initiative in policing offenders, for which see Christ 1990; Hunter 1994, 120, 134, shows that enforcement often lay in the hands of citizens, who were required to resort to self-help to prosecute criminals even within Athens. Nevertheless, Athenian magistrates had more power to enforce the law than is sometimes recognized by scholars, as argued by Harris 2007.

58. Reed 2003; Engen 2010; Isager and Hansen 1975; Hasebroek 1965.

59. See Bresson 2007, chapter 8, on private initiative driving the ancient Greek economy.

60. Hasebroek 1965, 21.

slaves out of Athens and to remove the ship from the harbor. (Dem. 33.9)

The collapse of Heracleides' bank caused the banker himself to go into hiding. His debtor, Apatourios, who had borrowed from Heracleides to cover an earlier overdue loan (Dem. 33.7), responded in turn by trying to remove the security for this defaulted loan, his ship and its slave crew, physically outside of the jurisdiction of the Athenian *polis*.

By escaping the legal reach of the state, one could enjoy property and profits with little fear of reprisal, which could only come in the form of *sula*, a measure of self-help. The ability to flee *polis* enforcement can be seen in Andocides' exile after he was convicted of defiling the sacred Herms, and it is entirely germane to note that while in exile he was able to support himself by engaging in maritime trade. Zenothemis at first was certainly trying to flee the jurisdiction of both the Syracusan and Athenian *poleis* by escaping with the money to his hometown of Massalia. Aphobus, Demosthenes' guardian, managed to keep the profits from embezzling his nephew's estate by physically leaving the jurisdiction of the Athenian courts, and settling down as a metic in Megara. If he had ever returned to Athens, of course, he would have been subject to *polis* enforcement, but only if he were careless enough to get caught.

This sort of difficulty in the enforcement of long-distance trade beyond the jurisdiction of a specific government was also characteristic of the early modern European economy. Braudel has spoken of the "impunity allowed by overseas trade—which was beyond supervision, given the distances between the points of sale and the individuals concerned in such exchanges."[61] Therefore, premodern maritime commerce was a dangerous world, which only became safer with the development of more sophisticated legal and monitoring methods in the modern world.

But even when one was within *polis* jurisdiction and third-party enforcement was possible, as in the case of the Athenian maritime courts, some of the individuals in the speeches trusted to deception and procedural trickery to avoid prosecution, to the point that they even returned to Athens after they had broken the law by violating the terms of their contracts.[62] Rather than trying to

---

61. Braudel 1982, 416.

62. The legal system in Athens was not comprehensive enough to protect against many of the tricks that could be employed in attempts to circumvent legal institutions. When Aphobus encumbered his land with debts so that Demosthenes could not recover the money owed to him, it was clear that he understood that using this trick would give him added time to remove his property and also make it more difficult for Demosthenes to collect his losses, according to Demosthenes at any rate (Dem. *Against Onetor* 1 and 2). When Demosthenes' guardians forced him to serve a

hide, some, like the brother traders Apollodorus and Artemo in Demosthenes *Against Lacritus*, returned to the city where they had made the agreement, apparently not very concerned about the possibility of state enforcement:

> ἐπειδὴ γὰρ ἀφίκοντο δεῦρο, εἰς μὲν τὸ ὑμέτερον ἐμπόριον οὐ καταπλέουσιν, εἰς φωρῶν δὲ λιμένα ὁρμίζονται, ὅς ἐστιν ἔξω τῶν σημείων τοῦ ὑμετέρου ἐμπορίου . . . καὶ τὸ μὲν πλοῖον ὥρμει ἐνταῦθα πλείους ἢ πέντε καὶ εἴκοσιν ἡμέρας, οὗτοι δὲ περιεπάτουν ἐν τῷ δείγματι τῷ ὑμετέρῳ.
>
> For when they arrived here, they did not sail into your harbor market, but rather put into the thieves' harbor,[63] which is outside the markers of your harbor market . . . and the ship was anchored there for more than twenty-five days, while these men themselves were walking around in your sample market. (Dem. 35.28–29)

By anchoring their ship in an illegal harbor, and then making their way into the market by foot, these brothers avoided detection and snuck back into the very city where they had violated the earlier contract. In the "sample market," the *deigma*, the moneylenders who had originally financed their trip, Androcles and Nausicrates, confronted them and demanded repayment. The brother of the borrowers who had stayed behind in Athens, Lacritus, responded by exploiting a loophole: that the ship which was carrying their cargo had been wrecked (Dem. 35.29–31), nullifying the original contract (35.11). The only hope the moneylenders had was to win their case in court by proving that the contract had not been followed.

Exploiting loopholes and technicalities in contract wording was a favorite trick of some of the more clever and unscrupulous. Dionysodorus and Parmeniscus also took advantage of the wording of their own contract to be able to keep the money and continue trading, likewise claiming that their ship sank (Dem. 56.21), and using this excuse to continue to trade at Athens with rented ships; Demosthenes, however, ingeniously seems to have exposed a fatal flaw in their argument, as they allegedly offered to repay the interest on the cargo from Egypt to Rhodes, though not from Egypt all the way to Athens; but they would

trierarchy in order to be permitted to bring his suit against them, they were using this as a means of discouraging him from taking legal action.

63. Isager and Hansen 1975, 171–72, say the φωρῶν λιμένα was a "pirate's harbor," not a "smuggler's harbor." Whatever the case, the point of the speaker's description is to show that the defendants were avoiding harbor officials and duties to try to illegally circumvent legal institutions to profit for themselves.

not have been liable for any interest at all if the ship had actually sunk (Dem. 56. 31–32). Phormion also returned to Athens to continue trading after breaking the terms of his own contract, exploiting a clause which gave the borrower the right to repay the loan to the *nauklêros* Lampis instead of the original lender; rather than actually paying Lampis, however, the two made a deal to split the money and then take their chances in the Athenian court should the issue ever arise (34.18, 35).

With the information problems of verifying the claims of these men, it was only their own mistakes that enabled them to be prosecuted. Phormion was found to be in violation of his contract before the ships' sinking, and likewise for Apollodorus and Artemo. Dionysodorus, as discussed above, was subverted by agreeing to repay the interest on part of the voyage when no interest would have needed to be paid at all in the event of the ship's destruction.

In the latter case, the deal offered by Dionysodorus to Dareius to repay the interest from Egypt to Rhodes is probably an accurate reflection of how contract violators would prefer to settle with their lenders. In the modern corporate business world, going to the courts is often the last resort in conflict resolution; side deals made between the companies in the absence of lawyers are the preferred way of resolving disputes to cut costs of litigation and avert the deterioration of relations between the two firms which would inevitably result.[64] Therefore, it may be that Dionysodorus was using a common strategy by trying to resolve this conflict with a compromise outside of court.

Moreover, even when the state did have the ability to enforce its laws, the slow pace of legal procedures often permitted individuals to whisk away disputed property before the judicial action itself.[65] Phaenippus took advantage of the time delay in the matter of his *antidosis* to sell the property in question, making a large profit while converting his produce to *aphanês*, or invisible, form (Dem. 42). Aphobus, the guardian of Demosthenes, similarly took advantage of the time involved in the legal procedures taken against him to liquidate his property, emptying the wine vats on his property, and perhaps also taking away his wards' manufacturing slaves with him to Megara, where he took up residence as a metic in order to enjoy his wealth outside the reach of the Athenian law courts. Apatourios attempted to sneak away from the Piraeus his ship

64. Granovetter 2001, 62.

65. Long protracted delays existed for other types of actions (see Cohen 2005, 301n58 for examples), but for maritime cases, the delays were eliminated, as part of the *dikai emmênoi*, cases to be settled with one month's time. In the Athenian maritime courts, foreign defendants were required to post pretrial bail or securities, and if they did not they would go to jail (Cohen 2005, 301). The *dikai emmênoi* reveal that the Athenian *polis* recognized the enforcement problems that encumbered maritime trade and attempted to resolve such conflicts in a quick and efficient manner.

and slaves that were about to be seized as security on a loan default, and after he failed, he resorted to arbitration to further delay the legal measures being taken against him (Dem. 33.14–22).

Clearly all these men thought that they could escape the law courts of Athens, and were so confident in their ability to do so that they even stayed in or returned to Athens after violating their contractual obligations. The plaintiffs in these cases were forced to resort to hiring Demosthenes to write speeches for them in order to be able to overcome the trickery of their borrowers.

This is not to say that there were no effective mechanisms for the enforcement of maritime trade contracts in ancient Greece. As North states, in the absence of effective third-party enforcement, it was still possible for lending and merchant businessmen to police their own ranks to a certain extent.[66] Indeed, if a merchant double-crossed a lender, there would be no way for that person to be able to engage in a business deal with that lender or anyone else who hears about the contract violation. Apatourios was slandered in the *emporion* by his former creditors who were trying to dissuade others from lending to him in their attempts to seize his ship and slaves (Dem. 33.6). Also, the moneylenders in the Piraeus in Lysias *Against Aeschines* were on the whole unwilling to lend to Aeschines, on account of the bad reputation he had acquired.[67] Demosthenes himself recognized the costs and benefits of ruining one's reputation for short-term gain: πολλῶν χρημάτων τὸ χρηστὸν εἶναι λυσιτελέστερόν ἐστιν, "Being honest is more profitable than a great deal of money" (Demosthenes 36.52). Therefore, the long-term benefits of remaining honest were definitely known to the ancient Greeks, many of whom were certainly willing to forgo the possibility of a quick profit to maintain long-term business relationships.[68] Reputation could be a powerful incentive to adhere to agreements.

But what if, as in the example of Protus above, one cared more for profit

66. North 1990, 55: "Ostracism of merchants who reneged on agreements . . . provide[s] incentives to parties to live up to agreements. Reputations, depending on the costs of information, provided parties in long-distance trade and impersonal exchange a mechanism to enforce agreements."

67. Lysias fragment 38.4 (Gernet and Bizos 2003).

68. For the awareness of reputation as being important in business, see the trader in Demosthenes *Against Phormion*, who made benefactions to Athens to secure a good reputation (34.38–40). The same man is astounded that Phormion did not gather witnesses when he was supposedly repaying the loan in the Bosporus as his contract permitted, because it would have secured him a great reputation for honesty in business dealings (34.29–30). Demosthenes also says πίστις ἀφορμὴ πασῶν ἐστι μεγίστη πρὸς χρηματισμόν, "Trust is the best capital of all for moneymaking" (36.44). In Demosthenes *Against Apatourios* lenders are said to have slandered their borrower in the *emporion* to ruin his reputation, in order to deny him new lines of credit (33.7–8). Aeschines in Lysias *Against Aeschines* had certainly acquired a bad enough reputation among money lenders in the Piraeus that they would not lend to him. For the importance of reputation in policing even the behavior of modern firms, see Williamson 1975, 108.

than for reputation? In this case, there would have been no reason to live up to one's agreements since the alternative provided more material return. Gossip and reputation were of course important for individuals who were concerned with keeping a good name, such as stationary moneylenders, but for those who were engaging in trade only as a short-term means of making money, it may have been more profitable to resort to deceptive behavior and then invest the profits into activities whose participants were entirely different from those members of the trading community who were aware of that individual's reputation. Zenothemis and Hegestratus clearly did not care more for their reputation among Syracusan lenders than the cash which they then had at their disposal in Massalia. Conversely, one could remain in the field of maritime trade, but change the cities in which one operated, or, as in the case of Zenothemis and Hegestratus, work cooperatively and use a partner as an intermediary to exploit the same moneylenders through an unknown associate.

In short, those individuals who did not care about a bad reputation were precisely those who were willing to exploit the imperfections of state enforcement in the open market. If one has already made a bad name for himself among the resident merchants and lenders of a given city, it is almost inevitable that he will leave the jurisdiction of this city as a matter of course. Therefore, for such individuals the limited third-party enforcement of cities would have carried little or no force anyway, and it is this lack of effective enforcement that characterizes much of ancient Greek mercantile trade behavior.

Perhaps many turned to trade as a means of making a quick profit, only to leave after they had made a small fortune. Zenothemis and Hegestratus certainly seem to have been treating their borrowing scam as a means to make money in a short-term stint in maritime trade. As Padget and McLean have shown for Renaissance Florence, many of the individuals who took up banking only engaged in this trade for a short period of time, on average only 8.2 years,[69] to make money quickly and then retire when they had accumulated enough wealth. Hesiod's father made his fortune in maritime trade but then bought land and retired. The merchants turned moneylenders discussed above likewise stayed in trade long enough to make their fortune, whereupon they retired. As described by game theory, individuals would have been more willing to honor a business relationship if they had an interest in maintaining that contact in the long term, and much less so if they perceived that they were dealing with someone for the last time.

With the limits to the enforcement that the state could provide for interna-

69. Padgett and McLean 2011, 19n44.

tional contracts, businessmen were left to their own devices to try to recover their losses through the institution of *sula*,[70] the forcible seizure of property from a debtor in another *polis*. This option, of course, was always available, but it required taking the time to track the cheater down and bring enough force to be able to execute the reprisal effectively. Moreover, it seems that some cities did not share the right of reprisals with each other (Dem. 35.13), and so there would have been safe havens for cheaters to hide even from *sula*. In the absence of effective state enforcement, individuals were forced to rely on themselves to protect their interests.

Contracts, Friends, and Family: Protecting Oneself on the Open Market

Moneylenders faced great risks when they handed their money over to maritime traders, who could do whatever they wanted once they had it in their hands. The speaker of Demosthenes *Against Dionysodorus* describes the difficult position moneylenders encountered every time they lent their money, as they were faced with an information problem due to the uncertainty that a borrower would repay the loan: "The borrower has the advantage over us in every respect."[71] Since the character of a borrower might not be known, the speaker continues, there is only one objective means to trust that loans might be repaid, namely the maritime court of Athens: τῷ οὖν ποτὲ πιστεύοντες καὶ τί λαβόντες τὸ βέβαιον, προϊέμεθα; ὑμῖν, ὦ ἄνδρες δικασταί, καὶ τοῖς νόμοις τοῖς ὑμετέροις, "And so, trusting in what and taking what as surety do we lend our money? In you, men of the jury, and in your laws" (Dem. 56.2). This speaker recognizes that there is no guarantee that a borrower will return his money, and that in such a situation, the only recourse a moneylender might have would be to the law courts of Athens. Therefore, a moneylender would want to ensure that he could turn to the courts in case his money were stolen, and so contracts were written to give the lender something tangible to use to recover his money with

70. The authoritative work on *sula* is still Bravo 1980. For a more recent treatment, see Lintott 2004.

71. ἡμῖν τοῖς τὴν κατὰ θάλατταν ἐργασίαν προῃρημένοις καὶ τὰ ἡμέτερ᾽ αὐτῶν ἐγχειρίζουσιν ἑτέροις ἐκεῖνο μὲν σαφῶς εἰδέναι, ὅτι ὁ δανειζόμενος ἐν παντὶ προέχει ἡμῶν. λαβὼν γὰρ ἀργύριον φανερὸν καὶ ὁμολογούμενον, ἐν γραμματειδίῳ δυοῖν χαλκοῖν ἐωνημένῳ (Dem. 56.1). A money borrower was in a much better position regarding information asymmetry than the lender of money, who would be forced to evaluate the trustworthiness of his potential business partner. A useful analog can be seen in the information uncertainties that arose based on the quality of coinage in the Athenian *agora*. In the case that a buyer had more than one type of coin, whose quality might be unknown (counterfeit, etc.), information asymmetries would arise in favor of the seller of goods (the receiver of money), for which see Johnstone 2011, 12–13.

state enforcement. With the advent of the Athenian *dikai emporikai*, a new level of enforcement was introduced, in which a written document could be used to support claims to private property.

Given the high risks for everyone trying to make a fortune in maritime commerce, merchants and financiers alike sought to reduce their exposure to risk and improve their bargaining position by gathering information.[72] Information problems with dealing with unknown or not-well-known partners in maritime trade can be usefully conceptualized in light of Geertz's description of the bazaar economy, where "information is poor, scarce, maldistributed, inefficiently communicated, and intensely valued. . . . The level of ignorance about everything from product quality and going prices to market possibilities and production costs is very high."[73] Granovetter shows how even in the corporate worlds of the United States and Japan in the 1980s, the information costs associated with finding new contacts in the open market actually cause businessmen to associate with known partners and create long-term trading relationships with a few trusted partners.[74] That the same phenomena existed in ancient Greece attests to the similar nature of social fabric that shaped the market economy at that time.

Problems of trust are what led the ancient Greeks to resort to written contracts in the first place, since they allowed for state enforcement through the law courts.[75] The speaker of Demosthenes *Against Phormion* says that lack of trust caused the defendant's lenders to make two contracts with him (ἀπιστοῦντες at Dem. 34.32). The money lender Demo in Demosthenes *Against Zenothemis* had an agreement, but no contract with Protus, and was then unable to produce written documentation to prove his ownership over the cargo he was claiming in Athens. Not having a written contract deposited with a third party exposed Demo to Zenothemis' attack when Protus escaped, since he was the star witness for Demo's case. Though state enforcement was not perfect, it was not even available without a contract, and so as a risk-reducing measure to avoid the treachery of business partners, lenders resorted to written contracts to decrease the chances of losing their money entirely. With a written contract, one could prove his property rights in court, and was therefore permitted to resort to self-help, which could be effective within the bounds of *polis* jurisdiction.[76]

---

72. Morley 2007, 33.

73. Geertz 1978, 29.

74. Granovetter 2001.

75. So says Aeschines in *Against Timarchus*: τὰς συνθήκας τῆς πρὸς ἀλλήλους ἀπιστίας ἕνεκα ποιούμεθα, ἵνα ὁ μὴ παραβὰς τὰ γεγραμμένα δίκην λάβῃ τῇ ψήφῳ παρὰ τοῦ παραβάντος (Aeschines 1.161).

76. As Harris 2007, 173n50, points out, in private suits, plaintiffs in Athens were allowed to

Lenders still wanted to engage in highly profitable bottomry loans, and they were willing to take the risks on the ship sinking or the borrower escaping. Maritime trade was dangerous however one was involved. But lenders did make attempts to reduce these risks as much as possible and thereby increase the chances of making a profit. Thus, it should come as no surprise that the speaker of Demosthenes *Against Apatourios* says that his co-lender wanted him to arrange things so that they were "as safe as possible" (ὡς ἀσφαλέστατα), for him (33.8). The desire for safety to offset risk was a central consideration for ancient Greek economic thought in general (see chapter 1), and so it should come as no surprise that contracts were a means of increasing the safety for the lender.

There were a number of ways in which contracts were written to reduce the risks for the lender.[77] First, security tended to be about twice the amount of the loan,[78] to ensure the lender that there would be ample property backing up a loan. Second, there were clauses that gave contracts precedence over laws in the cities where participants would be transacting business, to prevent any legislation from annulling the borrower's responsibility.[79] Third, clauses were introduced allowing the lenders *praxis*, power to collect, both in the city of the original contract[80] and sometimes also in the destination city,[81] to permit the lenders to take action without resorting to the legal system. Fourth, to increase the lender's trust in the borrower, penalties were also written into contracts in case of infractions.[82] In *Against Dionysodorus*, the borrowers Dionysodorus

---

seize defaulting debtors' property (see, e.g., Dem. 21.11; Theophemus and Euergus engage in a particularly forcible act of seizure at Dem. 47.52–61), which shows that self-help was indeed possible and effective within *polis* jurisdiction as long as the defaulting party could be found and overpowered. Goods are seized in a dispute over the security in a maritime trade deal at Dem. 32.20, even without the authority of a written contract.

77. Another way borrowers could ensure trust was to leave one of their partners behind in Athens, like Lacritus and Dionysodorus, while the other partner went with the ship. This enabled the lender to prosecute the partner who remained in the city in case of contract violation. Lenders also countered by sending representatives with the ship, or by sending letters to partners on the other side of a trade route (Dem. 34.8). These examples show pretty clearly, however, that these measures were also imperfect.

78. Dem. 35.18, Dem. 34.6.

79. See the clause stating that nothing will be "more authoritative" (*kurioteron*) than the agreement in the contract at Dem. 35.13; Cohen 2005, 298–99; Phillips 2009, 96–97. This clause is also found in numerous papyrus contracts, including *P.NYU* 3.15–16; *P.NYU* 468 R.11; *P.Eleph.* 1.13–14; *P.Tebt.* 104.39; *P.Oxy.* 1273.37.

80. In the contract at Dem. 35.12. The *praxis* clause is known from other contracts in the Demosthenic corpus at 34.27, 56.45; for the *praxis* clause in Egyptian papyrus contracts, see Wolff 1941.

81. For a clause giving lenders originating in Athens the right of *praxis* in the Bosporus, see Dem. 34.27.

82. Penalties were often built into contracts: see, e.g., Dem. 34.33, the time limit, ὑπερημερία, in Dem. 47.51, at Dem. 33.6 (time limit), and at Dem. 35.13 (time limit and interest rate increase), as well as the penalty of paying double in Dem. 56.20, 38.

and Parmeniscus wrote a clause penalizing themselves double the repayment price if they violated the contract's terms. Finally, many contracts specified the amount of interest which the borrower was to deliver upon completion of the voyage, ensuring a high profit for themselves, and laying the risk of loss upon the borrower.[83]

Because borrowers wanted to be able to pursue the most profitable opportunities possible, some contracts even had flexibility built into them. In the contract preserved in Demosthenes' speech *Against Lacritus*, this versatility can be seen in the increased interest that is specified for a voyage after the rising of Arcturus. This clause is a penalty, but also gives the borrower extra time in case he needs it. The borrower's choice can also be seen in the fact that although an outward cargo is specified (3,000 jars of Mendean Wine, 35.10), the return cargo is not (35.10–13), and referred to only vaguely as *chrêmata*, goods. Therefore, the borrower's choice was built into the contract itself, as it was in Demosthenes *Against Phormion*, where the contract gave the defendant the option of paying Lampis, the ship's *nauklêros*, rather than the moneylender in Athens (Dem. 34.34–35), freeing up Phormion to be able to make another deal in the Pontus region if he wanted.

The main way in which this was done was not through contractual wording, which could help only in case of the trader's returning to Athens where the contract could be used in the maritime courts, which did have true enforcement power. Nor did individuals want to depend on private reprisals and *sula*, which were only resorted to in the most extreme cases. Rather, it was through the creation and maintenance of trusted networks of business associates and personal contacts that individuals were best able to protect themselves in the world of ancient Greek maritime trade.

Since contracts and state enforcement were imperfect, a better way to protect effectively against potentially dangerous strangers in the open market was to buffer oneself through the creation of long-term business partnerships with trusted individuals, whether friends or family. It is hardly a coincidence that many of the trading partnerships we encounter in ancient Greece involved

83. Borrowers were protecting themselves, too, against big loss, which is why they took all the illegal measures I discussed above to protect themselves against unfair deals rigidly imposed by contracts in the face of changing market realities. As discussed above, Apollodorus the Phaselite trader is said to have lent the money he originally borrowed for his own trading voyage to a friend and fellow Phaselite *nauklêros*, doubtless because they were part of the same friendship and business partner networks. The speaker who indicts him, Androcles, attributes this rascality and knavery to the Phaselite people in general, who he says are involved in the most *dikai* in Athens of any other people, Greek or non-Greek (35.1–2).

family members,[84] and other business deals in the sources were often made between trusted business partners.[85] Slaves were some of a master's most loyal business associates (Lampis, Midas, Pasion, Phormion), and could attain positions of prominence in these circles of trust. National groups of merchants probably formed important networks of information,[86] and often seem to have worked together, including the Phaselite compatriot and friend to whom Apollodorus lent his borrowed money when he reached Pontus (Dem. 35.36).[87]

Even bankers, who (as I argued in chapter 3) often made high-interest loans to unreliable individuals to capitalize on every potential profitable opportunity, sometimes protected themselves through networks of trust, for example requiring introductions through known associates.[88] Pasion wanted unknown borrowers to be vouched for by current customers on at least two known occasions (Isoc. 17.4; Dem. 52.4), and is said to have accumulated a wide network of friends in his business (Isoc. 17.2). *Pistis* is explicitly said by Demosthenes to be the foundation for Phormion's business success (Dem. 36.44), and so trust was an important part of banking, which seems to be the most impersonal and open of ancient business practices. Since bankers were

84. See Reed 2003, 37n14, for trading partnerships among family members: catalog nos. 11 and 12, 19 and 20, 31 and 32, 49, 51 and 52, 11 and 12.

85. At Dem. 33.5, the borrowers are said to be well-known to the lender: τούτοις δὲ τοῖς ἐκ Βυζαντίου καὶ πάνυ οἰκείως χρῶμαι διὰ τὸ ἐνδιατρῖψαι αὐτόθι, "With these men from Byzantium, I am very much familiar from the time I spent there."

86. Compare the Byzantine traders who work together at Dem. 33.5.

87. Bang 2008, 241, agrees that merchants did try to form social networks to protect themselves against the vicissitudes of commercial life. These communal merchant organizations tended to be restricted to the sharing of information, mutual help in foreign lands, guarantee of burial, conviviality, and cultic activities. As in ancient Greece, they never developed into corporations. Foreign trading communities in particular served to forge contacts, vouch for new members, and performed other community strengthening activities. *Collegia* of cities' merchants were found in many *poleis*, and were in particular associated with cults (250). These associations also adjudicated private conflicts to police their members and maintain social order within the association (262–63).

88. Hasebroek 1965, 87, agrees: "The lending business of the Greek banker seems to have been largely confined to the occasional accommodation of personal friends, and his deposit business was no doubt equally restricted." The wide range of friends that Pasion is said to have had, however, shows that the term "friend" in this instance is rather inclusive, perhaps referring to trusted business associates. In this respect, bankers' and other merchants' reliance upon personal introductions for new contacts resembles the practice of expanding networks of contacts in *xenia*, or ritualized guest-friendship, and so may actually be derived from and related to the expansion of guest-friendship networks in the ancient Greek world. For introductions through intermediaries in guest-friend relations in ancient Greece, see Herman 1987, 47. In this respect, the social fabric of ancient Greek trade was similar to that of even early American rural communities: "Hasbrouck's early customers came from the neighborhood, and strangers hailing from beyond required an endorsement from a resident and partner-in-trade. Reputation thus pre-ceded economic interaction" (Bruegel 2006, 550).

actively involved in maritime finance,[89] they were also exposed to the risks of defaulting borrowers,[90] and so would have been wise to protect themselves.

Therefore, because merchants, moneylenders, and even bankers operated within personalized networks of contacts, they cannot be said to entirely conform with the principles of free market competition that are central to the simplified neoclassical models of economic behavior. Such market distortions are not solely characteristic of ancient Greece, however, but are also prevalent in the modern economy. Mark Granovetter has shown the importance of personalized contacts in modern American and Japanese corporate dealings,[91] and just as in premodern economies, relationships are used to curtail problems of information and trust. Geertz's discussion of the bazaar economy stresses the costs of information asymmetries, where relationship forming was not anti-profit-maximizing or economically irrational—rather, it was the result of the difficulties of trust and information acquisition.[92] The time needed to find new, more profitable contacts could be better spent doing something else, like making deals. Even modern firms tend to prefer repeated, long-term relationships with known contacts rather than incurring the high costs of gathering more information on new potential partners.[93] The problems of information that Geertz has illustrated for the bazaar economy are therefore equally applicable to the ancient Greek and modern economies.

The use of personalistic networks is not a sign of primitive economic development, therefore, but rather endemic to open market economies in general. Another historical parallel can be seen in Renaissance Florence, where business was frequently channeled through networks of personal contacts:

> In their riskiest business climates, Florentines tended to close ranks within intimate social relations for their strongest credit connections.

89. Bankers' active involvement in financing trade has been argued persuasively by Cohen 1992, 121–86, who, according to Reed 2003, 39, is correct, though too optimistic about certain examples at Dem. 27.11, which are in my opinion actually quite well-argued-for, unless they are perhaps business partners. See also Thompson 1982, 55n12. For earlier works which denied the role of banks in maritime finance, see Reed 2003, 39n24. Bankers financing trade are attested at, e.g., Dem. 33.4–7 (to finance credit purchase of ship), and 49.35–36 (banker finances merchandise bound for Athens). Perhaps up to half of the total value of known bank loans in ancient Greece was for trade, for which see Shipton 2008. This would make sense since many merchants were said to be the customers of the banker Pasion (Dem. 52.3).

90. Defaulting borrowers were especially dangerous for bankers, and are known to have caused the collapse of banks in ancient Greece (Dem. 45.64).

91. Granovetter 2001, has shown that the modern economy was more "embedded" than scholars such as Polanyi have allowed, and convincingly argues that the embeddedness often reserved for premodern economies was in fact a characteristic of all economic systems.

92. Geertz 1978.

93. Granovetter 2001, 62–64.

> Since Florentine families in international business were spread geographically all over Europe, some of the heaviest early fifteenth-century flow of international finance throughout Europe coursed through upper-class Florentine families' veins, making them very wealthy indeed. (Padgett and McLean 2011, 26)

Again contrary to the neoclassical model of impersonal markets, in fifteenth-century Florence personalistic markets predominated, which exhibit different features than the neoclassical model of the open, free market economy; instead of perfect access to information, it is exclusively shared by a limited number of individuals.[94] Restricting information and money to trusted contacts also concentrated and channeled the increased profits that accompanied such privileged access to lucrative opportunities. In these networks, restricting information was a way for sellers to maximize their own gains, which would be magnified within the group thanks to the exclusiveness of the information. As Osborne has argued the land leased by corporate groups in Attica seems to have been largely redirected to the actual group members who controlled the lease auctions, because they confined the news of these opportunities to themselves and other privileged insiders.[95]

Economic transactions served to cement personal contacts, rather than to make them impersonal, leading to an economic system strongly embedded in social relations, where cooperation was just as important as competition. So the invisible hand of the economy did not create a purely free, open market for all—instead, self-interested profit maximization within a world of limited government enforcement of contracts created a market system in which trust problems distorted the nature of impersonal exchange. Rather, the creation of networks of trusted contacts to reduce risk controlled access to opportunities to people who were part of these information networks. Individuals seeking profit on the open market were therefore barred from many of the most lucrative deals, which were restricted to certain circles. Therefore, separate channels of information existed independently of each other, each operating within different social networks, and lucrative news was a privilege of group members. Gaining a place in these protected networks was a difficult task since it often required a member of the group to introduce a new member and to risk his own reputation by bringing in someone new who could threaten the cohesiveness and safety of the trusted group of business contacts.[96]

94. Padget and McLean 2011, 46.
95. Osborne 1988.
96. Bourdieu 2001, 104.

Economic imbalances and asymmetries would have resulted from the creation of these social networks, and instead of opening up profitable opportunities to all, would have denied knowledge to all but those who were able to penetrate the group in one way or another. This is the heart of Polanyi's notion of embeddedness, the social fabric of economic activity.

Perhaps we can go further by applying Bruegel's insights into the social dynamics of economic relationships in early American farming communities, whose substantivist character he describes in detail.[97] Bruegel demonstrates how economic behavior was socially embedded and how the nature of these social bonds provided not just structure, but also an important impetus for, this economic behavior. Here Polanyi's emphasis on the concept of "embeddedness" can be seen in its full force:

> Of course, they were built on, and engendered, trust. But regular interaction also kept up pressure and the threat of sanctions. The cost of leaving a long-term relationship included a monetary as well as an intangible dimension. The inability to meet expectations put reputations at risk. The stigma diminished one's capacity to enter new partnerships. . . . Finally, long-term relationships in trade appeared convenient to partners-in-trade, but while trust accrued over time (though one might want to see the evolution of outstanding debts as time went by), pressure emanated from personal relations. (Bruegel 2006, 551–53)

Social pressures drove economic exchange. Since it was necessary to meet others' expectations in order to maintain one's reputation and relationships, and thereby ensure the future ability to enter into new partnerships, this social pressure may have been a significant factor in the economic decision-making process. The desire to maintain one's reputation as a receptive, approachable businessperson may have affected economic calculation and choice on a level that does not appear in the source material, and cannot be measured quantitatively.

With this continuous social pressure to maintain business relationships, individuals are operating under constraints not purely economic in character—that is, not just prices and profits. Rather, the need to appear as a ready and willing potential trade partner, who will generally be open to the opportunities for exchange which are presented, is of the utmost importance in such socially embedded trade conditions. If a businessman does not maintain his reputation as a trading partner receptive to new business possibilities presented by

97. Bruegel 2006.

partners, he may deprive himself of future opportunities for profit, since his partners, once refused, may turn to another more reliable contact when similar situations arise.

Moreover, since balanced reciprocity and favors are part of any social relationship,[98] the refusal to provide a favor for a business associate may be interpreted as a hostile act, and may jeopardize the future business deals available not just with that individual, but perhaps also others if they hear of a reluctant business partner. Therefore, reciprocity in the sense argued for by Polanyi, within an embedded, substantivist setting, could then affect individuals' behaviors in the sphere of the disembedded market operating according to formal economic rules. Both the embedded and disembedded realms are seen to be functioning in ancient Greece, just as they operated together in the rural communities of the early United States, and still do today in the modern economy. So for those who did care about their reputation, and who were more likely to be fixed in a single location, the social pressure to engage in transactions and remain a viable business partner would have been powerful.

As Bourdieu has argued, social capital is necessary to maintain one's standing as an active, viable player in the social network of economic interactions of which that person was a member:

> The profits that accrue from membership in a group are the basis of the solidarity that makes them possible . . . material profits . . . and symbolic profits. . . . It is the product of an endless effort . . . to produce lasting, useful relationships that can secure material or symbolic profits . . . the network of relationships is the product of investment strategies . . . aimed at establishing or reproducing social relationships that are directly usable in the short or long term. (103)

Staying connected with social networks required an investment of time and effort, a necessary cost to maintain the flow of information about and access to profitable opportunities provided by these relationships of trust. Therefore, the economic aims of a disembedded market system can be met through action within the social fabric of an embedded system. The two types are not mutually exclusive, but are instead complementary, coexisting as two poles on the spectrum of over- and under-socialized emphases in economic analysis:[99]

98. For the notion of balanced reciprocity, see Sahlins 1972, 219–30.
99. Granovetter 2001.

> Exchange transforms the things exchanged into signs of recognition and, through . . . the recognition of group membership that it implies, re-produces the group. . . . It reaffirms the limits of the group . . . beyond which the constitutive exchange—trade, commensality, or marriage—cannot take place. The reproduction of social capital presupposes an unceasing effort of sociability, a continuous series of exchanges in which recognition is endlessly affirmed and reaffirmed. (Bourdieu 2001, 104)

An unceasing effort of sociability, a continuous series of exchanges, is what Bourdieu says sustains the social capital needed to maintain membership in such groups. This, combined with Bruegel's notion of social pressure emanating from these relationships, illuminates some of the social aspects of economic networks. Social ties were a way of guaranteeing future economic exchange. Conversely, the economic primacy of these social relationships demonstrates the types of investments that were necessary to be successful in a hazardous trading environment: investments in the membership of a group are a form of protection against the dangers of the open market.

Because sustaining these relationships required constant effort, the social pressures which the networks created could also be taken advantage of by unscrupulous, profit-hungry borrowers; the need to maintain reputation and to maintain trading contacts in order to secure long-term financial success could be exploited by traders in search of funds. Personalistic market networks could be penetrated from the margins, and such an act of deception could even win the favor of a group's competitors, meaning that through damaging a link with one network, one could glide automatically into a new network of business contacts.[100]

In these situations, where lenders were approached by friends and repeated business partners,[101] their desire to maintain the relationship and their reputation may have been a significant factor in their decision to agree to make these loans. Thus, the deceptive borrowers were taking advantage of the pressure of social relations within the economy to manipulate the decision-making process of the lenders, who feel the demand to comply due to their desire to remain viable, active businessmen in the trading community. This was an economic drive, to sustain or to increase one's standing in the trading community

100. Such as seems to have happened when Protus sided with Zenothemis and the group of scoundrels in the Piraeus in Demosthenes *Against Zenothemis*.

101. Whenever a loan is made to unscrupulous borrowers in the sources, it is exclusively the borrowers that approach the lenders. See, e.g., Dem. 33.6, 35.6, and 56.5. It may be that these borrowers approached these lenders knowing that they could dupe them.

by showing that one was receptive to new opportunities and new potentially profitable partnerships. Social factors strongly affected the economic sphere in this respect, in that the necessity of maintaining reputation and relationships seems to have forced these men to make arrangements which may not have been entirely ideal. Thus, the social fabric of economic trade was a driving force in the economy, and the calculations were not merely numerical. Their ultimate goal may have been financial, but the means to maintaining and ensuring economic gain in the future was a careful assessment of the social pressures and opportunities in the market, and so monetary calculation had to go hand-in-hand with social calculation at all times.

In Demosthenes *Against Lacritus*, the borrowers used the lender's mutual acquaintances to penetrate their personal trade network to obtain a loan which otherwise may not have been accessible. Lacritus and his brothers were introduced to their prospective moneylender through the latter's friends, men who were known quite well to him.[102] They otherwise probably would not have been able to secure this loan, as the lender was a stranger, but presumably by exploiting the trust accumulated by an acquaintance of their own, they were able to use this person's trust to penetrate the lender's circle of trust at the margins. Therefore, as Granovetter points out for the modern business world, "While social relations may indeed often be a necessary condition for trust and trustworthy behavior, they are not sufficient to guarantee these and may even provide occasion and means for malfeasance and conflict on a scale larger than in their absence."[103] In short, social networks may have been a necessary, but not a sufficient, means of protecting oneself, and even the most close-knit network could be penetrated by free market opportunism at the fringes. Thus, the market could still find its way into these carefully guarded networks of trust.

This is as far as one can go with the evidence from ancient Greece, but nevertheless it fits entirely a broad pattern of behavior as presented by scholars of Renaissance Florence, farmers in the early American republic, and the modern economy in general: problems of trust led to the formation of personal business relationships which were mutually beneficial and restrictive. The very social nature of these relationships, however, exerted pressure to maintain them, leading perhaps to deals that were less than ideal for some individuals. These social networks warped the fabric of the open market, but were nevertheless vulnerable at their margins, and therefore did permit the free trade of neoclassical

102. Dem. 35.6.

103. Granovetter 2001, 58, who continues by showing that while the potential for malfeasance is always present in the market, the *level* of malfeasance in the market is much lower in comparison with breaches of trust within social networks (58–60).

market models to operate alongside, and also symbiotically overlap with, these personalistic networks.

Conclusions

In conclusion, as in other economic systems, unrestrained profit-maximizing behavior led to a distortion of the market in ancient Greece. While some tried to seek profit without regard for future reputation or the maintenance of contacts, others tried to sustain their long-term success in the highly profitable field of maritime commerce by protecting themselves against the dangers of free, impersonal trade in the open market. The result of these risk-reducing measures was an alteration of the market, in which opportunities were not open to all, but were rather restricted to individuals operating within personalistic networks. Therefore, instead of the perfect markets of neoclassical economics, characterized by free information and open competition, ancient Greek markets were contorted by kinship-centered partnerships that restricted the availability of information to members of protected circles of trust.

These networks, however, were not impenetrable. Rather, they were constantly in danger of being exploited at the fringes, where trust was weakest and where the problems of information and social pressure were most powerful. Although networks of business contacts could help to decrease the costs of loss, since they cushioned a businessman from exploitation, there was still a problem of trust which pervaded the lives of every ancient Greek businessman. Therefore, ensuring that these networks of contacts were as plentiful and as dependable as possible would have been of the utmost importance.

The market economy of the Greek world, as seen in international maritime commerce, had developed faster than the political and legal infrastructure that supported it. Personal initiative and enterprise, indeed an entrepreneurial spirit, had pushed the possibilities for making money in maritime commerce beyond the public structures for enforcement permitted by the political system of the *polis*. The market had become as sophisticated as it could have become within the peculiar economic world of the ancient Greek *polis*. Legal institutions were always a step behind the truly opportunistic and imaginative figures seen in the maritime court speeches of fourth-century Athens. If traders had just adhered to the rules governing trade, the market economy would have been perfectly suited to its institutional underpinning.

But this is not what happened; the drive for profits led to ever more clever and innovative strategies to surpass the bounds imposed by the law and contracts. The boldness with which individuals pursued profit is remarkable, and the aggregate behavior of ancient Greek traders created an expansion of the commercial sector of the ancient Greek economy and the other sectors that depended upon trade, such as finance and manufacturing. This expanded market economy was hazardous, however, since the reckless drive for profit maximization had pushed international trade beyond the point that it could be policed by individual *poleis*. Therefore, the politically fragmented Greek *polis* system, as an institutional structure, was by its very nature unable to intervene in, and therefore stabilize, the international markets of commerce and finance that had been created through the private initiative of individuals.

CHAPTER 5

Maximization in the Ancient Greek Economy

The ancient Athenians examined in this study exhibited great resourcefulness and ingenuity in coming up with innovative and sophisticated ways to make money. In their attempts to maximize their returns, many seem to have actually managed to achieve the aim of considerably expanding the overall wealth of their estates. Long-term growth over the course of one's career is a reliable sign of a wealth-maximizing approach to *oikonomia*. They also demonstrated the type of flexibility and profit-oriented choice based on the comparison of different investment options that is characteristic of individuals who are described as behaving in an economically rational manner in modern economic theory.

Many were even ruined in their quest for profit. Bankers were on the lookout for potentially gainful opportunities in their attempts to maximize their returns. But in order to keep their moneymaking machines going, some overextended themselves lending to risky borrowers, which eventually undermined the delicate balance of cash flows banks needed to survive, as the astonishingly high rate of bank failures suggests. In the dangerous world of maritime commerce, adventurous traders risked their lives at sea for profit, and merchants searched for news about lucrative opportunities at a frenetic pace to beat their competitors to sources of supply. They tried to maximize the number of transactions they could complete on individual trips and were remarkably versatile in responding to changing conditions. Sometimes it was more profitable to relend money borrowed from creditors to other merchants, creating short but risky chains of tenuous, overextended credit that could collapse in the blink of an eye. The market was volatile and filled with uncertainty; clever and deceptive individuals manipulated information and took advantage of the institutional fabric of the world of exchange with impressive creativity. Networks of trust were required to shield oneself from the perils of the open market, but could also be exploited to the ruin of those involved. Eventually some traders became stationary moneylenders themselves, which brought much risk but was the most sensible way to reinvest commercial profits since they were already familiar with the world of maritime trade and had preexisting networks of robust business contacts.

In the silver mining industry, huge fortunes were made, which spurred a silver rush and perhaps eventually an atmosphere of "irrational exuberance," to borrow a term from the modern economy. To maximize profits, ore washery owners experimented with technological innovations, ultimately leading to a highly efficient design that minimized water usage; likewise in smelting, an optimal level of cost minimization and silver maximization was achieved in the face of fuel constraints. Diversification allowed some to offset the risk of being overly concentrated in one type of moneymaking activity, while for others it was the means by which they expanded into lucrative new fields.

Indeed, maximizing income also explains much of Athenians' behavior in the field of agriculture. Phaenippus was certainly using his farm to make money.[1] The profits he received from just this one year's crop, 18,000 drachmas from barley (1,000 *medimnoi* at 18 drachmas)[2] and 9,600 drachmas for wine, even if they are reduced to more likely figures, are still enormous returns for an enterprise of any kind. Since this was such a productive *oikos*, it appears that Phaenippus was running this estate as a business, to make profit.[3] The fact that he was exploiting his resources to the fullest, he was probably trying to make as much money as he could with this farm, since he was cutting down and selling the timber on his property and expanding his available arable land. He also made the choice to grow wine on the better-watered portions of his estate, a cash crop that was regularly in high demand, as opposed to wheat which would have brought him a lower return.[4] And so, it seems that Phaenippus was, indeed, running his agricultural *oikos* as a moneymaking operation for profit, and all his decisions that can be reconstructed were designed to increase those returns. Or, even if these patterns were just invented for rhetorical purposes, they were supposed to be believable for an Athenian jury. In the lease inscriptions from Attica, wealthy Athenians seem to jump greedily at the chance to

1. For a detailed discussion of Phaenippus' farm, see Bresson 2007, 152–55; Osborne 2002; De Ste Croix 1966.

2. Dem. 42.40. Eighteen drachmas per *medimnos* was high but not unheard of. Demosthenes 34.39 preserves a price of 16 drachmas per *medimnos* during a food shortage. It may be that Phaenippus was hoarding his produce in order to sell it at the highest price he could, in which case his grain may have been more than a year's worth stored, and it may have been just such a huge windfall that alerted the speaker to challenge Phaenippus in an *antidosis*.

3. Phaenippus' estate is described as being quite large, large enough to have two huge threshing floors on his property, each a *plethron* in extent. He may have even rented out the use of these threshing floors to his neighbors or fellow demesmen, further exploiting the moneymaking potential of his property.

4. Osborne 2002, 122.

rent even small plots of land in their quest for quick profits in agriculture.[5] In the so-called *rationes centesimarum*, even expensive plots of land were snatched up by buyers at short notice; and large sums were paid for tracts in the sudden auctions recorded in the Attic Stelai, where there was no shortage of investors, such as the ready and eager buyers of Oionias' 81 talents of land in Euboea.[6]

Xenophon provides evidence that Greeks outside of Athens sought to maximize their profits and wealth in agriculture. In the *Constitution of the Spartans*, he describes the variety of ways non-Spartans made money: "For in the other cities everyone makes as much money as they can. For one farms, another captains a ship, another trades, and others are supported by crafts," ἐν μὲν γὰρ δήπου ταῖς ἄλλαις πόλεσι πάντες χρηματίζονται ὅσον δύνανται· ὁ μὲν γὰρ γεωργεῖ, ὁ δὲ ναυκληρεῖ, ὁ δ' ἐμπορεύεται, οἱ δὲ καὶ ἀπὸ τεχνῶν τρέφονται (7.1). This passage contains a number of important implications that must be unpacked. First, agriculture is included alongside manufacturing and trade as ways for Greeks to pursue their moneymaking ambitions, so on a conceptual level, here again farming is subsumed under the broader notion of *chrêmatistikê*, which is the primary category that unites the rest. Next, far from being merely an Athenian phenomenon, Xenophon states that in all Greek *poleis* except for Sparta, "everyone" is engaged in making money, the contrast being between the Spartiates as citizens forbidden from business, and every other *polis* where the citizen body does practice *chrêmatistikê*. Finally, in a quantitative sense, the phrase πάντες χρηματίζονται ὅσον δύνανται, "everyone makes as much money as they can," agrees with the statement of Aristotle that a wide portion of the citizen body devotes as much of their time to moneymaking activities as possible, or that they make as much money as they can. It is unclear whether ὅσον refers to time or money, but in either case, it seems to be echoing Aristotle's statements about widespread attempts at maximization. Elsewhere, in the *Poroi* passage discussed in the introduction chapter, Xenophon again lists trades as different ways people engaged in *chrêmatistikê*, which forms the broader category. He describes individuals who switch from occupation to occupation to go where the money is. He treats them not as farmers, traders, or craftsmen, but rather as *chrêmatistai*, moneymakers who evaluate these arts primarily on the basis of higher profits.

Outside of Athens, the rich inscriptional record of rural leases and sales

5. Osborne 1985, 54–59; 1988, 291.

6. For the *rationes centesimarum* as sales, see Lambert 1997; Andreyev 1974, 15–18, 44–45; and Lewis 1973. For a view that the transactions recorded in these inscriptions may be leases rather than sales (which seems less probable in my view), see Osborne 1985, 56–59. For the Attic Stelai, see Pritchett 1953; and Pritchett and Pippin 1956.

from very small *poleis* and villages illustrates the extent to which even the most remote areas had become monetized and connected to the cash-oriented economy of more commercialized *poleis*.[7] Property sales at fourth-century Tenos reveal multiple purchases of land, including one with forty-seven transactions ranging from sixty to eight thousand drachmas.[8] The Boeotian farmer who comes to barter with Dicaeopolis in the *Acharnians* is excited by the potential for a "great deal of profit,"[9] and Dicaeopolis later assures him that he "will profit."[10] As Bresson observes, in the Dodona tablets, farming and animal husbandry are primarily mentioned for their potential to create profit, which is the main criterion by which they are considered in the deliberations of those consulting the gods.[11] Therefore, agricultural *oikonomia* seems to have become incorporated into moneymaking activities throughout the Greek world and was largely aimed at the generation of wealth, and agriculture was no exception.

Thespiai in the late third and early second centuries BCE likewise published a series of land leases, in which it seems that both the price and the term of the lease was negotiable, and in which wealthier members of the community were eager to invest, often in more than one plot at a time, and renewed their contracts for long periods, up to twenty years.[12] The uses for these plots seem

7. Schaps 2004, 168–73, has argued that agriculture was not as thoroughly monetized as other fields of economic activity in classical Greece. However true this may be for some regions of the Greek world, nevertheless in the more commercialized regions monetization had so pervaded the field of agriculture that there were many opportunities for specialization for market production and profit from exchange. See Pernin 2014 for the temporal and spatial spread of monetized land transactions in the Greek world. As early as 427 BCE, agriculture is said to have been incorporated into the monetized economy of the Aegean, as Thucydides describes how in the aftermath of the Mytilenean revolt, Lesbos was divided into 3,000 *kleroi*, parcels, each given to an Athenian who was to receive a rent of 200 drachmas per year. He says that the Lesbians were forced to pay this rent in *argurion*, cash (Thucydides 3.50.2–3). The Attic Stelai, published just after the Hermokopidai incident in 415, expresses the agricultural produce and plots of land confiscated from the offenders in cash terms, the price paid by the buyers in the resulting auction. Other public documents, such as the *rationes centesimarum* attest that individuals in Athens were willing to pay huge amounts of cash for farm plots with little notice, doubtless confident in their ability to get more cash from them. Pericles, of course, was said to have sold all his produce in the market for cash (Plutarch, *Pericles* 16.4), apparently a real-world example of the so-called "Athenian style of householding, in which the estate's produce was sold in the market for cash, rather than being stored in the house all year (ps.-Aristotle, *Oikonomika* 1.6.2, 1344b31–33). Phaenippus in Demosthenes *Against Phaenippus*, is said to have sold 1,000 *medimnoi* of barley and 800 *metrêtes* of wine (Dem. 42.20). Osborne 2002, 128–29, argues convincingly that agriculture was very deeply integrated into the cash market economy at Athens, since so many liturgists needed to raise cash to meet state demands from agriculture. Reger 1994, 197–201, 205, 209, has shown that the prices for rents of estates at Delos were closely connected to the prices of the agricultural produce to be grown on them, barley and olives; this is as monetized a situation as one could imagine in the premodern world.

8. *IG* 12.5.872.

9. λάβοιμι μέντἂν κέρδος ἀγαγὼν καὶ πολύ (*Acharnians* 906).

10. κἂν τοῦτο κερδάνῃς ἄγων τὸ φορτίον (*Acharnians* 957).

11. Bresson 2016a, 167–68.

12. Osborne 1988, 292–93.

to have been purely agricultural, and those with *aulai*, stables, fetched a higher price on average, apparently because they were prized for the ability to raise livestock.[13] One particular stable was leased for 330 drachmas annually (12.5 percent its value), which indicates the types of profit it could be expected to make. The Rheneia estates owned by the Temple of Apollo at Delos were leased for an average of 1,300 drachmas a year in the 290s.[14] High status lenders,[15] many of whom appear as guarantors who already owned real estate, and some who were already known for other commercial activities,[16] showed interest in even small plots, and there was no shortage of demand for land by men of high wealth and status.[17] On Delos, auctions for the lease of Apollo's estates were highly competitive and driven by the hope for profit—one piece of land, for example, is said to have yielded 5,760 drachmas worth of crops in one year.[18] Deals were done in cash, and some estates' cash rents rose and fell with, and were therefore determined by, the market prices for barley.[19]

As Osborne observes, pastoralism was one of the primary moneymaking activities for the lessees of these estates, which perfectly illustrates the profit-oriented nature of their operation:

> Unlike crops with roots, sheep and cattle could quickly be acquired or disposed of for cash, along with the slaves who looked after them. Rapid entries to and exits from agricultural practice were therefore possible . . . the pattern of agriculture on the temple estates made an open ended commercial attitude to farming possible: the turn-over of estate leases makes it look as if some, at least, took advantage of that possibility.[20]

For the ambitious moneymaker, an opportunity such as a large estate lease could bring enormous profits. The size of the rents and the large crop production demonstrate how much money could be made. There was even a frantic bidding war for many of the estates, before Delian temple officials had to step in to stop the rapid increase,[21] in what could even be compared to a speculative

13. Osborne 1988, 295.
14. For the leases on Delos, see Kent 1948.
15. Osborne 1988, 299.
16. E.g., Diaktorides (Kent # 74), was a banker who leased temple land and a foundry. Another, Antigonos, who may have been a banker (Kent # 22), a lessee of temple land who also bought the contract for the harbor tax at another time, overextended his resources to the point that he became indebted to the temple.
17. Osborne 1988, 291.
18. Osborne 1988, 296.
19. Reger 1994, 197–201.
20. Osborne 1988, 302.
21. Kent 1948, 279–80; Reger 1994, 214–21.

bubble, since the default of lessees and the seizure of their land was the result of overcommitting resources beyond what the value of the property could sustain, to what was believed to be a more and more profitable venture. As with the Athenian silver rush, one could even say that here too ancient Greeks' "animal spirits" drove them to lengths of "irrational exuberance." Therefore, competition for these estates was intense because of the potential returns from the agriculture and animal husbandry that could be practiced on them. In the Delian economy, the scarcity of land certainly made the temple estate leases some of the best opportunities for lucrative investment, which explains why they were so valuable and sought-after, and the timely seizure of profitable enterprises can be seen in the rich men who so eagerly snatch up even small plots of land.[22]

Maximization is also attested in the archaeological record, where a number of households were entirely or primarily devoted to the production of goods for the market. House A v 9 from Olynthus, for example, seems to have devoted every available bit of sunlit space to the production of textiles, and at least four looms were set up in the house's well-lit areas to maximize the amount of productive space.[23] As Cahill notes, four looms are more than are needed for household consumption, and so this house seems to have been devoted almost entirely to the production of textiles for the market. The material record therefore corroborates the impression above that making money can be seen to have conceptually engulfed the larger mental category of traditional *oikonomia*, as households were widely considered to be mechanisms to create profit and wealth.

Other clear indications that Greeks considered growth to be desirable and natural for estates can be found in Athenian law. In the law governing the leasing of orphans' estates from the archon, it is required that any shortfall in what the guardians return to the orphan be repaid with interest added. Menecles leased from the archon an orphan's estate jointly with other guardians and was forced to pay interest on the amount he owed the orphan after his guardianship came to an end, which indicates that Athenian law considered that the wealth in an estate would normally be invested in productive enterprise.[24] But even more, just as the lease itself was expected to cause the estate to increase, and the *polis* required estate lessees to pay interest on top of the principal at the end of their administration, so the Athenians accepted the argument that

22. Osborne 1985, 54–59. Reger 1994, 218, describes competition for these estates as being "fierce."

23. Cahill 2002, 119.

24. For orphan estate leases see Cudjoe 2010; Leese 2016–2017.

orphans' estates would grow and produce profit under good management.[25] Demosthenes references this same expectation when he reckons the amounts his guardians owe him, saying that his estate could have doubled or tripled during the time they were managing it, and including the amount of interest that would have accumulated on his property during the time it was not being invested profitably.[26]

Moreover, these were not rare or exceptional patterns confined to the margins. Xenophon states that "everyone makes as much money as they can" in every *polis* other than Sparta, and his list of alternative investment options in the *Poroi* includes agricultural products, so these processes characterized not just the commercialized urban market, but even the rural countryside. I have argued elsewhere that market forces penetrated everyday life to such an extent, even into the hinterland, that the classical Athenians (the only citizen body for which we have any extant detailed source material) understood the basic principles of supply and demand and the way these forces were affected by behavior at the individual level.[27] Elsewhere, Olynthus, Hellenistic Delos, Babylon, Rome, and other places also reveal evidence for the operation of supply and demand, so these phenomena do not just characterize Athens alone.[28] As Polanyi notes (see introduction chapter), supply and demand result from groups of individuals behaving in an economically rational manner. Such a pattern of individual behavior could therefore be reasonably assumed for these other places outside of Athens as well.

And although Aristotle may be exaggerating when he says that "everyone engaged in money making will increase his wealth without limit," the Greeks describe the desire to make money as being hard-wired into the most primal regions of the *psychê*. Rather than being the characteristic of strange or unusual individuals, the drive to accumulate wealth was seen as being one of the core mental processes in the Greek mind. In the details of their character sketches of *chrêmatistai*, Aristotle and Plato add further support to the view that the aspiration to maximize wealth and profits was a widespread phenomenon in ancient Greece—they must have had enough exposure to build personal familiarity with traits associated with successful business; so much so that they echo precisely the characteristics that are described by Weber in his spirit of capitalism. Conceptually, *chrêmatistikê* had so fully pervaded daily life that it had engulfed

25. See Thür 2010, 15.

26. The Athenian law against *aergia* (idleness) assumes that an estate not being profitably managed could be made profitable with a change in management.

27. Leese 2017a.

28. As revealed by the analyses of price data by Reger 1994; Nevett 2000; Pirngruber 2017; Temin 2013.

the traditional purpose of everyday activities. Many arts had been subverted such that their end, *telos*, was money itself. Even traditional *oikonomia* was practiced to achieve πλοῦτος, wealth.

Psychological Impulses to Maximize Wealth in Greek Thought

It should not be a surprise that ancient Greeks sought to maximize profit and wealth because these behaviors stem from core psychological drives recognized by both archaic poets and classical philosophers. In the *Works and Days*, Hesiod gives valuable insight into the psychological impulses motivating economic behavior in Askra in the seventh century BCE.[29] He opens this poem with an account of two types of strife, *eris*, in the world: the first delights in mischief (28) and is harmful to people, while the second is better to mortals (18), because it forces them to work hard to improve their condition:

> ἥ τε καὶ ἀπάλαμόν περ ὁμῶς ἐπὶ ἔργον ἐγείρει·
> εἰς ἕτερον γάρ τίς τε ἴδεν ἔργοιο χατίζων
> πλούσιον, ὃς σπεύδει μὲν ἀρόμεναι ἠδὲ φυτεύειν
> οἶκόν τ' εὖ θέσθαι· ζηλοῖ δέ τε γείτονα γείτων
> εἰς ἄφενος σπεύδοντ'· ἀγαθὴ δ' Ἔρις ἥδε βροτοῖσιν.
> καὶ κεραμεὺς κεραμεῖ κοτέει καὶ τέκτονι τέκτων,
> καὶ πτωχὸς πτωχῷ φθονέει καὶ ἀοιδὸς ἀοιδῷ. (ll. 20–26)

> And this strife rouses the shiftless[30] man to work;
> for the one who is defective in his work looks upon another man who is rich,
> who is eager to plow and plant and set his house in good order.
> And neighbor is jealous of his neighbor who strives after wealth.
> This strife is good for mortals. Potter begrudges potter, builder
> vies with builder, beggar is jealous of beggar, as are bards of each other.

In this fascinating glimpse at life in an archaic agrarian village, Hesiod provides some of the earliest evidence for economic behavior in the ancient Greek

29. In the discussion that follows, my interpretation is almost entirely in line with that of Van Wees 2009 who sees Hesiod not as describing a world of barely self-sufficient peasants but rather that of fairly successful and well-off farmers.

30. *Apalamos*, which seems to mean "shiftless" or "helpless" here as elsewhere in archaic and early classical poetry, can also mean "foolish" (Page 1955, 315), which may also be implicit in Hesiod's use of the term in this passage.

world. It is not by mere whim or fancy that he opens the *Works and Days* with *eris* and the competition to excel in economic affairs. Indeed, the psychological response to seeing a wealthy neighbor is central to his argument in the poem: the wealthy man's *ploutos* and *aphenos* inspire *phthonos*, *zêlos*, and *kotos* in his neighbor. These feelings rouse the shiftless man to work, and to emulate his more successful peer. One who is eagerly working and accumulating wealth inspires the other who wants riches for himself by triggering some sort of anger or pain, which Hesiod depicts as an emotional sting. Here, the emotional response is perhaps best described as "rivalrous emulation," and Hesiod is not explicit in distinguishing between *kotos*, *phthonos*, and *zêlos*, but rather uses them as rough synonyms for the same envious, jealous, emulative behavior.[31]

To Hesiod, this is a meaningful and pointed statement that expresses a significant principle of human behavior—people are psychologically driven to emulate and compete with their neighbors, those who are perceived to be peers or close rivals. Indeed, by then elaborating with his list of people who pursue the same line of work (potters, builders, beggars, bards), Hesiod seems to be adding emphasis that his focus is not just on the feelings of rival farmers but on competition between peers in society more broadly. He conveys the idea that it is generally the case that whoever sees his rich peer or rival will feel the sting of envy and will try to emulate him. This rule moreover applies to everyone. By enumerating such diverse occupations, Hesiod demonstrates the universal nature of this psychological phenomenon; in each case, individuals are impelled by self-interested feelings of competition for wealth, desiring to have more and angry when they have less.

Because Hesiod connects this competition with the desire to be rich, such feelings are of the utmost importance for understanding ancient Greek economic behavior. Hesiod rephrases the same idea later in the poem: εἰ δέ κεν ἐργάζῃ, τάχα σε ζηλώσει ἀεργὸς πλουτεῦντα, "If you work, the lazy man will quickly envy you, because you are rich" (312–13). The causal aspect of the participle πλουτεῦντα is significant, as it specifies that the wealth is what elicits the emotional response. The man who looks upon his more successful and richer neighbor is awakened by *eris*, a competitive drive, to emulate (and surpass) him, *because* he is rich. "If you work, he *will* envy you," carries the implication that you *will* become rich.[32] Wealth is the natural result of working hard,

31. This is not a major issue methodologically, since each term can be interpreted accurately within its specific context, but it raises an important interpretive issue: each of these terms, *kotos*, *phthonos*, and *zêlos*, can have a negative connotation which is not entirely dissimilar or unrelated to the positive essence Hesiod emphasizes in the opening to the *Works and Days*.

32. The economic realities of life in Askra seem to have permitted growth and profit through intensifying effort.

and envy follows as a matter of course. Hesiod is asserting a universal rule of economic behavior, namely that work will create wealth, which in turn automatically triggers the emotional responses of envy and emulation. As Hesiod understands it, people are motivated by a twofold urge to accumulate wealth: they both desire wealth per se, and they also want to best their rivals. Those not moved by the former will be driven by the latter.

In his own psychological theories of human behavior, Aristotle has Hesiod's passage in mind as he delves into the distinction between the wide range of rivalrous and envious emotions in Greek thought.[33] Rather than simply using the terms as rough approximations for each other, however, Aristotle articulates subtle differences between them. *Phthonos*, to Aristotle, is approximate to "envy" or "jealousy,"[34] and is directed at notional equals or peers; people long for what others have, feel they have a right to own it themselves, and think the possession of it would increase their relative worth.[35] He directly cites Hesiod's words in the *Works and Days* to demonstrate that he was articulating the same sort of idea: that people envy their equals and peers when they see them in possession of something they themselves want (2.10.6). As for *zêlos*, he defines this as a more positive type of "rivalrous emulation," which is similar to Hesiod's idea of the good type of *eris*, wanting what one's equals have (2.11).[36] Furthermore, he specifies yet another emotion that denoted a positive type of jealousy, *nemesis*, the "righteous indignation" good people feel at seeing the undeserved good fortune of people who were unworthy (*Rhetoric* 2.9). So Aristotle agrees with Hesiod that in their economic affairs the Greeks were driven by deep-rooted emotional impulses to compete with their close peers.[37] For Aristotle, just as Hesiod described in the *Works and Days*, this type of emulous rivalry is particularly true in the relationships between notional equals, people considered to be peers and competitors in age, birth, place, reputation, and wealth.[38]

These ideas are also shared by other classical Athenian authors.[39] Plato's Socrates, referring directly to this passage of Hesiod, says that the people who

33. *Rhetoric* 2.9.1–2.11.7.

34. For the full range of ancient Greek emotions relating to envy and jealousy, see Walcot 1978; and Sanders 2014, who has laid out the full variety of envious, rivalrous, emulative, and jealous feelings in the ancient Greek mind, which range from the positive rivalrous emulation to the more negative emotions including something that resembles *Schadenfreude* and covetous and begrudging envy.

35. *Rhetoric* 2.9.3; 2.10.1–5.

36. This is the sense in which *zêlos* was received in later centuries by the Stoics, for example (Konstan 2003, 13).

37. *tois pelas* (toward those nearby) at *N.E.* 2.7.15, 1108b2.

38. *Rhetoric* 2.10. For the importance of equality in the emotions of envy and emulation, see Sanders 2014, 69–71; and Cairns 2003, 239–42.

39. See, e.g., Thucydides 6.16.

are most alike will be filled with feelings of rivalry and emulousness, while those who are most different are more likely to be friends.[40] Likewise, Xenophon classes envy among the hostile, warlike (*polemika*) parts of human nature, which sees individuals in conflict with each other: "Considering the same things to be good and pleasurable, they fight for them" (*Memorabilia* 2.6.21). This same passage connects *eris* to anger (*orgê*), greed (*pleonektein*), and envy (*phthonos*). For Xenophon, these are feelings which people must contend with in order to be friends, and it is only when envy, jealousy, and *Schadenfreude* are overcome, and the individual's interest is seen to be at one with another person's, that they can be called friends (2.6.22–23). Therefore, in the classical period, people who were perceived to be the closest peers were especially seen to be in direct competition with each other, precisely as Hesiod had said for neighbors in their economic affairs and people who shared the same occupations in archaic Askra.

Moreover, although the classical Greeks had a rich variety of such emotions with highly nuanced distinctions between them, they all seem to have overlapped conceptually in being connected with the envious desire to have another's wealth. Even the more positive emulative emotions of good people are linked with the desire for money, such as when Aristotle says people feel *zêlos* (*Rhetoric* 2.11.2–4) and *nemesis* (*Rhetoric* 2.9.8) toward other people's wealth. Indeed, when he wants to elaborate upon the nuances of such righteous indignation, he uses the example of how people feel more indignant at the honors attained by the newly rich than by old money to illustrate exactly what he means (2.9.9–11). *Nemesis* is so closely associated with wealth in his and his audience's mind that he thinks presenting the notion of "indignation" in terms of money will make it easiest for his audience to grasp the subtle distinctions he is trying to make between these emotions. As in Hesiod, there was a deep emotional response that ancient Greeks felt when observing the relative success or failure of their peers—they competed through wealth and wanted to acquire it for themselves.

This impulse was situated at the most elemental level in the *psychê*, as strife, competition, and the desire to win out over one's rivals were directly related to feelings of pleasure and pain in ancient Greek psychological theories of behavior. For Aristotle, envy (*phthonos*) and emulation (*zêlos*) were both a type of pain (*lupê*) at seeing a notional equal or peer who possesses something that one desires for him or herself (*Rhetoric* 2.9.3, 1386b16–20; 2.11.1, 1388a37–38). *Nemesis* is also a type of pain (*lupê*) to Aristotle, at seeing someone unde-

40. Plato, *Lys.* 215d.

serving enjoying something positive (*Rhetoric* 2.9). But Aristotle also considers feelings of deserved misfortunes of others, spite, and disdain, to be classed as "pleasures," similar to the German *Schadenfreude*, "pleasure at [another's] harm."[41] Therefore, feelings of pain could also overlap with, and even be closely accompanied by, pleasure. Plato describes the intimate relationship between *phthonos*, pain, and pleasure in the *Philebus*, when Socrates says that *phthonos* is both a "pain of the soul" and a "pleasure at the misfortunes of those close by" (48b8–12).[42]

Aristotle identifies pain and pleasure as the primary impulses to action in the Greek world, and the desire for money was driven by both; so there was a variety of urges to accumulate wealth from every point on the emotional spectrum. Aristotle's entire extensive discussion of the calculation of pleasure and pain in *Rhetoric* 1.11 is framed in terms of self-interested behavior, and as he states in the *Politics*, people both love themselves and they love money (2.5). Moreover, he says all people are selfish, and that loving oneself and one's accomplishments and possessions is a source of pleasure (*Rhetoric* 1.11.26, 1371b19–22), so individualistic self-serving wealth acquisition in competition with others was propelled by a complex combination of feelings of pain and pleasure deep in the Greek mind. Callicles in Plato's *Gorgias* expresses the perspective of pure self interest at the expense of others, and although Socrates disagrees with him, his attitudes must have been representative of enough people that the philosopher felt the need to argue against them with a moralizing agenda.

The essence of the self-interested economic competition in Hesiod's world can be seen in the work ethic he advocates and in the places he says that other people's goods trigger the motivation to work. First he indicates that Perses wants to strive after the wealth of others (34); later he bids Perses to be pious "so that you can buy another's farm and he not buy yours" (340–41). This statement suggests that both individuals are simultaneously trying to acquire each other's property and to avoid being bought out by each other.[43] It illustrates the twofold pleasure to satisfy both the covetous and begrudging envy of acquiring another person's farm and avoiding the loss of one's own to a competitor. Craving others' wealth is a motivation—the goal is to outdo the other person and take their property. In Hesiod's mind both Perses and his neighbor are aiming at the other's wealth and suspicious that the other is doing the same. This mutual suspicion therefore creates fear that another is trying to seize one's

41. Sanders 2014, 63.

42. For the full context of this idea, in reference to the joy one feels while watching comedy, see the discussion of this passage by Sanders 2014, 101–5.

43. Sanders 2014, 70, describes such behavior as "covetous envy."

own fortune; such attitudes are reminiscent of the conflict between peers over the same goods that Xenophon described above as being driven by the "warlike" parts of the brain. Likewise, Hesiod assumes that his audience would be acquisitive not only to attain their own material benefits, but even to expand their wealth at the expense of others.[44]

But not everything in Hesiod conforms to a Hobbesian model of self-interested individualistic competition; indeed he reveals that there were dual values of competition and social cooperation that coexisted in Askra. As with all economic systems, including the modern US, the ancient Greek economy was embedded in social relations, and the *Works and Days* is filled with references to social reciprocity that dominated everyday life. But there were limits to the social safety net and moral economy of mutual support; economic surplus was a requirement to be able to guarantee one's continued participation in the social interdependent realm of mutual reciprocity. Much of Hesiod's advice regarding social reciprocity is given not from an altruistic spirit, but one of calculated investment in *charis* because social capital can act as an important resource, especially during hard times.[45] Hesiod bids Perses to work hard to accumulate wealth and avoid poverty because there was a certain point at which one could no longer depend on the generosity of neighbors (397–400). Neighbors' continued goodwill was based upon the production of surplus and its regular investment in the system of mutual reciprocity that acted as a safety net. Work, Hesiod says, so that hunger may hate you and Demeter may fill your barn with food (299–301). In short, there were additional incentives to work beyond just the emotional drive for pleasure—wealth was needed to maintain the social interdependence without which one could not survive. Therefore, Hesiod promotes a work ethic not just to increase one's wealth but also to avoid the breakdown of social reciprocity and the starvation that will result.

This is not to say that Hesiod does not also advocate maintaining a minimum level of subsistence. At the very least he hopes his brother will aim at self-sufficiency, so that he will not plot against others to seize their wealth. But alongside this need to provide oneself with sustenance, there is another powerful psychological impulse to work—the emotional desire to emulate a neighbor. Once wealth is attained beyond a minimum baseline needed for survival, which is an absolute measure, it triggers a desire to achieve ever-increasing levels of success based not on biological needs but rather the surplus of one's

44. Scodel 2019, however, argues that the competition among farmers in Hesiod was not fixed-sum like other trades because the potential for growth was open to anyone willing to work.

45. Aristotle, *N.E.* 8.1.1–2, says that the poor man's only resource is friends. See Millett 1991, for the pervasiveness of social calculation in the ancient Greek world.

peers. Once unhitched from necessity, this relative measure of wealth becomes a driving force unto itself, and behaves according to its own rules, as explained by Hesiod.

Therefore, it was not just subsistence, the satisfaction of necessities that compelled individuals to work—they were also driven by pleasure and pain to acquire wealth, impulses that were located in the core regions of the Greek mind. Hesiod says "If the *thumos* in your heart desires wealth, do as I say, and work upon work upon work" (381–2), and "Through work men become rich in flocks and wealth" (308). Hesiod's advice in the *Works and Days* is largely directed at maximizing productivity on the farm, and one goal is to amass enough wealth that one is able to expand his overall possessions.[46] Alongside Hesiod, Theognis likewise identifies the *thumos* as the source for the urge to acquire wealth: οὔτε γὰρ ἂν πλούτου θυμὸν ὑπερκορέσαις "For you could not overly satisfy your heart with wealth" (1158).The mention of the *thumos* here is significant in that it connects directly to Aristotle's and Plato's theories of the mind discussed in chapter 1; as in those later authors, the *thumos* generates the yearning to accumulate far above the level of simple survival or safety. It is the desire within that drives people to seek wealth, both for its own sake and at the expense of others.

For Aristotle, feelings of envy and emulation had their roots in the "irrational desires" of anger and appetites, and he agrees with Plato in directly connecting pleasure, *epithumia*, with the drive to accumulate money. In the *Rhetoric* (1.10.9), he says that desire (*epithumia*) is what compels people to accumulate wealth and possessions; the poor desire to have wealth, and the rich want to acquire additional pleasures beyond what is necessary. Moreover, desire, *epithumia*, like anger (*orgê*), is an irrational longing or grasping (*orexis*) (1.10.8), meaning that there is a strong emotional impulse behind these drives. Aristotle's view of the causative relationship between anger (*orgê*) and envy or spite (*phthonos*) is well articulated by Viano, who says he conceptualized the confluence of these feelings in the sense of a "reactive emotional mechanism," and *thumos*, impulse, being at the root of competitive emotions.[47] In this respect, Aristotle seems to be in agreement with his teacher, Plato, who says that the spirited part of the soul (*epithumios*) creates *philotimia*, "envy" (*Republic* 586c). So the good feelings that money could buy outright were compounded by the additional pleasures that came with satisfying the emulative desires to accu-

46. Van Wees 2009, 448–50, agrees that Hesiod's goal is maximum productivity and profit seeking. As Scodel 2019, 46, puts it, once farmers in the *Works and Days* have secured subsistence, "Being the object of envy seems to be the main purpose of wealth."

47. Viano 2003, 90–91, 93–95.

mulate wealth. These desires (*epithumiai*) are associated with pleasure, according to Aristotle (*Rhetoric* 1.11.10), and although there is a difference between *thumos* and *epithumia*, both are still part of *orexis*, grasping or appetition in general.[48] Bias of Priene also explicitly connected profit with the feelings of pleasure in the mind; when asked what "delights" (τέρπεται) people most, he replied "making profit" (κερδαίνων).[49] For both the archaic poets and the classical period philosophers, there was a burning desire for wealth deep in the *thumos*, and they agree with that the insatiability of this passion was driven by the twofold urge to avoid pain and seek pleasure.

Furthermore, the direct connection between the lustful and gluttonous regions of the brain and money that classical authors drew is also stated by the archaic poets, who likewise felt that the Greek mind was wired to promote the endless accumulation of wealth. Such a level accelerates and rises with the increase of overall wealth since jealousy and envy, rather than need, precipitates the type of behavior depicted in this passage.

Because the craving for wealth was tied to the level of one's peers, it was not bound to any fixed baseline. Rather it was floating untethered, and as it was tied to the perception of the wealth of other individuals, peer competition could lead to a sort of seemingly unlimited wealth acquisition. Taylor has convincingly argued that poverty in Athens was likewise judged on a relative, instead of an absolute, measure of material well-being.[50] The Greeks' perception of economic success was tied not to minimum subsistence or survival needs, but was rather based on comparison with their family, friends, and neighbors. The relative measure of success vis-à-vis one's immediate competitors is central to Thorstein Veblen's theories of economic behavior:

> The usual basis of self-respect is the respect accorded by one's neighbours . . . it is necessary in order to his own peace of mind, that an individual should possess as large a portion of goods as others with whom he is accustomed to class himself; and it is extremely gratifying to possess something more than others. But as fast as a person makes new wealth . . . the new standard forthwith ceases to afford appreciably greater satisfaction than the earlier standard did . . . and when he has reached what may be called the normal pecuniary standard of the community . . . this chronic dissatisfaction will give place to a restless strain-

48. ἡ ὄρεξις εἰς τρία διαιρεῖται, εἰς βούλησιν καὶ θυμὸν καὶ ἐπιθυμίαν (*E.E.* 2.7.3, 1223a27–28).

49. Diog. Laert. 1.87.

50. Taylor 2017. Cecchet 2015 likewise demonstrates how the labels of rich and poor were highly subject to rhetorical manipulation.

> ing to place a wider and ever-widening pecuniary interval between himself and this average standard. . . . Relative success, tested by an invidious pecuniary comparison with other men, becomes the conventional end of action. (Veblen, 20–22)

Competition with one's closest rivals impels individuals to seek not just the satisfaction of wants, but rather to constantly increase their wealth relative to friends and neighbors. Psychological and emotional mechanisms can create an endless upward drive to accumulate wealth, which in turn becomes unhitched from absolute measures because one's peers can augment their own riches or be trying to increase the gap between that of their closest competitors as well as the average level of the immediate community. In the modern world, therefore, jealousy and envy spur competition for relative economic standing that can create an uncontrollable spiral of boundless wealth accumulation, which is precisely the complex series of interconnected processes described by archaic and classical Greek authors.

As Veblen argues, individuals regularly judge their own success based on comparison with those they identify as their closest peers and competitors, which he terms invidious pecuniary emulation. Wealth certainly brings security and comfort, but having more than others also brings esteem and honor, and people are driven by their invidious pecuniary emulation of others to amass as much money as possible. To Veblen, mainstream economists typically focus on the satisfaction of wants, and ignore the causes that lie behind the need to acquire more wealth endlessly across human societies. That well-known phenomenon from the twentieth-century United States, "keeping up with the Joneses," therefore, also directed economic behavior in ancient Greece. Scholars of ancient Greece are familiar with the widespread competitive emulation in the peer-polity interaction among *poleis*,[51] and Greek authors attest that the same type of competitiveness also existed at the individual level.

By constantly competing with their closest peers, the people they most frequently come in contact with and with whom they class themselves, individuals create an endless upward drive to accumulate ever more wealth and the esteem and honor that accompany it. Once people begin to be accustomed to a certain level of prosperity and honor, they seek to retain their position or improve it, and are disgusted by any loss of riches and the standing that they bring; Agamemnon's rage at losing Chryseis illustrates this reality in book 1 of the *Iliad*; his status is directly related to his possession of prizes, and specifically to

51. See, e.g., Ober 2015, 294.

having more than the other Greek leaders.[52] Veblen observed that once people become accustomed to a new level of lifestyle, this position becomes the new standpoint from which to compare oneself with others, an idea which finds a perfect echo in Aristotle's thought:

> ἡ πονηρία τῶν ἀνθρώπων ἄπληστον, καὶ τὸ πρῶτον μὲν ἱκανὸν διωβελία μόνον, ὅταν δ' ἤδη τοῦτ' ᾖ πάτριον, ἀεὶ δέονται τοῦ πλείονος, ἕως εἰς ἄπειρον ἔλθωσιν. ἄπειρος γὰρ ἡ τῆς ἐπιθυμίας φύσις, ἧς πρὸς τὴν ἀναπλήρωσιν οἱ πολλοὶ ζῶσιν.
>
> The baseness of people is insatiable, and on the one hand first a two-obol dole is sufficient, but when this then becomes one's own, always they want more until they come to an extent that is unbounded. For the nature of desire has no limit, which is the thing most people live to fulfill. (*Politics* 2.7.19, 1267b2–6)

As Aristotle says, once a higher standard of living has become habitual, people then try to accumulate more, and are ceaselessly striving after the next level, which is ἄπειρον, "boundless."

Indeed, far from being a purely modern phenomenon, the Greeks themselves thought that these feelings of invidious pecuniary emulation were deeply rooted in the Greek cultural *psychê*, as stated by Achaemenes to Xerxes in Herodotus:[53] "It's typically Greek to envy success and hate being outdone" (Hdt. 7.236.1).[54] Greeks strove to emulate their peers because they were jealous of their wealth; *eris*, competition for personal success, was the force that fueled the economic behavior of these individuals.[55]

Such eagerness to excel in economic affairs is tied in with competition in general, which, of course, was widely celebrated in Greek culture, and wealth is explicitly said to have created *phthonos* throughout Greek sources of the archaic and classical period. The earliest attestation of envy at another's wealth is found in Homer (*Odyssey* 18.15–19), and likewise in Hesiod it is precisely the richness of one's neighbor that elicits this same response. In epinician poetry, Pindar likewise connects wealth and envy: ἴσχει τε γὰρ ὄλβος οὐ μείονα φθόνον (*Pyth.* 11.29). Herodotus says that the Athenians seized the land of the Pelas-

52. See, e.g., Donlan 1979.

53. Walcot 1978, 11.

54. Translation by Waterfield, 1998.

55. Konstan 2003 rightly warns that ancient Greek emotions may not precisely equate to modern feelings of jealousy; nevertheless the term "jealousy" is close enough to the emotional response Hesiod is describing to act as a rough approximation.

gians because they were jealous (*phthonos*) of how well farmed it was (Hdt. 6.137). Plato states in the *Laws* that *phthonos* would cease to exist if wealth and poverty were eliminated (679c). In the Mytilenian Debate, Diodotus says that personal profit, *kerdos*, directly gives rise to *phthonos* (Thuc. 3.43.1). Therefore, rather than just cooperation at the individual level, self-interested principles of individualistic competition drove Greek economic behavior. Like their archaic predecessors, a wide range of classical Greek authors conceptualized *phthonos* in the sense of covetous feelings for others' wealth.

As in the passages cited above, Aristotle repeats elsewhere that people are naturally selfish (*Rhetoric* 1.11.26), but far from just condemning self-interested behavior, he also says that people who seek individualistic aims are right to do so.[56] He even praises the pursuit of self-interested gain as a virtue, saying it is prudence (*sophrosynê*) to deliberate about what is good for oneself and achieve it (*N.E.* 6.5.2). He is explicit that effective *oikonomia* is essential to pursuing one's own welfare and that it is right to seek one's advantage (*N.E.* 6.8.4), so Aristotle also sees these feelings as being positive. Indeed, he even sees the feeling of *nemesis*, "righteous indignation," as being morally acceptable, and even a positive characteristic of good people, when it is directed against the good fortune of those who are undeserving (*N.E.* 2.7, 1108b1–4).

Hesiod also sees the competition for personal wealth as a good thing. Indeed, he describes this type of *eris* in economic affairs as beneficial specifically because he believes that those who do not want to work will instead resort to unjust means to acquire wealth.[57] The envy of others' riches and the desire to best them was often so strong that some even were led to steal from others; as he says, the lazy man's heart turns to mischief when he is lacking his livelihood (498–99), and he focuses in great depth on people who plot against their peers to plunder the wealth of others rather than work hard for it themselves. The desire for profit (*kerdos*) drives people to trample upon honor (323–24), and Hesiod warns his brother to avoid base gain, because it is equal to *atê* (352), declaring that wealth should not be seized, *harpakta* (320). Zeus and the rest of the gods bring down the house of an unjust person, who is only successful for a short time (325–26). The unjust seizure of wealth was also practiced at the highest levels of society, among the bribe-devouring *basileis* who apparently awarded Perses the greater share of their inherited property (38–39, 220–21). Hesiod devotes much attention to how the unjust city will be torn apart, while the just city will prosper (225–47). He knew this from his own personal experi-

56. *N.E.* 6.8.4. For his well-known condemnations of selfish gain at the expense of the common good, see, e.g., Meikle 1996.

57. Scodel 2019, 40, agrees.

ence, because his brother Perses was turning to conflicts (*neikea*) in order to seize other people's wealth (29–34). This type of *neikos* had penetrated even into his family and put the two brothers in conflict with each other (35). No wonder he says "even with your brother get a witness," since trust cannot be depended upon even within the family (370–72). The self-interested drive for wealth ruptured even the most intimate bonds of kinship.

This intrafamilial strife was characteristic of Hesiod's Iron Age race in which parents quarreled with children, and brothers fought among each other (182–85), so Hesiod saw the unjust seizure of wealth as having saturated every level of his society. To Hesiod, the principles of competition, work, and accumulation were what uniquely characterized Iron Age human existence, and he wishes he had lived sometime earlier or later than his own present time (174–75). The Golden Age is clearly contrasted by its lack of pain, strife, and labor (91), and was also free from the *zêlos* that plagued humanity during the Iron Age (195). Individualistic competition and self-interested acquisition can be seen in Hesiod's advice to Perses and his description of the relationship between neighbors—these terms frame the entire discussion and lay at the foundation of the values Hesiod uses in his rhetorical strategies. Many of his attempts at persuasion involve individualism and the pursuit of profit rather than cooperation, sharing, and mutual support.

Broader Patterns of Wealth Acquisition: Unjust Seizure of Wealth

Nor was it only in Hesiod's Askra that the unjust seizure of wealth broke down the social bonds that held the *polis* together; Solon also reports the same processes at work in late seventh- and early sixth-century Athens. Although his beliefs about the psychological drives to acquire riches are more implicit than Hesiod's, he undeniably agrees that people were motivated by wealth to such an extent that they would turn to injustice, even to the point of stealing it from others and destroying the social bonds that held the *polis* together, which ultimately led to civil war. This behavior and psychology at the individual level therefore explains broader patterns of economic behavior and wealth acquisition that created some of the best-known political conflicts in ancient Greece.

Solon depicts in Athens the exact situation Hesiod wanted to avoid. As part of his account of the forces that led to the crisis of late seventh- and early sixth-century Athens,[58] echoing Hesiod, Solon says that god-given wealth is the best

58. For Solon's political poetry, see Irwin 2005. For economic explanations of the Athenian

(1.9–10), that which is earned justly: "While I desire to have wealth, I do not want to acquire it unjustly" (1.7–8). But those whom he targeted in his moralizing philosophy did not share his sentiments. He says that citizens who obey money were destroying the city (3.1–6); they were seizing wealth (*kleptousin eph'arpagê*) from each other, and disregarding justice, causing civil conflict (3.13–14). In one place Solon says that wealth drives people to *hybris* (5.9), and in another that insolence from acquiring wealth turns people to injustice, *hybris*, and creates misery for the *polis* (3.6–8). The *dêmos* understands no *koros* (satiety), according to Solon, and grows rich trusting in unjust deeds (3.9–11), causing conflict within kinship groups (*emphylon stasis*), even to the point of reducing fellow citizens to slavery (3.19–25). Just as Hesiod said for Askra, wealth gained unjustly or through *hybris* results in *atê* (1.13), and the punishment for such acts (*tisis*) comes from Zeus (1.17–32). Profit comes from the gods, as does the retribution for its unjust seizure (1.74–76). The frequent echoes of Hesiod in Solon's poetry indicate that the latter recognized the same psychological forces and the consequences of those drives—in his time, people were behaving just as Hesiod described.

Likewise, in sixth-century Megara, Theognis says that citizens were deceiving each other and ripping the city apart for the sake of selfish profit. His wrath was directed against the non-elite, lower classes and nouveaux riches citizens of the city, whom he refers to as the base born (*kakoi*).[59] Theognis blames the *kakoi* for committing unjust acts for base gain and breaking down the social cohesion of the *polis* at the expense of the noble classes (the *agathoi*):

οὐδεμίαν πω, Κύρν', ἀγαθοὶ πόλιν ὤλεσαν ἄνδρες,
ἀλλ' ὅταν ὑβρίζειν τοῖσι κακοῖσιν ἅδηι
δῆμόν τε φθείρουσι δίκας τ' ἀδίκοισι διδοῦσιν
οἰκείων κερδέων εἵνεκα καὶ κράτεος·
ἔλπεο μὴ δηρὸν κείνην πόλιν ἀτρεμέ' ἧσθαι,
μηδ' εἰ νῦν κεῖται πολλῆι ἐν ἡσυχίηι,
εὖτ' ἂν τοῖσι κακοῖσι φίλ' ἀνδράσι ταῦτα γένηται,
κέρδεα δημοσίωι σὺν κακῶι ἐρχόμενα.
ἐκ τῶν γὰρ στάσιές τε καὶ ἔμφυλοι φόνοι ἀνδρῶν. (*Elegies* 42–50)

Noble men have never destroyed a polis,
but [this happens] whenever it is pleasing to the *kakoi* to commit *hybris*

crisis at the time of Solon, see Morris 2002; Forsdyke 2006.

59. For Theognis' observations, see Von Reden 2003, 183–84.

and they destroy the people and give justice to criminals
for the sake of their own personal profits and power.
Expect that that city will not sit unshaken for long,
Not even if it now lies in great peace,
Whenever these things become dear to *kakos* men,
Profits coming along with harm to the people.
For from such things arise discord and the murder of men among their
own kin.

Selfish profits and power—these were driving the *kakoi* to commit *hybris* and injustice in Theognis' mind. Particularly noteworthy is the emphasis Theognis places on personal, self-interested profits, as his use of the adjective οἰκείων to modify κερδέων seems to be deliberate and significant. Furthermore this behavior was so prevalent that it was destroying the *dêmos* and upsetting the political and social order. Far from an isolated phenomenon or just the actions of a select few, Theognis depicts this self-interested pursuit of profit as occurring on a large scale—the upward economic and social mobility of this class of nouveaux riches was affecting Megarian society in general, and undermining the cohesion of the overall *polis*.

Perhaps worst of all to Theognis was the fact that this conflict was not restricted only to warfare between classes, but even penetrated within *phyla*, among members of the same kinship groups (*stasies te kai emphyloi phonoi*), an unmistakable echo of the problems that Solon identified at Athens. As in Hesiod and Solon, *hybris* is here intimately associated with the unjust pursuit of profit, a sign that the people were motivated by the same underlying psychological drives to acquire wealth. Even the social bonds of friendship were being perverted and distorted for the sake of personal gain. The *kakoi* once were living with deer skins wrapped around them, but now they live in the city, having improved their economic and social status, to the point that some might even seem to be a friend. But Theognis warns against becoming intimate with such men because their mind is without trust (61–66). You should flee the *kakos* man like a bad harbor rather than make him your companion (113–14). These people never knew justice or laws, and so may seem to be friends, but are only filled with treachery. Such individuals were deceiving each other for personal gain (59), and were said by Theognis to be seizing (*harpazousin*) wealth by violence (677); this verb may even be a direct reference to Hesiod's use of the term to describe the type of wealth-seeking that destroys justice in the city (*harpakta*). As in Hesiod's description of the Iron Age, in Theognis' Megara the selfish competition for wealth and status was dissolving even the most intimate of social and kinship bonds.

Common elements recur in these Greek authors' depictions of the urge to acquire wealth, which suggests that there was a similar pattern of behavior throughout the archaic period in Boeotia, Megara, and Athens. As Hesiod, Solon, and Theognis stated, the desire for riches was powerful and they all saw people pursuing it without any limits, whether to satisfy their needs or to outdo their rivals. Some were so consumed by their lust for wealth that they valued it over the benefits of social relationships and reputation. Blinded by their desire for private profits, these individuals not only created strife and political instability within their communities, but even transgressed the bonds of family and kinship. So to Hesiod, self-interested competition for economic gain through hard work was a good thing because it allowed one to avoid injustice, hence his strong work ethic.

The link between the unjust pursuit of profit and social unrest, which was so widely decried by the archaic poets, was repeated by authors throughout the classical period as well. This type of selfishness with respect to wealth was so widespread in ancient Greece that it had a name: *pleonexia*, or greed. As Ryan Balot has argued, greed and injustice were inextricably linked in the Greek mind from the archaic through the classical period. While describing the civil war in Corcyra in his own voice, Thucydides himself explicitly associates the desire for wealth with not only just *phthonos*, but also *philotimia* and *philonikia* (competition), which he connects with *pleonexia*, greed (Thuc. 3.82.8). In Euripides' *Suppliants*, Theseus describes different types of people who destroy their fellow citizens through their self-serving actions—those who seek power, those who destroy their fellow citizens through their thirst for personal profit, the rich who still want more, the poor who are filled with envy (235–45). Some even tried to justify having more than others on the basis of natural law, such as Callicles in Plato's *Gorgias*, who argued that being selfishly greedy and having more than others (*pleonektein*) was justifiable and defensible.[60] *Pleonexia* in the sense of having more than one's proper share meant that other people were unjustly deprived of what they deserved. Föllinger demonstrates convincingly that Plato is consistent in depicting *pleonexia* as being the aggregate manifestation at the *polis* level of the overall pattern of individuals' self-interested maximization of their own economic interests.[61] Plato preserves a common saying that being unjust is profitable if you get away with it (*Republic* 392b); such behavior could manifest itself in voluntary contracts, where it pays to violate trust because the unjust man always makes more money than the just (*Republic* 343d). Likewise, Aristotle

60. See Balot 2001, 5–21, for a discussion of Callicles.
61. Föllinger 2016, 61.

notes that the motive behind injustice is gain (*N.E.* 5.2.6), and says it is the mark of the unjust man that he takes the larger share (*N.E.* 5.1.9).

In Xenophon's discussion of the Thirty Tyrants, their greed for private profit was what drove them to kill their fellow citizens (*Hellenica* 2.4.21–42), the epitome of injustice. He states that greed was at odds with honor and friends, and destroyed social ties in the exact same way Hesiod, Solon, and Theognis described (*Hellenica* 2.3.33).[62] As Herodotus states, even tyrants were susceptible to *phthonos*, so there was no threshold at which one would stop competing for increased wealth and status (and trying to extend the distance between oneself and those below him)—not even among those who had achieved the highest station in society.[63]

Some people simply wanted to have more than others, and would even go so far as to take it forcibly, destroying their reputations and honor to continually outdo other people. Aristotle and Plato echo the sentiments of the archaic poets in saying that it was best to acquire wealth in a way that did not involve taking it from other people. In their day, the seizure of money from others through plunder was still a way of life for many. As Plato puts it, the propensity to be either a trader or a pirate depends on a person's personality type since the two pursuits are merely different means of attaining riches (*Laws* 8.831e). How someone might seek money depended on their circumstances, and Aristotle lists piracy and brigandage among the various occupations people turn to as a way of making their living (*Politics* 1.8.7–8). Thucydides agrees that people turn to plunder for profit to secure their livelihood if the circumstances dictate (Thuc. 1.5.1). As Aristotle says, men want what is noble, but choose what is profitable (*N.E.* 8.13.8), a very pragmatic, instrumental view of the world that does not conform to the prescriptions of moralizing philosophy or poetry. Therefore, classical period authors drew the same links between greed, injustice, and the political and social upheavals that such selfish behavior created as their archaic predecessors.

Oligarchy as a form of government was even theorized as arising from a political environment that promoted individualistic pursuit of self-interested gain. According to Plato, greed was the reason for oligarchic governments' very existence, and was an anti-democratic vice; the oligarchic man, who was wealthy and sought only to increase his wealth at the expense of the community, had no place in democratic *poleis* (*Republic* 548a–b, 555b). As Aristotle puts it, oligarchy is the form of government that emerges when wealth is most

62. For a discussion of these passages, see Balot 2001, 217–19.
63. Hdt. 3.80.3.

highly honored (*Nicomachean Ethics* 8.10.3). One reason he devotes so much attention to *chrêmatistikê* in the opening of the *Politics* is because he thought that citizens were pursuing their own self-interested economic benefit to the point that they were interfering with the overall interests of the *polis*. Citizens were spending so much time on making money that they were neglecting the collective social welfare, and when the wealthy become too numerous or their personal fortunes increase too much, the government becomes oligarchic (πλειόνων γὰρ τῶν εὐπόρων γινομένων ἢ τῶν οὐσιῶν αὐξανομένων μεταβάλλουσιν εἰς ὀλιγαρχίας, *Politics* 5.3.8, 1303a). Therefore, at the macro level of the *polis*, the very structure of the government was seen to be susceptible to the forces of individualistic wealth acquisition by its citizens.

This same dynamic malleability at the macro *polis* level is also observable in the social and political upward mobility that were possible in ancient Greece. As discussed above, scholars have identified the emergence of a class of nouveaux riches in a number of *poleis* whose concerted efforts at accumulating wealth allowed them to raise their economic and social status.[64] Individuals who achieved wealth and status through their moneymaking successes are attested as early as Theognis, who says that poor men can become rich very quickly.[65] At least some people advanced socially in archaic Megara through their economic success, and the fruits of their labor often came in the form of prestigious marriage alliances with families of the noblest classes. Moreover, Solon's establishment of property classes allowed for social and political mobility through wealth acquisition as far back as early sixth-century Athens. Many families seem to have accomplished the difficult task of raising themselves into the liturgical class or into higher Solonian wealth classes through specializing in individual fields of production in the long term.[66] For some Greeks, the political and social rewards alone were incentive enough to justify a long-term wealth-maximizing strategy. Speaking also of his own experience in seventh-century Amorgos, Semonides states that "There is no mortal who does not expect to come as a friend to wealth and blessings next year,"[67] so this pattern of upward mobility and the emergence of nouveaux riches is widely attested across the archaic Greek world, as was the expectation that one could become wealthy.

Classical Athens, of course, preserves the best evidence for this social mobility. Nausikydes is said by Xenophon to have elevated himself up into the

64. Connor 1971; Davies 1981, 68–72; Kron 1996, 84–85 and 111–27.

65. *Elegies* book 1, 662–63.

66. See, for example, Raubitschek 1949, 401, for the dedicator of the monument on the Athenian Acropolis who seems to celebrate his moving from the class of the *thetes* into the *zeugitae* in early fifth-century Athens.

67. Semonides fr. 1.6–10. See Campbell 1967, 185–86.

liturgical class through his milling business.[68] He then converted much of his money into cattle and pigs, possibly as an investment in additional profitable property since his mill was already so successful. Timodemos was a banker who became a citizen and liturgist. As discussed above mining alone seems to have been responsible for the membership of many families in the liturgical class. Davies argues that Nicias' father Nikeratos probably made the money in the mines which initially brought his family into the upper strata of the Athenian elite.[69] Demostratos' family owned a smelting oven in the Laureion region, which seems to have lifted them out of obscurity into the liturgical class.[70] Diodoros son of Simos and his own son Simos seem to have become liturgists from their mining efforts,[71] as did many others.[72]

A new social and political elite arose in fifth- and fourth-century Athens, represented especially by the individuals whose low origins and commercial success were insulted in comedy and public discourse. Cleon's father owned a workshop of slave tanners, which gave the family its fortune,[73] and his meteoric rise to the top of the Athenian political elite is perhaps the best known example. Isocrates' wealth is said to have come from a workshop of slave flute makers,[74] just as Hyperbolos' father raised his family up with his lamp-making business.[75] Anytos inherited a tannery and shoemaking workshop from his father which contributed to his family's wealth.[76] Iphicrates' father was said to be a cobbler,[77] Agyrrhios' a carpenter,[78] and Phocion's a pestle maker whose prosperity allowed his family to hold the generalship forty-five times.[79]

An entire class of individuals advanced their families socially and politically through their economic success, which demonstrates the scale and prevalence of long-term wealth maximization in ancient Greece. Even if these individuals were not able to get the absolute greatest return out of every venture, the fact that so many were able to accomplish impressive economic advancement over the course of their lives is highly suggestive of the successful maximization of wealth during their lifetimes. Though the actual day-to-day management strat-

68. Xenophon, *Memorabilia* 2.7.6.
69. Davies 1971, inv. # 403.
70. Davies 1971, inv. # 3623.
71. Davies 1971, inv. # 3953.
72. See, e.g., Davies 1971, inv. # 525, 2419, 3953, 4048, 4329, 4386, 4718, 5232, 9057, 9719, 14100, 14164.
73. Davies 1971, 318–19.
74. Davies 1971, 246.
75. Davies 1971, 517.
76. Davies 1971, 41.
77. Davies 1971, 248 (inv # 7737).
78. Davies 1971, 279.
79. Davies 1971, 559.

egies and operations of these individuals will never be known, the weight of the evidence of this class of nouveaux riches in the aggregate is indicative of long-term wealth maximization on a mass scale by a large number of individuals in Athens and other Greek cities, from the archaic period onward.

Diversity of Personality Types

At the same time, however, not all Greeks in every *polis* behaved in the same manner economically. Herodotus says that most Greeks esteem their tradesmen less than their other citizens, especially the Spartans, while the Corinthians were the least prejudiced against trades (2.167). Moreover, as the author of the pseudo-Aristotelian *Oikonomika* states, Athenian agriculture was dominated by production for the market, which suggests that the predominant mode of exchange in fourth-century Athens for agricultural goods was in the monetized economy, while Spartan *oikonomia* was different.[80] So there were some dissimilarities between the ways individuals in various *poleis* approached specific economic activities.

Likewise, with the lack of a free land market in ancient Greece, an institutional particularity of the *polis* system, those barred from owning land (i.e., metics) would be forced to turn to commercial opportunities and would more likely demonstrate maximizing behavior in the market. Whoever could own land would have a choice—either to seek maximum profits in the commercial realm or to eschew market behavior and focus on accumulating cultural and social capital to try to secure marriage alliances and dowries in the marriage market.

Moreover, the wide variety of personality types discussed in ancient Greek sources also indicates that not all Greeks wanted to maximize their profits and wealth in the long term. On the contrary, the impression to be gained from the pseudo-Platonic dialogue *Eryxias* and philosophers' preference scales indicates that many ancient Greeks also preferred good health to having money.[81] Plato's Socrates in the *Republic* says that there are three main types of people, *philoni-*

80. Pseudo-Aristotle, *Oikonomika* 1.6.2, 1344b31–33.

81. For philosophers' preference scales, see Aristotle, *N.E.* 1.4.6. But this preference for health should not be taken as a sign of an alien *mentalité*—modern individuals also have a variety of opinions about how money measures up to other good things. In a 2017 survey of 1,000 Americans by Charles Schwab in which 65 percent responded that they defined wealth as being in good health, while only 35 percent considered wealth as having a lot of money. Even in the modern US there is no single overarching *mentalité* that defines our economic behavior and distinguishes us from the Greeks.

koi (lovers of victory), *philosophoi* (lovers of wisdom), and *philokerdoi* (lovers of profit).[82] Although one of these three is focused on money, the other two are not, and have different aims. These types of person each correspond with a part of the brain in Plato's theory of the mind. But Plato also adds a fourth type, the *philotimoi* (lovers of honor), which complicates his tripartite model. Moreover, the extreme pursuit of profit at the expense of honor and shame are presented by Theophrastus in *Characters* as an abnormal stereotype in his description of the person characterized by "shameful profiteering," *aischrokerdeia*. As these authors reveal, there was tremendous diversity aside from those the Greeks classified as *chrêmatistai*.

Aristotle's descriptions of liberality and meanness, in which he includes greed, parsimony, and love of base gain, suffice to convey the wide range of behavioral patterns with respect to money that were observable in the Greek world (*Virtues and Vices* 5.4–7.12, 1250b25–1251b17). Elsewhere he states that liberality is a middle state between the extremes of meanness and prodigality in the attitudes toward spending wealth (*Nicomachean Ethics* 2.7.4, 1107b9–14); within a more extended discussion he reveals a variety of characteristics, each with subtle particularities and nuanced distinctions (*Eudemian Ethics* 3.4.1–7, 1231b28–1232a18). Some characters are more inclined to seek profit in certain situations, while others are more or less generous in different contexts, and all vary in their proclivity for calculation. So not everyone was trying to seek maximum profit and wealth all the time.

Nevertheless, such objections should not be taken too far. They miss the point and they obfuscate a reality that is far more dynamic and complex than an either-or situation. On the one hand they demonstrate that a single monolithic mentality did not characterize the Greeks in their economic behavior, who instead had a variety of personality types and attitudes toward profit seeking as in the modern world. Furthermore, Aristotle states that people value honor not for its own sake but for the other benefits it brings (*Nicomachean Ethics* 8.8.2). This inversion of means and ends shows the fluid nature of these elements in the Greek mind.

Social and cultural capital were far more dynamic than when they are simply depicted in opposition to financial interests, because they could be transformed into economic capital in a number of ways. For example, marriage alliances could bring both security and an instant injection of financial liquidity in the form of dowry, so marriage was often the largest and most important

82. *Republic* 581a–d.

economic decision ancient Greeks ever faced. Social and cultural capital could be converted into profitable marriage alliances that were unavailable to those who were conspicuously devoted to seeking profits in the marketplace.

Evidence of athleticism, education, high culture, leisure, and noble status opened up access to the largest transfers of wealth through dowry and marriage alliances at the highest levels of the elite;[83] Herodotus says that Megacles beat Hippoclides son of Tisander for the hand of Agariste, the daughter of Cleisthenes, tyrant of Sicyon, due to his manners and deportment during the competition among the suitors. Megacles also just happened to be the son of the first four-horse chariot race victor from Athens, Alcmaeon, and it was at the four-horse chariot race that Cleisthenes announced the competition for his daughter's hand. An Olympic victory, therefore, could be the sign of noble status that guaranteed the most profitable and secure social bonds and the largest dowries, so the love of *nikê* may have been seen as a means to other things. In other words, it could be more profitable in the long term to aim at victory or honor than to be patently seeking after money itself. These traits could be translated into social connections that provide both economic security (*asphaleia*) and profit, two of the most highly desirable factors that shaped the ancient Greek economic decision-making process, as discussed in chapter 1.

Indeed, Xenophon says that the man who does nothing but make money all day is not a good friend, who "because of his lust for making money makes no leisure for anything else but from where he is able to make profit," ὅστις διὰ τὸν ἔρωτα τοῦ χρηματίζεσθαι μηδὲ πρὸς ἓν ἄλλο σχολὴν ποιεῖται ἢ ὁπόθεν αὐτός τι κερδανεῖ (*Memorabilia* 2.6.3–4). Such a person who takes moneymaking to an extreme is antithetical to the traits desirable in a friend—self-interested, individualistic, and focused on profit rather than reciprocity and fostering relationships.

Not every estate owner was willing to do everything necessary to maximize income, as seen in Socrates' conversation with Aristarchus in Xenophon's *Memorabilia*. Aristarchus, a member of the Athenian elite whose fortune like so many others was ruined by the Peloponnesian War, became so overrun by his female relatives that he fell into difficult financial straits. In this anecdote, Xenophon depicts Socrates as providing sound advice to Athenians who were forced to confront the new economic and political realities in the wake of the Peloponnesian War, which saw the collapse of huge fortunes, particularly in Attic agriculture and mining in the Laureion region, which were largely unavailable

83. Leese 2017a.

to the Athenians during the final phase of the war due to the Spartan occupation of Deceleia.[84]

Socrates advises Aristarchus to turn his household into a business by employing his female relatives as weavers producing for the market in order to survive financially. He could be as successful as other individuals who have secured long-term success from specializing in textiles,[85] as well as most of the Megarian population, who make a living by producing a specific type of cloak.[86] But Aristarchus' response is initially negative. He says that the success of Socrates' examples is dependent upon slave labor, whereas his female relatives are not trained as weavers, but rather were educated in the manner of the well-to-do: ὁ μὲν δούλους τρέφει, ἐγὼ δ' ἐλευθέρους . . . ὁ μὲν γὰρ τεχνίτας τρέφει, ἐγὼ δ' ἐλευθερίως πεπαιδευμένους, "That man feeds slaves, but I support free people . . . he supports craftsmen, while I support people educated in the manner of free people."[87] This emphatic contrast between slave and free reveals the most prominent values and considerations in Aristarchus' mind. Framing his response in such terms, he illuminates his fuller cultural and social context, a concern about appearing "slavish" that is repeated by another down-and-out interlocutor in the *Memorabilia*, Eutherus. The rhetoric of freedom and slavery is an important opposition in Greek thought and discourse with respect to how their culture framed the economic opportunities at their disposal. Their cultural conceptualization of freedom as being the antithesis of slavery influenced some to avoid certain types of employment.

So the contrast in his mind between free and slave may be based on the perception that maximizing productivity in weaving was associated with slave labor. After all, Xenophon says that teaching a female slave wool working (*talasias*) can double her value for the household.[88] Moreover, the term "wool worker" was sometimes also conceptually associated with prostitution.[89] In Aristarchus'

84. Thuc. 7.27–28 describes the great decline in Athenian power due to the Spartan occupation of Deceleia, saying that afterward the Athenians were deprived of their entire hinterland during the entire year. The result of this would be a collapse in agricultural productivity and consequently wealth based on agriculture in Attica. With landowners unable to produce crops or even to mobilize their land as collateral for alternative investments, many agricultural fortunes seem to have been decimated. Thucydides says that the wealthiest (many of whom were farmers) were suffering the most from the war (8.48), as does the Old Oligarch, who says that farmers wanted to end the war (Pseudo-Xenophon, *Ath. Pol.* 2.14). Aristophanes' *Acharnians* is filled with references to the struggles of farmers during the Peloponnesian War. For a detailed discussion with references, see Hanson 1998, 136–37.

85. For textile specialization in ancient Greece, see Bresson 2007, 196–99.

86. Xen., *Mem.* 2.7.6. See Osborne 1995, 27–43, for a discussion of this passage and the scholarly debates about citizen prejudices against engaging in slave-like labor.

87. Xen., *Mem.* 2.7.3–4.

88. *Oeconomicus* 7.41.

89. Wrenhaven 2009.

household, there are signs that the women themselves asserted their own agency to protect their collective interests and avoid the potential drop in their status that would have resulted from exposing themselves to the slander of weaving for market production.[90] Aristarchus certainly recognizes their collective resentment as a powerful force.[91] Indeed, these women were raised as members of the leisure class, in which case they would have resisted their leisure being taken away, and deplored labor to the point that they themselves probably employed the rhetoric of slavery metaphorically to denounce their drop in status. From this perspective it is of the utmost importance that Aristarchus' relatives do not work—they enjoy a life of unproductive leisure, which was a sign of their elite upbringing. Aristarchus also seemingly feared the loss of his own standing that would inevitably result from his female relatives' need to become producers for the market. This drop in status would negatively affect the marriage prospects of his female relatives. Aristarchus already would have been hard pressed to provide dowries, so he was in a bind, potentially needing to find husbands for some and lacking the necessary money for dowries, while also not wanting to sacrifice the social and cultural capital that could yield the most profitable marriage alliances. Earlier wealth had allowed his family to achieve the highly desirable goal of leisure; this was an investment of money into a lifestyle and the cultural and social capital that accompanied it. It was not so much that Aristarchus was employing them—but rather that he was taking away their leisure, which was an important conspicuous mark of their high standing.

So Aristarchus was initially taken aback by Socrates' proposal since he was still coming to terms with the new economic realities. His values, which were formed during the heyday of fifth-century prosperity, had not yet adjusted to the poverty he was experiencing in the wake of Athens' economic disaster. The bubble had burst and he did not know how to adapt. Changing circumstances required that Aristarchus and his female relatives abandon the aversion to labor that characterizes the leisure class in order to recover financially. But then as his decisive rhetorical strategy, Socrates asks Aristarchus if it is shameful (*aischron*) that his freeborn household is less prosperous than the slave-staffed estate of Ceramon. Combining shame with this comparison of relative wealth is a calculated move to elicit an emotional impulse in Aristarchus to increase his productivity, and it works, much like the sting of envy that spurs the *apalamos* in Hesiod to work as he looks upon his wealthier neighbor.

90. Although citizen women certainly were widely praised for their weaving abilities throughout Greek culture, the focus of Aristarchus' remarks is meaningful for this specific context and his family's unique standing and circumstances.

91. Xen., *Mem.* 2.7.12.

But these leisure class attitudes, while not "rational" according to textbook economic theory, are not inconsistent with a system that is also driven by the economically rational maximization of profit. Indeed, the two types of behavior both coexist comfortably in the modern world, as argued so convincingly by Thorstein Veblen. In Edith Wharton's masterpiece, *The House of Mirth*, the protagonist Lily Bart also expresses disdain for lower-class activity, but her opinions are not evidence of a nonentrepreneurial *mentalité* that characterized late nineteenth-century New York. Likewise, similar attitudes had become so widespread in twentieth-century England, the birthplace of modern industrial capitalism, that Martin Wiener was able to write an entire book entitled *The Decline of the Industrial Spirit*.[92] Aristarchus is not expressing a disdain for productive activity that was uniquely Greek. Veblen and Wharton both remarked on its pervasiveness throughout American society during the most extreme, unfettered period of modern capitalism. Wiener argues that the British slid away from the industrial-capitalistic mindset of the nineteenth and early twentieth centuries, so mentalities are not monolithic or static but shift according to circumstances. This aversion to conspicuously market-oriented activity was not something that was specifically Greek that prevented further economic development or investment in profitable enterprise in the manner of a nonproductive *mentalité*; on the contrary, it is also pervasive within modern capitalistic societies.[93]

Therefore, the Aristarchus episode does not illustrate a significant difference between the modern and ancient economy. As Figueira argues, Finley overlooked many important factors about Aristarchus when emphasizing his reluctance to employ his female relatives as wool workers, especially the fact that he had just lost all of his properties, which he may have previously managed "aggressively," and Aristarchus did indeed follow Socrates' advice in the end.[94] Figueira points out that Aristarchus also weighs the costs of borrowing to pay for subsistence against the benefits of borrowing to start a business, which he eventually chooses. Aristarchus is not so constrained in his mentality or rigid in his leisure class views that he is not able to be persuaded, but his thoughts are rather quite malleable. Socrates is able to sway him by appealing to values that are positive in Greek cultural thought: justice, prudence, friendship, *charis*, honor, and profit. Another argument Socrates employs is that Aristarchus will improve familial bonds of affection: "You will love them when you see that they are profitable to you," ἐκείνας φιλήσεις, ὁρῶν ὠφελίμους σεαυτῷ οὔσας.

92. Wiener 2004.
93. As argued by Finley 1985, 272n55.
94. Figueira 2012, 669–70.

Finally, honor can be retained by all parties involved because weaving is generally a culturally acceptable economic activity for women in ancient Greece, even though it might also invite slander within the leisure class.

This entire conversation is therefore an economic deliberation about increasing profit and maximizing utility, so it is not only the specific content of this debate that is important, but also the very nature of the deliberation itself. In this conversation Xenophon provides insight into the economic decision-making process and the wide range of factors a Greek estate owner might have to consider, including weighing the benefits of employing female relatives in market production and the potential decrease in social capital such a choice would cause. Moreover, here once again the ancient Greeks exhibit behavioral patterns similar to those described by Thorstein Veblen in the modern world. The leisure of the women of the household was an important mark of status because it demonstrated that they were wealthy enough to avoid labor. Women's leisure in patriarchal societies is seen as an extension of a man's in Veblen's view, so a male citizen would receive cultural and social capital by forgoing the potentially profitable labor of his female relatives. Market-oriented behaviors were a liability in the marriage market at the highest levels,[95] so it is likely that Aristarchus was weighing the benefits of employing his female relatives in productive activity against the loss of status that would close opportunities for more profitable and noble marriage alliances. In the end, Socrates recommends a smart compromise aimed at maximizing utility, which more accurately reflects the full range of considerations that modern economists now incorporate into their theories than pure monetary calculation.

Moreover, there is voluminous evidence that Aristarchus' aversion to employing the free ladies of his household in productive activities was not shared by many Greeks, as illustrated by their discussions of the ideal wife. For Greek men, whose voices are almost exclusively what survive from antiquity, choosing the right wife meant the difference between a happy, prosperous household and one that is characterized by grief and misery. Hesiod goes into some detail on exactly how to go about picking a wife for the household;[96] while the good wife can be the greatest blessing for a man's house, the bad wife is equally baneful, and can fill a man's life with sorrow. Wives are often seen to be an economic liability, which shows how central material considerations were to the evaluation of women's role in the household in the *Works and Days*.[97]

As discussed above, a wife who helped increase the estate and enabled it to

95. Leese 2017a, 42–44.
96. *Works and Days* 695–705.
97. Zeitlin 1995, 67–68.

grow by controlling her consumption and being an active, industrious member of the household, was the focus of much of the discussion in Xenophon's *Oeconomicus*, where Ischomachus dedicates a great deal of attention to the process of training one's wife so that she becomes an "equal" member in the productive and profitable household. Likewise, Pseudo-Aristotle's *Oikonomika* advocates treating one's wife as an equal partner in the management of an estate, outlining a natural division of labor according to gender, and even instructing men to temper their own behavior in order to retain their wives' good will and benevolence.

Wives who control their consumption and contribute to the management of the household are consistently depicted as the ideal, not only in Xenophon's *Oeconomicus* and Pseudo-Aristotle's *Oikonomika*, but in other Greek literature as well. In Lysias 1.7, the same praise of meticulous control of expenditure and consumption coupled with accurate account keeping that was seen in Plutarch's account of Pericles' slave manager Euangelos appears in discussions of the speaker Euphiletus' wife. He describes his wife as being "the best of women, for she was an impressive household manager, sparing and administering everything with precision," πασῶν ἦν βελτίστη: καὶ γὰρ οἰκονόμος δεινὴ καὶ φειδωλὸς ἀγαθὴ καὶ ἀκριβῶς πάντα διοικοῦσα. The repeated emphasis on frugality and precision, both here and in Plutarch's account of Pericles' manager Euangelos, suggests that these were widely recognized to be the values of successful and praiseworthy wives and slave managers. The fact that these values are the focus of his positive evaluation of his wife suggests that these were precisely the qualities which the jury would have considered to be desirable as well.

Gorgias reportedly said that a woman's *aretê* was to run a household well.[98] Wives were seen to be crucial to successful household economy, both from a consumptive and productive perspective. One who depletes the family's resources is a curse, while one who helps the estate thrive is praised. This impression from literature is corroborated by the evidence from classical Greek funerary epitaphs, which echo the praise given by Euphiletus for his wife while she still conformed to the ideal of industriousness and their consumptive restraint.[99] Two praise a woman for her "industriousness" (ἐργάτις),[100] the latter of which also described her in the same way as Euphiletus, "sparing" (φειδωλός). The most common compliment for a deceased woman, however, is "prudent," "temperate," or "self-controlled," in the terms σώφρων and σωφροσύνη.[101] Thus,

98. Plato, *Meno* 71e.

99. See *IG* II^2 11162, which praises a wife for her consumptive restraint.

100. *CEG* 491, 537.

101. See, e.g., *CEG* 494, 495, 516, 518, and 525. Σώφρων and σωφροσύνη are often used of

temperance, moderation, self-control, frugality, and industriousness were all seen as the defining and most praiseworthy qualities with which to remember these women who were missed so dearly by their families. These traits were absolutely indispensable in a good moneymaker, according to Plato, whom he describes as "sparing and industrious" (φειδωλὸς εἶναι καὶ ἐργάτης), so wives were praised for precisely the qualities that were considered to be important for making money.[102] The moneymaking and the stingy man (φειδωλός) are equated in Plato's discussion,[103] and the term for sparing (*pheidomenos*) also features prominently among the traits in Plato's description of the oligarchic man in the passage discussed above (see chapter 1), so moneymaking and thrift were closely associated. The fact that men celebrated their wives for frugality and productivity shows that increasing one's estate was seen as a major preference for ancient Greek household owners. Therefore, a profitable household was considered an ideal situation, one which was certainly not achieved by some, but was probably the goal of many.

Picking a wife, in the minds of ancient Greek men, could mean the difference between a prosperous and profitable household and one in financial ruin. Semonides, of seventh- or sixth-century BCE Amorgos, says in a misogynistic poem on women that there are some wives who spend all their time eating and consuming the *oikos'* resources, or else refuse to do any work, neglecting the house and its finances, and are said to be made from dogs, asses, pigs, and other animals.[104] Others, however, have the nature of the industrious bee, and can be quite a boon, causing the property of the household to flourish and increase.[105] These are the only women Semonides praises in this poem; the rest are either insulted exclusively or have abuse interspersed with reserved praise.

Praising wives for their ability to help an estate to increase and grow financially is an important insight into the economic mind of the ancient Greek male household owner. If ancient Greek men identify thrift, frugality, self-control, and industriousness as the characteristics that are praiseworthy in a wife, and lavishness and laziness as faults, then it is clear that they considered a woman's role to be extremely important in determining the fate of the household. The fact that financial responsibility and the growth of the estate are central in their discussions of women's qualities shows that these were the traits that were idealized in ancient Greece. Wives were largely judged in material terms, based

sparing or restraint in money, appetites, expenditures, pleasures, and luxury, which is how Plato says that the majority of people, οἱ πολλοί define it (*Gorgias* 491d).

102. Plato, *Republic* 554a5.

103. Plato, *Republic* 555a.

104. Semonides 7 in Campbell 1967.

105. θάλλει δ' ὑπ' αὐτῆς κἀπαέξεται βίος (Semonides 7.85).

on whether they could help or harm; the instrumental evaluation of a wife's qualities can be seen in Hesiod's statement that there is nothing a man can have that is better than a good wife or worse than a bad one.[106] Conceptually, women's behavior was often evaluated according to material criteria, their value summed up in economic terms.

But it should be no surprise that monetary considerations pervaded marriage since social relationships were often exploited by Greeks for economic benefits, and even the bonds of kinship were affected by economic concerns.[107] Paul Millet has described Greeks as being "coolly calculating" in the way they assessed the wide range of benefits they could reap from friends since relationships acted "as a form of insurance in a world of capricious fortune."[108] Social bonds provided an invaluable safety net against disaster, as seen in Hesiod's advice to Perses. But friendship was also calculated in such fine economic terms that friends and the benefits they brought could be conceived as having a "precise cash equivalent,"[109] as seen in Socrates' advice in Xenophon, *Memorabilia* 2.4. Aristotle discusses the economic benefits of friendship in depth, including its potential for creating financial profit (*N.E.* 8.3.1–4.2), and devotes all of book 9 of the *Nicomachean Ethics* to calculating the gains that could be made from friends.[110] Polanyi's notion of embeddedness illustrates the complex intertwining of these different spheres of life, and as I have argued economic factors influenced nonfinancial considerations, an interconvertability of cultural, economic, and social capital that also characterizes the modern world.[111]

Furthermore, the emphasis on different types of cultural and social capital may have varied according to the different proportions of agricultural as opposed to trading opportunities in the various *poleis*. In highly commercialized cities like Corinth, openly making money by trading in the market may have been more profitable than accumulating social and cultural capital, whereas in more agricultural areas where the control of land was more important, securing marriage alliances and social connections could yield greater returns and security in the long run. Xenophon's comment in the *Constitution of the Spartans* further illustrates how many people spent their money on clothing, not the continuous reinvestment in production.[112] With the opportunities

106. *Works and Days* 702–3.

107. See, e.g., Davies 2002.

108. Millett 1991, 120–21.

109. Millett 1991, 116.

110. For a recent discussion of the utility of friendship, see van Berkel 2019.

111. Leese 2017a.

112. Cf. Xenophon's observation that men often like to invest their money in horses, and women in jewelry (*Poroi* 4.6).

for social mobility and marriage alliances, however, cultural capital had the potential to repay far more handsomely than endlessly expanding commercial activities.[113] Visible signs of success, such as being a wealthy farmer, could provide cultural capital.[114]

Aristotle also states that people created the new forms of moneymaking in their quest for unlimited bodily pleasure: "This other type of moneymaking has come because of this. For with enjoyment being in excess, they seek the production of excessive enjoyment," καὶ τὸ ἕτερον εἶδος τῆς χρηματιστικῆς διὰ τοῦτ' ἐλήλυθεν. ἐν ὑπερβολῇ γὰρ οὔσης τῆς ἀπολαύσεως, τὴν τῆς ἀπολαυστικῆς ὑπερβολῆς ποιητικὴν ζητοῦσιν (*Politics* 1.9.16–17, 1258a7–9). However, he immediately precedes this comment by saying "but even those people who do desire to live well seek this in respect to the pleasures of the body" (ὅσοι δὲ καὶ τοῦ εὖ ζῆν ἐπιβάλλονται τὸ πρὸς τὰς ἀπολαύσεις τὰς σωματικὰς ζητοῦσιν); those people who aim at what he defines as "the good life" still seek to maximize their returns.

Even in Sparta wealth was frequently an important consideration in marriage alliances, so the opposition between social/cultural spheres and the economic should not be taken too far. Indeed, *philochrêmatia*, the love of money, was not even able to be overcome in Sparta where the pursuit of wealth by male citizens had been outlawed (*Politics* 2.9.13, 1270a14–15). The drive for self-interested wealth accumulation, which had earlier been responsible for economic inequality and was replaced by a communistic ethic, was unable to be repressed. Xenophon laments the return of individualistic economic behavior at Sparta, where he says that people in his day boast about their possessions (*Lak. Pol.* 14.3). Therefore, even when this instinct was legislated against, individuals still found ways to amass personal wealth in violation of a collectivistic ethos, and inequality prevailed in Sparta by the classical period.[115] Spartan women were legally permitted to own property, and by the Hellenistic period women were the wealthiest members of society (Plutarch, *Agis* 4–7). Women continued to engage in moneymaking activities while the male citizens were constrained by law, which demonstrates that it was not men alone who were motivated by self-interested economic desires. The law was necessary to compel Spartan citizens to control their innate drives, so the external power of the state was the only force capable of checking these urges. Nevertheless, even in the face of legislation and social sanction, Spartans persisted in seeking economic gains, whether it was citizen men in secret or women openly. Therefore, the collective

113. Leese 2017a.
114. Scodel 2019.
115. Hodkinson 2000.

social ethos that defined Spartan "equality" was an artificial construct that was able to intervene and check individualistic behavior only to a limited extent; the latter was more deeply hard-wired into the brain than the former. In the end, it was the self-interested pursuit of wealth that prevailed. Both within Sparta itself and also throughout the rest of the Greek world in which Sparta was situated, the innate urges and values that promoted selfish wealth acquisition were more powerful than those that attempted to counter them.

Safety, Honor, and Social Mobility: The Benefits of Wealth

Nor is it difficult to see why wealth was so desired in ancient Greece. As Hesiod says in *Works and Days*, people even take to the seas to seek their living because χρήματα γὰρ ψυχὴ πέλεται δειλοῖσι βροτοῖσιν, "Wealth is life to wretched mortals" (686). And as he warned Perses, starvation is the inevitable result of not working hard and accumulating wealth. Moreover, Theognis says that it is better to die than to live poor (351–54), because wealth helps to bring release from the pains and cares that were so prevalent in ancient life: Εἴη μοι πλουτοῦντι κακῶν ἀπάτερθε μεριμνέων ζώειν ἀβλαβέως, "Let it be possible for me to live wealthy without harm and far from evil worries."[116] Wealth itself, therefore, helped to alleviate much of the uncertainty and anxiety that plagued people living in a premodern society where the chance of starvation and death was ever present.[117] Theognis sums up the benefits of wealth in such an uncertain world very well: Οὔ σε μάτην, ὦ Πλοῦτε, βροτοὶ τιμῶσι μάλιστα·ἦ γὰρ ῥηϊδίως τὴν κακότητα φέρεις, "Not in vain, Ploutos, do mortals honor you most, for you bear hardship easily" (523–24).[118] With the phrase, κακῶν ἀπάτερθε μεριμνέων, "far from evil worries," he reveals that he wished he could avoid precisely the characteristics that distinguish the current Iron Age from the Golden Age of humanity in Hesiod. Among the Iron Age's defining features are the μερίμνας "worries" that the gods imposed on humans (178), unlike the time when humans lived apart from evils, κακῶν (115); Theognis' choice of words may be a direct reference to the Golden age in which people lived ἄτερ κακῶν, "apart

116. *Elegies* 1.1152–53.

117. This is not to say that famines and food crises in the ancient world were a constant feature of everyday life, for which see Garnsey 1988, 6–40. Nevertheless, the threat of bad harvest was very real and required effective strategies of risk buffering especially among the members of the population who were living at or near subsistence. For peasant subsistence strategies, see Garnsey 1988, 43–88; Gallant 1991. Even in the modern world starvation and famine are a constant threat in some communities, for which see Sen 1983.

118. Herodotus attributes this same sentiment to Solon (Hdt. 1.32).

from evils" (91). Wealth not only satisfied the desire for gain, but also reduced the impact of hardships, pains, and worries, which were so common in this Iron Age, and even helped to recover some of the feelings of peace and security that characterized the Golden Age of humanity.

But wealth conferred more than just material benefits; as Theognis says, it also engendered respect in the community: Πᾶς τις πλούσιον ἄνδρα τίει, ἀτίει δὲ πενιχρόν, "All honor a rich man but dishonor a poor one" (621). Honor came to those who became rich. Hesiod concurs, πλούτῳ δ' ἀρετὴ καὶ κῦδος ὀπηδεῖ, "Excellence and praise attend wealth" (311), and he implies later that admiration also comes with wealth (482). The esteem that accompanied wealth was so widespread in fourth-century BCE Athens that Plato in the *Republic* says that some individuals "honor nothing other than wealth and those who are wealthy,"[119] and "the rich man is honored by many" (582c). Far from approving of the esteem which moneymaking and wealth brought to its possessors, however, Plato decries this practice, since the noble and good then become deprived of the esteem which they rightfully deserve, usurped by those who could merely make money (550e–551a).[120]

But *hoi polloi* would not adhere to Plato's prescriptions because wealth could bring honor. As Aristotle says, those who are especially jealous are those who highly value honor,[121] so the drive to emulate would have been particularly strong among such individuals, and money was an important means to acquiring it. Alcaeus even goes so far as to say "Money maketh man; no pauper can be noble or held in honor."[122] Because this saying is attributed to a Spartan, Aristodamos, it reveals that wealth brought honor not only in the rest of the Greek world, but even in Sparta, the *polis* to adopt the most extreme anti-wealth legislation. Aristotle says that those whom we honor are those who do not live dependent upon others but work for themselves, including farmers and *autourgoi*, self-employed folk (*Rhetoric* 2.4.10, 1381a19–23). Therefore, honor could be achieved by realizing a specific economic mode of life, and even those aiming at social esteem could have seen money as the best means of attaining it.

After accumulating enough wealth, one could even join the ranks of the elite, which is a central theme of Theognis' poetry as he describes the develop-

119. καὶ τιμᾶν μηδὲν ἄλλο ἢ πλοῦτόν τε καὶ πλουσίους (Plato, *Republic* 553d).

120. Notions of the rich as wicked in their exploitation of others are common in Greek literature: in Plato *Laws* 742b–743a, the idea is stated that only scoundrels, and never good people, are rich. This same idea is repeated throughout Aristophanes' *Ploutos* (passim), and the notion that the richest people are also the most wicked is stated in the pseudo-Platonic dialogue *Eryxias* 392b–393a.

121. Walcot 1978, 18.

122. Χρήματ' ἄνηρ, πένιχρος δ' οὐδ' εἶς πέλετ' ἔσλος οὐδὲ τίμιος (F. 360). Translation by Page 1955, 315.

ing socioeconomic situation of sixth-century Megara: Πλοῦτε, θεῶν κάλλιστε καὶ ἱμεροέστατε πάντων, σὺν σοὶ καὶ κακὸς ὢν γίνεται ἐσθλὸς ἀνήρ, "Wealth, most beautiful and pleasing of all the gods, with you even one who is base becomes a noble man" (1117–18). Indeed, in archaic Megara, the newly rich had become successful in penetrating the upper classes of society, who "honor wealth" to the point that it "has mixed the race"—that is, different classes.[123] Thus, social mobility and desirable marriage alliances were tangible benefits of becoming rich, particularly in a world in which it was possible for lower classes to surpass their aristocratic neighbors in material well-being.

To a certain extent, wealth and profit had even succeeded in trumping the aristocratic notion of *aretê*: Πλήθει δ' ἀνθρώπων ἀρετὴ μία γίνεται ἥδε, πλουτεῖν, "For the majority of people this is the only excellence: to be wealthy" (698–99). Socrates expresses a similar sentiment in Plato's *Apology*, where he claims that he has spent his life trying to convince Athenians that they should aspire not to economic prosperity, but rather to improving their character: Οὐκ ἐκ χρημάτων ἀρετὴ γίγνεται, ἀλλ' ἐξ ἀρετῆς χρήματα, "Excellence does not arise from wealth, but rather wealth from excellence" (Plato, *Apology* 30b). Clearly others had the opposite notion, that *aretê* resulted from wealth;[124] they did not learn his lesson. Many people conflated riches with *aretê*, in Socrates' mind, or thought that excellence could be gained through wealth. Aristotle agreed that *aretê* was a worthy end to pursue (*N.E.* 1.5.5–6), and it seems that many tried to attain it through money. Socrates tried to persuade the Athenians that money could not buy *aretê*, but few listened. To a philosopher, such an idea would be outrageous, but it was *hoi polloi* who made up the majority of society, and whose behavior is more representative of ancient Greeks as a whole. And it should come as no surprise that people so eagerly desired money, since it brought so many tangible benefits: honor; security against hardships; freedom from toil, pain, and worry; social mobility; profitable marriages; even *aretê*.[125]

In conclusion, the drive to accumulate wealth was multipronged in ancient Greek theories of human psychology. First, biological need and poverty natu-

123. χρήματα μὲν τιμῶσι· καὶ ἐκ κακοῦ ἐσθλὸς ἔγημε καὶ κακὸς ἐξ ἀγαθοῦ· πλοῦτος ἔμειξε γένος (189–190).

124. For a further discussion of Socrates' notions of *aretê*, see Aristotle, *E.E.* 1.5.15, 1216b.

125. There are some stray passages in *Works and Days* that seem at first glance to indicate a competing anti-wealth attitude, such as Hesiod's statement that the bribe-devouring *basileis* are "fools and do not know how much more the half is than the whole, and how much of a great benefit there is in mallow and asphodel" (40–41). This passage must be considered alongside Hesiod's strictures to avoid base gain (352), and wealth seized by force (321), and are in stark contrast with Hesiod's otherwise positive evaluation of gain earned through hard work, and should therefore be read only in the context of his advice to his brother Perses, who has shamelessly seized the greater part of their father's estate. For the historicity of Hesiod and Perses, see West 1978, 30–40; Griffith 1983, 37–65; Edwards 2004, 20–25.

rally required people to secure their subsistence. But this was just the beginning. People were also motivated by the desire to satisfy a complex array of appetites, especially the corporal pleasures of food, drink, leisure, and sex, which could be infinite. Such passions provided the impetus for so many Greeks to acquire wealth beyond the level of subsistence that Plato called the "appetitive" element in the brain the "money-loving" part. Next, and different in type, though perhaps even more contributive to the insatiable thirst for wealth, was the range of emotions of emulation, envy, and rivalry that also drove people to strive for riches far beyond their daily needs. Subsistence was not the aim for these people, but rather the need to outdo, and be victorious among, their notional competitors and closest peers; this competition for *ploutos* alone could give rise to a cycle of accumulation that knew no bounds, emulation which acted as an endless upward drive to acquire ever-increasing levels of wealth.

Emulation warped the mind's perception of one's true economic situation, to the point that the wealthiest Greeks believed they were poor and wanted nothing more than to continue to multiply their wealth. *Pleonexia* is often translated as "greed," which obscures an important element in the root meaning: to have more, not just in the absolute sense (accumulating more and more), but also in the relative sense (having more than other people). Greed, and the desire to have more than others, was a potent force in ancient Greek society, and some like Callicles in Plato's *Gorgias* even tried to rationalize this lust and justify it based on natural law.

Finally, wealth also brought honor and power, in addition to security and safety from hardship, which could themselves motivate even (or especially) the richest to seek ways of further expanding their fortunes. Pain also was a powerful impulse, especially envy and the indignation at seeing one's peers being more successful. "Shame" was the term Xenophon's Socrates used to prick Aristarchus and goad him to increase his household's productivity, similar to the emotional sting that spurred farmers to work hard, in Hesiod's words. Some Greeks were also driven by an insatiable lust for pleasure, which explains why the urge to acquire wealth is often classed in the same category as other *epithumiai* such as the desire for food, drink, and sex, the most basic carnal pleasures. Any combination of two or more of these wants (or emotional triggers) could easily create an endless craving for money and the things it could provide. This vast multitude of distinct urges or impulses were major forces at the individual level that drove the operation of the ancient Greek economy as a system, one that was largely directed at continuously increasing wealth acquisition.

The desire to pursue riches was a utility-maximizing measure, one that predated the invention of coinage, as Hesiod's description of the life of the Golden

Age of humanity demonstrates. And although his focus is more on ways in which these divinely created (and ordained) emotions affected the mundane lives of mortals on earth, he credits the gods with the underlying causality of these emotional forces; Hesiod thereby reveals Greek cultural views that the self-interested drive for wealth was at the very root of their religious views and cosmology. A strong work ethic was necessary to aspire to the lifestyle of the gods and Golden Age of humanity, the ideal life of prosperity free from pain and toil in the Greek cultural mind.

But even replicating the blissful conditions of the Golden Age was not sufficient to placate this relentless yearning to accumulate. Bacchylides states that wealth cannot provide everything, and in particular cannot surpass the benefits of health and good fortune. But diseases and poverty must also be absent in order to enjoy life, and those who are able to avoid these pains can most closely approximate the lifestyle of the Golden Age. Nevertheless, the trouble-free life of the Golden Age was not enough to bring contentment: "The rich man desires great things just as the more humble desires lesser things; but it is not sweet for mortals to live in easy comfort, but always they seek to attain the things that flee before them," ἶσον ὅ τ'ἀφνεὸς ἱμείρει μεγάλων ὅ τε μείων παυροτέρων· τὸ δὲ πάντων εὐμαρεῖν οὐδὲν γλυκὺ θνατοῖσιν, ἀλλ' αἰεὶ τὰ φεύγοντα δίζηνται κιχεῖν (1.62–67). Having good things in abundance never satisfies completely, and even those who are very rich and living in effortless comfort are constantly trying to acquire more, always grasping at what is fleeting. As Hesiod would put it, the curse of the Iron Age is that even those blessed with plenty are not satisfied with what they have but always seeking to grasp at the things that elude them.

The things one does not have become the object of desire, and trigger a drive to add continuously, propelling people to seek more. Trying to attain what is at the next level, always grasping at what is just beyond their reach, in an attempt to provide satisfaction and peace of mind is depicted by Bacchylides as a yearning that cannot be fulfilled. The echoes with Thorstein Veblen are unmistakable: in his theory people are plagued with "chronic dissatisfaction" with their lot: the next highest level is always the target of individual success, and those who surpass their peers then scramble to increase the gap between themselves and their closest competition.

And so this grasping emotion, which inspires the rich to reach farther and farther at an ever-expanding set of objects, is able to account for the desire to accumulate endlessly. "Grasping" is also the emotion described by Aristotle above in his use of the term *orexis*, and when he says that "the masses grasp at profit rather than honor:"[126] οἱ γὰρ πολλοὶ μᾶλλον ὀρέγονται τοῦ κέρδους ἢ τῆς τιμῆς. Here his choice of the verb ὀρέγονται, "grasp at," echoes precisely the psychology Xenophon attested in the *Constitution of the Spartans* where it denotes the general drive to seek wealth by Greeks as "grasping for money" (χρημάτων ὀρέγεσθαι). In this same passage, Xenophon uses another equally significant term to describe the acquisitive behavior of Greeks overall: "eagerness" or "yearning" (*spoudasteos*). This same term appears twice in the passage opening the *Works and Days* in which Hesiod discusses the actions of the wealthy neighbor who, though already rich, is eagerly working for more wealth and thereby inspires the nearby onlooker to emulate his behavior.[127] Solon (or Theognis) also selects the term "eager" or "yearning" (σπεύδουσι) to depict the mindset of these already rich individuals who strive after additional wealth: "For those of us who now have the greatest wealth yearn for twice as much; who could satisfy them all?" (οἳ γὰρ νῦν ἡμῶν πλεῖστον ἔχουσι βίον, διπλάσιον σπεύδουσι. τίς ἂν κορέσειεν ἅπαντας;).[128] From the archaic to the classical period, therefore, it seems that the same psychological processes within the Greek mind drove people to attempt to accumulate wealth endlessly.

The overall effect of these mental impulses is clear: as Aristotle states, most people are avaricious (*N.E.* 4.1.37), and this avarice is insatiable (*Politics* 2.7.19–20, 1267b1–9). And like the later philosophers, Theognis emphasizes the unique nature of wealth, which alone cannot be satisfied: πλὴν πλούτου παντὸς χρήματός ἐστι κόρος, "There is satiety in every good thing but wealth" (596). Of all the pleasures and desires, it was only the yearning for wealth that was unable to be filled. Solon's famous maxim that "There is no bound to riches for mortals" (πλούτου δ' οὐδὲν τέρμα πεφασμένον ἀνθρώποισιν),[129] while perhaps technically impossible, nevertheless accurately conveys the practical reality he observed around him. As mentioned in chapter 1, Antisthenes describes the compulsion to accumulate endlessly as being hard-wired in the very *psychê*, which is also where he says poverty is located. Mental distortions cause even very rich people to believe that they are poor, not based on an absolute baseline, but rather on a comparison with their peers. To Veblen, as to Aristotle, this

126. *Politics* 6.4.3, 1318b17.

127. πλούσιον, ὃς σπεύδει μὲν ἀρόμεναι ἠδὲ φυτεύειν οἶκόν τ' εὖ θέσθαι· ζηλοῖ δέ τε γείτονα γείτων εἰς ἄφενος σπεύδοντ' (*Works and Days* 22–24).

128. Theognis 226–28; Solon F 13 (West 1972, 72–74).

129. Solon F1 l. 71 (Campbell 1967).

never-ending yearning to attain a higher level of wealth knows no bounds and can spiral out of control as people try to keep increasing their economic and social standing. Therefore, it seems that in ancient Greece as in the modern world, a continuously expanding desire to acquire wealth was observed in the economic behavior of the people. No wonder Plato calls this insatiable yearning a "hunger in the soul," which many Greeks sought to feed in an endless cycle of accumulation.

Conclusions

Long-term maximization of both profit and wealth are amply attested in ancient Athens and beyond. This evidence appears in a variety of contexts and levels of society, at each scale of focus as one zooms in from big-picture political and social trends within and across *poleis*, to the general estate and business management of private citizens, and finally down to the more minute decisions made by individuals within specific economic transactions. Not only the economic strategies individuals employed in their *oikonomia*, but also the multiple superlatives authors use to describe maximizing profit and wealth, support the conclusion that ancient Greeks behaved in an economically rational manner. Many seem to have deliberately chosen between alternative options to maximize income; although trial and error and experimentation by testing the waters for different production options may have been the rule, this does not alienate the ancient Greeks from modern corporate strategies.[1] Aristotle even articulates the means-to-ends relationship of rational choice in a manner akin to modern economic theorists.[2]

Moreover, when Plato labels one of the three core regions of the *psychê* the "money- or profit-loving portion," he is providing a glimpse into Greek behavior that would otherwise remain hidden. *Chrêmatistikê* was such an all-encompassing part of daily life that it had conceptually absorbed even some of the most elemental of human activities. Economically rational thought was far from being alien to their culture or "mentality"; the Greeks themselves, in their

1. Trial and error is still today used by the modern firm as part of the profit-maximizing process, for which see Macve 1985, 250. North 1990, 79, agrees that modern corporations still rely upon trial and error, and not just computations, in their quest to maximize profits: "Maximizing activity by the firm results from learning by doing and investing in the kinds of skills and knowledge that will pay off." Thus, rather than merely depending upon calculations, the modern firm must try a combination of different approaches, as seems to have been the case in ancient Greece. Trial and error was also recognized as the key to success in the ancient world: see, e.g., Columella 1.4.5, on the need for experimentation to increase profitability on the Roman farm.

2. *Politics* 1.9.15–16, 1257b38–1258a9.

own theories of the mind, identified these mental processes as being hard-wired into the *psychê* and argued that they stood among the main forces driving the behavior of individuals in their society. The competition for economic success was encouraged by Greek cultural values, the pursuit of honor, fame, and social capital. In their cultural system of conceptualization, at the very roots of their cosmology and accounts of anthropogony, self-interested economic accumulation was central to their notions of individual behavior. During the Iron Age of humanity, conflict between individuals for economic resources penetrated even the most intimate of kinship bonds within the family itself.

Ancient Greeks felt such a strong desire for money because it was the ultimate utility-maximizing device. Not only satisfying pleasures and eliminating pains, money also provided safety, honor, leisure to enjoy other interests, and power. For others, the pursuit of money was not just considered a means to achieving other ends like relieving pain or achieving pleasure, but was seen as being an end unto itself. It alone could be converted into practically any form, and was a safe mechanism to store wealth to allow individuals to weather market fluctuations. It could be put to any use in response to changing external circumstances and the multiple internal transformations in preferences that occur over the course of an individual's lifetime. Being wealthy allowed Greeks to resemble most closely the life of humans during the Golden Age and that of the gods on Mount Olympus; but even these conditions were insufficient to check the desire to "grasp at" what was ever just beyond one's reach. An insatiable "eagerness" or "yearning" compelled many to amass wealth endlessly. Therefore maximization is not an anachronistic retrojection onto ancient evidence, but was described by the Greeks themselves as stemming from their own innate fundamental psychological processes.

Alongside the profit and wealth maximization of *homo oeconomicus*, however, other patterns of economic behavior also appear prominently. In ancient Greece as in the modern world, self-interested rationality existed in conjunction with social interests, and was driven by irrational emotional impulses at the most elemental level. So what does all this mean? First, scholars must incorporate economic rationality into their full panoply of theoretical tools, including behavioral economics, economic anthropology and sociology, game theory, peasant studies, and Veblen's leisure class. Separately, these models are far too simplistic and schematic to account for the full complexities of individual behavior; only together can they accurately elucidate the rich texture of intertwined cultural, economic, and social interests in a holistic manner.

There will always be scholarly resistance to economic rationality, as there has been since John Stuart Mill first introduced the concept in his 1836 article,

"On the Definition of Political Economy; and on the Method of Investigation Proper to It."[3] Furthermore, the arguments in favor of cultural specificity are well-founded. But as McCloskey states, the emphasis on profit in neoclassical economics should be seen as "a complement to what is missing from an anthropological approach" that focuses on culture.[4] Similarly, even behavioral economists who seek to explore nonrational behavior such as Akerlof and Shiller, whose work focuses on the emotionally driven "animal spirits" of Keynes, recognize that this irrationality coexists alongside economic rationality in all people.[5] Behavioral economics experiments therefore have opened intriguing new avenues of research in human psychology and behavior, but nevertheless have not supplanted the central model of rationality that lies at the heart of economics.[6] Emotional and irrational aspects of human behavior are intertwined symbiotically with rationality in the same individuals. Kahneman, moreover, argues that the thinking process of individuals varies by situation: more emotional when it is fast, impulsive, unconscious, and reactive, but more deliberate and logical when it is slower and more conscious.[7] People have "two selves" that behave, think, and decide differently based on the context.

Just as the Greek philosophers observed, the presence of irrational behavior does not preclude rationality; both are needed to explain human behavior. Cultural and social factors likewise illuminate nonmaximizing behaviors, but they do not refute economic rationality—rather they coexist simultaneously within the same economic systems and indeed the same individuals. Economic anthropologists and sociologists have been advocating a more nuanced, hybrid approach that emphasizes both economic and social concerns for decades.[8] Gudeman notes that the two realms "complement each other," "may be institutionally and tactically interwoven," and "most of us use both realms of economy every day."[9] Therefore although certainly not a sufficient explanation for the full complexity of individual behavior, economic rationality is a necessary one that must be included alongside other behavioral models.

Taking an extreme position on either side is not satisfactory—culture and economic rationality need to be examined together. The culture-rationality

3. See Persky 1995.

4. McCloskey 1996, 127.

5. Akerlof and Shiller 2009, 3.

6. As Wittman puts it, behavioral economics "is an interesting area of investigation, but at present, the results are not sufficiently compelling to overturn the analysis based on rational actors" (2005, 12).

7. Kahneman 2011.

8. See, e.g., Granovetter 2001, and Parry and Bloch 1989, on the long- vs. short-term transactional orders.

9. Gudeman 2001, 11–12.

opposition is a relic of the debates in which "it was often assumed that the antonym of rationality is relativism."[10] Sahlins' critique of radical individualism embodies this refusal to retroject modern behavioral assumptions onto other societies;[11] eschewing individualism might be more appropriate for other cultures than ancient Greece, however, for which methodological individualism is often the most accurate heuristic approach, as I have argued above. As seen in the dispute between Hesiod and his brother, conflict among individuals for economic resources penetrated even the most intimate social relationships, within the family itself. The rupture of kinship bonds amid the self-interested competition for material gain features prominently in the numerous speeches of Isaeus concerning inheritance, the dispute between Apollodorus and his brother, as well as between Demosthenes and his uncle and cousins. As Hesiod describes it, the level of perceived wealth in ancient Greece was tied to that of one's neighbors and peers, and the emotional impulses of pain and pleasure that drove wealth acquisition to unbounded levels lay at the core of Greek behavior in their everyday life. These fundamental psychological processes in the mind that powered the engine of their economy arose from a clear distinction between the self and others. Therefore, fears of violating Greek cultural specificity by employing methodological individualism do not seem grounded in the realities of the evidence for Greek behavior, but rather in the assumptions which oversimplified theoretical models impose upon that evidence.[12]

Sahlins' point in *Cosmologies of Capitalism*, on the other hand, is compelling—each culture's cosmology is unique and complicates the application of modern social science models. Although I have shown that Greek cosmology and their view of the individual's place in the universe do not depart definitively from economic rationality, there must have been something distinctive to their culture and *Weltanschauung* that characterizes their thought and behavior as Greek. Cultural particularism must remain a central methodological approach. But it is often difficult to determine what is specific to Greek culture. Such a task would require extensive research in a number of different areas. The precise differences between Greek thought and our own (as well as the diversity within Greek thought and that of other premodern cultures), needs to be the focus of a series of comprehensive and systematic analyses. Culturally specific conceptions and notions can only be identified through examinations at the finest level of detail in discrete studies and in com-

10. Lloyd 2018, 8. For the rationality vs. relativism debates of the twentieth century, see Trigger 2003, 3–14.

11. Sahlins 2004, 142–43.

12. Seaford 2004, 292–301, also argues for individualism in ancient Greece.

parative perspective, as Lloyd has done with China. Moreover, Sahlins' challenge that "culture constitutes utility" should be addressed with careful consideration, though problems with defining "culture" are myriad to begin with. In short, thick description is desirable, but overly schematic treatments of all types destroy particularism, even if scholars' exclusion of rationality is motivated by their desire to achieve relativism. Ancient Greece's rich cultural texture should be integrated into economic history, but as I have argued, this is only possible without rejecting economic rationality.

This book shows how rationality and irrationality were interconnected and fed into each other; irrational behavior and emotions actually fueled long-term wealth maximization, much in the way that Weber described for the spirit of modern capitalism. And if examples of irrationality are found, scholars must resist the temptation to use blanket labels to describe the Greeks' entire mental universe or cultural mentality. Such statements are provocative and attention-grabbing, but do as much violence as assuming that Greeks were entirely rational. Indeed, as Lloyd demonstrates, the very terms rational and irrational are highly problematic, since they are often "deployed polemically, serving as a prime weapon to defeat opponents, whose ideas and practices, once labeled 'irrational,' can be disqualified from serious consideration."[13] Such binaries are often mobilized by scholars and philosophers to win arguments within the contexts of disputes,[14] oversimplifications that obscure the complexities of ancient evidence far more than the open-minded acceptance of all gradations of detail. The rational/irrational polarization that appears so frequently throughout scholarship on the economy and the premodern world in general is itself an unhelpful distinction because when scholars employ these terms they necessarily (even if unintentionally) reinforce the modern/premodern divide. If scholars believe rationality is peculiar to the modern West, they will interpret evidence to fit that biased perspective.

Profit maximization existed alongside social and cultural aims as well as irrationality within the same individuals, as it does in the world today. As Wittman puts it, "The concept of rationality is rather trivial . . . people generally choose what they prefer. However . . . rationality in combination with other simple ideas produces non-obvious and deep insights."[15] For example, I have argued elsewhere that ancient Greeks pursued profit and wealth maximization not just in a crude sense but even at the finer details of information manipula-

13. Lloyd 2018, 94.
14. Lloyd 2018, 39, 56.
15. Wittman 2005, 12.

tion described in Geertz's bazaar economy model,[16] which demonstrates the efficacy of a nuanced approach that situates economically rational behavior within a specific cultural and institutional context.[17] New Institutional Economics, with its focus on institutions and information problems can, indeed, yield fruitful research, even if scholars eschew the controversial arguments that efficiency determines institutional success and survival.

Wittman describes economic rationality as "trivial," and I would even take it a step further—the term "rationality" does not even need to be used most of the time in economic history—at best it is tautological, and at worst it recreates the "Primitive" or "Savage Mind." Maximizing behavior can be emphasized, but without the massive transformative causal force often attributed to it. Furthermore, for analytical precision, instead of "irrational," which reinforces the modern/premodern dichotomy, scholars could employ phrases like "non-profit-maximizing" or "forgoing maximum profit to secure other benefits like cultural and social capital." Such descriptions are more accurate, less loaded with baggage, do less violence to the past, and respect the agency of the ancients rather than depicting them as deficient. My position might best be described as "anti-anti-rationalism"—a term I use in homage (and as a complement) to Geertz's "anti-anti-relativism."[18] It is best to proceed with both eyes wide open.

Furthermore, the notion of *mentalité* (as it has been traditionally employed) needs to be completely reassessed, as it seems to buckle under the weight of the variety of ancient attitudes toward moneymaking activity. Indeed, as Humphreys recognized, "mentality" changes with prevailing circumstances, especially proximity to and opportunities for commercial exchange.[19] This dynamic view, in which *mentalité* is not monolithic or static, is a more accurate depiction of a complex reality, since we know markets were pervasive in the ancient Greek world.[20] It also agrees with Weber's overall impression that two different economic systems seemed to coexist in the ancient Greek world—one highly commercialized and market-oriented, and the other rural and primitive operating according to the "natural" economy of the peasant: "Much of ancient history centres round those cities whose ships were engaged in international trade . . . alongside the highly developed commercial economy of these towns there existed—exactly opposite in character—the natural economy of the primitive peasants of the interior."[21] Peasant studies was designed by Chayanov

16. Leese 2017b.
17. Geertz 1979.
18. Geertz 1984.
19. Humphreys 1978, 71.
20. Harris and Lewis 2016.
21. Weber 1976, 391–92.

to explain the rules of economic contexts that operated without wages, rents, prices, which much of the Greek world did have, so both market and nonmarket behavioral theories need to be considered in any analysis.

Because different types of economic behavior operated simultaneously within the same individuals, a variety of models are needed to account for both a single person's full behavioral spectrum and to characterize the personality types that fall into separate patterns across an overall population. As Arnold states in his succinct critique of *mentalité*:

> The problem—but perhaps also the solution—with *mentalité* is that the people of the past are as different from us as we are *from ourselves*. At certain moments they—and we—cohere around patterns of behaviour, and the historian can certainly seek out those patterns; but they are neither entirely the same nor entirely different from us.[22]

The existence of non-profit-maximizing personality types cannot be taken to support a pre-rational *mentalité* in ancient Greece. Their own diversity is analogous to our own. People are not confined to just one group or category of behavior, but are dynamic and fluid, each individual a unique combination of traits that respond differently to various situations, but all seeking ends in a manner we would call maximizing utility.

Lloyd has demonstrated convincingly that the notion of mentality is a gross oversimplification of the mental diversity in the ancient Greek world,[23] and this perspective needs to be explicitly integrated into economic history. The recent bestseller *Sapiens* by Harari represents the traditional view that a radical shift in approaches to business caused and coincided with the rise of modernity.[24] But it is not just outdated, nonspecialist, or general works—some of the most sophisticated NIE scholarship still falls back on the theory that premodern peoples had a distinctive mentality and that as part of the psychological transformation in early modern Europe, people increasingly behaved in an economically rational manner like modern individuals, a sort of cognitive revolution that was a significant contributing factor in the rise of the modern economy.[25]

In light of these issues, the applicability of theoretical paradigms central to the history of capitalism and influenced by Marx and Weber must be reexam-

22. Arnold 2000, 109.

23. Lloyd 1990.

24. See, e.g., Harari 2015, 310–15.

25. See, e.g., Boldizzoni 2011, 56–60, who criticizes Greif 2006 for basing many of his arguments on the rise of individualism and Genoese merchants acting as *homines oeconomici*.

ined. First, with the pervasiveness of self-interested competition, methodological individualism is not as problematic as is often argued, because the social bonds within which ancient Greeks are supposed to have been embedded break down once the individuals within them come into competition with each other. The modern notion of the self seems not so foreign to that of the Greeks as is often claimed. Moreover, Weber's spirit of modern capitalism can be observed in ancient Greece, as well as the self-interested individualistic behaviors often attributed to later capitalism; therefore, mentality, psychological transformations, and epiphanies of rationality need to be completely reconsidered as causal forces in long-term economic change.

Furthermore, institutional innovations must be explicitly separated from mentality because scholars often conflate the effects of these different phenomena: "It cannot yield the conclusion that there were significant Greek and Roman markets in capital and wage-labour, because we know there were not. Without them it is vain to harp on about the evidence for Athenian 'entrepreneurship', 'risk-taking', and so forth, because, even granting that there were things which can reasonably be described in these terms, they cannot have been anything more than marginal."[26] Within this rigid Marxist theoretical framework the validity of such behavior is trivialized because the model does not permit mental actions that do not fit a predetermined set of institutional variables. This study has shown that Greeks did take risks and act as entrepreneurs using the institution of slavery, without the need for free wage labor markets.[27]

Obviously the ancients did not achieve modern industrial capitalism, but Greek behavior does satisfy more flexible, alternative definitions of capitalism that emphasize innovation, endless accumulation, and the continuous reinvestment of profit into additional productive enterprise.[28] Weber once described ancient Greece's economy as a "flowering of capitalism," and called some Greeks "capitalists" who employed a rational approach in their moneymaking behavior.[29] If capitalism is defined as the continuous reinvestment of profits into additional productive enterprise, then some Greeks certainly do merit this label.[30] The Greeks' achievements in *kapêlikê* and commerce, which made these fields "more technical," attest to the innovative spirit that created a rising arc of

26. Meikle 1995b, 181.

27. As Wallerstein (1974, 400) argues, slave labor is not inconsistent with a capitalist economic system.

28. Grassby 1999, 5.

29. Weber 1976, 76, 191.

30. Weber 1976, 48, provides an even looser definition: "Were these developments really part of an economic structure which we can call 'capitalist'? . . . capital always means wealth used to gain profit in commerce. Otherwise the term loses any classificatory use."

technical sophistication in their eyes. So also do the individuals whose creativity led them to experiment with increasingly efficient silver ore washeries and to push the limits of the opportunities provided by contract and legal loopholes, as seen in such practices as *epidaneisis*.

By entering into dialogue with less static, more dynamic definitions of capitalism that do not rely upon mental transformations and instead explore often overlooked fundamental aspects of economic behavior, such as those of Jason Moore who emphasizes the creation of cheapness,[31] scholars of antiquity can make significant contributions to the big-picture history of economic development. Wiener describes twentieth-century England as experiencing a "decline of the industrial spirit"[32]—mentality is neither static nor monolithic but experiences ebbs and flows, dynamic expansions and rebounds that fit Veblen's account of leisure class aspirations and then the subsequent shift in attitudes that accompanies attaining that status. In these models, ancient and modern mentality are not so different as to constitute an insurmountable barrier of alien ideas impossible for the other to conceive.

The notions of modernity and individualism are reified constructs that have taken on causal force and explanatory power of their own, and distract from more accurate causes of economic development. The premodern/modern dichotomy that emerges from modernization theories is ultimately rooted in teleological accounts of progression by stages that dominated nineteenth-century scholarship based on evolutionary models.[33] As Latour argues so compellingly, the binary ways of organizing reality for analytical and cognitive simplicity, such as those that result in such dichotomies as modern and premodern, are gross distortions of both our own sophistication and other peoples' backwardness.[34] The scholars who have performed the closest empirical studies of the critical period of transition to the rise of the modern economy have been among the most convincing and fiercest critics of the theory of a new mentality.[35] There simply does not seem to be compelling evidence for a psychological transformation at the time it was supposed to have happened. Plus, such claims are even more problematic when one considers that we do not even have a clear idea of what makes modern thought unique anyway.[36]

31. Moore 2015.
32. Wiener 2004.
33. Tilly 1984.
34. Latour 1993. Moore and Patel 2017, similarly object to the widespread use of binaries in studies of capitalism.
35. E.g., Roper 1994; Grassby 2001.
36. Geertz 2000.

In their analysis of long-term economic change, therefore, scholars should redirect their attention away from theories of mental transformations, psychological shifts, and rational epiphanies and toward institutional and technological factors. Institutional innovations can create changes so profound that they can *appear* to result from a new mentality.[37] Great care is needed, however, because the effects of institutions and technology can be overestimated. Double-entry bookkeeping, for example, is often extolled as a prerequisite for the calculation of profit necessary in modern capitalism. But as Braudel and Macve demonstrate convincingly, not only was this type of accounting not sufficient for rational choice, it was often not even used in the economic decision-making process of businesspeople for centuries after its invention.[38] Misinterpreting the causal effects of institutions and technology can result in yet another form of teleological determinism.

In Aristotle's discussion of innovations, he explicitly credits the mental drives to build up ever-increasing levels of wealth as being responsible for the technical advances that he observed. He attributes the original cause that gave rise to new types of *chrêmatistikê* not to the invention of coined money, but to the desires innate within the Greek mind. These new means of accumulating wealth in the form of coinage emerged afterward as a result of, and to satisfy, preexisting mental forces. The impulse to maximize wealth preceded and precipitated the invention of these novel mechanisms for making money and increasing profit. Moreover, the broader economic patterns of wealth maximization and "endless accumulation" that fueled the inequality described by archaic period authors existed before coinage. As Solon shows, the idea of infinite acquisition was not engendered by the innovation of coined money, but predated it.[39] Psychological processes gave rise to new instrumental means of acquisition, not the other way around. Therefore the invention of coined money facilitated, rather than engendered, the goal of maximizing wealth, which existed in the Greek mind previously.

Nevertheless, with institutional and technological innovation, new behaviors are possible, but scholars must be extremely careful in distinguishing the effects of such changes from cognitive capabilities. Coined money increased the sophistication of calculation and comparability, but as Weber notes, the finer precision resulting from new technical instruments may have been more a matter of degree, rather than type.[40] Quantitative improvements can be sig-

37. Chandler 1990, 2, describes how a "new subspecies of economic man" appeared with the institutional advances of managerial business enterprise in the late nineteenth century.

38. Braudel 1982, 575; Macve 1985, 257–58.

39. See, however, the fascinating discussion by Seaford 2004, 190–216.

40. Weber 2009, 6.

nificant enough to appear to create qualitatively different effects. Institutions like the corporation, when combined with rationality, eventually resulted in profound transformations,[41] but many of the most significant changes were unintended and unlikely developments. For example, the origins of the firm arose not from a rational epiphany, but as protective measures to consolidate group interests in the face of outside pressure—Padgett and McLean do not associate the advances that laid the origins for the institution of the firm with a new mentality, as is often posited in teleological accounts, but rather an organic development addressing the needs of a specific context.[42] From the perspective of intent, this institution's later success was largely an inadvertent, unforeseen consequence when combined with a particular set of circumstances. It is of the utmost importance that scholars use great caution to separate institutional and technological advances from mentality in order to avoid teleology.

Removing mental transformations and the survival of institutions based on efficiency are important steps toward avoiding teleological accounts for the rise of modern capitalism, which in turn lump ancient Greeks together with every other premodern culture. The Greek economy must be contextualized in its position between the Neolithic and Industrial Revolution. But the assumption that psychological metamorphoses were necessary for institutional or technological advances further feeds deterministic and teleological explanations. Braudel strongly argues against giant leaps in mentality as being prime causes in the long-term process that brought about modern capitalism,[43] and instead emphasizes the "step by step," slow, incremental changes that occurred over the centuries.[44] In his account, long-term economic development was largely the accidental result of unique (often unintended) combinations of factors, and even when all the ingredients are in place for an industrial revolution, it still might not happen. To achieve a nonlinear and nonteleological approach, regression and cyclical patterns must feature prominently. Perhaps human evolutionary models, which are now depicted in bush-like form with a multitude of possible endpoints of development, can be helpful in envisioning economic progress in the long run. From this perspective, it is easy to visualize a broad diversity in the resulting configurations of different patterns of economic change and performance, each *telos* depending on the specific particularities of a given historical context, rather than a series of progressively less primitive stages all advancing inevitably toward modern industrial capitalism.

41. Reed 2003, 80.
42. Padgett and McLean 2006, 1543–44.
43. Braudel 1982, 402.
44. Braudel 1982, 228.

Bibliography

Acton, Peter, *Poiesis: Manufacturing in Classical Athens* (New York: Oxford University Press, 2014).

Acton, Peter, "Industry Structure and Income Opportunities for Households in Classical Athens," in E. Harris, D. Lewis, and M. Woolmer (eds.), *The Ancient Greek Economy: Markets, Households and City-States* (Cambridge: Cambridge University Press, 2016), 149–65.

Adams, Charles Darwin, *Lysias: Selected Speeches* (Norman: University of Oklahoma Press, 1970 [1905]).

Aeschines, *Speeches*. Translated by C. D. Adams (Cambridge, MA: Harvard University Press, 1919).

Akerlof, George A., and Robert J. Shiller, *Animal Spirits: How Human Psychology Drives the Economy, and Why It Matters for Global Capitalism* (Princeton: Princeton University Press, 2009).

Amemiya, Takeshi, "Comment on Davies," in J. G. Manning and Ian Morris (eds.), *The Ancient Economy: Evidence and Models* (Stanford: Stanford University Press, 2005), 157–60.

Amemiya, Takeshi, *Economy and Economics of Ancient Greece* (London: Routledge, 2007).

Andreau, Jean, and Jérôme Maucourant, "À propos de la 'rationalité économique' dans l'Antiquité gréco romaine: Une interprétation des thèses de D. Rathbone," *Topoi* 9.1 (1999), 47–102.

Andreau, Jean, J. France, and S. Pittia (eds.), *Mentalités et choix économiques des Romains* (Pessac: Ausonius, 2004).

Andreyev, V. N., "Some Aspects of Agrarian Conditions in Attica in the Fifth to Third Centuries B.C.," *Eirene* 12 (1974), 5–46.

Apostle, Hippocrates, and Lloyd Gerson, *Aristotle's Politics* (Grinnell, IA.: Peripatetic Press, 1986).

Arnaoutoglou, Ilias, *Ancient Greek Laws: A Sourcebook* (New York: Routledge, 1998).

Arnold, John H., *History: A Very Short Introduction* (Oxford: Oxford University Press, 2000).

Atack, Jeremy, Fred Bateman, and William Parker, "The Farm, the Farmer, and the Market," in Stanley L. Engerman and Robert E. Gallman (eds.), *The Cambridge Economic History of the United States*, vol. 2 (Cambridge: Cambridge University Press, 2000), 245–84.

Austin, M. M., and P. Vidal-Naquet, *Economic and Social History of Ancient Greece: An Introduction* (Berkeley: University of California Press, 1977).

Axelrod, Robert, *The Evolution of Cooperation* (New York: Basic Books, 1984).
Badian, Ernst, "The Road to Prominence," in Ian Worthington (ed.), *Demosthenes: Statesman and Orator* (New York: Routledge, 2000), 9–44.
Balot, Ryan K., *Greed and Injustice in Classical Athens* (Princeton: Princeton University Press, 2001).
Bang, Peter F., *The Roman Bazaar: A Comparative Study of Trade and Markets in a Tributary Empire* (Cambridge: Cambridge University Press, 2008).
Bang, Peter F., "The Ancient Economy and New Institutional Economics," *JRS* 99 (2009), 194–206.
Baptist, Edward, "Toxic Debt, Liar Loans, Collateralized and Securitized Human Beings, and the Panic of 1837," in Michael Zakim and Gary J. Kornblith (eds.), *Capitalism Takes Command* (Chicago: University of Chicago Press, 2012), 69–92.
Beresford, James, *The Ancient Sailing Season* (Leiden: Brill, 2013).
Bissa, Errietta, "Investment Patterns in the Laureion Mining Industry in the Fourth Century BCE," *Historia* 56.3 (2008), 263–74.
Bissa, Errietta, *Governmental Intervention in Foreign Trade in Archaic and Classical Greece* (Leiden: Brill, 2009).
Blaug, M., *Economic Theory in Retrospect*, 5th ed. (Cambridge: Cambridge University Press, 1997).
Boardman, John, "Trade in Greek Decorated Pottery," *OJA* 7.1 (1988), 27–33.
Bogaert, Raymond, *Banques et banquiers dans le cités grecques* (Paris: A. W. Sijthoff, 1968).
Bogaert, Raymond, "Notes critiques et économiques sur deux discours démosthéniens (XXVII, 9 et XXXIV, 10)," in *Studien zur alten Geschichte: Siegfried Lauffer zum 70. Geburtstag am 4. August 1981 dargebracht von Freunden, Kollegen und Schülern* (Rome: Bretschneider, 1986), 49–66.
Boldizzoni, Francesco, *The Poverty of Clio: Resurrecting Economic History* (Princeton: Princeton University Press, 2011).
Bolkestein, H., *Economic Life in Greece's Golden Age* (Leiden: Brill, 1958).
Bourdieu, Pierre, "The Forms of Capital," in Mark Granovetter and Richard Swedberg (eds.), *The Sociology of Economic Life* (Boulder: Westview Press, 2001), 96–111.
Bourdieu, Pierre, *The Social Structures of the Economy* (Cambridge: Polity Press, 2005).
Braudel, Fernand, *Civilization and Capitalism 15th–18th Century*, vol. 2, *The Wheels of Commerce* (New York: Harper and Row, 1982).
Braudel, Fernand, *Civilization and Capitalism 15th–18th Century*, vol. 3, *The Perspective of the World* (New York: Harper and Row, 1984).
Bravo, Benedetto, "Sulân: Représailles et justice privée contre des étrangers dans les cités grecques," *Annali della scuola normale superior di Pisa*, serie 3, 10.3 (1980), 675–983.
Bresson, Alain, *La cité marchande* (Paris: Diff. De Boccard, 2000).
Bresson, Alain, *L'économie de la Grèce des cités: Fin VIe–Ier siècle a. c. I. Les structures et la production* (Paris: A. Colin, 2007).
Bresson, Alain, *L'économie de la Grèce des cités: Fin VIe–Ier siècle a. c. II. Les espaces de l'échange* (Paris: A. Colin, 2008).
Bresson, Alain, *The Making of the Ancient Greek Economy: Institutions, Markets, and Growth in the City-State* (Princeton: Princeton University Press, 2016a).
Bresson, Alain, "Women and Inheritance in Ancient Sparta: The Gortynian Connection," *Studi Ellenistici* 30 (2016b), 9–68.

Bresson, Alain, and François Bresson, "Max Weber, la comptabilité rationnelle et l'économie du monde gréco-romain," in Hinnerk Bruhns and Jean Andreau (eds.), *Sociologie économique et économie de l'antiquité: À propos de Max Weber* (Paris: Centre de recherches historiques, 2004), 91–114.

Brooks, Charles E., *Frontier Settlement and Market Revolution: The Holland Land Purchase* (Ithaca: Cornell University Press, 1996).

Bruegel, Martin, "The Social Relations of Farming in the Early American Republic: A Microhistorical Approach," *Journal of the Early Republic* 26.4 (2006), 523–53.

Brun, J.-P., *Archéologie du vin et de l'huile de la préhistoire à l'époque hellénistique* (Paris: Errance, 2004).

Burford, Alison, *Land and Labor in the Greek World* (Baltimore: Johns Hopkins University Press, 1993).

Burke, Edmund, "The Economy of Athens in the Classical Era: Some Adjustments to the Primitivist Model," *TAPA* 122 (1992), 199–226.

Burke, Peter, *The French Historical Revolution* (Cambridge: Polity Press, 2015).

Cahill, Nicholas, *Household and City Organization in Olynthus* (New Haven: Yale University Press, 2002).

Cairns, Douglas, "The Politics of Envy: Envy and Equality in Ancient Greece," in David Konstan and N. Keith Rutter (eds.), *Envy, Spite, and Jealousy: The Rivalrous Emotions in Ancient Greece* (Edinburgh: Edinburgh University Press, 2003), 235–52.

Campbell, David, *Greek Lyric Poetry* (London: Macmillan, 1967).

Cargill, Jack, *The Second Athenian League: Empire or Free Alliance?* (Berkeley: University of California Press, 1981).

Carlsen, Jesper, "Estate Managers in Ancient Greek Agriculture," in Vincent Gabrielsen (ed.), *Ancient History Matters: Studies Presented to Jens Erik Skydsgaard on His Seventieth Birthday* (Rome: L'Erma di Bretschneider, 2002), 117–26.

Cartledge, Paul, "Introduction and Notes," in Xenophon, *Hiero the Tyrant and Other Treatises* (London: Penguin Books, 1997).

Cartledge, Paul, "The Economy (Economies) of Ancient Greece," in Walter Scheidel and Sitta von Reden (eds.), *The Ancient Economy* (New York: Routledge, 2002), 11–32.

Casson, Lionel, *The Ancient Mariners* (Princeton: Princeton University Press, 1991).

Cecchet, Lucia, *Poverty in Athenian Public Discourse: From the Eve of the Peloponnesian War to the Rise of Macedonia* (Stuttgart: Franz Steiner, 2015).

Chandezon, Christophe, "Some Aspects of Large Estate Management in the Greek World during Classical and Hellenistic Times," in Zosia Archibald et al. (eds.), *The Economies of Hellenistic Societies: Third to First Centuries BCE* (Oxford: Oxford University Press, 2011), 96–121.

Chandler, Alfred, *Scale and Scope: The Dynamics of Industrial Capitalism* (Cambridge, MA: Belknap Press of Harvard University Press, 1990).

Chandler, Alfred, *The Visible Hand: The Managerial Revolution in American Business* (Cambridge, MA: Belknap Press of Harvard University Press, 1992).

Chayanov, A. V., *The Theory of Peasant Economy* (Homewood, IL: R. D. Irwin, 1966).

Christ, Matthew R., "Liturgy Avoidance and Antidosis in Classical Athens," *TAPA* 120 (1990), 147–69.

Christ, Matthew R., "Legal Self-Help on Private Property in Classical Athens," *AJP* 119 (1998), 521–45.

Christ, Matthew R., *The Bad Citizen at Athens* (Cambridge: Cambridge University Press, 2006).

Christesen, Paul, "Economic Rationalism in Fourth-Century BCE Athens," *Greece and Rome* 50.1 (2003), 31–56.

Clinton, Kevin, *Eleusis: The Inscriptions on Stone*, vol. 1 (Athens: Archaeological Society at Athens, 2005).

Clinton, Kevin, *Eleusis: The Inscriptions on Stone*, vol. 2 (Athens: Archaeological Society at Athens, 2008).

Coase, Ronald, "The Nature of the Firm," *Economica* 4.16 (1937), 386–405.

Coase, Ronald, "The Problem of Social Cost," *Journal of Law and Economics* 3.1 (1960), 1–44.

Cohen, Edward, *Ancient Athenian Maritime Courts* (Princeton: Princeton University Press, 1973).

Cohen, Edward, "Athenian Finance: Maritime and Landed Yields," *Classical Antiquity* 8.2 (1989), 207–23.

Cohen, Edward, "Commercial Lending by Athenian Banks: Cliometric Fallacies and Forensic Methodology," *CP* 85 (1990), 177–90.

Cohen, Edward, *Athenian Economy and Society: A Banking Perspective* (Princeton: Princeton University Press, 1992).

Cohen, Edward, *The Athenian Nation* (Princeton: Princeton University Press, 2000).

Cohen, Edward, "An Unprofitable Masculinity," in Paul Cartledge, Edward Cohen, and Lin Foxhall (eds.), *Money, Labour, and Land: Approaches to the Economics of Ancient Greece* (New York: Routledge, 2002), 100–112.

Cohen, Edward, "Commercial Law," in Michael Gagarin and David Cohen (eds.), *The Cambridge Companion to Ancient Greek Law* (Cambridge: Cambridge University Press, 2005), 290–304.

Cohen, Edward, *Athenian Prostitution: The Business of Sex* (Oxford: Oxford University Press, 2015).

Connor, W. R., *The New Politicians of Fifth-Century Athens* (Princeton: Princeton University Press, 1971).

Conophagos, Constantin, *Le Laurium antique et la technique grecque de la production de l'argent* (Athens: Ekdotike Hellados, 1980).

Cox, Cheryl Anne, *Household Interests: Property, Marriage Strategies, and Family Dynamics in Ancient Athens* (Princeton: Princeton University Press, 1998).

Crosby, Margaret, and John Young, "Greek Inscriptions," *Hesperia* 10.1 (1941), 14–30.

Cudjoe, R. V., *The Social and Legal Position of Widows and Orphans in Classical Athens* (Athens: Centre for Ancient Greek and Hellenistic Law, Panteion University of Social and Political Sciences, 2010).

Darnton, Robert, *The Great Cat Massacre and Other Episodes in French Cultural History* (New York: Basic Books, 1999).

Davies, John K., *Athenian Propertied Families, 600–300 B.C.* (Oxford: Clarendon Press, 1971).

Davies, John K., *Wealth and the Power of Wealth in Classical Athens* (New York: Arno Press, 1981).

Davies, John K., "Temples, Credit, and the Circulation of Money," in Andrew Meadows and Kirsty Shipton (eds.), *Money and Its Uses in the Ancient Greek World* (Oxford: Oxford University Press, 2001), 117–28.

Davies, John K., "The Strategies of Mr. Theopompos," in Paul Cartledge, Edward E. Cohen, and Lin Foxhall (eds.), *Money, Labour and Land: Approaches to the Economies of Ancient Greece* (New York: Routledge, 2002), 200–208.

Davies, John K., "Classical Greece: Production," in W. Scheidel, I. Morris, R. Saller (eds.), *The Cambridge Economic History of the Greco-Roman World* (Cambridge: Cambridge University Press, 2007), 333–61.

Davis, Morton D., *Game Theory: A Nontechnical Introduction* (Mineola, NY: Dover, 2012).

Donlan, Walter, "The Structure of Authority in the Iliad," *Arethusa* 12 (1979), 51–70.

Duncan-Jones, R., *The Economy of the Roman Empire: Quantitative Studies* (Cambridge: Cambridge University Press, 1982).

Duncan-Jones, R., *Structure and Scale in the Roman Economy* (Cambridge: Cambridge University Press, 1990).

Edwards, A. T., *Hesiod's Ascra* (Berkeley: University of California Press, 2004).

Eidinow, Esther, *Oracles, Curses, and Risk among the Ancient Greeks* (Oxford: Oxford University Press, 2007).

Elster, Jon, "Marxism, Functionalism, and Game Theory: The Case for Methodological Individualism," *Theory and Society* 11 (1982), 453–82.

Elster, Jon, *Nuts and Bolts for the Social Sciences* (Cambridge: Cambridge University Press, 1989).

Engen, Darel Tai, *Honor and Profit: Athenian Trade Policy and the Economy and Society of Greece, 415–307 B.C.E.* (Ann Arbor: University of Michigan Press, 2010).

Engen, Darel Tai, "Democracy, Knowledge, and the Hidden Economy of Athens," *Journal of Economic Asymmetries* 8.1 (2011), 93–107.

Faraguna, Michele, "Calcolo economico, archivi finanziari e credito nel mondo greco tra VI e IV sec. a. C.," in Koenraad Verboven, Katelijn Vandorpe, and Véronique Chankowski (eds.), *Pistoi dia tèn technèn: Bankers, Loans, and Archives in the Ancient World; Studies in Honour of Raymond Bogaert* (Leuven: Peeters, 2008), 33–58.

Feinman, Gary, "Reframing Ancient Economies: New Models, New Questions," in Manuel Fernandez-Gotz and Dirk Krausse (eds.), *Eurasia at the Dawn of History: Urbanization and Social Change* (Cambridge: Cambridge University Press, 2016), 139–49.

Figueira, T. J., "Karl Polanyi and Ancient Greek Trade: The Port of Trade," *AW* 10.1 (1984), 15–30.

Figueira, T. J., "Sitopolai and Sitophylakes in Lysias' 'Against the Grain Dealers': Governmental Intervention in the Athenian Economy," *Phoenix* 40 (1986), 149–71.

Figueira, T. J., "Economic Thought and Economic Fact in the Works of Xenophon," in F. Hobden and C. Tuplin (eds.), *Xenophon: Ethical Principles and Historical Enquiry* (Leiden: Brill, 2012), 665–87.

Finkelstein, Moses I., "Ἔμπορος, ναύκληρος, and κάπηλος," *CP* 30 (1935), 320–36.

Finley, M. I., "Aristotle and Economic Analysis," *Past and Present* 47 (1970), 3–25.

Finley, M. I., *The Ancient Economy* (Berkeley: University of California Press, 1973).

Finley, M. I., *Studies in Land and Credit in Ancient Athens, 500–200 B.C.: The Horos-Inscriptions*, reprinted with a new introduction by Paul Millett (New Brunswick, NJ: Transaction Books, 1985. First published 1951 by Rutgers University Press [New Brunswick, NJ]).

Fisher, Nicholas, "'Independent Slaves' in Classical Athens and the Ideology of Slavery," in Constantina Katsari and Enrico Dal Lago (eds.), *From Captivity to Freedom:*

Themes in Ancient and Modern Slavery (Leicester: University of Leicester, School of Archaeology and Ancient History, 2008), 121–46.

Föllinger, Sabine, *Ökonomie bei Platon* (Berlin: De Gruyter, 2016).

Fornara, Charles, *Translated Documents of Greece and Rome*, vol. 1, *Archaic Times to the End of the Peloponnesian War* (Cambridge: Cambridge University Press, 1983).

Forsdyke, Sara, *Exile, Ostracism, and Democracy: The Politics of Expulsion in Ancient Greece* (Princeton: Princeton University Press, 2005a).

Forsdyke, Sara, "Riot and Revelry in Archaic Megara: Democratic Disorder or Ritual Reversal?" *JHS* 125 (2005b), 73–92.

Forsdyke, Sara, "Land, Labor, and Economy in Solonian Athens," in J. H. Blok et al. (eds.), *Solon of Athens: New Historical and Philological Approaches* (Leiden: Brill, 2006), 334–50.

Foxhall, Lin, "Access to Resources in Classical Greece," in Paul Cartledge, Edward E. Cohen, and Lin Foxhall (eds.), *Money, Labour and Land: Approaches to the Economies of Ancient Greece* (New York: Routledge, 2002), 209–20.

Foxhall, Lin, *Olive Cultivation in Ancient Greece* (Oxford: Oxford University Press, 2007).

Foxhall, Lin, and H. A. Forbes, "*Sitometreia*: The Role of Grain as a Staple Food in Classical Antiquity," *Chiron* 12 (1982), 75–92.

Francotte, Henri, *L'industrie dans la Grèce ancienne* (Brussels: Société belge de librairie, 1900).

Franklin, James, *The Science of Conjecture: Evidence and Probability before Pascal* (Baltimore: Johns Hopkins University Press, 2001).

Frier, Bruce W., *Landlords and Tenants in Imperial Rome* (Princeton: Princeton University Press, 1980).

Gabrielsen, Vincent, "Phanera and Aphanes Ousia in Classical Athens," *Classica et Mediaevalia* 37 (1986), 99–114.

Gabrielsen, Vincent, *Financing the Athenian Fleet: Public Taxation and Social Relations* (Baltimore: Johns Hopkins University Press, 1994).

Gabrielsen, Vincent, "Brotherhoods of Faith and Provident Planning: The Non-Public Associations of the Greek World," *Mediterranean Historical Review* 22.2 (2007), 183–210.

Gabrielsen, Vincent, "Profitable Partnerships: Monopolies, Traders, Kings, and Cities," in Sofia Archibald et al. (eds.), *The Economies of Hellenistic Societies: Third to First Centuries BC* (Oxford: Oxford University Press, 2011), 216–50.

Gallant, T. W., *Risk and Survival in Ancient Greece: Reconstructing the Rural Domestic Economy* (Stanford: Stanford University Press, 1991).

Garlan, Y., *Slavery in Ancient Greece*, revised and expanded edition, translated by Janey Lloyd (Ithaca: Cornell University Press, 1988).

Garnsey, Peter, *Famine and Food Supply in the Graeco-Roman World* (Cambridge: Cambridge University Press, 1988).

Garnsey, Peter, *Cities, Peasants, and Food in Classical Antiquity* (Cambridge: Cambridge University Press, 1998).

Gauthier, Philippe, *Un commentaire historique des Poroi de Xénophon* (Paris: Droz, 1976).

Geertz, Clifford, "The Impact of the Concept of Culture on the Concept of Man," in *The Interpretation of Cultures: Selected Essays by Clifford Geertz* (New York: Basic Books, 1973), 33–54.

Geertz, Clifford, "The Bazaar Economy: Information and Search in Peasant Marketing," *American Economic Review* 68.2 (1978), 28–32.

Geertz, Clifford, "Anti Anti-Relativism," *American Anthropologist*, n.s., 86.2 (1984) 263–78.

Geertz, Clifford, "The Way We Think Now: Toward an Ethnography of Modern Thought," in *Local Knowledge: Further Essays in Interpretive Anthropology* (New York: Basic Books, 2000), 147–63.

Gernet, Louis, and Marcel Bizos, *Lysias: Discours* (Paris: Les Belles lettres, 2003).

Ginzburg, Carlo, *The Cheese and the Worms: The Cosmos of a Sixteenth-Century Miller* (Baltimore: Johns Hopkins University Press, 1980).

Goette, Hans Rupprecht, Ὁ ἀξιόλογος δῆμος Σούνιον (Athens: M. Leidorf, 2000).

Goldthwaite, Raymond, *The Economy of Renaissance Florence* (Baltimore: Johns Hopkins University Press, 2009).

Goody, Jack, *The Domestication of the Savage Mind* (Cambridge: Cambridge University Press, 1977).

Graham, Benjamin, *The Intelligent Investor: A Book of Practical Counsel*, rev. ed., updated with new commentary by Jason Zweig (New York: Harper Business Essentials, 2003).

Granovetter, Mark, "Economic Action and Social Structure: The Problem of Embeddedness," in Mark Granovetter and Richard Swedberg (eds.), *The Sociology of Economic Life* (Boulder: Westview Press, 2001), 51–76.

Grassby, Richard, "The Rate of Profit in the Seventeenth Century," *English Historical Review* 83 (1969), 721–51.

Grassby, Richard, "English Merchant Capitalism in the Late Seventeenth Century: The Composition of Business Fortunes," *Past and Present* 46 (1970), 87–107.

Grassby, Richard, *The Business Community of Seventeenth-Century England* (Cambridge: Cambridge University Press, 1995).

Grassby, Richard, *The Idea of Capitalism before the Industrial Revolution* (Cambridge: Cambridge University Press, 1999).

Grassby, Richard, *Kinship and Capitalism: Marriage, Family, and Business in the English-Speaking World, 1580–1740* (Cambridge: Cambridge University Press, 2001).

Greif, Avner, *Institutions and the Path to the Modern Economy* (New York: Cambridge University Press, 2006).

Griffith, Mark, "Personality in Hesiod," *Classical Antiquity* 2 (1983), 37–65.

Gudeman, S., *The Anthropology of Economy: Community, Market, and Culture* (Malden, MA: Blackwell, 2001).

Günther, Sven, "Framing the Financial Thoughts of Aeneas Tacticus: New Approaches of Theory to Economic Discourses in Antiquity," *Journal of Ancient Civilizations* 29 (2014), 77–86.

Hanson, V. D., *Warfare and Agriculture in Classical Greece* (Berkeley: University of California Press, 1998).

Harari, Noah, *Sapiens* (New York: Harper Collins, 2015).

Harding, Phillip, *Didymos on Demosthenes* (Oxford: Oxford University Press, 2006).

Harding, Phillip, *The Story of Athens* (New York: Routledge, 2008).

Hargreaves Heap, Shaun, *Rationality in Economics* (New York: Blackwell, 1989).

Harris, Edward M., "When Is a Sale not a Sale? The Riddle of Athenian Terminology for Real Security Revisited," *Classical Quarterly* 38.2 (1988), 351–81.

Harris, Edward M., "The Liability of Business Partners in Athenian Law: The Dispute between Lycon and Megacleides (Dem. 52.20–21)," *Classical Quarterly*, n.s., 39.2 (1989), 339–43.

Harris, Edward M., "Workshop, Marketplace and Household," in P. Cartledge, E. Cohen, and L. Foxhall (eds.), *Money, Labour and Land: Approaches to the Economies of Ancient Greece* (London: Routledge, 2002), 67–99.

Harris, Edward M., "Who Enforced the Law in Classical Athens?," in Eva Cantarella (ed.), *Symposion 2005: Vorträge zur griechischen und hellenistischen Rechtsgeschichte (Salerno 14.–18. September 2005)* (Vienna: Austrian Academy of Sciences Press, 2007), 159–76.

Harris, Edward M., "Response to Gerhard Thür," in Edward Harris and Gerhard Thür (eds.), *Symposion 2007: Vorträge zur griechischen und hellenistischen Rechtsgeschichte* (Vienna: Austrian Academy of Sciences Press, 2008), 189–202.

Harris, Edward M., "Finley's Studies in Land and Credit Sixty Years Later," *Dike* 16 (2013a), 123–46.

Harris, Edward M., "Were There Business Agents in Classical Greece? The Evidence of Some Lead Letters," in Uri Yiftach-Firanko (ed.), *The Letter Law, State, Society and the Epistolary Format in the Ancient World* (Wiesbaden: Harrassowitz, 2013b), 105–24.

Harris, Edward M., "The Meaning of the Legal Term Symbolaion, the Law about Dikai Emporikai and the Role of the Paragraphe Procedure," *Dike* 18 (2015), 7–36.

Harris, Edward M., "The Legal Foundations of Economic Growth in Ancient Greece," in E. Harris, D. Lewis, and M. Woolmer (eds.), *The Ancient Greek Economy: Markets, Households and City-States* (Cambridge: Cambridge University Press, 2016), 116–46.

Harris, Edward M., "The Rule of Law and Economic Growth in Ancient Greece," in Edward M. Harris and Mirko Canevaro (eds.), *The Oxford Handbook of Ancient Greek Law* (Oxford: Oxford University Press, 2020), https://doi.org/10.1093/oxfordhb/9780199599257.001.0001

Harris, Edward M., and David M. Lewis, "Introduction," in Edward M. Harris, David M. Lewis, and Mark Woolmer (eds.), *Markets, Households, and City-States in the Ancient Greek Economy* (Cambridge: Cambridge University Press, 2016), 1–40.

Hasebroek, Johannes, *Trade and Politics in Ancient Greece* (New York: Biblo Tannen, 1965).

Heilbroner, Robert L., *The Worldly Philosophers: The Lives, Times, and Ideas of the Great Economic Thinkers*, revised 7th ed. (New York: Simon and Schuster, 1999).

Herman, Gabriel, *Ritualised Friendship and the Ancient Greek City* (Cambridge: Cambridge University Press, 1987).

Hodges, Richard, *Primitive and Peasant Markets* (New York: Blackwell, 1988).

Hodkinson, Stephen, *Property and Wealth in Classical Sparta* (London: Duckworth, 2000).

Horden, Peregrine, and Nicholas Purcell, *The Corrupting Sea* (Oxford: Blackwell, 2000).

Humphreys, S. C., *Anthropology and the Greeks* (New York: Routledge, 1978).

Hunter, Virginia J., *Policing Athens: Social Control in the Attic Lawsuits* (Princeton: Princeton University Press, 1994).

Irwin, Elizabeth, *Solon and Early Greek Poetry: The Politics of Exhortation* (Cambridge: Cambridge University Press, 2005).

Isager, Signe, and M. H. Hansen, *Aspects of Athenian Society in the Fourth Century BC* (Odense: Odense University Press, 1975).

Jameson, Michael, "Agriculture and Slavery in Classical Athens," *CJ* 73 (1977), 122–41.

Jameson, Michael, "Attic Eschatia," in Vincent Gabrielsen (ed.), *Ancient History Matters: Studies Presented to Jens Erik Skydsgaard on His Seventieth Birthday* (Rome: L'Erma di Bretschneider, 2002), 63–68.

Jansen, J. N., *After Empire: Xenophon's Poroi and the Reorientation of Athens' Political Economy* (PhD diss., University of Texas, 2007).

Johnstone, Stephen, *A History of Trust in Ancient Greece* (Chicago: University of Chicago Press, 2011).

Jones, Donald W., *Economic Theory and the Ancient Mediterranean* (Malden, MA: Wiley Blackwell, 2014).

Jones, John Ellis, "The Laurion Silver Mines: A Review of Recent Researches and Results," *G and R* 29.2 (1982), 169–83.

Kahneman, Daniel, *Thinking, Fast and Slow* (New York: Farrar, Straus and Giroux, 2011).

Kahneman, Daniel, and Amos Tversky, "Prospect Theory: An Analysis of Decision under Risk," *Econometrica* 47 (1979), 263–91.

Kakovogiannis, E., "Σουνιακά-Λαυρεωτικά," *Arch. Delt.* 32A (1982), 182–217.

Kazakévich, Emily Grace, "Were the χωρὶς οἰκοῦντες Slaves?" edited by Deborah Kamen *GRBS* 48 (2008), 343–80.

Kehoe, Dennis P., "Economic Rationalism in Roman Agriculture," *JRA* 6 (1993), 476–84.

Kehoe, Dennis P., *Investment, Profit, and Tenancy: The Jurists and the Roman Agrarian Economy* (Ann Arbor: University of Michigan Press, 1997).

Kent, J. H., "The Temple Estates of Delos, Rheneia, and Mykonos," *Hesperia* 17 (1948), 243–338.

Kindelberger, Charles, *A Financial History of Western Europe* (London: Allen and Unwin, 1984).

Kirchgässner, G., *Homo Oeconomicus: The Economic Model of Behavior and Its Applications in Economics and Other Social Sciences* (New York: Springer, 2008).

Kirchner, Johannes, *Prosopographia Attica* (Berlin: G. Reimeri, 1901).

Knigge, Ursula, *Der Bau Z, mit einem Beitrag von Karin Tancke* (Munich: Hirmer, 2005).

Konstan, David, "Before Jealousy," in David Konstan and N. Keith Rutter (eds.), *Envy, Spite, and Jealousy: The Rivalrous Emotions in Ancient Greece* (Edinburgh: Edinburgh University Press, 2003), 7–27.

Korver, J., "Demosthenes gegen Aphobus," *Mnemosyne* 10 (1942), 8–22.

Kroll, John H., "What about Coinage?," in John Ma, Nikolaos Papazarkadas, and Robert Parker (eds.), *Interpreting the Athenian Empire* (London: Duckworth, 2009), 195–210.

Kron, John Geoffrey, *Landed and Commercial Wealth at Classical Athens, 500–300 B.C.* (PhD diss., University of Toronto, 1996).

Kron, John Geoffrey, "Classical Greek Trade in Comparative Perspective," in Edward M. Harris, David M. Lewis, and Mark Woolmer (eds.), *Markets, Households, and City-States in the Ancient Greek Economy* (Cambridge: Cambridge University Press, 2016), 356–80.

Lambert, S. D., *Rationes Centesimarum: Sales of Land in Lykourgan Athens* (Leiden: Brill, 1997).

Lang, Mabel, "Numerical Notation on Greek Vases," *Hesperia* 25.1 (1956), 1–24.

Lang, Mabel, *The Athenian Agora*, vol. 21, *Graffiti and Dipinti* (Princeton: Princeton University Press, 1976).

Lanni, Adriaan, *Law and Justice in the Courts of Classical Athens* (Cambridge: Cambridge University Press, 2006).

Latour, Bruno, *We Have Never Been Modern* (New York: Harvester Wheatsheaf, 1993).

Lauffer, Siegfried, *Die Bergwerkssklaven von Laureion* (Wiesbaden: F. Steiner, 1979 [1955–1956]).

Leese, Michael, "Lysias and a Forgotten Law on the Administration of Orphans' Estates in Classical Athens," *Dike* 19/20 (2016–2017), 107–24.

Leese, Michael, "An Economic Perspective on Marriage Alliances in Ancient Greece," in Dennis Kehoe and Thomas McGinn (eds.), *Ancient Law, Ancient Society: Essays Presented to Bruce W. Frier* (Ann Arbor: University of Michigan Press, 2017a), 32–45.

Leese, Michael, "*Kapêloi* and Economic Rationality in Fourth-Century BCE Athens," *Illinois Classical Studies* 42.1 (2017b), 41–59.

Lewis, David M., "Attic Manumissions," *Hesperia* 28.3 (1959), 208–38.

Lewis, David M., "The Athenian Rationes Centesimarum," in M. I. Finley (ed.), *Problèmes de la terre en Grèce ancienne* (Paris: Mouton, 1973), 181–212.

Lewis, David, "Behavioural Economics and Economic Behaviour in Classical Athens," in M. Canevaro, A. Erskine, B. Gray, and J. Ober (eds.), *Ancient Greek History and Contemporary Social Science* (Edinburgh: Edinburgh University Press, 2018), 15–46.

Lintott, Andrew, "*Sula*: Reprisal by Seizure in Greek Inter-Community Relations," *CQ*, n.s., 54.2 (2004), 340–53.

Lloyd, G. E. R., *Demystifying Mentalities* (Cambridge: Cambridge University Press, 1990).

Lloyd, G. E. R., *The Ambivalences of Rationality: Ancient and Modern Cross-Cultural Explorations* (Cambridge: Cambridge University Press, 2018).

Lohmann, Hans, *Atene: Forschungen zu Siedlungs- und Wirtschaftsstruktur des klassischen Attika* (Cologne: Böhlau, 1993).

Loomis, William, *Wages, Welfare Costs, and Inflation in Classical Athens* (Ann Arbor: University of Michigan Press, 1998).

Lytle, Ephraim, "Ἡ θάλασσα κοινή: Fishermen, the Sea, and the Limits of Ancient Greek Regulatory Reach," *Classical Antiquity* 31.1 (2012), 1–55.

Lyttkens, Carl Hampus, *Economic Analysis of Institutional Change in Ancient Greece: Politics, Taxation and Rational Behavior* (New York: Routledge, 2013).

MacDonald, Paul K., "Useful Fiction or Miracle Maker: The Competing Epistemological Foundations of Rational Choice Theory," *American Political Science Review* 97. 4 (2003), 551–65.

MacDowell, Douglas M., *Demosthenes the Orator* (Oxford: Oxford University Press, 2009).

Macve, R., "Notes on de Ste. Croix's 'Greek and Roman Accounting,'" in Paul Cartledge and F. D. Harvey (eds.), *Crux: Essays in Greek History Presented to G.E.M. de Ste. Croix* (London: Duckworth, 1985), 233–64.

Markides, Constantinos C., "Corporate Refocusing," *Business Strategy Review* 4.1 (1993), 1–15.

Markides, Constantinos C., "Diversification, Restructuring, and Economic Performance," *Strategic Management Journal* 16.2 (1995), 101–18.

Mayer, Enrique, *The Articulated Peasant: Household Economies in the Andes* (Boulder: Westview Press, 2002).

McCloskey, Donald M., "The Economics of Choice: Neoclassical Supply and Demand," in Thomas G. Rawski et al. (eds.), *Economics and the Historian* (Berkeley: University of California Press, 1996), 122–58.

Meijer, Fik, and Onno Van Nijf, *Trade, Transport, and Society in the Ancient World: A Sourcebook* (New York: Routledge, 1992).

Meikle, Scott, *Aristotle's Economic Thought* (Oxford: Oxford University Press, 1995a).

Meikle, Scott, "Modernism, Economics, and the Ancient Economy," *Proceedings of the Cambridge Philological Society* 41 (1995b), 174–91.

Meikle, Scott, "Aristotle on Business," *CQ*, n.s., 46.1 (1996), 138–51.

Meikle, Scott, "Modernism, Economics, and the Ancient Economy," in Walter Scheidel et al. (eds.), *The Ancient Economy* (Edinburgh: Edinburgh University Press, 2002), 233–50.

Meyer, Elizabeth, *Metics and the Athenian Phialai-Inscriptions* (Wiesbaden: Steiner, 2009).

Mickwitz, G., "Economic Rationalism in Graeco-Roman Agriculture," *English Historical Review* 52 (1937), 577–89.

Millett, Paul, "Maritime Loans and the Structure of Credit in Fourth-Century Athens," in P. K. Garnsey, K. Hopkins, and C. R. Whittaker (eds.), *Trade in the Ancient World* (Berkeley: University of California Press, 1983), 36–52.

Millett, Paul, "Hesiod and His World," *PCPhS* 30 (1984), 84–115.

Millett, Paul, "Sale, Credit, and Exchange in Athenian Law and Society," in P. Cartledge, P. Millett, and S. Todd (eds.), *Nomos: Essays in Athenian Law, Politics, and Society* (Cambridge: Cambridge University Press, 1990), 167–94.

Millett, Paul, *Lending and Borrowing in Ancient Athens* (Cambridge: Cambridge University Press, 1991).

Moore, Jason W., *Capitalism in the Web of Life: Ecology and the Accumulation of Capital* (New York: Verso, 2015).

Moore, Jason W., and Raj Patel, *A History of the World in Seven Cheap Things* (Berkeley: University of California Press, 2017).

Moreno, Alfonso, *Feeding the Democracy* (Oxford: Oxford University Press, 2007).

Moreno, Alfonso, "The Attic Neighbor: The Cleruchy in the Athenian Empire," in J. Ma, N. Papazarkadas, and R. Parker (eds.), *Interpreting the Athenian Empire* (London: Duckworth, 2011), 211–21.

Morley, Neville, *Trade in Classical Antiquity* (Cambridge: Cambridge University Press, 2007).

Morris, Ian, "Hard Surfaces," in Paul Cartledge, Edward E. Cohen, and Lin Foxhall (eds.), *Money, Labour and Land: Approaches to the Economies of Ancient Greece* (London: Routledge, 2002), 8–43.

Morris, Ian, "Archaeology, Standards of Living, and Greek Economic History," in J. G. Manning and Ian Morris (eds.), *The Ancient Economy: Evidence and Models* (Stanford: Stanford University Press, 2005), 91–126.

Morris, Ian, and Joe Manning, "Introduction," in J. G. Manning and Ian Morris (eds.), *The Ancient Economy: Evidence and Models* (Stanford: Stanford University Press, 2005), 1–46.

Morris, Ian, Richard Saller, and Walter Scheidel, "Introduction," in W. Scheidel, I. Morris, and R. Saller (eds.), *The Cambridge Economic History of the Greco-Roman World* (Cambridge: Cambridge University Press, 2007), 1–12.

Munn, M., *The Defense of Attica: The Dema Wall and the Boiotian War of 378–375 BC* (Berkeley: University of California Press, 1993).

Mussche, Herman, "Insula 3," in H. F. Mussche, et al. (eds.), *Thorikos IX, 1977/1982* (Brussels: Peeters Publishers, 1990), 12–62.

Mussche, Herman, "Thorikos during the Last Years of the Sixth Century B.C.," in W. D. E. Coulson et al. (eds.), *The Archaeology of Athens and Attica under the Democracy* (Oxford: Oxford University Press, 1994), 211–15.

Mussche, Herman, *Thorikos: A Mining Town in Ancient Attika* (Ghent: Ecole archéologique en Grèce, 1998).

Nevett, Lisa, "A Real Estate 'Market' in Classical Greece? The Example of Town Housing," *ABSA* 95 (2000), 329–43.

North, Douglass, *Structure and Change in Economic History* (Cambridge: Cambridge University Press, 1986).

North, Douglass, *Institutions, Institutional Change, and Economic Performance* (Cambridge: Cambridge University Press, 1990).

Ober, Josiah, *Fortress Attica: Defense of the Athenian Land Frontier 404–322 B.C.* (Leiden: Brill, 1985).

Ober, Josiah, *Democracy and Knowledge: Innovation and Learning in Classical Athens* (Princeton: Princeton University Press, 2008).

Ober, Josiah, "Public Action and Rational Choice in Classical Greek Political Theory," in Ryan K. Balot (ed.), *A Companion to Greek and Roman Political Thought* (Oxford: Oxford University Press, 2009), 70–84.

Ober, Josiah, "Wealthy Hellas," *Transactions of the American Philological Association* 140.2 (2010), 241–86.

Ober, Josiah, *The Rise and Fall of Classical Greece* (Princeton: Princeton University Press, 2015).

O'Halloran, Barry, *The Political Economy of Classical Athens: A Naval Perspective* (Leiden: Brill, 2018).

Osborne, Robin, *Demos: The Discovery of Classical Attika* (Cambridge: Cambridge University Press, 1985).

Osborne, Robin, *The Classical Landscape with Figures* (London: George Philip, 1987).

Osborne, Robin, "Social and Economic Implications of the Leasing of Land and Property in Classical and Hellenistic Greece," *Chiron* 18 (1988), 279–323.

Osborne, Robin, "The Economics and Politics of Slavery at Athens," in A. Powell (ed.), *The Greek World* (New York: Routledge, 1995), 27–43.

Osborne, Robin, "Pots, Trade and the Archaic Greek Economy," *Antiquity* 70 (1996), 31–44.

Osborne, Robin, "Pride and Prejudice, Sense and Subsistence: Exchange and Society in the Greek City," in Walter Scheidel and Sitta von Reden (eds.), *The Ancient Economy* (New York: Routledge, 2002), 114–32.

Osborne, Robin, "The Economics and Politics of Slavery at Athens," in Eric W. Robinson (ed.), *Ancient Greek Democracy: Readings and Sources* (Oxford: Blackwell, 2004), 265–80.

Osborne, Robin, "Archaic Greece," in Walter Scheidel et al. (eds.), *The Cambridge Economic History of the Greek and Roman World* (Cambridge: Cambridge University Press, 2007), 277–301.

Padgett, John F., and Paul D. McLean, "Organizational Invention and Elite Transformation: The Birth of the Partnership Systems in Renaissance Florence," *American Journal of Sociology* 111.5 (2006), 1463–1568.

Padgett, John F., and Paul D. McLean, "Economic Credit in Renaissance Florence," *Journal of Modern History* 83.1 (2011), 1–47.

Page, D. L., *Sappho and Alcaeus* (Oxford: Clarendon Press, 1955).

Parry, Jonathan P., and Maurice Bloch, "Introduction: Money and the Morality of Exchange," in Jonathan P. Parry and Maurice Bloch (eds.), *Money and the Morality of Exchange* (Cambridge: Cambridge University Press, 1989), 1–32.

Pearson, Lionel, *Demosthenes: Six Private Speeches* (Norman: University of Oklahoma Press, 1972).

Pernin, Isabelle, *Les baux ruraux en Grèce ancienne: Corpus épigraphique et étude* (Lyon: Jean Pouilloux, 2014).

Persky, Joseph, "Retrospectives: The Ethology of Homo Economicus," *Journal of Economic Perspectives* 9.2 (1995), 221–31.

Phillips, David, "Hypereides 3 and the Athenian Law of Contracts," *TAPA* 139.1 (2009), 89–122.

Pirngruber, Reinhard, *The Economy of Late Achaemenid and Seleucid Babylonia* (Cambridge: Cambridge University Press, 2017).

Polanyi, Karl, *The Great Transformation* (New York: Farrar and Rinehart, 1944).

Polanyi, Karl, "Aristotle Discovers the Economy," in Karl Polanyi et al. (eds.), *Trade and Market in the Early Empires* (Glencoe, IL: Free Press, 1957a), 64–94.

Polanyi, Karl, "The Economy as Instituted Process," in Karl Polanyi et al. (eds.), *Trade and Market in the Early Empires* (Glencoe, IL: Free Press, 1957b), 243–69.

Polanyi, Karl, *The Livelihood of Man* (New York: Academic Press, 1977).

Pomeroy, S. B., *Xenophon Oeconomicus: A Social and Historical Commentary*, with a new English translation (Oxford: Clarendon Press, 1994).

Pritchett, W. Kendrick, "The Attic Stelai: Part I," *Hesperia* 22.4 (1953), 225–99.

Pritchett, W. Kendrick, and Anne Pippin, "The Attic Stelai: Part II," *Hesperia* 25 (1956), 178–328.

Rathbone, Dominic, *Economic Rationalism and Rural Society in Third-Century A.D. Egypt: The Heroninos Archive and the Appianus Estate* (Cambridge: Cambridge University Press, 1991).

Rathbone, Dominic, and Sitta Von Reden, "Mediterranean Grain Prices in Classical Antiquity," in Robertus van der Spek, Bas van Leeuwen, and Jan Luiten van Zanden (eds.), *A History of Market Performance: From Ancient Babylonia to the Modern World* (London: Routledge, 2015), 149–235.

Raubitschek, A. E., *Dedications from the Athenian Akropolis: A Catalogue of the Inscriptions of the Sixth and Fifth Centuries B.C.*, edited with the collaboration of Lillian H. Jeffrey (Cambridge, MA: Archaeological Institute of America, 1949).

Reed, C. M., *Maritime Traders in the Ancient Greek World* (Cambridge: Cambridge University Press, 2003).

Reger, Gary, *Regionalism and Change in the Economy of Independent Delos, 314–167 B.C.* (Berkeley: University of California Press, 1994).

Reger, Gary, "The Price Histories of Some Imported Goods on Independent Delos," in J. Andreau, P. Briant, and R. Descat (eds.), *Économie antique: Prix et formation des prix dans les économies antiques* (Saint-Bertrand-de-Comminges: Musée archéologique départemental, 1997), 53–72.

Roper, Lyndal, *Oedipus and the Devil: Witchcraft, Sexuality, and Religion in Early Modern Europe* (New York: Routledge, 1994).

Rosivach, Vincent, "'Talasiourgoi' and 'Paidia' in 'IG' 22 1553–78: A Note on Athenian Social History," *Historia* 38.3 (1989), 365–70.

Rosivach, Vincent, *The System of Public Sacrifice in Fourth-Century Athens*, American Classical Studies 34 (Atlanta, GA: Scholars Press, 1994).

Rosivach, Vincent, "Classical Athens: Predatory Democracy? Hidden Oligarchy? Neither? Both?" *New England Classical Journal* 41.3 (2014), 168–94.

Sahlins, Marshall, *Stone Age Economics* (Chicago: Aldine-Atherton, 1972).

Sahlins, Marshall, *Culture and Practical Reason* (Chicago: University of Chicago Press, 1976).

Sahlins, Marshall, "Cosmologies of Capitalism," in *Culture in Practice: Selected Essays* (New York: Zone Books, 2000), 415–70.

Sahlins, Marshall, *Apologies to Thucydides: Understanding History as Culture and Vice Versa* (Chicago: University of Chicago Press, 2004).

Sallares, Robert, *The Ecology of the Ancient Greek World* (Ithaca: Cornell University Press, 1991).

Salviat, F., "Le vin de Thasos: Amphores, vin et sources écrites," Supplement 13, *BCH* (1986), 145–95.

Sanders, Ed, *Envy and Jealousy in Classical Athens: A Socio-Psychological Approach* (Oxford: Oxford University Press, 2014).

Saunders, Trevor, *Aristotle: Politics Books I and II* (Oxford: Clarendon Press, 1995).

Schaps, D. M., *Economic Rights of Women in Ancient Greece* (Edinburgh: Edinburgh University Press, 1979).

Schaps, D. M., *The Invention of Coinage and the Monetization of Ancient Greece* (Ann Arbor: University of Michigan Press, 2004).

Schefold, Bertram, "The Applicability of Modern Economics to Forms of Capitalism in Antiquity: Some Theoretical Considerations and Textual Evidence," *Journal of Economic Asymmetries* 8 (2011), 131–63.

Scheidel, Walter, Ian Morris, and Richard Saller (eds.), *The Cambridge Economic History of the Greco-Roman World* (Cambridge: Cambridge University Press, 2007).

Scodel, Ruth, "Hesiodic Eris and the Market," in Cynthia Damon and Christoph Pieper (eds.), *Eris vs. Aemulatio: Valuing Competition in Classical Antiquity* (Leiden: Brill, 2019), 29–52.

Scott, James C., *The Moral Economy of the Peasant: Rebellion and Subsistence in Southeast Asia* (New Haven: Yale University Press, 1976).

Seaford, Richard, *Money and the Early Greek Mind: Homer, Philosophy, Tragedy* (Cambridge: Cambridge University Press, 2004).

Sen, Amartya K., "Rational Fools: A Critique of the Behavioral Foundations of Economic Theory," *Philosophy and Public Affairs* 6.4 (1977), 317–44.

Sen, Amartya K., *Poverty and Famines: An Essay on Entitlement and Deprivation* (Oxford: Clarendon Press, 1983).

Sen, Amartya K., "Maximization and the Act of Choice," *Econometrica* 65.4 (1997), 745–79.

Shanks, Michael, *Art in the Early Greek State* (Cambridge: Cambridge University Press, 1999).

Sharfman, Keith, "The Law and Economics of Hoarding," *Loyola Consumer Law Review* 19.2 (2006), 179–93.

Shiller, R. J., *Irrational Exuberance* (Princeton: Princeton University Press, 2000).

Shipton, Kirsty, "The Private Banks in Fourth-Century B.C. Athens: A Reappraisal," *CQ* 47 (1997), 396–422.

Shipton, Kirsty, *Leasing and Lending: The Cash Economy in Fourth-Century BC Athens* (London: Institute of Classical Studies, School of Advanced Study, University of London, 2000).

Shipton, Kirsty, "Banks as Money Lenders: The Banks of Classical Athens," in Koenraad Verboven, Katelijn Vandorpe, and Véronique Chankowski (eds.), *Pistoi dia tèn technèn: Bankers, Loans, and Archives; Studies in Honour of Raymond Bogaert* (Leuven: Peeters, 2008), 93–114.

Simon, H. A., "A Behavioral Model of Rational Choice," *Quarterly Journal of Economics* 69 (1955), 99–188.

Simon, H. A., *Economics, Bounded Rationality and the Cognitive Revolution* (Brookfield, VT: E. Elgar, 1992).

Spitaels, P., "Insula 3: Tower Compound 1," in P. Spitaels, et al., (eds.), *Thorikos VII, 1970–1971* (Brussels: Peeters Publishers, 1978), 39–110.

Stadter, Philip, *A Commentary on Plutarch's Pericles* (Chapel Hill: University of North Carolina Press, 1989).

De Ste. Croix, G. E. M., "Demosthenes' Timêma and the Athenian Eisphora in the Fourth Century B.C.," *Classica et Mediaevalia* 14 (1953), 30–70.

De Ste. Croix, G. E. M., "Studies in Greek and Roman Accounting," in A. C. Littleton and B. S. Yamey (eds.), *Studies in the History of Accounting* (London: Arno Press, 1956), 14–74.

De Ste. Croix, G. E. M., "The Estate of Phainippus (ps.-Dem. xlii)," in Ernst Badian (ed.), *Ancient Society and Institutions: Studies Presented to Victor Ehrenberg* (Oxford: Blackwell, 1966), 109–14.

De Ste. Croix, G. E. M., "Ancient Greek and Roman Maritime Loans," in H. Edey and B. S. Yamey (eds.), *Debt, Credits, Finance, and Profits: Studies in Honour of W. S. Baxter* (London: Sweet and Maxwell, 1974), 41–59.

Swedberg, Richard, and Mark Granovetter, "Introduction," in M. S. Granovetter (ed.), *The Sociology of Economic Life*, 2nd ed. (Boulder: Westview Press, 2001), 1–19.

Taylor, Claire, *Poverty, Wealth, and Well-Being: Experiencing Penia in Democratic Athens* (Oxford: Oxford University Press, 2017).

Temin, Peter, *The Roman Market Economy* (Princeton: Princeton University Press, 2013).

Thaler, R. H., *Quasi Rational Economics* (New York: Russell Sage Foundation, 1991).

Thompson, Wesley, "The Athenian Investor," *RSC* 26 (1978), 403–23.

Thompson, Wesley, "The Athenian Entrepreneur," *L'Antiquité classique* 51 (1982), 53–85.

Thonemann, Peter, "Who Made the Amphora Mountain?" *Times Literary Supplement*, no. 5758, August 9, 2013, 10–11.

Thür, Gerhard, "How to Lease an Orphan's Estate in Classical Athens," *Annals Fac. L. Belgrade* 7 (2010), 7–19.

Thür, Gerhard, "Transaction Costs in Athenian Law," in Dennis P. Kehoe, David Ratzan, and Uri Yiftach (eds.), *Law and Transaction Costs in the Ancient Economy* (Ann Arbor: University of Michigan Press, 2015), 36–50.

Tilly, Charles, *Big Structures, Large Processes, Huge Comparisons* (New York: Russell Sage Foundation, 1984).

Titchener, Frances B., *An Historical Commentary on Plutarch's Life of Nikias* (PhD diss., University of Texas, 1988).
Tod, M. N., *A Selection of Greek Historical Inscriptions*, vol. 2, *From 403 to 323 B.C.* (Oxford: Clarendon Press, 1948).
Todd, S. C., *The Shape of Athenian Law* (Oxford: Clarendon Press, 1993).
Trevett, Jeremy, *Apollodorus the Son of Pasion* (Oxford: Clarendon Press, 1992).
Tridimas, George, "Homo Oeconomicus in Ancient Athens: Silver Bonanza and the Choice to Build a Navy," *Homo Oeconomicus* 30.4 (2013), 435–58.
Trigger, Bruce G., *Understanding Early Civilizations: A Comparative Study* (Cambridge: Cambridge University Press, 2003).
Tucker, Robert C. (ed.), *The Marx-Engels Reader*, 2nd ed. (New York: Norton, 1978).
Tzochev, Chavdar, "The Markets, Amphora Trade and Wine Industry: The Case of Thasos," in Edward M. Harris, David M. Lewis, and Mark Woolmer (eds.), *Markets, Households, and City-States in the Ancient Greek Economy* (Cambridge: Cambridge University Press, 2016), 230–53.
van Berkel, Tazuko Angela, *The Economics of Friendship* (Leiden: Brill, 2019).
Van Wees, Hans, "The Economy," in Kurt Rauflaub and Hans Van Wees (eds.), *A Companion to Archaic Greece* (Chichester: Wiley-Blackwell, 2009), 444–67.
Veblen, Thorstein, *The Theory of the Leisure Class* (New York: Macmillan, 1899).
Viano, Cristina, "Competitive Emotions and the *Thumos* in Aristotle's *Rhetoric*," in David Konstan and N. K. Rutter (eds.), *Envy, Spite and Jealousy: The Rivalrous Emotions in Ancient Greece* (Edinburgh: Edinburgh University Press, 2003), 85–97.
Vlassopoulos, K., review of *The Rise and Fall of Classical Greece*, by J. Ober, *BMCR*, 2016.03.04.
Von Neumann, J., and O. Morgenstern, *Theory of Games and Economic Behavior* (Princeton: Princeton University Press, 1944).
Von Reden, Sitta, *Exchange in Ancient Greece* (London: Duckworth, 2003).
Walcot, Peter, *Envy and the Greeks: A Study of Human Behaviour* (Warminster: Liverpool University Press, 1978).
Wallerstein, Immanuel, "The Rise and Future Demise of the World Capitalist System: Concepts for Comparative Analysis," *Comparative Studies in Society and History* 16.4 (1974), 387–415.
Wang, Donni, review of *The Making of the Ancient Greek Economy: Institutions, Markets, and Growth in the City-States*, by Alain Bresson, *BMCR*, 2016.07.35.
Wang, Donni, *Before the Market: The Political Economy of Olympianism* (Champaign, IL: Common Ground, 2018).
Waterfield, Robin, *Herodotus. The Histories* (Oxford: Oxford University Press, 1998).
Weber, Max, *The Agrarian Sociology of Ancient Civilizations* (London: NLB, 1976).
Weber, Max, *The Protestant Ethic and the Spirit of Capitalism* (New York, 2009).
Wermuth, Thomas S., "New York Farmers and the Market Revolution: Economic Behavior in the Mid-Hudson Valley," *Journal of Social History* 32 (1998), 179–96.
West, M. L. (ed), *Iambi et Elegi Graeci ante Alexandrum cantati vol. II* (Oxford: Clarendon Press, 1972).
West, M. L., *Hesiod: Works and Days* (Oxford: Oxford University Press, 1978).
Whitehead, David, *Hypereides: The Forensic Speeches* (Oxford: Oxford University Press, 2000).

Wiener, Martin J., *English Culture and the Decline of the Industrial Spirit, 1850–1980* (Cambridge: Cambridge University Press, 2004).

Williamson, Oliver, *Markets and Hierarchies* (New York: Free Press, 1975).

Wittman, Donald, *Economic Foundations of Law and Organization* (Cambridge: Cambridge University Press, 2005).

Wolf, Eric, *Peasants* (Englewood Cliffs, NJ: Prentice-Hall, 1966).

Wolf, Eric, *Europe and the People without History* (Berkeley: University of California Press, 1982).

Wolff, Hans Julius, "The Praxis-Provision in Papyrus Contracts," *TAPA* 72 (1941), 418–38.

Wood, Ellen Meiksins, *Peasant Citizen and Slave: The Foundations of Athenian Democracy* (New York: Verso, 1988).

Woolmer, Mark, "Emporoi kai nauklēroi: Redefining Commercial Roles in Classical Greece," *Journal of Ancient History* 3.2 (2015), 150–72.

Wrenhaven, Kelly L., "The Identity of the 'Wool-Workers' in the Attic Manumissions," *Hesperia* 78 (2009), 367–86.

Xenophon, *Hiero the Tyrant and Other Treatises*, translated by Robin Waterfield with introduction and notes by Paul Cartledge (London, 1997).

Young, John, "Country Estates at Sounion," *Hesperia* 25.2 (1956), 122–46.

Zafirovski, Milan, and Barry B. Levine, "Economic Sociology Reformulated: The Interface between Economics and Sociology," *American Journal of Economics and Sociology* 56.3 (1997), 265–85.

Zeitlin, Froma, "Signifying Difference: The Myth of Pandora," in Richard Hawley and Barbara Levick (eds.), *Women in Antiquity: New Assessments* (New York: Routledge, 1995), 58–74.

Zouboulakis, Michel S., *The Varieties of Economic Rationality* (New York: Routledge, 2014).

Zweig, Jason, "Commentary," in Benjamin Graham, *The Intelligent Investor: A Book of Practical Counsel*, rev. ed., updated with new commentary by Jason Zweig (New York: Harper Business Essentials, 2003).

General Index

Index Locorum